SPRINGBOARD FOR PASSING THE GED SCIENCE TEST

REVISED

GLENCOE
McGraw-Hill
New York, New York Columbus, Ohio Mission Hills, California Peoria, Illinois

GED • GED • GED • GED • GED • GED • GED • GED • GED • GED • GED • GED • GED

GED PROGRAM AUTHORS

Linda Barnes
Downers Grove, Illinois

Adrienne Breen
Northbrook, Illinois

Jane McLachlan Brown
South Dartmouth, Massachusetts

Mary T. Brown
Morrisville, New York

Philip Carona
Dickinson, Texas

Ellen Credille
Chicago, Illinois

Patricia Magaw Fuhs
Arlington Heights, Illinois

Jane Haasch
Waupaca, Wisconsin

Rita Milios
Toledo, Ohio

Coley Mills
Chicago, Illinois

Rena Moran
Flossmoor, Illinois

Stephen L. Volkening
Joliet, Illinois

CONSULTANTS

Pamela Bliss
Grayslake, Illinois

Kathryn Boesel-Dunn
Columbus, Ohio

Toby G. Cannon
Nashville, Tennessee

Lee Chic
San Carlos, California

Della Colantone
Skillman, New Jersey

John Grabowski
Staten Island, New York

Cynthia A. Green
Dallas, Texas

Esther Gross
Morrilton, Arkansas

Theodore M. Harig
Union Grove, Wisconsin

Linda L. Kindy
Little Rock, Arkansas

Mary Malone Kirsch
Ossining, New York

Ed A. Mayfield
Lexington, Kentucky

Pat Mitchell
Dallas, Texas

Laura Morris
Tallahassee, Florida

Marcia Mungenast
Upper Montclair, New Jersey

Evelyn H. Nunes
Richmond, Virginia

Ann Kuykendall Parker
Nashville, Tennessee

Phyllis Rosner
Yorktown Heights, New York

Yvonne E. Siats-Fiskum
Elkhorn, Wisconsin

Robert T. Sutton
Charlotte, North Carolina

Carole Thompson
Alexandria, Virginia

Imprint 1996

Send all inquiries to:
Glencoe/McGraw-Hill
936 Eastwind Drive
Westerville, OH 43081

ISBN 0-02-802064-2

4 5 6 7 8 9 10 DBH 00 99 98 97 96

Text Acknowledgments

Directions for GED Science Test are adapted from pp. 31, 32 of the OFFICIAL GED PRACTICE TESTS, Form AA, 1991 Edition. Copyright © 1987, American Council on Education. All rights reserved. Reprinted by permission of the GED Testing Service, Center for Adult Learning and Educational Credentials, American Council on Education.

Skills Survey **16** From PHYSICS AND HUMAN AFFAIRS by Art Hobson. Copyright © 1982 by John Wiley & Sons, Inc. Reprinted by permission.

Biology **25** From SCOTT, FORESMAN BIOLOGY by Irwin L. Slesnick et al. Copyright © 1985 Scott, Foresman and Company. **33** From SCOTT, FORESMAN LIFE SCIENCE by LeVon Balzer et al., p. 282. Copyright © 1987 Scott, Foresman and Company. **39** Paul Lewis and David Rubenstein, THE HUMAN BODY. New York: Grosset and Dunlap, 1971, p. 126. **39** Adelle Davis, LET'S HAVE HEALTHY CHILDREN. New York: Harcourt Brace Jovanovich, Inc., 1972, p. 239. **40** From SCOTT, FORESMAN LIFE SCIENCE by LeVon Balzer et al., p. 320. Copyright © 1987 Scott, Foresman and Company. **40** From SCOTT, FORESMAN BIOLOGY by Irwin L. Slesnick et al., p. 521. Copyright © 1983 Scott, Foresman and Company. **44** From SCOTT, FORESMAN BIOLOGY by Irwin L. Slesnick et al., p. 531. Copyright © 1985 Scott, Foresman and Company. **45** From SCOTT, FORESMAN LIFE SCIENCE by LeVon Balzer et al., p. 28. Copyright © 1987 Scott, Foresman and Company. **51** From SCOTT, FORESMAN LIFE SCIENCE by LeVon Balzer et al., p. 46. Copyright © 1987 Scott, Foresman and Company. **52** From SCOTT, FORESMAN BIOLOGY by Irwin L. Slesnick et al., p. 122. Copyright © 1983 Scott, Foresman and Company. **52–53** From SCOTT, FORESMAN BIOLOGY by Irwin L. Slesnick et al., p. 126. Copyright © 1983 Scott, Foresman and Company. **54** From "A Stupid Cell With All the Answers" by Natalie Angier. DISCOVER, November 1986. Copyright © 1986 Time Inc. All Rights Reserved. Reprinted by permission of *Discover* magazine. **59** Ron Wilson, HOW THE BODY WORKS. New York: Larousse and Co., Inc., 1978, p. 68. **60** Margery and Howard Facklam, FROM CELL TO CLONE. New York: Harcourt Brace Jovanovich, Inc., 1979, p. 95. **61** From SCOTT, FORESMAN LIFE SCIENCE by LeVon Balzer et al., p. 399. Copyright © 1987 Scott, Foresman and Company. **62–63** From SCOTT, FORESMAN BIOLOGY by Irwin L. Slesnick et al., p. 220. Copyright © 1985 Scott, Foresman and Company. **73** David Attenborough, LIFE ON EARTH: A NATURAL HISTORY. Boston: Little, Brown and Company, 1979, p. 76. **74–75** From "They've Got Rhythm" by David M. Schwartz. NATIONAL WILDLIFE, December 1986-January 1987. Copyright © 1986 by the National Wildlife Federation. Reprinted by permission. **77** From SCOTT, FORESMAN LIFE SCIENCE by LeVon Balzer et al., p. 139. Copyright © 1987 Scott, Foresman and Company. **80** From SCOTT, FORESMAN LIFE SCIENCE by LeVon Balzer et al., pp. 200–201, 204–206. Copyright © 1987 Scott, Foresman and Company. **82** Victor Berge, as told to Henry Wyshan Lanier, PEARL DIVER. New York: Doubleday & Co., Inc., 1930. **92** From "The Dam Builder Is At It Again!" by Phillip Johnson. NATIONAL WILDLIFE, June-July 1984. Copyright © 1984 by the National Wildlife Federation. Reprinted by permission. **111** From SCOTT, FORESMAN LIFE SCIENCE by LeVon Balzer et al., p. 85. Copyright © 1987 Scott, Foresman and Company.

Earth Science **117** From SCOTT, FORESMAN EARTH SCIENCE by Jay M. Pasachoff et al., p. 46. Copyright © 1986 Scott, Foresman and Company. **128** From SCOTT, FORESMAN EARTH SCIENCE by Jay M. Pasachoff et al., p. 132. Copyright © 1986 Scott, Foresman and Company. **129** From SCOTT, FORESMAN LIFE SCIENCE by LeVon Balzer et al., p. 394. Copyright © 1987 Scott, Foresman and Company. **134** From SCOTT, FORESMAN EARTH SCIENCE by Jay M. Pasachoff et al., p. 404. Copyright © 1986 Scott, Foresman and Company. **134** From SCOTT, FORESMAN EARTH SCIENCE by Jay M. Pasachoff et al., p. 425. Copyright © 1986 Scott, Foresman and Company. **135** Herbert H. Gross, Ph.D., WORLD GEOGRAPHY. Chicago: Follett Publishing Company, 1980, p. 124. **135** Jonathan Weiner, PLANET EARTH. New York: Bantam Books, 1986. **148** From SCOTT, FORESMAN EARTH SCIENCE by Jay M. Pasachoff et al., p. 279. Copyright © 1986 Scott, Foresman and Company. **152** Edward Teller, ENERGY FROM HEAVEN AND EARTH. San Francisco: W. H. Freeman and Company, 1979, p. 173.

Chemistry **174** From SCOTT, FORESMAN PHYSICAL SCIENCE by Jay M. Pasachoff et al., pp. 256–57. Copyright © 1986 Scott, Foresman and Company. **179** From SCOTT, FORESMAN PHYSICAL SCIENCE by Jay M. Pasachoff et al., p. 253. Copyright © 1986 Scott, Foresman and Company.

Physics **199** From SCOTT, FORESMAN PHYSICAL SCIENCE by Jay M. Pasachoff et al., p. 415. Copyright © 1986 Scott, Foresman and Company. **219** From SCOTT, FORESMAN PHYSICAL SCIENCE by Jay M. Pasachoff et al., p. 395. Copyright © 1986 Scott, Foresman and Company.

Posttest A **238** From SCIENCE IN THE WORLD AROUND US by William C. Vergara. New York: Harper & Row, 1973. Reprinted by permission of the author. **248** Figure after "The Elusive Mechanism Circadian Clock" by Carl Hirschie Johnson and J. Woodland Hastings. AMERICAN SCIENTIST, January-February 1986, p. 30. Reprinted by permission. **250** Maurice A. Corrigy, "New Production Techniques for Alberta Oil Sands." SCIENCE, 1986.

Illustration Acknowledgments

Positions of illustrations are shown in abbreviated form as follows: top *(t)*, bottom *(b)*, left *(l)*, right *(r)*.

6 From HEALTH by Ruth Ann Althaus et al., p. 98. Copyright © 1987 Scott, Foresman and Company. **9** From HEALTH by Ruth Ann Althaus et al., p. 337. Copyright © 1987 Scott, Foresman and Company. **20** Skin Cancer Foundation, American Cancer Society. Reprinted by permission. **25** From SCOTT, FORESMAN BIOLOGY by Irwin L. Slesnick et al. Copyright © 1985 Scott, Foresman and Company. **37** From A WOMAN'S GUIDE TO GOOD HEALTH AFTER 50 by Marie Feltin. Copyright © 1987 Scott, Foresman and Company and American Association of Retired Persons. **46** From SCOTT, FORESMAN BIOLOGY by Irwin L. Slesnick et al., p. 79. Copyright © 1983 Scott, Foresman and Company. **48** From SCOTT, FORESMAN BIOLOGY by Irwin L. Slesnick et al., p. 88. Copyright © 1983 Scott, Foresman and Company. **56** From SCOTT, FORESMAN LIFE SCIENCE by LeVon Balzer et al., p. 375. Copyright © 1987 Scott, Foresman and Company. **62** From SCOTT, FORESMAN BIOLOGY by Irwin L. Slesnick et al., p. 220. Copyright © 1985 Scott, Foresman and Company. **70** From SCOTT, FORESMAN BIOLOGY by Irwin L. Slesnick et al., p. 79. Copyright © 1983 Scott, Foresman and Company. **72** *(l)* From SCOTT, FORESMAN LIFE SCIENCE by LeVon Balzer et al., p. 135.

Contents

What You Should Know About Preparing for the GED Test

What Is the GED Test?

The initials GED stand for General Educational Development. You may have heard the GED Test called the High School Equivalency Test. That is because the test measures your ability against that of graduating high-school students. If you pass, you will earn a certificate that is the *equivalent* of a high-school diploma. You do not have to go back to school to get it. That's quite an opportunity, if you think about it!

Why Take the Test?

Every state in the Union, the District of Columbia, nine United States territories or possessions, and many Canadian provinces and territories use GED Test results as the basis for giving high-school equivalency credentials. A credential is something that credits a person with an achievement. GED credentials give credit for achieving the same amount of learning as high-school graduates. Those credentials are accepted for employment, promotion, and licensing just as high-school diplomas are.

There's another good reason for taking the test. Many colleges and universities now accept satisfactory GED Test scores in place of high-school grades to admit students.

Who Takes the Test?

In this country about 40 million people over eighteen do not have high-school diplomas. This means that almost 22 percent of the adult population of the United States has not graduated from high school.

In recent years more than one-half million people each year have taken the GED Test. A lot of people must think it makes good sense to have a high-school equivalency credential.

Getting Ready for the GED Test

If you are not already enrolled in a GED preparation program and would like help preparing for the test, you should make some phone calls. The office of the superintendent of schools or your local vocational school, community college, or adult education center is a good place to contact. Ask if there are GED preparation courses available nearby. A call or two should be enough to get the information.

Many people prefer to study on their own rather than in a class. If you are one of those independent spirits, you can still benefit by calling one of the places suggested above. You may ask for information on the GED Test and about fees, application forms, and test times. If, however, you can't get the information you need, write to the following address:

General Educational Development
GED Testing Service of the American
Council on Education
One Dupont Circle NW
Washington, DC 20036

What's the GED Test Like?

Most questions on the GED Test are multiple-choice, and there are five answer choices for each. You will need only to mark one of the five answer spaces for each question. You also have to write a short essay for the Writing Skills Test.

The GED Test measures whether you have mastered the skills and general knowledge that are usually acquired in a four-year high-school education. However, you are not expected to remember many details, definitions, and facts. Therefore, being out of school for some time should not be a handicap at all.

The five subtests on the GED Test have been created to test whether an adult has the knowledge and skills that the average high-school graduate has in these areas:

Test 1: Writing Skills
Test 2: Social Studies
Test 3: Science
Test 4: Interpreting Literature and the Arts
Test 5: Mathematics

The GED Test does not base your score on your ability to race against the clock as some tests do. You will have plenty of time to finish each subtest. Even so, you will want to work steadily and not waste any time. It is important that you answer every question, *even if you just guess,* because your score depends on the number of answers you get right.

Now read on to find out more about the GED Science Test.

The GED Science Test

What's on the Test?

The GED Science Test contains 66 multiple-choice questions and takes about 95 minutes to complete. The number of questions from each area of science is shown here.

Biology	33 questions
Earth Science Chemistry Physics	33 questions

Biology is the study of life—from the smallest cell to the largest animal. It also studies the relationship between living things and their environment. That environment is itself the focus of earth science. Earth science deals with the land, air, and water on our planet. Chemistry involves matter—the tiny particles that make up matter and how those particles come together to form the things we see, including ourselves. And finally, physics is the study of matter *and* energy, including heat, light, electricity, and atomic energy.

On the GED Science Test, items from the different areas are not kept separate. You'll find questions about biology, earth science, chemistry, and physics all mixed together. That is not really a problem because the skills required to answer the questions are the same regardless of which branch of science the information is about. The Posttests in this book will show you how easy it is to go from a question about one branch of science to another.

On the GED Science Test, you'll find single questions that include all the information you need right there. You'll also see longer articles or visuals (graphs, tables, and diagrams) followed by several questions. All these questions test your ability to understand, apply, analyze, and evaluate the information you have just read.

Life Experience: A "Plus" for GED Test Takers

If you've been out of school for a while, you may be anxious about preparing for the GED Science Test. You may think that you've forgotten how to study, or you may feel that you're just not good at science. If that sounds like the kind of thinking you've been doing, you're forgetting one very important thing you've got on your side: all the *experience* you have. The information you've learned just from everyday life is the kind of information that the GED Science Test is most concerned with.

For example, perhaps you follow the news stories about the effects of pollution, toxic-waste clean-ups, and acid rain. Or maybe you have an indoor or outdoor garden and know how to plant, fertilize, and reproduce plants. If so, you've got a start on understanding biology. If your indoor garden is in a window that faces south because you know it gets more sun there, you're applying a principle from earth science. What about making cake batter with cake mix, water, and eggs or taking milk of magnesia for an upset stomach? If you do such things, you're dealing with physical and chemical properties. And if you know a little about electrical circuits and fuses, or how to use a crowbar to lift a heavy object, or that lifting the lid off a kettle will let some of the built-up steam out and reduce the temperature, you already know a bit about physics.

In addition to these practical experiences, perhaps you like to watch science programs on television or to read popular science magazines (or the science section that is part of many Sunday newspapers). If so, you already feel "comfortable" with scientific topics, and that is a big head start toward preparing for the GED Science Test.

Keep this in mind: You don't need to remember all the scientific terms and formulas that are taught in high school to pass the GED Science Test. Instead, most of the questions on the test let you put your experience to work for you. Working through this book will help you learn to apply your experience to your preparation for the GED Science Test.

The Scientific Method and the GED Test

Long ago many people, including doctors, believed that the shape of a plant indicated whether it was useful as a medicine. A flower that resembled a human heart was administered to patients with heart problems. A plant with a root shaped like a human kidney was prescribed for patients with kidney ailments. Seeds that were shaped like teeth were vigorously chewed to get rid of toothache. However, since the plants did not contain any ingredients that could actually heal or cure, the belief gave many patients false hope.

The belief that certain plants could heal whatever they resembled seems silly now. It is a good illustration of mistakes that can occur when the *scientific method* is not followed. What is the scientific method? It is a way of thinking and studying about something carefully and logically. It involves a set of attitudes and procedures that can be followed to discover knowledge about the world.

Although the name *scientific method* suggests that it is used only in a laboratory, that is far from the truth. In fact, you may have used something like the scientific method many times without realizing it. The thought process that lies behind the scientific method is so valuable and important that the GED Science Test will test your ability to identify when and how it can be applied.

The scientific method is made up of five steps: (1) observing and identifying a problem, (2) forming a hypothesis, (3) conducting an experiment, (4) interpreting the results, and (5) drawing a conclusion. Scientists follow this procedure strictly in their research. However, it may be easier to understand the five steps if their use is applied to a common consumer problem.

Take, as an example, a couple who are on a tight budget. They want to be sure to get the most value for their food dollar. Here is how they might use the scientific method.

Observing and identifying a problem: The couple is trying to decide which kind of bread—diet or regular—to buy. The diet bread appeals to them because it has only half the calories of regular bread. On the other hand, the diet bread costs twice as much. They read the list of ingredients on both packages and discover that both kinds have the same ingredients. They compare the appearance of the breads. In color and texture, they seem very much the same, yet the slices of diet bread seem smaller. They decide that the problem is this: Which type of bread will provide the best value?

Forming a hypothesis: The next step is to form a *hypothesis,* or a possible explanation, about which kind is better and why. Since the slices of diet bread are smaller and a loaf actually costs *twice* as much as the regular bread, the consumers feel that it is probably not as good a value. They form the hypothesis that the regular bread is the best value.

Experimenting: To test their hypothesis, the man and woman bring a loaf of each type home and weigh a slice of each on their kitchen scale. The slice of regular bread weighs two grams. The diet slice weighs only one.

Interpreting the results: From the "experiment," the couple have discovered that the two products are the same except in weight. The diet bread weighs only half as much. In other words, the diet bread has half as many calories per slice just because there is only half as much bread per slice. Yet the diet bread costs twice as much.

Drawing a conclusion: On the basis of their "experiment," the couple conclude that their hypothesis was correct: the regular bread is the better value.

Of course, the questions investigated in scientific laboratories are far more complex than that example, and the equipment used for observations and true experiments is much more sophisticated. Yet the same five steps guide researchers as they seek the answers to scientific questions about the world. And when the same hypothesis has been proved by experiments over and over, it comes to be accepted as a general explanation called a *theory.*

You can see how the five steps of the scientific method are used by scientists and can be applied to your practical decision making. Remember them when you take the GED Science Test too.

How to Use This Book

What Is a Springboard?

You probably already know what a real springboard can do for athletes such as divers and tumblers. A springboard is used to increase the height of their leaps. In the same, this *Springboard* is your take-off point for making the big leap—passing the GED Science Test. This book starts each lesson at a very basic level. Then it brings you right up to the point where you can answer questions like those on the actual GED Test.

Taking the Skills Survey

The Skills Survey can be used as a pretest to show you how much you know already. It has one-third the number of multiple-choice questions as the GED Science Test. The passages and questions are very much like those on the actual GED Test, and the skills they measure are the same. Taking the Skills Survey and then carefully reading the answer explanations will show you which skills you need to work on. When you come to a lesson in the book that teaches one of those skills, you can give more of your time and attention to it. In that way you can plan your studies to meet your own special needs.

All of the answers for the Skills Survey are labeled according to the cognitive levels of Bloom's Taxonomy, another way of classifying the types of questions on the GED Test. For example, a question may be labeled **AP,** which means that it involves application of the topic information. Questions labeled **CP** involve comprehension, those labeled **AN** require analysis, and **EV** questions require evaluation of the information given. The actual GED Test will contain questions at all of these levels. Cognitive level labels, as explained above, also have been added to the Extra Practice questions and to the Posttests in this book. Keys have been provided at the bottom of the answer pages for your reference.

Polishing Your Thinking Skills

Many people who plan to take the GED Science Test are surprised to learn that it's more important to think clearly and reason out problems carefully than to know all about biology, earth science, chemistry, and physics. This book puts special emphasis on the reading and thinking skills that are tested on the GED Science Test. Every lesson focuses on a particular skill—that is, a special way of understanding, analyzing, or evaluating reading passages, graphs, and diagrams. You'll practice each thinking skill using examples from the science content area that you study in the first part of the lesson.

This special two-part lesson organization, which combines skills and content, will help make your study interesting and meaningful. And the book gives you more than one chance to practice each thinking skill tested on the GED Science Test. If you look closely at the table of contents, you'll notice that almost all the skills—whose names appear in red—are presented at least once after they are introduced. For example, notice that understanding cause-and-effect relationships is introduced in biology lesson 5, and that the same skill is also the focus of earth science lesson 15 and physics lesson 25. This "recycling" technique allows you to learn a skill and then practice it again using examples from a different science area.

Pay extra attention to the second half, or skills section, of each lesson. The heads for this section are printed in red so that you can find them easily. Do the skills in the order in which they are presented in this book, study the explanations and examples of each skill carefully, and answer the multiple-choice questions at the end of each skills section just as you would if you were taking the real test. If you follow these suggestions, you'll probably have no trouble getting a good score on the GED Science Test.

Working the Lessons

The lessons in this book carefully guide you through all the steps you need to understand the material. Each lesson is easy to read and understand. First it presents content matter about a particular scientific topic with plenty of examples and illustrations. Important new terms appear in **bold** type and are defined right in the text. The new words are also listed with their definitions in a *Coming to Terms* section. Although you do not have to memorize these terms, you'll probably find it helpful to learn their meanings. You can do this by reading each definition twice, thinking about it, and then reading it again.

Then comes a *Warm-up,* a short exercise that asks you to restate in your own words the content matter you have just read. Each lesson has several *Warm-up* exercises, so you'll get plenty of practice in summarizing by writing sentences and paragraphs.

The second part of the lesson introduces a thinking or reading skill that you'll need for the test. In *Here's an Example,* you'll find one or more specific examples of how to use the skill that was just explained. A section called *Try It Yourself* lets you see if you have understood what you've just read. It gives you the opportunity to use the skill yourself in reading a passage or graphic; then it explains how you should have gone about doing so. You'll also find many *Test-Taking Tips.* These are practical suggestions about how to answer certain types of questions that often appear on the GED Science Test.

Each lesson then introduces a very important step, one that helps you leap from a lower level to a higher, GED, one. This step is a special section called *On the Springboard.* It has a passage or graphic and one or two multiple-choice questions that are similar to those on the GED Test (but not quite as difficult). On the Springboard is not only a jumping-off point but also a step that helps you gain confidence in your ability to answer questions like those on the actual test. If you have any problems answering the Springboard questions correctly, this book will tell you exactly what to review before going on. After all, you need to be in top shape before taking the final leap.

That leap is the section called *"The Real Thing."* There you will find a passage or graphic and questions like those on the GED Test. Because you've just completed On the Springboard, your chances of success with "The Real Thing" will be greatly increased.

Checking Your Answers

You can check your answers to the *Warm-up* quickly and easily in the *Sample Warm-up Answers.* These answers are found at the bottom of the page that has the questions, usually in the same column. Use the sample answers as guides; your answers may differ because your thoughts and the way you express them are your own.

Answers for On the Springboard and "The Real Thing" multiple-choice questions in each section are near the end of the section, after all the lessons. Solid red strips run along the edges of these pages to help you locate them quickly. On these pages you'll find not only each correct answer but also an explanation of why that answer makes sense. Reading the explanation, even if you got the answer right, will help you check your thinking and strengthen what you have already learned. It will also add confidence in your ability to make good judgments.

Keeping Track

After the answer explanations for "The Real Thing" multiple-choice questions in each lesson, you'll find a Keeping Track box that will help you do just that—keep track of how well you are doing. There you can record how many "Real Thing" answers you got right. Once you've finished all "The Real Thing" questions in a section, you can transfer your scores to the Keeping Track chart that follows the explanations. You'll be able to see which skills you've learned and which ones you need to review before you go on.

Taking Advantage of the Extra Practice

Following each subject section is some Extra Practice for that particular content area of the GED Science Test: biology, earth science, chemistry, and physics. These sections measure the same skills that the GED Test measures. Doing the Extra Practice for a section lets you know whether you've learned the skills needed to do well in that area on the GED Test.

Charting Your Progress

The Progress Chart on the inside back cover is for you to keep a record of how many multiple-choice questions you got correct in the Extra Practice for each section. Notice how many correct answers you need to get a passing score, a good score, and a very good score. A good or very good score means you are ready to go on to the next section. If you just barely get a passing score or less, take the time to go back over those lessons that gave you trouble.

Taking the Posttests

After you've finished studying all four content areas, done the Extra Practice, and reviewed any material you need to, make an appointment with yourself to take the first of the two Posttests. When you finish, check your answers. Then find your score and the explanation of your results.

If you pass, you are ready to take the GED Science Test. If you don't, you can use the Skill Chart on page 257 to determine which sections of the book to review before you take the second Posttest.

Using the Index

When you need to review certain skills, the Index at the back of this book can help you. It lists all the important topics in the book and the numbers of the pages on which the topics are discussed. In addition, all the terms whose definitions appear in Coming to Terms throughout the book appear in the Index in **bold** type. That will help you locate and review their meanings.

How to Read Scientific Diagrams, Tables, and Graphs

About one-third of the items on the GED Science Test refer to visual materials such as diagrams, tables, and graphs. Knowing how to read and interpret these will help you succeed on the test.

Diagrams

Some GED science items will test your ability to understand, summarize, and work with information given in a diagram. A diagram is an illustration that shows the outlines of an object or area so that you can see how its parts fit or work together. It is specially designed to help you gather information quickly.

The first step in reading a diagram is to read the title if there is one. It tells the topic of the diagram. Next, look at the general shape of the object or area represented in the diagram. Then look at the separate parts. In many diagrams different colors or gray shadings are used to help you distinguish the different parts from each other. Notice where they are placed in relation to each other. If labels are given, read them carefully. Labels help you understand how the different parts work together within the whole item represented.

Read the title of the diagram below. Notice the general shape of the item represented. Read the labels. Then use information from the diagram to answer the questions that follow.

Parts of the brain

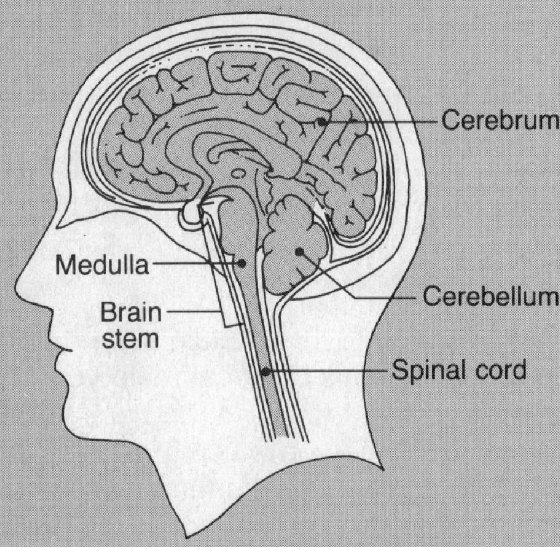

1. What is the name of the largest part of the brain? ______________________

2. The lowest part of the brain stem is a small bulb called the ______________________.

3. The spinal cord is a nerve cable that extends down from the ______________________.

You can check your answers with those given below.

Answers
1. cerebrum **2.** medulla **3.** brain stem

Many scientific principles involve understanding how one step leads to another. A diagram is an excellent way to picture a process like that. Directional arrows show your eye the next steps in the process.

Study the diagram below. First read its title; then notice the direction pointed out by the arrows. Start at the top, read the first label, and follow the directional arrows to the next label and then the next.

Control of Breathing Rate

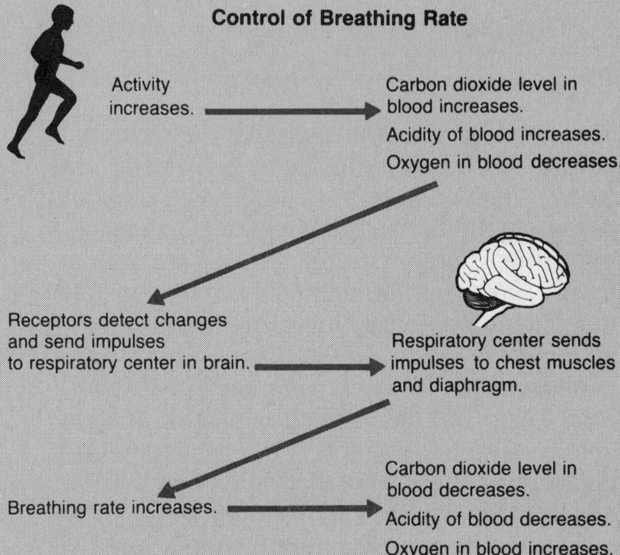

Use information from the diagram to answer the following questions.

1. What happens to the blood right after a person's activity level increases? ______________________

____

2. When does the breathing rate increase?

____

Answers
1. Carbon dioxide and acidity increase while oxygen decreases. **2.** The breathing rate increases once the respiratory center has sent impulses to the chest muscles and diaphragm.

When the labels and arrows are arranged in a circle, you know that the process being diagrammed is a cycle, in which one step leads to the next, with no beginning or end.

Sometimes a diagram allows you to see both the inside and the outside of an object at the same time. Can you figure out the diagram of a beaver lodge below?

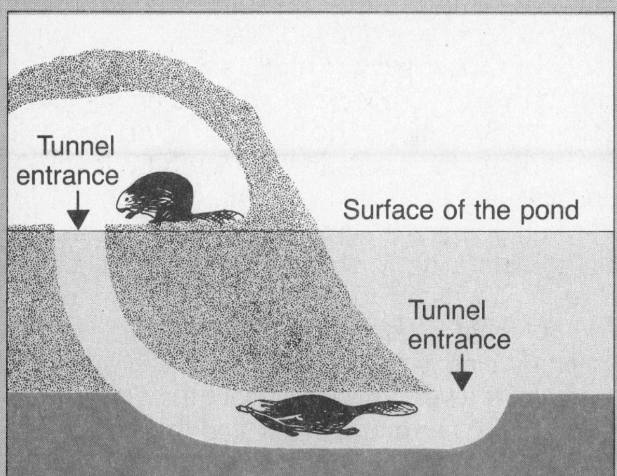

Now use the diagram to answer these questions.

1. Is the beaver home entirely under water?

---

2. How do the beavers enter and leave the home?

Tables

Some items on the GED Science Test are based on tables. A table is made up of columns of figures, names, or other information given briefly. Each column has a heading to show the kind of information it contains. At the left of the table is a list of items. Each item applies to a row across the table.

As with other visual aids, it's a good idea to preview a table before you attempt to answer any questions about it. Read the title to discover what the topic is. Read the headings and items to see what kind of information about the topic is given, how much is given, and in what order it is arranged.

The Planets

Planet	Diameter		Rotation Period
	Miles	Kilometers	
Mercury	3,007	4,840	59 d
Venus	7,705	12,400	243 d
Earth	7,917	12,742	23 h 56 m
Mars	4,225	6,800	24 h 37 m
Jupiter	88,730	142,800	9 h 50 m
Saturn	75,060	120,800	10 h 14 m
Uranus	29,600	47,600	10 h 49 m
Neptune	27,700	44,600	15 h 40 m
Pluto	8,900	14,400	16 h

What is the topic of the table? Can you see that the title tells you the topic is the planets? Does the table give information about the sizes of the planets? Yes, according to one of the column headings, the diameter of each planet is given in miles and kilometers. Does the table tell how many satellites each planet has? No, there is no heading about satellites.

To find a particular statistic, put one finger on the appropriate heading at the top of that column. Locate the item—in this case, the name of a planet—on the left. Move your finger down and your eyes across until they meet. The information you find matches a heading with an item.

Use that method to answer this question: Is the length of a day on Mars, as measured by the rotation period, shorter or longer than an Earth day?

To answer that question, find the column that lists the rotation periods. Then find the figure that tells the length of one rotation of Earth and the figure that tells the length of one rotation of Mars. When you contrast the two, you can tell that Mars's rotation is 41 minutes longer than Earth's. So the answer is *longer.*

Graphs

On the GED Science Test, you will also find a number of items that require you to gather and use information from a circle graph, bar graph, or line graph. Each graph on the GED Science Test presents information from one of the four areas of science tested: biology, earth science, chemistry, or physics.

Answers
1. No, it is partially above the water level. **2.** A tunnel leads from the outside of the lodge under the water into the bottom of the lodge.

Circle Graphs Circle graphs, sometimes called pie graphs, are always made in the shape of a circle. Different-sized portions, or slices, of the circle represent parts of a whole amount. A circle graph allows you to see how the different amounts of the parts compare with each other and with the whole.

Study the circle graph below, beginning with the title. Then answer the questions that follow it.

Elements in the Earth's Crust

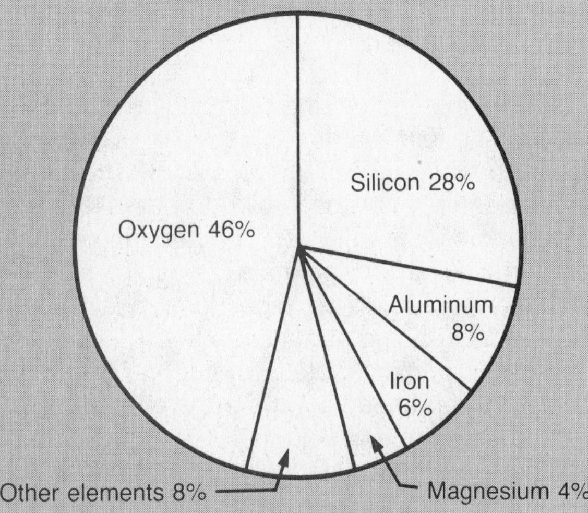

1. What kind of information does the graph give?

____

____

2. List the elements in the earth's crust in order from largest percentage to smallest percentage.

____

____

Some circle graphs are not labeled with percentages. In that case, you must estimate each percentage from the size of the portion. For example, if a portion of a circle graph is about one-fourth of the circle, then you know the portion is about 25 percent of the whole. Remember that the whole of a circle graph always equals 100 percent. The graphs at the top of the next column will help you visualize what other percentages look like on a circle graph.

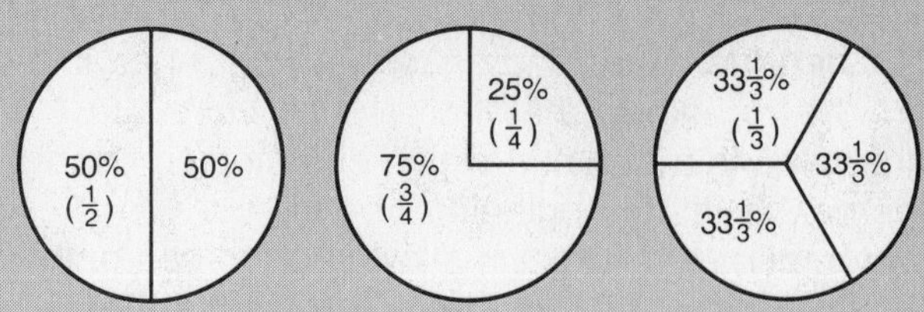

Bar Graphs A bar graph shows comparisons. Bars of different lengths let you compare amounts for the people or things represented. Labels along the side and bottom of the graph show what is being compared and give measurements so that you can note the amounts yourself. Sometimes the bars run across from left to right, and sometimes they run from the bottom up.

When you come across a bar graph, read the title to determine what the graph is about. Next, note the labels along the side and bottom to find out what is being compared and what kind of information is being given. Then you are ready to answer questions about the graph.

Study the bar graph below and then answer the questions that follow it.

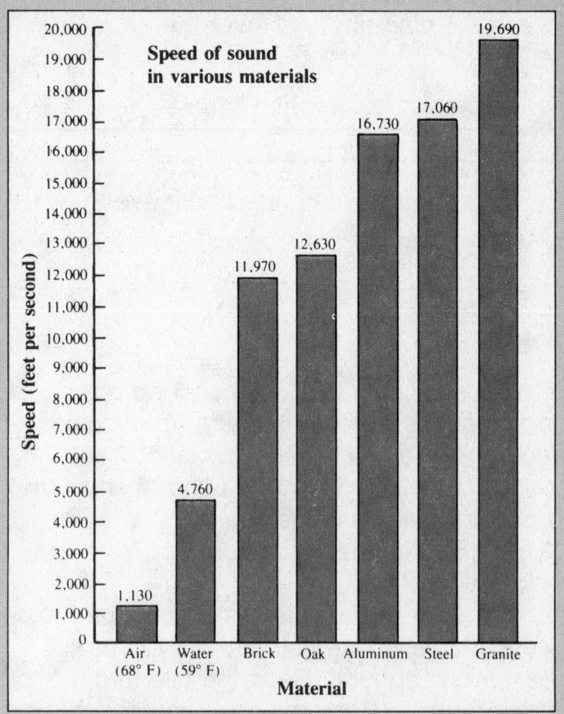

Answers
1. It tells the elements that make up the earth's crust.
2. oxygen, silicon, aluminum, iron, magnesium, and other elements

1. What do the bars on the graph show?

2. How many feet per second does sound travel through steel?

3. Which material does sound travel through more quickly—air or brick?

4. Which does sound appear to travel through most quickly—gases such as air, liquids such as water, or solids such as wood?

Often two or more bars are used to compare two or more groups of people or things. In such cases, you have to pay particular attention to which group is represented by which bar. Sometimes the labels will appear right inside the bars. If not, a *key* will give you that information. The key appears within the graph or next to it and tells what people or things are represented by each bar.

Read this double-bar graph.

Death Rate of Smokers and Nonsmokers

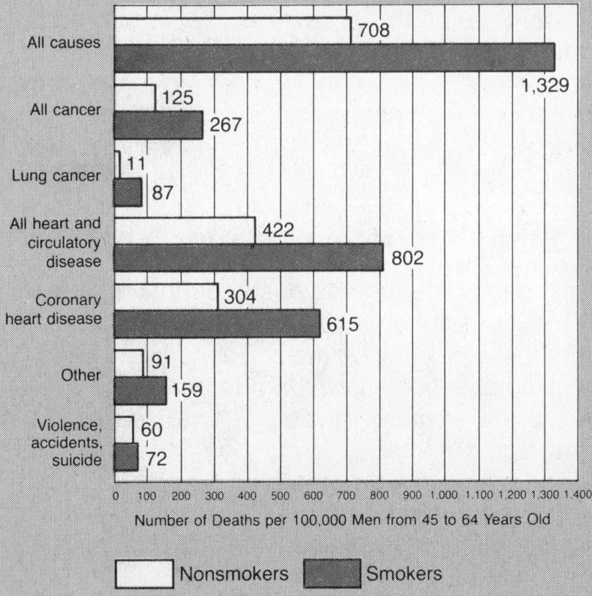

Now complete these sentences about the graph.

1. The labels on the left side list different __________ of death.

2. The numbers along the bottom represent the number of __________.

3. Cancer kills __________ smokers than nonsmokers.

4. What does the evidence show about the causes of death among smokers and nonsmokers?

Line Graphs A line graph shows changes or trends. As with other graphs, you need to begin reading a line graph with its title to see what the topic is. Then, as you do with a bar graph, read the labels on the side and bottom to see what kind of information is given along each dimension. In some line graphs, straight lines extend outward from the sides and bottom. Those lines crisscross and form a grid, which makes it easier for you to locate the information you need.

Look carefully at the line graph below. When you have read the title and labels, notice how points are marked along the grid. Those points are joined with a line to help you see the general change. Use information from the graph to answer the questions that follow it.

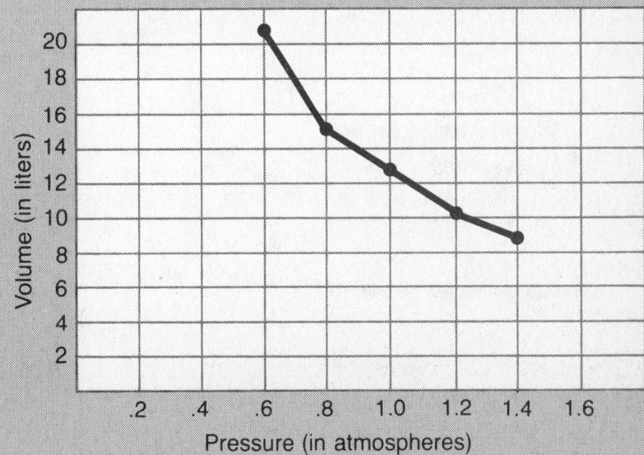

Relationship of Pressure and Volume of Oxygen at 25° C

Answers
1. how fast sound travels through various materials
2. 17,060 **3.** brick **4.** solids

Answers
1. causes **2.** deaths per 100,000 men aged 45 to 64
3. more **4.** More smokers than nonsmokers die from all the causes of death listed.

1. What is being measured along the left side of the graph?

---

2. What is being measured along the bottom of the graph?

---

3. Approximately what is the volume of the oxygen at 1.2 atmospheres of pressure?

---

4. In general, what happens when the pressure on the gas is increased?

Some line graphs show change in more than one item by using more than one line. To avoid confusing readers, each line is drawn differently. Usually a key is given within the graph or next to it to show what each line represents.

Preview the graph below, including the title, labels, and key. Then read the graph by following each line from its starting point at the left to its end point at the right. Use information from the graph to answer the question below it.

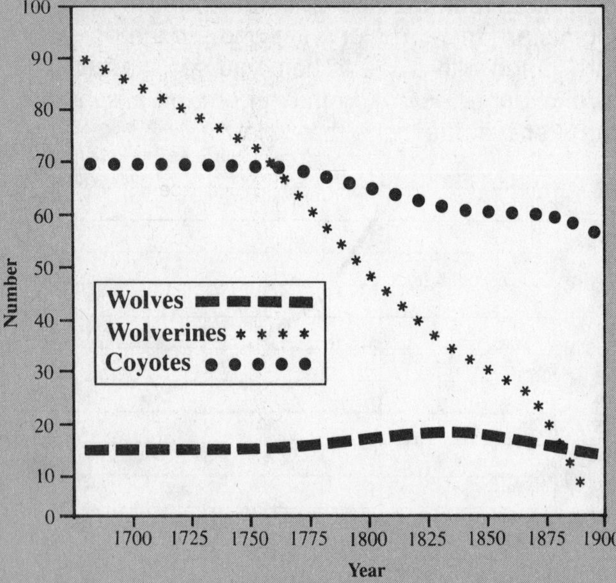

Based on the trends shown by the populations of all three predators, which animal was most likely the first to vanish from Bay County?

Answers
1. volume of oxygen in liters 2. pressure measured in units called atmospheres 3. about 10 liters 4. The volume decreases.

To answer the question, you first need to notice the general trends shown in the graph. From 1700 to 1900, all three predators showed a decline in population. If the trends continued, it can be predicted that all three predators would in time have vanished from Bay County. Which would disappear first? You can predict that it would be the one whose line takes the sharpest downward plunge—the wolverine.

Test Anxiety: How to Cope with It

When you think about actually taking the GED Test, you may feel anxious. This is perfectly normal. Plenty of people—no matter how prepared, intelligent, or self-confident they may be—feel test anxiety.

Test anxiety can make you so afraid of failing that you put off studying. It can make you panic so that you do not think clearly. You may begin to jump from one area to the next in an impossible attempt to learn everything at once without any plan.

Test anxiety can work against you during the test too. You may feel so anxious that you can't concentrate on the questions. That is the most dangerous result of test anxiety. Just when you need every bit of energy, you waste that energy thinking, "I didn't answer the last question fast enough," or "I'm probably behind everyone else now," or "I never did understand this."

Making Anxiety Work for You

Most people do get nervous about taking a test. The successful ones are those who make that nervousness work *for* them. Test anxiety can actually help you if you learn to channel it correctly. For example, anxiety can cause many people to put their noses to the grindstone and spend plenty of time preparing for a test. They try harder to answer the test questions—even difficult ones. Their anxiety makes them alert and careful.

If you use this book properly, you can avoid the build-up of harmful test anxiety. You can make your anxiety work for you by using your energy to prepare thoroughly for the exam.

As you work through this book, be honest in grading yourself on the sections called On the Springboard and "The Real Thing." You can fool yourself by saying, "Oh, I marked answer 5, but I thought it might be 3, so I'll give myself credit for that answer." But if you do this, you will begin to feel uneasy. You may doubt that you really have covered the material. Then you have created your own test anxiety. So don't rush your study. The extra time it takes you to review sections is well worth it.

Positive Thinking Can Raise Your Scores

While you've been away from school, you've done many things that show your basic strengths. You may have held down a job; received raises or promotions; had children; supported a family; bought, built, or rented a home; saved some money; traveled; acquired interesting hobbies; or made good friends. However, when facing a new challenge, like a test, you may forget that you've done such things. You may feel unsure of yourself because now you're entering unknown territory—and the ground begins to feel shaky!

Look at the Accomplishments Chart below. Take time now to write down five things you've done that you feel good about. Don't think, "I'm proud of that, but it's too silly to write down." Be honest and put down whatever you want. After all, no one but you has to see your list.

Once you've written your list, ask yourself if any of those things took hard work, courage, patience, or the ability to put your experience to work for you. Then put checks in the boxes where you deserve them.

If you start feeling bad about your abilities later, come back to this chart and take another good look at those checks. Then tell yourself that you have no reason to feel bad.

Feeling depressed or anxious takes a surprising amount of energy. By thinking positively, you will find it easier to prepare for this new challenge in a steady, organized way.

Relax!

Following that order is not always as easy as it might seem. If you are one of the many people who feel anxious about taking a test, you can *learn* to relax.

Exercise can be one of the best ways to relax your mind. You might try jogging or doing simple stretching exercises for fifteen minutes after each study session. Don't think about what you have just studied. For this short period of time, think only of how you will soon pass the GED Test.

Another way to relax is to find a quiet spot where you can be alone for fifteen minutes after every study session. Close your eyes. Think about how you are working steadily to pass the GED Test and that you will soon achieve your goal.

Still another way to relax is to tense and then relax your muscles. For example, you might try tensing your muscles while saying to yourself, "I am working hard to pass the GED Test." Then relax your muscles and say, "And I am going to

Accomplishment	Hard work	Courage	Patience	Experience
1.				
2.				
3.				
4.				
5.				

pass it soon." Each time, appreciate the relaxation for a little while and think about how good it feels to be working toward something you want.

Research shows that people forget less of what they have studied if they relax immediately after studying. That's another good reason to do one of the relaxation activities right after studying for the GED Test.

The Endurance Factor

Some people confuse two things: studying in a steady way and studying until they are tired or bored or both. You will be wasting a lot of your time if you study too long or if you study when you are too tired to concentrate.

Decide before you begin to study what hours you will set aside each day to prepare for the GED Test. Probably you should spend between forty-five minutes and two hours per session. You can choose to study once or, if you have the time, two or even three times a day.

Set up your schedule so that you can use your periods of greatest energy for study. Some people study best in the early morning hours. You will have to decide which times are best for you.

If you have a job, try to make use of your lunch hour and coffee breaks. If you take a bus or train to work, you can use your travel time for study. If you do this regularly, chances are you'll be able to squeeze in a surprising amount of extra study time.

Remember, whenever you feel yourself concentrating poorly or when you feel tired, close your book and do something else. You might do some of the relaxation exercises mentioned earlier.

Tips for Passing the GED Science Test

Long-Range Planning

1. As you prepare for the GED Science Test, keep in mind that what you are learning will benefit you for the rest of your life, not just until you pass the test. Certainly, passing the test is foremost in your mind right now, and it should be. But don't assume that once the test is over, you will no longer use what you are learning. Consider the skills you are now mastering to be a permanent part of your life. This attitude will help you value what you learn. It will also give you a greater sense of purpose as you prepare for the GED Test.

2. Give yourself plenty of time to prepare for the GED Science Test. Don't think you can do all your studying in one weekend. Your brain can't continue to work at its peak if you cram too much into it at once.

3. If you think you might have a vision problem, have your eyes checked before you begin to study for the test. All your knowledge and ability may not help if you have trouble seeing and end up misreading some of the questions.

4. Be sure that your study conditions help you, not hold you back. Check to see that you have good lighting. Use a desk or table that is large enough for all your study materials. Make certain that you are not too warm or too cold. If you are, you may not be able to concentrate as well as you could. Use a comfortable chair that supports your back well.

5. Keep all your study materials in one place and have them ready before you sit down to study. You will probably want to have plenty of pencils, pens, paper, a notebook or folder, and, of course, a dictionary.

6. Begin slowly and build your endurance. Don't spend more than an hour each time you study until you are sure that covering this amount of material doesn't wear you out. Preparing for the GED Science Test is, in this sense, like preparing for running a marathon race.

7. As you study, take notes. If you jot down main ideas and important facts, you reinforce what you are learning. Then later you can use these notes to review. But be careful not to write down too much. Too many notes are just as bad as no notes at all. If you are in a GED class, your notes can also help you keep track of questions to ask your teacher. Take time to think carefully about his or her answers. Make sure that you really do understand what has been explained. Don't be afraid to ask for further explanations. The first big step in understanding something is being able to ask questions about it.

8. People study best at different speeds. This book will help you decide how long to spend on each section. The answer explanations, Keeping Track charts, and Progress Chart can help you judge your progress and decide if you are moving at the right pace. Make the most of these self-checks as you work through the lessons.

9. Be sure to review what you have studied each day. It is easy to forget what you have read if you do not go over it once more before closing your book. You can review by going through your notes, by looking at the headings in your book, and by asking yourself to explain what was covered in each section. Try explaining aloud to yourself, as if you were a teacher talking to a class, the important ideas that you just read. This builds your confidence. You won't just *think* you know it—you can actually *hear* that you know it. This is probably the best way to see whether you really understood what was being taught.

10. Put your newly-acquired reading and thinking skills to use in your daily life. Practice with other reading that you do on the job or at home.

Short-Range Planning—The Last 24 Hours

1. If you have prepared for a long time in advance, do something relaxing the night before the GED Test. You might want to go to a movie or to a sports event.

2. Getting a good night's sleep before the exam is one of the best things you can do for yourself. Cramming is not wise for any exam. It doesn't make sense at all for the GED Test. To pass the GED Test, you must read and think carefully and use common sense. A good night's sleep will help you do just that.

3. It's not smart to drink too much coffee or soft drinks with caffeine or take any other kind of stimulant. After an initial "high," you may begin to feel nervous or tired. This jittery sensation won't help you concentrate.

4. Steer clear of tranquilizers as well. Even though they help you feel less nervous, they will also affect your ability to think quickly and read carefully. The trade-off is just not worth it when you're taking an important test.

5. Don't dress too warmly when you go to take the test. Psychologists have found that if people feel slightly cool, they tend to do better on a test. You may become drowsy if you are too warm.

6. If you are left-handed, get a desk with a left-handed writing board. Ask the examiner about this before the exam, if possible.

During the Test

1. No matter how much or how little people study for a test, they often go into it with the attitude they developed toward test taking long ago. Some students get too rattled to make good use of what they have learned with all their study. Others pride themselves on not getting nervous and take the test without being serious about it. They trust that their good luck will see them through and don't really give the test their complete attention. What is the best attitude to take during the GED Test? The best attitude is to be very serious about doing your best, but never panic.

2. The people who give the GED Test know that many people are anxious about taking the test. They will make every effort to make you feel at ease. Before you begin the test, they will let you know where the rest rooms and smoking areas are located. They will also try to make sure that the testing room is quiet and at a comfortable temperature and that the lighting is good. A wall clock will probably be in the room. If not, about every fifteen minutes the examiner will announce the time remaining during the test. Even so, you may want to wear a watch so you will know exactly how much time you have to finish.

3. Some GED questions are missed only because test takers don't mark answer sheets correctly. In some places the answers are corrected by a machine that can recognize only a completely filled-in space as a correct answer. If the machine sees an answer that is marked in some other way—like this  or like this  or like this  —it cannot count that mark as a correct answer.

Remember that the machine is fair. However, if you confuse it with markings that it does not understand, it will mark your answer wrong even if it is correct. To avoid this, fill in the space so that the answer is definitely clear, but not so hard that you can't erase later if you want to change an answer. Check to make sure you have not made any extra marks near that answer or filled in any other space in that row of choices.

4. Put both the answer sheet and the test booklet on your desk so that they are easy to see and reach. Keep your place by putting one hand near the multiple-choice question you are working on and the other hand next to the number of that question on the answer sheet. Otherwise, one of your hands must move back and forth from the answer sheet to the test booklet. This wastes time and increases your chances of making an error.

5. Try to answer every multiple-choice question on the test. Your score will be based on the number of answers you get right. You do not get any points taken off for making wrong answers. *So don't be afraid to guess.* Try to answer every question on the exam.

6. Each multiple-choice question counts exactly the same when the final score is being determined. Don't spend too much time on a difficult question and then leave others blank. Try to ration your time.

7. Try to answer each multiple-choice question for yourself *before* you read the five possible choices. After you decide what you think the answer should be, match your idea to the five choices and pick the one that is most similar.

8. You may first want to go through and answer the questions that are easy for you. Then you can go back and answer those that take more time. *Warning:* If you follow this suggestion, be very careful to mark the answer space whose number is the same as that of the question you are answering. Test takers often skip one question, say number 19, but they forget to skip an answer on the answer sheet. Then, when they mark the answer for question number 20, they put that answer by mistake in the space for number 19. You can probably guess what happens next—their answers to all the following problems are also in the wrong spaces. If they don't catch the problem, they can actually fail the test just because of this mix-up. *Make sure that you have the right answer in the right answer space.* When you do skip a question, make a very light *X* beside the number for it on your answer sheet so that you can find it easily when you come back. Remember to erase the *X* when you've answered the question.

9. From time to time, breathe deeply and stretch. Did you know that stretching is the most natural exercise to help you feel refreshed and relaxed?

10. On multiple-choice tests that have five answer choices, like the GED Science Test, you can sometimes see quite easily that three of the choices are wrong. Then it becomes a problem of deciding between two very logical-looking options. If you really can't make up your mind about which of two good options is best, follow your intuition. By answering this way, you have a better than 50 percent chance of getting the right answer. Hunches, after all, are one way of arriving at perfectly good conclusions.

11. Don't choose any answer on the basis of its number. In other words, don't choose answer (3) just because it's been a while since you chose the third answer. On the other hand, if you think choice (1) is the correct answer, choose it even if the answer right before it was also (1).

12. Try to stick to your first impressions. Don't change your answer once you've marked it unless you are certain it is wrong.

13. Some people work faster, though not necessarily more accurately, than others. If you finish early, don't turn in your test. Use every minute you have to go back and check your answers. Go over each mark to see that you have filled in the correct space. Some students get poor scores just because they are careless. They know that the correct answer is, say, (2), but they accidentally mark the space for (1) or (3). Be sure to check before turning in your exam to see that the answer you have marked is really the number of the answer you have chosen.

Make a date with yourself to reread this section the day before you take the GED Science Test. With these tips and all the study aids this book provides fresh in your mind, you should pass the test with flying colors.

Skills Survey

<u>Directions</u>

On the following pages is a Skills Survey. Here is where you get the chance to show yourself how much you already know.

Don't look at this Skills Survey as a test. That may only make you nervous, and you won't do as well as you otherwise would. Instead, look at this Skills Survey as a personal guide. First, it is a guide to what is on the GED Test. It has passages, diagrams, a graph, and a table from the four science areas: biology, earth science, chemistry, and physics. It has the same kind of multiple-choice questions that the GED Test has. And it asks you to use many of the same skills that the GED Test does. That is the second way in which you can use this survey as a guide. The survey shows you which skills you are already good at, which skills you need to practice, and which skills you need to learn.

To use this guide correctly, you will need to be good to yourself. Get yourself a comfortable chair next to a desk or table in a well-lighted area. Most important, demand some peace and quiet. You will want to be able to concentrate so you can work to the best of your ability.

There is no time limit on this survey. Reading information and answering questions quickly are skills in themselves. They are skills you will get to practice as you work through the lessons, the Extra Practice sections, and the two Posttests in this book. For now, forget about the clock.

Read each passage or graphic on the Skills Survey carefully. Next read the questions and answer as many as you can. Try to answer every question.

If this is your own book, you can mark your answers in the answer circles after the questions. Completely fill in the circle of the number you have chosen as the correct answer. For example, if you think the fourth choice is the correct answer to a question, fill in oval 4 like this:

Filling in the oval completely will give you practice in marking an answer sheet correctly. That will help you when you go to take the actual GED Science Test.

If this is not your book, number a separate sheet of paper from 1 to 22. You can write the number of each answer you have chosen after the number of the question.

Are you ready to find out how much you already know? Then turn the page and start the Skills Survey.

Directions: Choose the one best answer to each question.

1. A particular kind of fungus survives in soil and infects plants through their roots. The fungus plugs the water-conducting tubes in the plant roots. The leaves of the plants will eventually wilt because they are giving off more water than the roots can take in.

   Which of the following actions would probably be most effective in controlling this fungus-caused disease?

   (1) spraying the plants
   (2) watering the plants even more
   (3) fumigating the soil
   (4) cutting off the roots of the plants
   (5) misting the leaves of the plants

   ① ② ③ ④ ⑤

2. In physics, the work done by a force acting on an object can be measured by multiplying the force by the distance that the object moves.

   Based on that principle, in which of the following situations is work actually done?

   (1) A man holds his seven-pound baby for ten minutes.
   (2) A person pushes against a wall for ten minutes.
   (3) A child pulls a wagon around the yard.
   (4) A meteor travels at 10,000 miles per hour through space, where the gravitational force is zero.
   (5) A 3,000-pound car is held six feet above the ground by a lift.

   ① ② ③ ④ ⑤

Items 3–4 are based on the following table and information.

Sources of Radiation in the United States

Source	**Dose per Person (millirems per year)**
Natural	
Cosmic rays, U.S. average	44
Sea level, 41 millirems	
Denver (5,000 ft), 70 millirems	
Rocks and soil, U.S. average	40
Atlantic coastal plains, 23 millirems	
Rocky Mountains, 90 millirems	
Internal consumption	18
Total from natural sources, U.S. average	102
Artificial	
Fallout from weapons tests	4
Nuclear power	0.003
Medical uses	72
Miscellaneous (e.g., television screens)	4
Total from artificial sources, U.S. average	80
TOTAL from all sources, U.S. average	182

How much radiation a person can safely be exposed to has been debated for years. No one knows what the maximum safe amount is. Scientists currently think that exposing the whole body one time to less than 25,000 millirems has no directly demonstrable effects on health. However, it is definitely known that doses above 100,000 millirems damage the blood-forming tissues, and doses over 500,000 millirems cause death within a few weeks. On the other hand, the effects of repeated small doses of radiation over a period of time are not known and are the source of controversy.

3. Based on the information given, which of the following statements is true about the natural background radiation along the ocean?
   (1) It is less than the natural background radiation at high elevations.
   (2) It is due to fallout from weapons tests and nuclear power plants.
   (3) It is greater than the amount of radiation due to medical use.
   (4) It is approximately equal to that due to nuclear power.
   (5) Each year people along the ocean receive enough natural background radiation to cause damage to their blood.

   ① ② ③ ④ ⑤

4. A man refuses to have dental X rays taken because of the information given. Which of the following beliefs best explains his decision?
   (1) Scientists can be depended upon to know the truth.
   (2) X rays should never have been discovered.
   (3) It is better to be safe than sorry.
   (4) Scientists are mistaken about the amount of radiation in one dose that is fatal.
   (5) X rays should be replaced by cosmic rays.

   ① ② ③ ④ ⑤

5. Plants are producers of food. Animals that eat plants are considered first-order consumers; animals that eat plant-eating animals are second-order consumers; animals that eat animals that have fed on plant-eating animals are third-order consumers; and so on.

   A man can eat a dinner of lettuce salad and beefsteak because he is a
   (1) producer
   (2) producer and first-order consumer
   (3) first-order consumer alone
   (4) first-order and second-order consumer
   (5) second-order consumer alone

   ① ② ③ ④ ⑤

6. Below are five phrases from a brochure describing a resort hotel on the Pacific Ocean.

   A. clearest waters on the coast
   B. most beautiful beaches
   C. best seafood available

   Which of the claims above could be proved by scientific analysis?
   (1) A only
   (2) B only
   (3) C only
   (4) A and B only
   (5) A and C only

   ① ② ③ ④ ⑤

GO ON TO THE NEXT PAGE.

Items 7–10 are based on the following information.

Proteins are large organic molecules found in all living things. They serve many different purposes and can be classified according to their function. Below, five types of proteins are defined.

(1) antibodies = proteins in the blood and body fluids that can protect the body from infections

(2) enzymes = proteins that speed up chemical processes that occur in living things

(3) hormones = proteins carried by the blood or other body fluids that act as messengers to produce effects in other body systems

(4) structural proteins = proteins that are part of the framework and coverings of living things

(5) transport proteins = proteins that bind to other substances and carry them to different parts of the body

Each item following describes the function of a specific protein within the body. For each item, select the type of protein that is best illustrated by the example.

7. Skin, hair, nails, and hooves are made up mostly of keratin.
   Keratin is one of the proteins called
   (1) antibodies
   (2) enzymes
   (3) hormones
   (4) structural proteins
   (5) transport proteins

   (1) (2) (3) (4) (5)

8. High levels of Immunoglobulin M molecules appear in a person's blood during an illness.
   Immunoglobulin M molecules belong to the group of proteins called
   (1) antibodies
   (2) enzymes
   (3) hormones
   (4) structural proteins
   (5) transport proteins

   (1) (2) (3) (4) (5)

9. In red blood cells, hemoglobin combines with oxygen and distributes it to all tissues throughout the body by means of the bloodstream.
   Hemoglobin functions in the body as one of the
   (1) antibodies
   (2) enzymes
   (3) hormones
   (4) structural proteins
   (5) transport proteins

   (1) (2) (3) (4) (5)

10. Epinephrine is produced by the adrenal gland. Once it is released into the bloodstream, it alerts the body and prepares it for action by slowing digestion and stimulating the muscular and nervous systems.
    Epinephrine belongs to the group of substances called
    (1) antibodies
    (2) enzymes
    (3) hormones
    (4) structural proteins
    (5) transport proteins

    (1) (2) (3) (4) (5)

Items 11–12 are based on the following information.

A useful rule in chemistry is "like dissolves like." For example, gasoline will dissolve oil because these two are similar types of substances. Water will dissolve carbon dioxide, but it will not dissolve kerosene. The reason that "like dissolves like" has to do with whether the molecules carry small electrical charges. Molecules with small charges at their ends are called polar. Water is a polar substance. Molecules without charges are nonpolar. Gasoline, oil, and kerosene are nonpolar substances. Some substances have molecules with one polar end and one nonpolar end.

11. Vinegar dissolves readily in water. Based on the information above, what must be true of vinegar?

    (1) It will dissolve in kerosene.
    (2) It is a nonpolar molecule.
    (3) It is a kind of oil.
    (4) It will not dissolve carbon dioxide.
    (5) It carries an electrical charge.

12. Soapy water can remove grease stains. Based on the information above, which of the following facts could be used to explain this observation?

    (1) Grease dissolves readily in nonpolar substances.
    (2) Soap changes the chemical composition of water.
    (3) Soap can change the charge on a molecule.
    (4) Soaps have molecules with polar and nonpolar ends.
    (5) Nonpolar molecules do not dissolve in water.

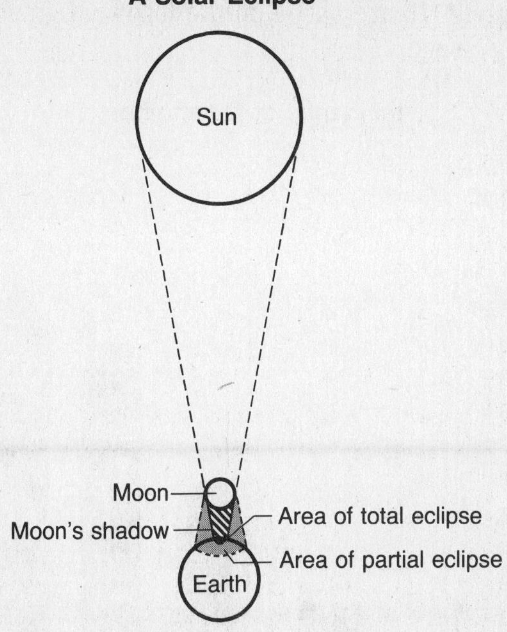

13. In an area of total eclipse, the moon almost totally blocks out the sun's rays from a portion of the earth, as shown in the diagram above. What would happen if the moon were farther away from the earth than it is?

    (1) The area of partial eclipse would disappear.
    (2) The area of total eclipse would be smaller.
    (3) Half the earth would be in either total or partial eclipse.
    (4) The moon could not cause an eclipse.
    (5) The moon would produce a shadow on the sun.

GO ON TO THE NEXT PAGE.

Items 14–16 are based on the following graph and passage.

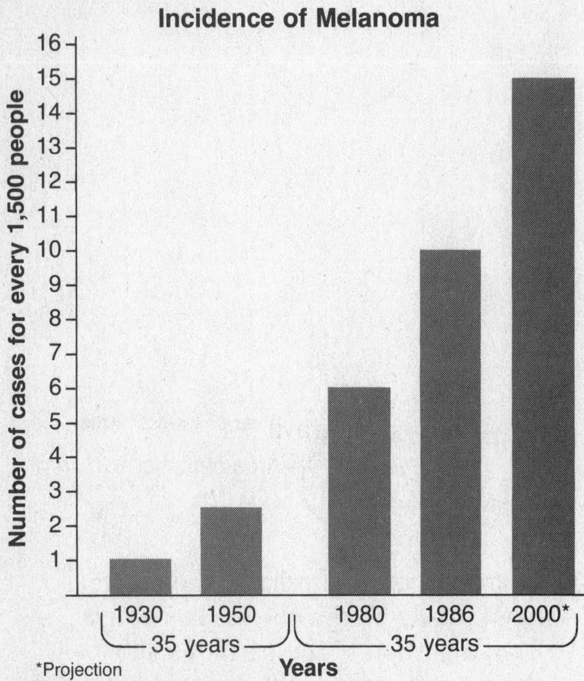

Source: Skin Cancer Foundation, American Cancer Society. Reprinted by permission.

Three types of skin cancer are associated with exposure to sunlight. Two types—basal-cell and squamous-cell carcinomas—probably result from accumulated skin damage by sunlight over a long period of time. These types of skin cancer are nearly 100 percent curable *if* detected and removed in their early stages. A third type of cancer, rarer than the others, is believed to be due to severe blister-type sunburns received years earlier, before or during the teenage years. This type of cancer is called melanoma.

The cause of all three types of skin cancer is usually the portion of sunlight called ultraviolet light (UVL). It is strongest during the noonday hours. Human skin contains some natural protection against the UVL portion of sunlight. When the skin is exposed to sunlight, special skin cells called melanocytes release melanin, a dark pigment that protects us by absorbing and scattering the UVL. Given too much UVL, however, the melanocytes become cancerous cells. This results in the often fatal form of cancer called melanoma. People who naturally have very little melanin in their skin are most at risk. For example, the rate of melanoma for whites is ten times higher than the rate for African Americans.

UVL has many other effects besides tanning the skin and causing skin cancers. Research has linked UV light to cataracts, premature aging of the skin, and less active immune systems.

Shade is the best possible protection against UVL. Cover-up clothing and sunscreen lotions will effectively reduce the amount of UVL the skin is exposed to. Clouds actually filter out only about 20 percent of UVL and cannot be counted on to reduce the risk of sunburn.

14. Which of the following best summarizes the relationship between sunlight and cancer?

(1) The occurrence of cancers associated with exposure to sunlight is increasing.
(2) Skin cancer begins with severe sunburns during the teenage years.
(3) UVL is the agent in sunlight that causes sunburn and three types of skin cancer.
(4) People who are dark-skinned or who tan easily are much less likely to get skin cancer.
(5) Skin cancers occur only in people who spend too much time in direct sunlight.

15. Given the predicted rate for melanoma on the graph, what assumption are scientists making?

(1) The population will increase by the year 2000.
(2) African Americans will lose their resistance to melanoma by the year 2000.
(3) A cure for melanoma is far off in the future.
(4) People will continue to sunbathe in the year 2000, despite scientists' warnings.
(5) In recent decades a large number of young people have suffered blistering sunburns.

16. A twenty-year-old woman with skin that tans easily sunbathes all day one Saturday but is careful to use sunscreen from 11:00 to 2:00. What is wrong with her logic?

(1) She doesn't need sunscreen because her skin tans easily.
(2) She doesn't need sunscreen because she is past her teenage years, when the cause of melanoma begins.
(3) The sunscreen is not effective during noonday hours.
(4) UVL is present in sunlight at all times of the day.
(5) She should begin using sunscreen at 10:00 rather than 11:00.

(1) (2) (3) (4) (5)

---

17. Bacteria can be classified according to their need for oxygen. Some bacteria require oxygen for their life processes. Some bacteria die in the presence of oxygen. Others do not need oxygen but can use it if it is available.

A hospital laboratory technician wants to grow a bacterial sample in a long tube of a gelatin-like material. The particular bacterium is not harmed by oxygen, but it does not need oxygen to live. Where will the bacteria grow in the tube?

(1) only at the surface of the gelatin
(2) nowhere in the tube
(3) only along the sides of the tube above the gelatin
(4) at the very bottom of the gelatin
(5) throughout the tube

(1) (2) (3) (4) (5)

18. Gravity is a force that exists between all objects in the universe. It is measured as the force of attraction between objects. When two objects approach each other, their gravity affects their motion. The more mass an object has, the greater its attraction.

If a planet in our solar system did not follow a predicted orbit around the sun, which of the following explanations could account for this?

(1) The planet is larger than expected.
(2) An unknown object is passing close to it.
(3) The force of gravity is not strong enough to hold the planet in orbit.
(4) The planet is moving quickly away from the sun.
(5) The planet has no moons.

(1) (2) (3) (4) (5)

19. An inert material does not react with anything. If clothes could be made from an inert fabric, which of the following would be true?

(1) The clothing could be dyed many bright colors.
(2) The clothes would be resistant to staining.
(3) Strong bleach would ruin the fabric.
(4) The clothes would catch fire easily.
(5) The fibers would be strong and durable.

(1) (2) (3) (4) (5)

GO ON TO THE NEXT PAGE.

Items 20–22 refer to the following passage and diagram.

Lake Nyos in Cameroon, Africa, fills the crater of one of the many dormant volcanoes in the country. On the night of August 21, 1986, people in the village near the lake heard rumbling like the sound of distant thunder. Suddenly a gas cloud arose from the lake. The cloud was made up mainly of carbon dioxide (CO_2) and perhaps small amounts of carbon monoxide and hydrogen sulfide. Within minutes the cloud of gas settled in the village in the valley below because CO_2 is heavier than air. At least 1,700 people and many animals died, most of them suffocating in their sleep.

Currently two possible explanations for the event have been offered: (1) A small volcanic eruption occurred at the bottom of the lake, releasing gases from deep within the earth. (2) Gas from decaying plant and animal matter and from cracks in the lake bottom became trapped at the bottom of the lake and then was suddenly released. Although the second explanation is favored by many geologists, no one knows what sort of disturbance was responsible for stirring up the lake. Possibilities include an earthquake, a landslide, or a small eruption.

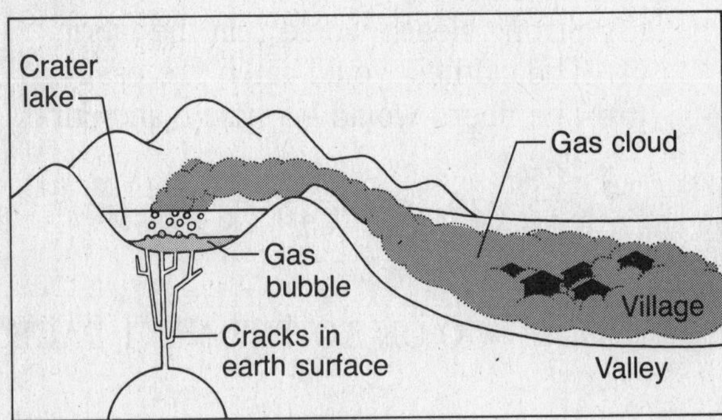

20. Which of the following statements best summarizes the known events that led to the deaths described in the passage?
   (1) CO_2 gas from the depths of Lake Nyos displaced the air in the valley.
   (2) A landslide near Lake Nyos buried many people.
   (3) An earthquake created a large bubble of poisonous gas.
   (4) CO_2 formed a bubble in the lake and was released into the air when the lake was dramatically disturbed.
   (5) Poisonous gases were formed when a volcanic eruption occurred in the bottom of Lake Nyos.

21. Which of the following statements is a hypothesis about the cause of the cloud?
   (1) CO_2 can mix with small amounts of carbon monoxide and hydrogen sulfide.
   (2) CO_2 accumulated at the bottom of the lake and was trapped for a while by the waters above.
   (3) CO_2 is heavier than air.
   (4) CO_2 is present within the earth beneath dormant volcanoes.
   (5) CO_2 can suffocate people by forcing the air away.

22. Which of the following situations would most likely have helped avoid the high death rate?
   (1) if the people had had a warning system for earthquakes
   (2) if the village had been built in the hills above the lake
   (3) if swimming and fishing in the lake had been forbidden
   (4) if a retaining wall had been built to prevent landslides
   (5) if the level of the lake water had been kept lower

END OF EXAMINATION

Answers: Skills Survey

1. (3) The disease is caused by the fungus. Since the fungus lives in the soil and invades the plants from the soil, the soil would be the best place to try to get rid of the fungus. **AN**

2. (3) The child does work because he or she applies a force to the wagon by pulling it, and the wagon moves the distance around the yard. In all the other options, either no force is applied (4) or the object is not moved (1), (2), and (5). **AP**

3. (1) This is the only correct statement. Both cosmic rays and radiation from the rocks and soil are lower at the level of the ocean than they are in mountainous regions. **EV**

4. (3) This option indicates that the man would rather wait until the risks due to small-dose radiation over a long period of time are known. **EV**

5. (4) When a man eats a lettuce salad, he is eating a plant; in other words, he is being a first-order consumer. When he eats a beefsteak, he is eating an animal that grazes on plants, so he is being a second-order consumer. **CP**

6. (1) This option could actually be proved by doing scientific tests that measure the cloudiness of the water. The other options are opinions and could not be tested by scientific methods. **AN**

7. (4) Keratin makes up materials that are body coverings, so it fits the definition of structural proteins. **AP**

8. (1) Immunoglobulin molecules appear in the blood during an illness. Antibodies protect against infection this way. **AP**

9. (5) Only a transport protein could combine with a substance like oxygen and distribute it throughout the body. **AP**

10. (3) Epinephrine is a hormone because it is released into the bloodstream so it can produce an effect somewhere else in the body. **AP**

11. (5) A substance that dissolves in water must be a polar molecule with a small electrical charge. **CP**

12. (4) The polar end of the soap dissolves in the water; the nonpolar end dissolves the greasy stain. **AN**

13. (2) Look at the diagram carefully to see what exactly happens when a total eclipse occurs. The moon is between the earth and the sun and is just far enough away from the earth to block all the sun's rays above one section of the earth. If the moon were closer to the sun, more of the sun's rays would be able to shine past the moon, so the area under a total eclipse would be smaller. **AP**

14. (3) UVL is believed to be the portion of sunlight that is responsible for skin damage and cancers. That statement best summarizes the cause-effect relationship between sunlight and skin cancer. **CP**

15. (5) The passage suggests that melanoma occurs in adults who received bad sunburns when they were young. In order for the large increase in melanoma that the graph shows to occur in the year 2000, young people must have recently been suffering such sunburns. **AN**

16. (4) Ultraviolet light (UVL) is strongest during the noonday hours, but it always makes up a portion of sunlight throughout the day. Therefore, before 11:00 and after 2:00 the woman would be exposing her unprotected skin to sunlight with UVL. **EV**

17. (5) Because the bacterium can live with or without oxygen, it will grow throughout the tube, regardless of how much oxygen is present. **AP**

18. (2) Gravity is the attraction between two objects. If the planet does not follow its expected orbit, it must be attracted by another object. No other option takes into account the effect of gravity on the planet's orbit. **AN**

19. (2) This option indicates that the fabric does not react with substances that stain. An inert fabric also would *not* react with dye (1), bleach (3), or flame (4). However, a nonreactive fabric might fray or tear (5). **AN**

20. (1) This option states only the *known* facts. All the other options suggest that the cause of the disaster or the source of the gas is understood. The passage states that these questions have not been answered yet. **CP**

21. (2) A hypothesis is a suggested explanation. Option (2) is a hypothesis suggested by the scientists studying the lake after the deaths occurred. All the other options are facts that have been scientifically proved. **AN**

22. (2) The people and animals were killed because the carbon dioxide gas cloud was heavier than air and therefore slid down into the valley village, pushing the air out and up. If the village had been built in the hills over the lake, it might have stayed above the carbon dioxide. **AP**

CP = Comprehension **AP** = Application **AN** = Analysis **EV** = Evaluation

Answer Key

Now circle the number of each item you got wrong on the answer key below.

1. (3)
2. (3)
3. (1)
4. (3)
5. (4)
6. (1)
7. (4)
8. (1)
9. (5)
10. (3)
11. (5)
12. (4)
13. (2)
14. (3)
15. (5)
16. (4)
17. (5)
18. (2)
19. (2)
20. (1)
21. (2)
22. (2)

Using the Survey Results

How did you do on the Skills Survey? Here's a chart to show you the skills that were tested by the questions. By comparing the answers you got wrong with the chart, you can see which skills you need to concentrate on when you study the lessons in this book. The chart also shows which lessons give you instruction and practice in those areas.

If you had difficulty reading and understanding the material even before you tried to answer the questions, pay close attention to Lessons 1, 2, and 3. They will help you develop your basic reading skills. And if you had trouble understanding the diagrams and graph, be sure to study "How to Read Scientific Diagrams, Tables, and Graphs" on pages 5–10.

You will probably want to work through every lesson, of course. That will help you develop skills that weren't tested directly on the Skills Survey as well as strengthen the skills you already have. Those new and strengthened skills will improve your chances of passing the GED Science Test.

Question Number	Skill	Lesson
1, 13, 22	Seeing cause-effect relationships	5, 15, 25
2, 7, 8, 9, 10	Applying ideas	6, 19, 24
3, 5	Restating information	2, 12
4	Understanding the role of values in beliefs and decision making	18, 23
6, 21	Distinguishing between facts, opinions, and hypotheses	8, 20, 26
11, 17, 19	Working with conclusions	7, 14, 21
12, 18	Evaluating data	10, 22, 27
14, 20	Summarizing	4, 13
15	Recognizing assumptions	9, 16
16	Seeing faulty logic	11, 17, 28

Biology

What do a racehorse, a cancer cell, a prize-winning rose, and you all have in common? All would be studied by biologists because you and the others are all *alive.* Biology is the study of living things, of how they relate to each other, and of how they relate to their environment. You yourself are dealing with biology when you care for a houseplant, garden, lawn, or crop; when you visit the doctor to find out what germ or virus is making you feel sick; or when you see the effects of pollution on the environment.

Biology on the GED Science Test deals with those and other issues concerning living things. There are 33 multiple-choice questions in all about biology. However, you don't need a great deal of biological knowledge to answer them. Most of the information you need to answer every question will be given to you right there, in an article, a graph, a diagram, or a table. What you need to be able to do is read and understand biological information so that you can use it to answer multiple-choice questions.

For example, biologists sometimes use long, unfamiliar words to describe things. If a GED question uses such a word, it will also define it for you, as in this item.

Different biochemical reactions occur inside an organism to keep it alive. Anabolic reactions build up complex substances from smaller ones. Catabolic reactions break down complex substances into simpler ones.

Which of the following is an example of a catabolic reaction?

(1) An old red blood cell is filtered out of the bloodstream by the liver.
(2) Proteins are assembled in cells from small units called amino acids.
(3) When a person eats more food than he or she needs, small sugar molecules are linked together and stored in the liver or muscles.
(4) Blood flows from a cut on a person's hand.
(5) Starch from a potato becomes smaller, simpler sugar molecules during digeston.

(1) (2) (3) (4) (5)

Anabolic and *catabolic* are long, scientific words that might scare off some people. Yet both are defined in the paragraph before the question. The main idea of that information is simply that one of the processes that takes place in an organism (an anabolic reaction) involves the build-up from small substances to large ones, while the other (a catabolic reaction) is the opposite; it involves the breakdown of large substances into small ones. If you understand that idea, you can answer the question. You just need to find which of the five options describes a larger substance being broken down into smaller ones. The answer is (5).

Some reading passages on the GED Science Test will be fairly long—perhaps articles of several paragraphs. Such a biology article will be followed by several multiple-choice questions. Visual aids such as graphs, tables, and diagrams often appear on the test, either by themselves or with paragraphs that help explain them. Here's an example of such a diagram.

How Predation Controls Population

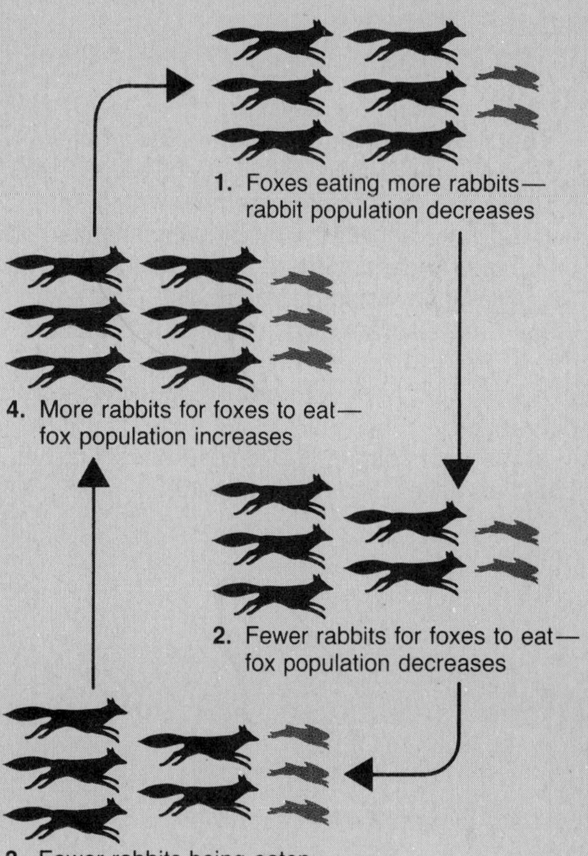
1. Foxes eating more rabbits—rabbit population decreases
2. Fewer rabbits for foxes to eat—fox population decreases
3. Fewer rabbits being eaten—rabbit population increases
4. More rabbits for foxes to eat—fox population increases

To read that diagram, you begin with the first drawing on top and then follow the arrows down and around to understand how the cycle of population control works. Now look at a GED-level question that could be asked about that diagram.

Settlers in an area want to control the rabbit population because the rabbits are destroying vegetable crops. Some settlers want to introduce into the area a wild cat that feeds on rabbits. If they do, which of the following would most likely occur?

(1) The number of rabbits in the area will actually increase.
(2) The number of foxes in the area will increase.
(3) The number of both rabbits and foxes in the area will decrease.
(4) The number of foxes and rabbits will remain steady.
(5) The number of cats in the area will remain steady.

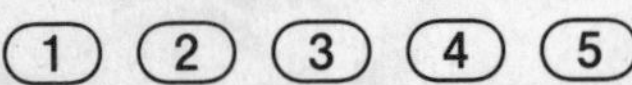

That item is asking you to analyze a cause-and-effect relationship: What effect would the cats have in the area? Since they would eat some of the rabbits, the rabbit population would decrease. And since there are fewer rabbits, the fox population would decrease also. The second step in the diagram gives you that information. Therefore, the best answer to the question is (3). The number of both rabbits and foxes would decrease.

In the next column is a second question that could be asked about the diagram.

Increased hunting of foxes in the area will lead to less successful vegetable crops.

Based on the diagram and information, which of the following statements would justify that conclusion?

(1) Hunters will ruin the vegetable fields.
(2) The decrease in foxes will cause an increase in rabbits.
(3) People will be too busy hunting to care for their vegetable crops.
(4) People will no longer need vegetables for food because they can eat fox meat.
(5) Foxes will dig into vegetable fields to avoid the hunters.

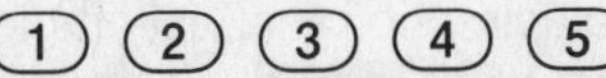

To answer that question, you need to judge supporting evidence for a statement. Increased hunting of foxes will probably lead to a decrease in the fox population. Fewer foxes lead to more rabbits, according to steps 2 and 3 of the diagram. More rabbits would most likely cause more damage to the vegetable crops. So option (2) supports the conclusion given at the beginning of the question. There is no information given to make you think that any of the other options is true.

Questions like those ask you to use your thinking skills as well as your reading skills. The following section in this book will help you develop and polish both those kinds of skills using information on biological topics that you'll probably find interesting to read about and satisfying to know. With polished skills and comfort in reading about biology, you'll be well prepared to answer the biology questions on the GED Science Test.

LESSON 1

The Human Body: Input and Output

Biology is the study of living things, and perhaps no living thing is as fascinating as yourself, a human being. Inside a human body are many parts that work together to keep the person alive. All the parts are organized into different systems. The first section of this lesson explains how two of the body's systems take in things that the body needs. Before you read, take a moment to look at the Warm-up at the end of the section. Keep it in mind to help you look for important information in the section.

Input

You probably are aware that humans need to breathe air in order to live. Actually, it's not air itself that people need but a certain gas that air contains—oxygen. The job of the human **respiratory system** is to bring air into the body, take the oxygen from it, and get rid of waste gases formed by the body that it does not need.

The respiratory system, like the body's other systems, includes a number of **organs** that help it do its job. Think of what happens when you breathe. You may already know that the air you take in travels from your nose through the windpipe (or trachea) into your lungs. The nose, windpipe, and lungs are just three of the organs of the respiratory system. Take time to look at the drawing and the other organs that it names.

Respiratory System

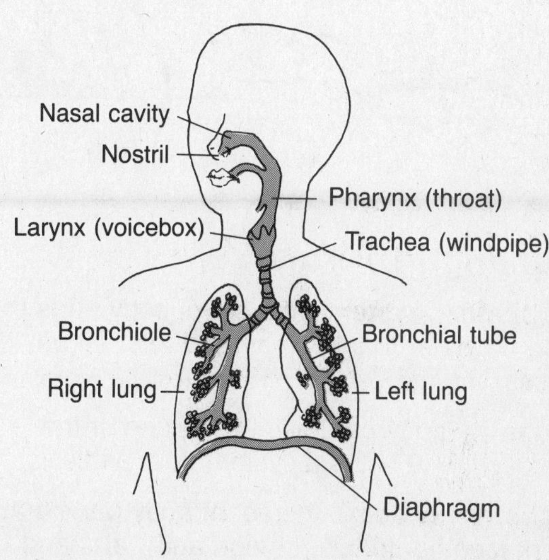

What other things must the body take in to stay alive? You're probably thinking, "Food and water, of course." The **digestive system** takes in food and water. It also breaks down the food into incredibly small particles that the body can use. Look at the diagram of the digestive system. It names the digestive organs and summarizes how they carry out the process of digestion.

Digestive System

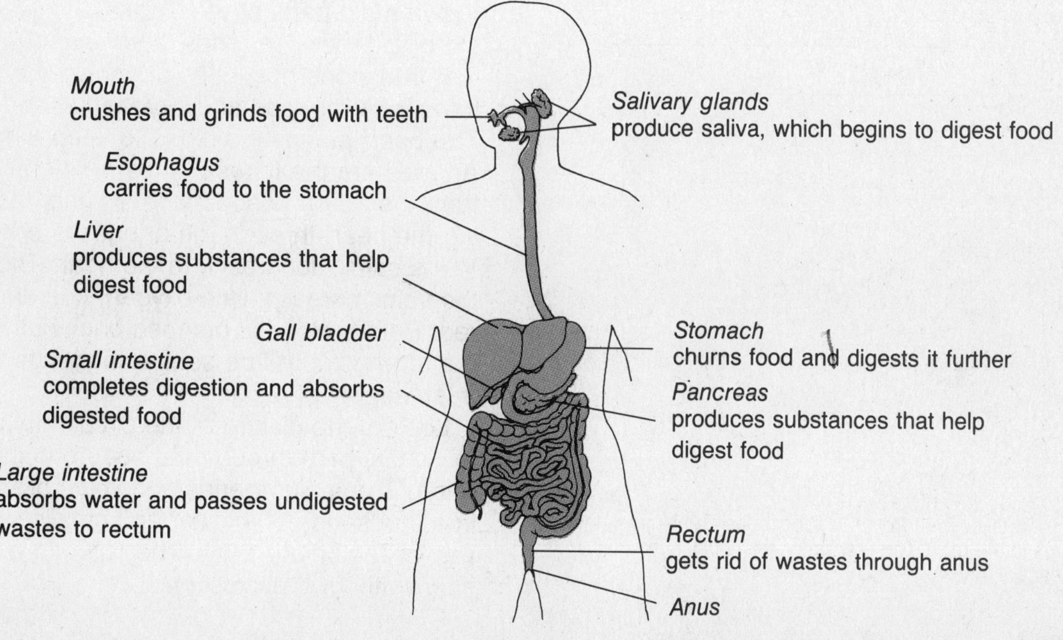

Coming to Terms

respiratory system the set of body parts that work together to take in air and release waste gases

organ a body part, such as a lung or the stomach, that helps a system do a particular job

digestive system the set of body parts that work together to take in food and water and break the food down into usable particles

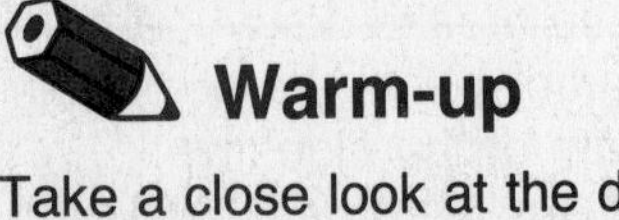

Warm-up

Take a close look at the diagram of the digestive system. Then write a few sentences that describe what the stomach and the liver do.

____

____

____

____

Sample Warm-up Answer
The stomach takes food from the esophagus and helps digest it by churning the food. The liver produces substances that help digest the food.

You have just learned how food and oxygen get into the body and how the digestive system makes food usable. But how do food and oxygen get to the parts of the body that need them? The next section will answer this question for you. Glance at the Warm-up question before you begin. It will help you focus on important information as you read.

Transportation

The **circulatory system** is the body's transportation and delivery system. With the help of the circulatory system, food and oxygen travel through the body. The word *circulatory* comes from the word *circulate,* which means "to go around." The circulatory system goes around the body bringing oxygen from the lungs and digested food from the intestines to all parts of the body. It carries away waste substances. It also carries particles that help fight disease.

The main parts of the circulatory system are the blood, heart, arteries, and veins. Like a river that transports boatloads of goods, the blood transports the food and oxygen needed for life. The heart pumps the blood to keep it moving. Arteries are the tubes that carry the blood away from the heart. Loaded with oxygen, blood leaving the heart through the arteries is bright red. Veins carry blood back to the heart. Blood in the veins contains little oxygen. It is dark bluish-red. Before blood is pumped back out through the arteries, it will be sent to the lungs for a fresh supply of oxygen.

Look at the picture of the circulatory system. Notice its path through the body and its main parts. The main arteries and veins branch out into thousands of smaller and smaller tubes that are far too tiny to draw. They cannot even be seen without a microscope.

Circulatory System

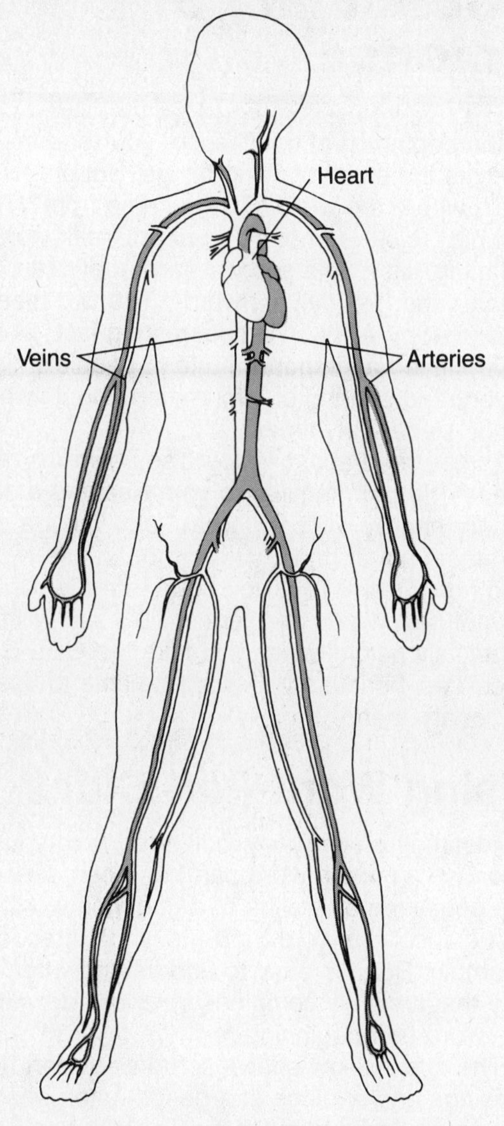

Coming to Terms

circulatory system the system of body parts that transports oxygen, digested food, waste products, and other body chemicals

---

Warm-up

In a sentence or two, tell why blood leaving the heart is bright red, while blood entering the heart is dark bluish-red.

____

____

____

____

So far you have read about the human body's input—the things it takes in and uses. In the next section, you will look at an opposite body function—output. Before you go on to this section, look ahead to the Warm-up questions. They will help you focus on some main points as you read.

Output

You have seen how the digestive and respiratory systems bring needed substances into the body. But their work does not end there. The body must also get rid of materials that it doesn't need.

As you have read, the respiratory system gets rid of waste gases. Whenever you breathe out, you are getting rid of gases that your body does not use.

The digestive system gets rid of undigested food that the body cannot use. This waste passes through the rectum and the anus. Some waste water leaves the body through the skin as sweat. But a whole other system is needed to get rid of waste materials in the blood. This system is the **urinary system.**

The diagram on the next page shows the main organs of the urinary system. A major artery brings blood to both kidneys. A major vein carries the cleaned, filtered blood away.

Sample Warm-up Answer
Blood leaving the heart through the arteries is bright red because it is loaded with oxygen. Blood entering the heart through the veins contains little oxygen, so it is less red.

Urinary System

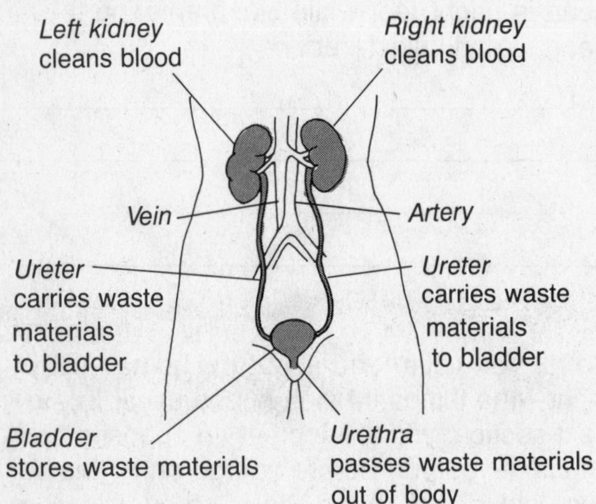

Coming to Terms

urinary system the system of body parts that removes waste materials from blood and then gets rid of them

Warm-up

Write a sentence or two of your own to answer each question below.

1. What is the special function of the urinary system?

____

____

2. According to the diagram of the urinary system, what happens to the "output" of the kidneys?

____

____

____

____

Sample Warm-up Answers
1. The urinary system cleans waste materials from the blood and eliminates them. **2.** Waste materials leave the kidneys through ureters. They go into the bladder and leave the body through the urethra.

Understanding the Vocabulary of Science

At the beginning of this lesson, you read that biology is the study of living things. But do you know where the word *biology* came from? The first part, *bio-*, is from an ancient Greek word meaning "life." The second part, *-logy*, can mean either "study" or "word." The two meanings of *-logy* point up an interesting fact: words have played an important role in people's discovery and sharing of information about living things since early times.

As you read about biology, some words may seem long or unfamiliar to you. Keeping a dictionary nearby will be a great help. But if a dictionary is not at hand, you can often use two kinds of clues to help you figure out the meanings of new words and terms. This skill will be especially helpful when you take the GED Science Test because you won't be able to use a dictionary then.

Using Word-Part Clues

Sometimes a word may look strange to you only because a certain word part has been added to the beginning or ending of a common word. At first glance, the word *redo* may look strange, for example. But it is easy to understand when you see that it simply combines the word *do* with the word-part beginning *re-*.

The chart below shows some word-part beginnings and endings that people often attach to everyday words to make new words. You've already seen and heard many of them; you even use them yourself when you talk.

Word Part	Meaning	Example
dis-	do the opposite of	*dis*infect
in-, im-, ir-	not	*in*direct *im*balanced *ir*regular
in-, im-	in; inside	*in*put *im*plant
multi-	many	*multi*layered
non-	not	*non*human
pre-	before	*pre*mature
re-	again back toward	*re*produce *re*act
trans-	from one to another; across	*trans*fusion
un-	not	*un*polluted

-able	able to ___ or to be ___ed	adapt*able*
-ion, -tion, -ation,	the process of ___ing	digest*ion* absorp*tion* form*ation*
-ive	having to do with ___ing	connect*ive*
-ize	to make ___	immun*ize*
-ment	the act of ___ing	develop-*ment*
-ory	having the job of ___ing	circulat*ory*
-ous	full of ___; having ___	cancer*ous*

Notice that sometimes when a word part is added to a word, the spelling of the word changes a bit to make the new word easier to say. For example, adding *-ation* to the word *classify* creates *classification,* and adding *-ive* to *destroy* makes *destructive.*

In addition to those common word parts, other parts are often added to each other to create many scientific words. You've already read about two such word parts: *bio-* and *-logy.* Here are a few more examples.

Word Part	**Meaning**	**Example**
derm-	skin	*derm*atology
hyper-	over; too much	*hyper*active
micro-	small	*micro*scope
thermo-	heat	*thermo*meter
zoo-	animals	*zoo*logy

You don't really need to learn the meanings of such scientific word parts. But the more scientific material you read, the more you'll notice that certain word parts tend to appear often.

Remember also that some long words are just a combination of shorter words. Examples of such words are *starfish, underlying, backbone, seawater,* and *overpopulated.*

As you read material about biology and other scientific fields, you can sometimes break down long words into word parts or word combinations to figure out what the unfamiliar words mean.

Here's an Example

In the short paragraph below, each *italicized* word is made up of either two smaller words or a familiar word with a word part added at the beginning or ending.

■ Within the nasal *passageway* are small *threadlike* hairs called cilia. The cilia are responsible for the *filtration* of *impurities* from the air we breathe in.

You can see that *passageway* and *threadlike* are made up of two smaller words: *passage* and *way,* and *thread* and *like.* Dividing them helps make their meaning clear. *Filtration* is made up of *filtrate* plus the ending *-ion,* which means "the process of." In other words, the cilia are responsible for the process of filtrating, or filtering, the air. *Impurities* is made up of the beginning *im-,* which means "not," plus the word *purities.* Impurities, therefore, are substances that are not pure.

Try It Yourself

In this sentence, look for three words that contain added word parts. Try to decide what each means.

■ Discouragement is turning to hope as many heart diseases that were once incurable are now treated by corrective surgery.

Did you identify *discouragement* as having two added word parts? You know that *dis-* means "not" and *-ment* means "the process of." Putting those two ideas together, you can see that *discouragement* means "the process of losing courage, or heart." The *in-* at the beginning of *incurable* means "not." If you realize that *cur* is actually *cure* and *-able* can mean "able to be," you can figure out that *incurable* means "not able to be cured." Finally, did you spot *corrective* as a combination of the word part *-ive* and the word *correct?* Its meaning is "having the job of correcting."

Using Context Clues

Sometimes an unfamiliar word simply cannot be broken into parts that you can recognize. In such cases, the **context** of the word can often help you. The context of a word is made up of the words and sentences that surround it. Often the context of an unfamiliar word will help you figure out its meaning. For a word that has more than one meaning, its context will help you decide which meaning is intended.

Coming to Terms

context the words and sentences that surround a word

Here's an Example

Very often in scientific material, a word is directly defined by its context, as in these sentences.

- *Metabolism* is the sum of all the processes that occur in an organism to keep it alive.
- *Bile,* the greenish-yellow liquid made by the liver, helps digest food.

In the second sentence, notice how the words after the comma tell you exactly what bile is. Sometimes this kind of definition in context will be set off by parentheses or dashes instead of one or two commas.

In this next sentence, you are given specific examples of what a more general term means.

- Heart attacks, heart failure, and other *cardiac* problems can be fatal.

Because heart attacks and heart failure are given as examples of cardiac problems, you can tell from the context that *cardiac* must mean "having to do with the heart."

In this last example, the surrounding details can give you a clue to the meaning of *immune.*

- Your body structure and chemistry make you naturally *immune* to many diseases. Such diseases can harm other animals and plants, but they cannot survive in the human body. Your body resists invasion by them.

The first sentence does not give much help with the word *immune.* But remember that context always includes the surrounding sentences. The next two sentences tell you that the body can resist certain harmful diseases. That context can help you see that *immune* means something like "able to resist disease."

Try It Yourself

See if you can figure out the meaning of the **bold** word in this sentence.

- **Allergens** such as pollen, dust, and animal hair can irritate the respiratory systems of some people.

Did you see that pollen, dust, and animal hair were given as examples of allergens? The fact that those items cause allergic reactions in some people ("can irritate the respiratory systems") is a clue that allergens are things that cause allergic reactions. Now use context clues to help you decide which meaning of the word *minute* is intended in this sentence.

- The small intestine contains hundreds of **minute,** fingerlike projections that aid digestion.

Minute can mean "a unit of sixty seconds of time," or it can mean "very small." Which meaning does it have in the sentence? The sentence discusses small projections in the intestine. The word's context, then, indicates that the second meaning—"very small"—is the meaning intended here.

☑ A Test-Taking Tip

You will not be allowed to use a dictionary when you take the GED Science Test. You'll have to use context clues and word-part clues to figure out the meanings of words. Word-part clues may help you figure out the meaning of a word you've never seen before. However, even if you can use such clues, or if you feel you know the meaning of a word without using them, it's always best to read a word *in context* as well. Context clues can help you make sure that you understand how the word is being used.

On the Springboard

Items 1–2 refer to the following passage. Use word-part and context clues to decide word meanings.

Kidney failure may occur when there is a lack of oxygen. Renal failure may also occur when there is a severe fall in blood pressure. Whatever causes the kidneys to fail, the result is the same: a build-up of wastes and toxins. Without treatment, the patient dies. When possible, doctors use a kidney transplant to treat the patient. In other cases, they use an artificial kidney.

1. The term *renal* refers to which of the following items?

   (1) oxygen
   (2) kidneys
   (3) blood

   ① ② ③

2. As used in this passage, *transplant* means

   (1) repotting a plant with new soil
   (2) moving a kidney from one person to another
   (3) removing waste products from the blood

   ① ② ③

The answers to On the Springboard are on page 103.

How did you do? Were you able to decide the correct meanings of *renal* and *transplant?* If you feel confident of your skill in using word-part and context clues, keep on going and try the GED-level "Real Thing." If you're not sure, review this section and then practice using vocabulary clues by rereading the information on body systems in the first part of this lesson.

"The Real Thing"

Items 1–2 refer to the following passage.

When blood flow through an artery decreases, the living tissue that depends on that particular artery can die. Heart attacks can occur when vessels are filled with sebaceous material. Such fatty deposits hinder the normal flow of blood to the heart muscle. Strokes occur when vessels do not bring blood to a certain part of the brain.

1. What are the vessels referred to in the article?

   (1) special medical devices
   (2) drinking glasses used in hospitals
   (3) tubes that conduct blood
   (4) organs that pump blood
   (5) separate parts of the heart

   ① ② ③ ④ ⑤

2. One cause of heart attacks is the accumulation in the circulatory system of

   (1) too much blood
   (2) living tissue
   (3) heart muscle
   (4) fatty substances
   (5) waste material

   ① ② ③ ④ ⑤

Check your answers and record your score on page 105.

☑ A Test-Taking Tip

If you come across a word on the GED Science Test that you don't know, try to use word-part and context clues to figure out its meaning. If you still cannot determine its meaning, don't worry about it. Just keep reading and concentrate on understanding as much as you can. If you let yourself get upset or frustrated just because you don't understand a word or a phrase, you may miss the answers to questions you would otherwise get right.

LESSON 2

The Human Body: Control and Movement

You have read that a human body has a number of systems and organs that support life. In this lesson you'll learn about two vital systems at the center of all the body's systems. Take a moment now to look at the Warm-up activity at the end of the first section. Keep it in mind as you read.

Control

With all the activity that goes on in the human body, something has to be in control. Control of body systems is the job of the **nervous system.**

The brain is the main organ of the nervous system. A bundle of nerves called the spinal cord runs from the brain down the back. From this spinal cord, a network of millions of nerves stretches to all parts of the body. These nerves bring electrical messages to the brain. Some of these messages are perceived by the brain as pain, heat, sight, sound, smell, or taste. Others communicate the activities of all the various parts of the body.

The brain, in turn, sends electrical messages back along the nerves. Often the messages go to the organs of the body to control their activities. In such cases a person is not even aware of the messages.

The diagram in the next column gives you an idea of what the nervous system looks like.

Nervous System

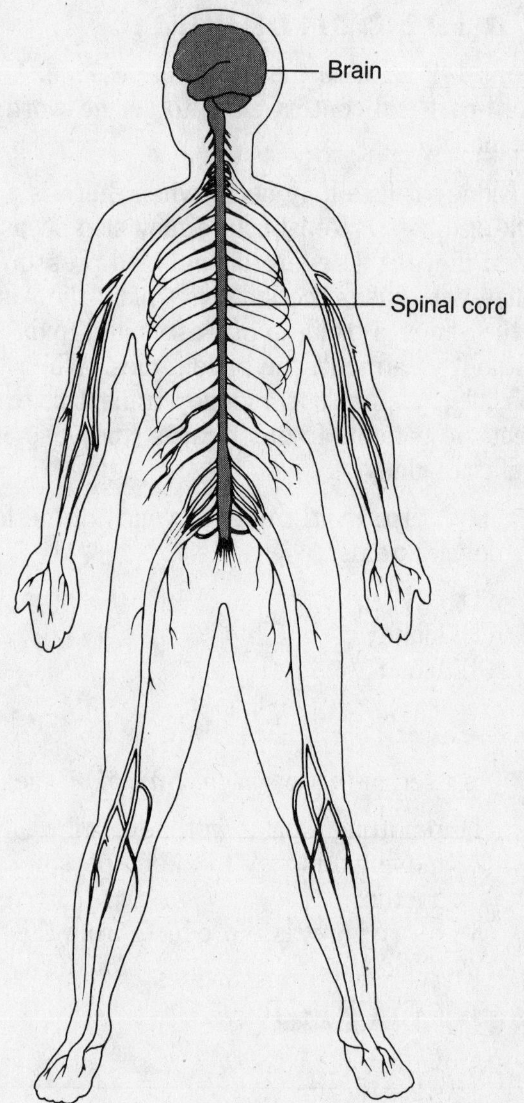

In addition to the nervous system, another system helps control the body's activities. Certain body glands release chemicals called **hormones** into the bloodstream, where they are transported by the circulatory system. These hormones influence other parts of the body. This system of glands and hormones is known as the **endocrine system.** On the next page is a diagram that shows you some glands of the endocrine system and what each one does.

Endocrine System

Pituitary
regulates other endocrine organs; controls growth

Parathyroids
control the amount of calcium in the blood, which influences blood clotting, bone and teeth development, and nerve activity

Thyroid
controls growth and rate of body's activities

Thymus
helps body fight infection

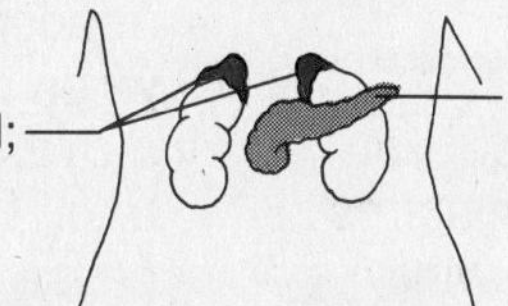

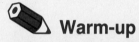

Adrenals
regulate water and salt in blood; help body react in emergency

Islets of Langerhorns
control sugar level in blood

In addition to the glands pictured, females have two ovaries that produce female hormones. In males, the testes produce male hormones.

Coming to Terms

nervous system the body system that controls other body systems through the brain and spinal cord

hormones chemicals that circulate through the bloodstream and influence the functions of all the organs

endocrine system all the hormone-producing glands in the body

Warm-up

Look at the diagram of the nervous system. Then write a short paragraph describing it.

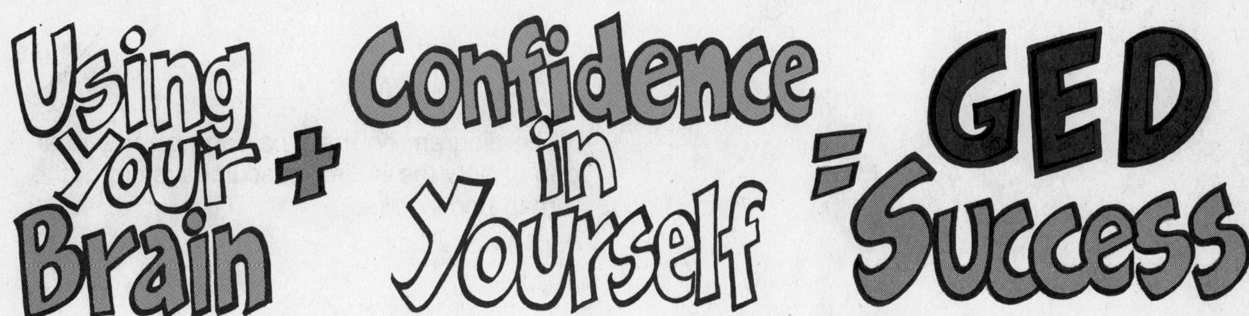

Sample Warm-up Answer
The brain is located in the head and is the main organ of the nervous system. From it, the spinal cord runs down the back. From the spinal cord, millions of nerves go to almost every part of the body.

The activities of the endocrine system, like those of the digestive and circulatory systems, are mostly chemical actions. You are unaware of them most of the time as you go about the normal routines of your day. You are well aware, however, of many of the movements your body makes. In fact, you decide what some of them are going to be. Before you read about movement in the human body, glance at the Warm-up question. It will help you focus your reading of this section.

Movement

Two special systems work together to help you move parts of your body. One of these systems is the **skeletal system,** shown in the drawing.

Skeletal System

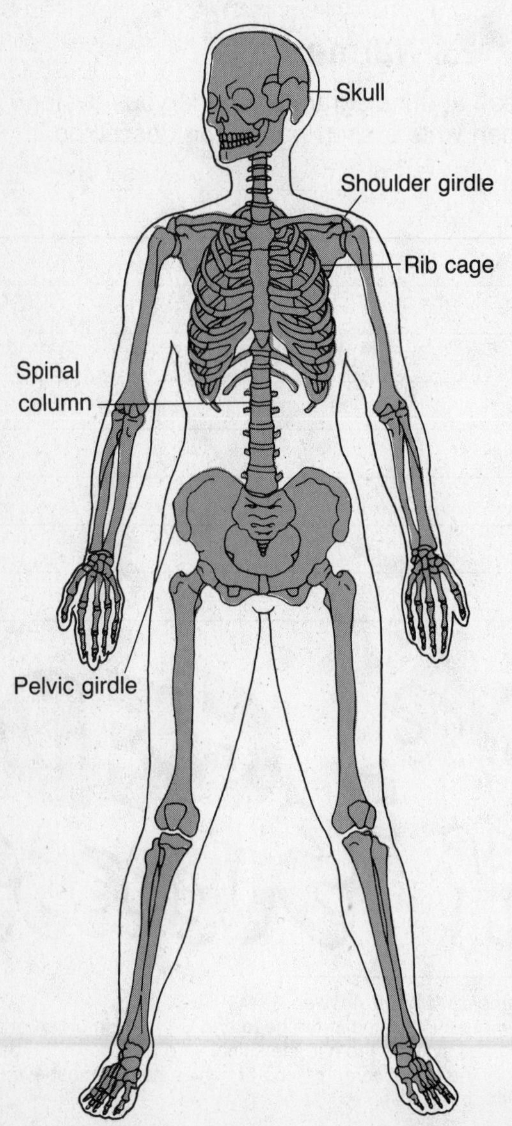

It's easy to see how the bones of the human skeleton provide a framework for the body and protect its organs. The skull shelters the brain, and the spinal column protects the spinal cord. The bones of the rib cage, in turn, curve around parts of the respiratory, digestive, and circulatory systems.

Where two bones meet, they form a joint. Some joints of the skeletal system can move; you move the joints at your knees, elbows, wrists, and fingers often. All of these joints are different and make it possible for you to make a variety of movements.

The **muscular system** is the second system needed to make the body move. Bones move when the muscles that are connected to them move. When muscles attached to bones contract, or shrink, they pull on the bones and cause joints to bend. This bending moves bones from one position to another. Messages from your nervous system tell the skeletal muscles when to contract and when to relax. Take a moment to look at the diagram below, which shows how muscle action causes bones to move.

Muscle action

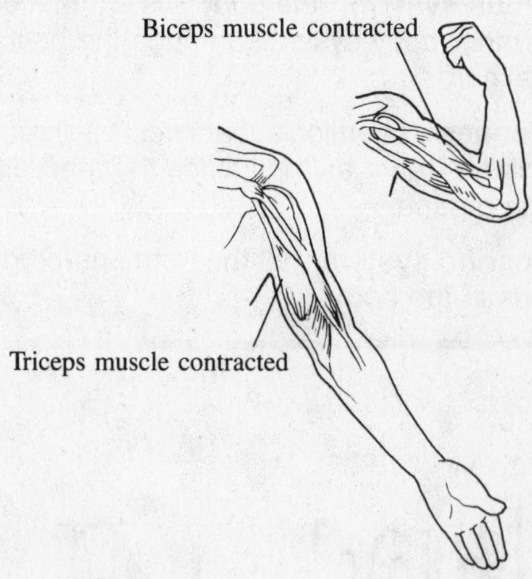

The diagram on the next page gives you an idea of how the entire muscular system of the human body looks.

Muscular System

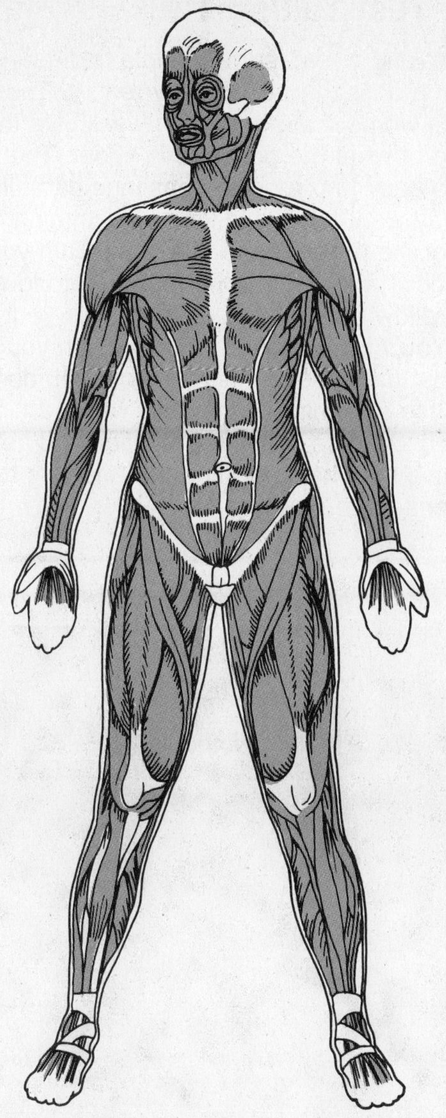

In addition to its skeletal muscles, the human body also has two other kinds of muscles. Smooth muscles help make up organs such as arteries and the stomach. The cardiac muscle makes up the heart. The heart, in fact, is really one big muscle.

Coming to Terms

skeletal system the framework of bones that supports the body and protects its organs

muscular system the system of muscles that are attached to bones of the skeleton or make up organs of the body

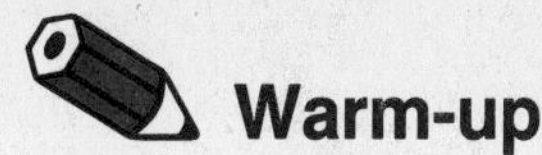

Warm-up

Use a sentence or two to explain the functions of the skull and spinal column.

____

____

____

____

Skimming for Information

At one time or another, you've probably found it necessary to locate specific information in something you have read. What do you do when you want to locate such information? Chances are, you skim.

When you skim, you don't try to reread every idea in the reading material. Instead, your eyes sprint over the lines of print, looking for key words and phrases.

Here's an Example

First read this sentence for yourself.

■ The head of a newborn baby is very large in proportion to the rest of its body.

If you were skimming that sentence, these key words and phrases would probably catch your eye.

head . . . newborn baby . . . large . . . rest of body

In addition to the words listed above, your eye might also stop at the word *proportion.* Longer words often stand out in a sentence and sometimes may indicate an important idea or term. Unfamiliar words may also stand out and suggest that word-part clues or context clues will come in handy.

These facts about skimming are important because they make it useful when you are looking for information to answer a test question.

Sample Warm-up Answer
The function of the skull is to shelter the brain. The function of the spinal column is to protect the spinal cord.

Try It Yourself

Try skimming the entire paragraph that the sentence in Here's an Example came from. As you skim, look for this specific information: How large is the human brain at birth, at six years, and in the adult?

■ The head of a newborn baby is very large in proportion to the rest of its body. At birth, a human brain weighs about 14 ounces. By the age of six, it has grown to nearly full size. A human adult's brain weighs a little over 3 pounds.

You may have noticed that the information you were seeking actually was fairly easy to find because two of the answers were numbers. Numbers tend to stand out from a page of print, as do symbols (such as quotation marks), capital letters, and special print such as *this* or **this.**

Did you spot that a human brain weighs 14 ounces at birth and 3 pounds in adulthood? What about at age six? As you skimmed, your eyes should have picked up "six" in the next-to-last sentence. After that, perhaps you noted "nearly full size." That is the information you were looking for.

☑ A Test-Taking Tip

On the GED Science Test, when you need to find specific information to answer a question, keep in mind that certain features of the printed page, such as numbers, capital letters, and special type, can sometimes lead you quickly to the place where the information is given.

☑ A Test-Taking Tip

When taking a test, some people find it helpful to skim a passage *before* they read it. They pick out words and phrases that will give them an idea of what the passage is about. Then they go back and read the passage carefully. You may want to try this kind of skimming on some of the passages in this book. Run your finger down the page from upper left to lower right. Follow the tip of your finger with your eyes. You'll be surprised at how much you can tell about the passage. And even if you decide not to use skimming in this way when you take the GED Science Test, the practice you get skimming may help you find the answers to questions more quickly.

Restating Information

"Will you give Larry a message for me? Tell him that . . ."

Have you ever taken such a message for someone else? If so, you probably wanted to make sure that you understood what was being said. When you finally passed on the message, you may not have used exactly the same words that you heard. But the words you did use told the important points of information.

The same thing is true about reading materials in science. You want to be able to understand the information in them, not memorize them exactly as written. If you can understand an idea, you can discuss it in your own words and answer questions about it. You'll be able to recognize when information is being restated accurately.

Here's an Example

Read this sentence carefully. Determine what information it is giving.

■ The muscles of the head, trunk, and limbs are known as voluntary muscles, for they contract and produce movements in response to conscious efforts of will.

Now read this statement. It gives the same information using different words.

■ Skeletal muscles are called voluntary because you can choose to contract them.

The second statement gives the same information because skeletal muscles *are* muscles of the head, trunk, and limbs. The words "you can choose to contract them" say the same thing as "contract and produce movements in response to conscious efforts of will." The second statement is an accurate rewording of the first.

Try It Yourself

Suppose you need to find the view of a nutritionist in this article. Use your skimming skills to find the quotation. Then see how well you can recognize a restatement of that quoted idea.

■ Rickets is a bone disease that may develop in children who have not received enough calcium or vitamin D. In areas of the world where severe malnutrition exists, children may show the effects of bone disease before the age of three. According to one famous nutritionist, "If the diet is made adequate, faulty bone structure can be improved as long as growth continues, but the superior development possible had no dietary insult occurred will probably never be achieved."

To find the quotation you were looking for, did you watch for the quotation marks?

Now look at the two sentences below. Which one best restates the information contained in the quotation?

Superior bone structure can never be achieved even with a proper diet.

A proper diet in people who are still growing can improve bad bone structure but not totally reverse damage.

Did you choose the second sentence as the best restatement of the information? The first sentence misinterprets the nutritionist's view and omits an important idea—the idea that a proper diet *can* improve bone health in a person *if* that person is still growing. The second sentence, however, includes all the ideas of the quotation but says them with different words.

On the Springboard

Items 1–2 refer to the following passage. Practice reading for understanding so that you will be able to recognize questions and answers that restate information.

A body gland makes and secretes chemicals. For example, sweat glands make sweat that travels through ducts to the skin. Similarly, salivary glands make saliva that goes through ducts to the mouth. Other glands, such as the thyroid gland and adrenal gland, are endocrine glands. They do *not* release chemical substances through ducts. Instead, these ductless glands release their chemicals directly into the bloodstream. The blood then carries these chemicals, called hormones, to specific target organs. The hormones control the body's growth, use of energy, and reproduction. You do not know when an endocrine gland is releasing hormones, but you can see and feel the results.

1. The human body's salivary and sweat glands release chemical substances by way of

   (1) ducts
   (2) hormones
   (3) the bloodstream

   (1) (2) (3)

2. According to the information in the passage, which of the following statements best describes the work of the endocrine glands?

   (1) You see evidence of the endocrine glands as they release substances into the bloodstream.
   (2) Without your immediate awareness, endocrine glands affect your growth, energy, and reproductive functions.
   (3) The glandular action that humans feel is related to hormones and ducts leading to the bloodstream.

Check your answers to On the Springboard on page 103.

Did you remember to skim for the specific information asked for in the first question? Were you able to pick out the restated information from the last two sentences in the passage for question 2? If so, you are ready to try "The Real Thing." If you had trouble, it would be a good idea to review this skill section before you go on.

“ The Real Thing ”

Items 1–2 refer to the diagram and information below.

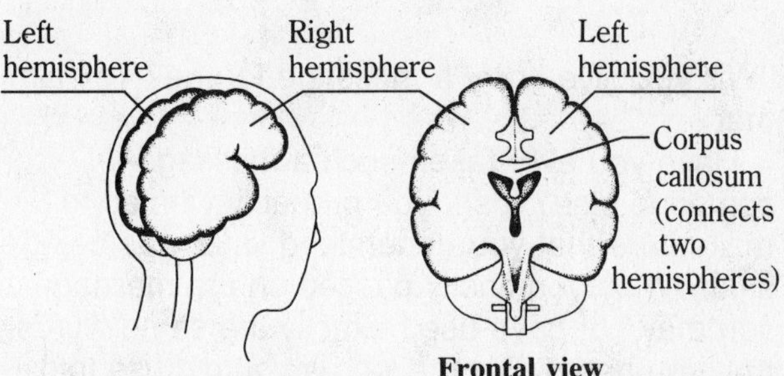

Frontal view

The cerebrum of the brain is divided into two hemispheres. The right hemisphere controls the left side of the body; the left hemisphere controls the right side.

Scientists have known for over one hundred years that the two hemispheres are not identical, but they did not have much information about the differences. Recent research has shown that the differences between the two hemispheres are concerned with the most basic mental processes. In general, the left hemisphere is responsible for logical, orderly thinking, while artistic and creative functions originate in the right hemisphere. Brain lateralization is not exactly the same for everyone, but the information is helping scientists to better understand various brain disorders and behavior difficulties.

1. The two hemispheres of the brain are characterized by

(1) logic
(2) identical thought processes
(3) creativity
(4) disorders
(5) different modes of thinking

2. According to the information given, knowledge of brain disorders is aided by research into

(1) behavior difficulties
(2) the two-sidedness of the brain
(3) basic mental processes
(4) the right hemisphere of the brain
(5) the corpus callosum

Check your answers and record your score on page 105.

LESSON 3

Cells

In the last two lessons you learned about life-supporting activities in your own body. Now you will begin to look at other aspects of life, in and around you. In the next section you'll see how life started on earth. Pay special attention to the different kinds of substances that help make up all living things. But first you may want to look at the Warm-up activity at the end of the section. It will help guide you to important information as you read.

The Beginning of Life

Imagine the world millions of years ago, before humans or any other forms of life existed. First, violent earthquakes and boiling volcanoes ruled the land. Then the rains came—rains so long and hard and heavy that they formed the oceans. After millions of years, the sun shone through a sky made greenish blue by **molecules** of ammonia, methane, water, and other substances. A molecule is the smallest particle of a compound that has all the properties of that compound.

At some point in time, energy from lightning or sunlight caused the existing molecules to combine and form more complicated substances. Among these were **organic** molecules such as **amino acids.** Organic molecules are ones that contain carbon, which is necessary for life.

Amino acids and other organic materials eventually fell from the sky with rain and collected in lakes and pools. Here they combined in many more and different ways. Amino acids combined to make **proteins,** which give shape to all living things and do the chemical work inside them. Eventually, certain combinations became living **cells,** the smallest units of life. All the different forms of life on earth today came from these first cells.

What made the cells different from all the other things around them? In other words, what made them alive?

First, the cells could *grow:* they took in food to make new material.

Second, they could *reproduce.* That is, they could create new cells that were very much like themselves.

Third, the cells could *respond* to their surroundings.

Fourth, the cells could *use energy* to grow, reproduce, and respond. They got this energy from the food they took in.

Today all living things are made up of cells. All living things grow, reproduce, respond, and use energy.

Coming to Terms

molecule the smallest particle of a compound that has all the properties of that compound

organic containing carbon, which is needed for life

amino acids the building blocks of proteins

proteins the complex substances that help make up the shape of all living things and carry out the work in them

cell the smallest unit of life. Cells make proteins from amino acids.

Warm-up

Write four sentences to describe the characteristics of cells that show they are alive.

Sample Warm-up Answer
Cells grow by using food to make new material. Cells reproduce, or make new cells like themselves. They respond to their environment. Cells use energy to do all these things.

In the next section you'll find out about the different parts that make up a cell. Preview the Warm-up to help you focus on important points as you read.

What a Cell Looks Like

You just learned that all living things are made up of cells. Some animals and plants consist of only one cell. Others are made up of many cells. The body of the average human adult, for example, has more than 10,000,000,000,000 (ten trillion) cells. In fact, if you had a penny for every cell in your body, you could spend four million dollars *every day* for the next sixty-eight years and still have money left over!

Most cells are extremely small, far too small to see with just your eyes. Yet the largest cells can certainly be seen, since they are the yolks of birds' eggs.

Cells vary in shape too. They can look like cubes, saucers, rods, coils, snowflakes, footballs, or trees; some cells even have no particular shape at all. And when a plant or an animal is made up of many cells, the cells develop into special groups, each with a particular job, or function. These groups make up the systems of the body that you read about in the last two lessons.

The shape of a cell often depends on its function. Here are the shapes of some of the special cells in the human body.

Some Special Body Cells

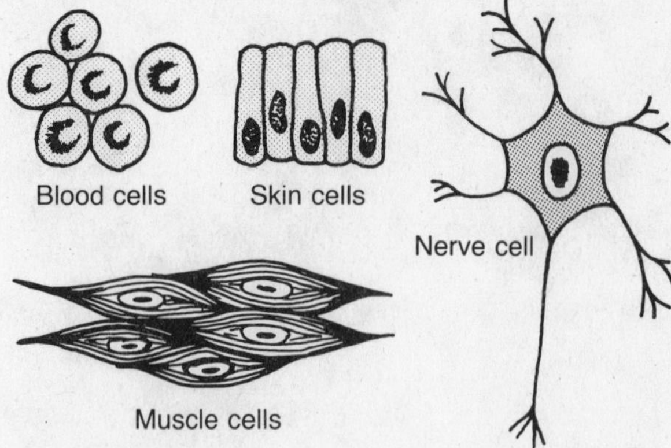

So cells differ in size, shape, and function. But almost all cells have many of the same basic parts. Look at this example of a "typical" cell found in a human or other animal.

"Typical" Animal Cell

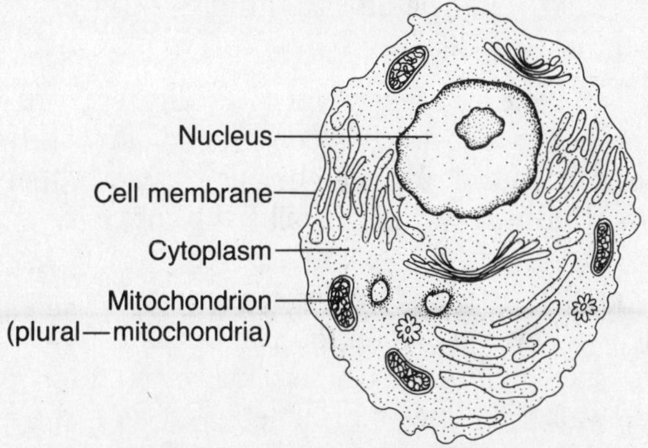

The **cell membrane** separates the cell from its surroundings. The **nucleus** is like the brain of the cell. It directs the cell's activities. The **cytoplasm** is a clear, jellylike fluid made mostly of water that contains many tiny structures. The names of the structures are not as important as the job each one does.

For example, the mitochondria are sometimes called the power plants of the cell. They change food into energy. Other structures in the cytoplasm are the manufacturers. They make the proteins that the cell needs to live and grow. Still other structures help the cell break down materials, store and release substances, or reproduce itself.

Coming to Terms

cell membrane the thin boundary that separates a cell from its surroundings

nucleus a structure inside a cell that controls the activities of the cell

cytoplasm the clear, jellylike fluid inside the cell membrane

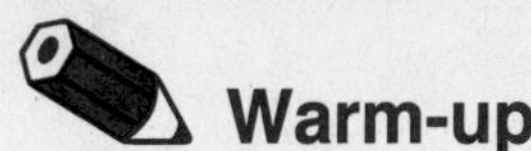

Warm-up

Write a sentence to answer this question: In what three ways do cells differ from one another?

Finding the Main Idea

Finding the **main idea** of a paragraph or longer passage is an important skill in understanding scientific writing. The main idea is the controlling thought, the single most important message that the written material contains. Sometimes you will find the main idea clearly stated in a single sentence, usually in the first or last sentence of the selection.

Coming to Terms

main idea the single most important thought of a piece of writing

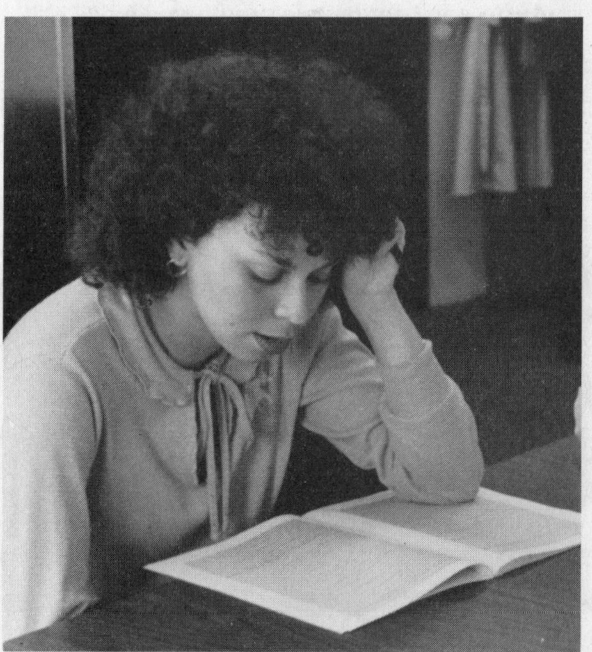

Sample Warm-up Answer
Cells have different sizes, shapes, and functions.

Here's an Example

In the paragraph below, one sentence gives the main idea the paragraph develops.

■ Different degrees of nerve responses are possible, depending on the number of nerve cells, or neurons, stimulated and the rate of stimulation of each neuron. For example, you can apply a light or a heavy touch to an object. The touch depends on the number of motor neurons involved in the action. You can tell the difference between lukewarm, warm, and hot water because your sensory neurons carry more impulses per second as the temperature of the water increases.

In that paragraph, the main idea is that different degrees of nerve responses occur. The first sentence states this controlling thought right at the beginning. The rest of the sentences in the paragraph go on to support that main idea by explaining and giving examples of it.

Try It Yourself

Now read the paragraph below. One of its sentences clearly states the main idea. See if you can find it.

■ A cell's nucleus controls its food intake, its growth, and its elimination of waste materials. In addition, protein created by small structures in the nucleus dictate what work the cell will do. The nucleus tells the cell when to prepare to duplicate itself and how to complete the duplication process. Clearly, the nucleus is the control center of the cell.

Which sentence did you choose? You were correct if you said that the last sentence states the main idea. Take time to reread it. Then notice how the sentences that lead up to the last one support the idea by showing how the nucleus controls a cell.

On the Springboard

Item 1 refers to the following paragraph. Decide which sentence states the main idea as you read. You will be asked to find a restatement of this idea.

The general appearance of a plant tells you whether or not its cells contain enough water. Each individual plant cell begins to swell when it is filled with water. As all the plant cells swell, they push against their cell walls. That action keeps the stem and leaves firm and upright. However, when the plant cells lack water, each cell begins to shrink away from its cell wall. The leaves become less rigid and begin to drop off. The stem of the wilting plant loses strength and bends over or buckles easily.

1. Which of the following sentences best states the main idea of the entire paragraph?

   (1) Plants should be watered regularly.
   (2) Falling leaves and drooping stems indicate that a plant needs water.
   (3) The concentration of water in a plant's cells is revealed by the way the plant looks.

   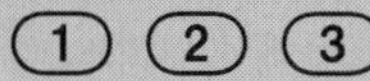

Check your Springboard answer on page 103. Then go on to read about the details that help support a main idea.

Seeing Patterns of Details

You've just seen how one sentence in a paragraph or passage can state a main idea while other sentences support the main idea. These sentences add details—supporting details—that help you understand the main idea.

Generally a selection will contain only those supporting details most closely related to the main idea. Sometimes the supporting details occur in a certain order in the reading selection. As a reader, you can use the order, or pattern, to help you concentrate and understand the relationships among the details. For instance, if a passage begins by saying that there are two types of cell division, you can direct your reading toward finding out what those two types are and how they may be alike and different. If you realize you are reading about a process, you can look for the details to be the ordered steps of the process.

Here's an Example

The paragraph below contains details arranged according to time order. It describes a series of steps to be performed one by one in a given order. As you read the paragraph, notice how time order helps you picture the process in your mind and so better understand it.

■ To prepare a slide for viewing onion cells under a microscope, first gather the necessary equipment: an onion, a microscope, a glass slide and coverslip to cover the specimen, tweezers, paper towel, a medicine dropper, and iodine. Second, put a drop of water on the slide. Next, use the tweezers to remove a thin layer of skin from the inside of the onion. Tear off a small piece, lay it on the drop of water, and cover it with the coverslip. Then place a drop of iodine on one edge of the coverslip. Hold a small piece of paper towel on the other side to draw the iodine across the onion skin. The iodine will tint the skin, allowing the individual cells to be seen as you look through the microscope.

The details in that paragraph are the steps of a process carefully ordered. The words *first, second, next,* and so on help you picture how the steps follow each other.

Try It Yourself

The passage that follows discusses the role vitamin C plays in the human body. It gives three functions, arranged in the order of importance. As you read the passage, decide if the details follow a pattern from least important to most important, or the other way around.

■ Vitamin C serves a number of different functions in the body. Some of these functions have been proven, and some are still being explored. Its main known function is to help form and maintain the "cementing" material between body cells. We also know that it is needed for healthy teeth and gums. Recently, there has been growing evidence that large doses of vitamin C can help prevent cancer and heart disease.

Did you realize that the first sentence stated the main idea? It was also a clue that the rest of the paragraph would detail the known functions of vitamin C. Because the first supporting sentence begins with "Its main known function . . . ," you should have realized that the most important *proven* function was being given first. The next known function is less important than the first. And the last one—about cancer and heart disease—is yet to be proven, so it is placed at the bottom of the list of *known* functions. Did you see that pattern as you read?

On the Springboard

Items 2–3 refer to the following passage. In the passage, two things are compared and contrasted. Use that pattern of organization to help you understand the information.

Normal red blood cells are round with a slight depression in the center. This round, smooth shape allows the red blood cells to pass easily through very small blood vessels. Sickle-cell anemia is an inherited disease in which the red blood cells are bent into shapes that look like sickles. Sickle-shaped red blood cells get caught in very small blood vessels. A person with sickle-cell anemia suffers from poor circulation, painful cramping, and a shorter life expectancy.

2. According to the passage, sickle cells differ from normal red blood cells in

   (1) shape
   (2) color
   (3) function

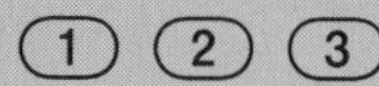

3. What is the poor circulation of a person with sickle-cell anemia due to?

   (1) too few blood cells in the vessels
   (2) the tightening and cramping of the blood vessels
   (3) the inability of the cells to pass through blood vessels

   ① ② ③

You can check your answers to On the Springboard on page 103.

Have you noticed how different patterns help you see the relationships among ideas? In "The Real Thing" that follows, one of the passages will divide a general topic into two specific categories and describe each one separately. Use this classification pattern to help you understand the information and answer the questions. The other passage in "The Real Thing" will use a pattern that you've already seen an example of.

☑ A Test-Taking Tip

Questions on the GED Science Test will not ask you to identify different patterns of details. But if you can see how the information you are reading on the test is organized, you can more easily understand and remember what you read.

"The Real Thing"

Item 1 refers to the following passage.

Biologists classify cells as simple and complex. Simple cells are called prokaryotic, which means "before the nucleus." The cells are so simple that their internal structures float freely inside the cell membrane. Complex cells, called eukaryotic, carry on the same life processes that prokaryotic cells do, but the material directing their activities is contained within a nuclear membrane. In addition, many different kinds of internal structures are encased in their own membranes within the cell membrane.

1. What is the classification of cells primarily based on?

   (1) the presence of a nucleus
   (2) the presence of a cell membrane
   (3) the life processes they carry on
   (4) the direction of their activities
   (5) their floating internal structures

   ① ② ③ ④ ⑤

Items 2–3 refer to the following diagrams and information.

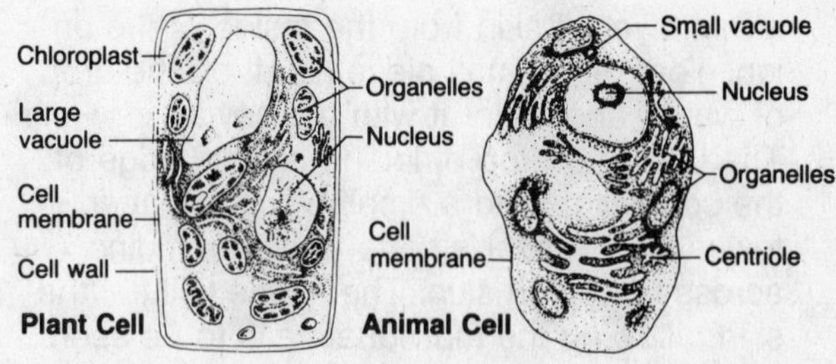

Plant and animal cells are alike in many ways. In both, a cell membrane holds together the contents of the cell. The membrane also allows nutrients to enter and wastes to exit. Both plant and animal cells contain cytoplasm, the clear, jellylike substance in which float the nucleus and other structures called organelles.

Unlike animal cells, however, a typical plant cell also has a cell wall; eventually the cell walls of the many cells of a plant make up its stem. Also unlike animal cells, plant cells contain chloroplasts, small structures that allow the plant to make its own food.

2. Which of the following is one way in which plant and animal cells are similar?

   (1) They are approximately the same size.
   (2) Both make their own food.
   (3) Both contain inner centrioles.
   (4) They have some of the same structures.
   (5) They have either a cell wall or a cell membrane.

   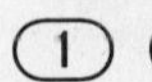    

3. One way in which plant and animal cells are different is that a plant cell has

   (1) organelles
   (2) a nucleus
   (3) cytoplasm
   (4) a cell membrane
   (5) a cell wall

      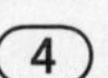 

Check your answers and record your score on page 105.

LESSON 4

Cell Activities

You have read that a cell is the smallest, basic unit of life. How do such small cells perform the functions of life? You will begin to see how they do in the next section as you learn how a cell takes in the things it needs to live. First read the Warm-up question at the end. Keep it in mind as you read.

Moving into and out of a Cell

Your body takes in food, air, and water. It uses them and then gets rid of the waste materials. A cell must do the same. In fact, it is because the cells in your body do these things that your body as a whole does them.

You learned that a membrane encloses a cell and separates it from its surroundings. How, then, do substances get into and out of the cell?

The molecules that make up the membrane of a cell have extremely small spaces between them. And extremely small molecules of other substances, like oxygen, can pass through these spaces. But the membrane doesn't let just any small molecule in. The cell can use chemical means to keep out molecules that it doesn't want.

A cell's membrane must deal with more than just small molecules, however. The cell requires food molecules and other substances too large to enter through the spaces. And sometimes it needs to release large proteins it has made. How do these substances get through the membrane?

In most animal cells, the molecules that make up the membrane will actually help move other molecules in and out. The whole process is something like a revolving door. The different stages of the diagram show how it works.

Moving a Particle into a Cell

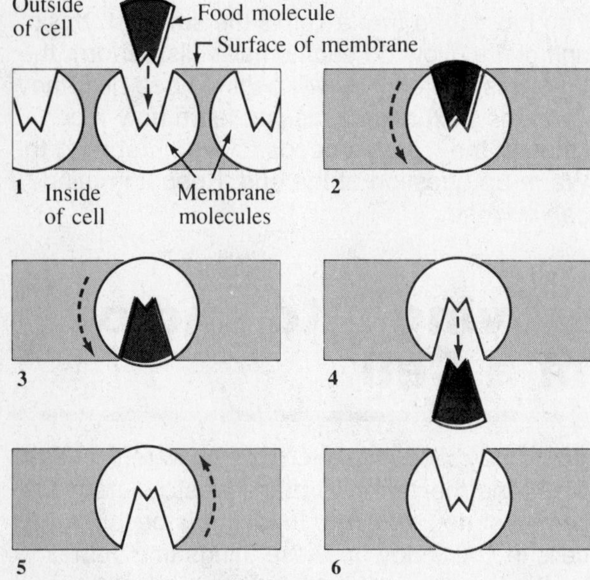

Molecules usually try to even things out. If there are more molecules of a particular substance on one side of a cell membrane than on the other, the molecules will try to move from the side with more molecules to the side with fewer. (Imagine that you opened the door to a closet that was filled with sand. Would the sand particles stay inside the closet, or would they even things out by half-burying you?)

Sometimes, though, a cell needs to keep an uneven state. It may need fewer molecules of a substance than are on the outside, or it may need more. In a sense, it needs to open and close the closet door very quickly once in a while to let a few particles in or out. In such cases, the "revolving door" process is used. Both small and large molecules can get a ride through the membrane whenever the cell requires it.

Remember, all of this activity is going on in a thing so small that it takes several *million* cells just to make up the skin on the palm of your hand.

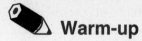

Warm-up

In what two ways can molecules get in and out of a cell? Write your answer in a brief paragraph.

____

____

____

____

____

The following section tells you how a cell breaks down the food it has taken in to get the energy it needs. Before you read, notice that the Warm-up will ask you about the order in which the steps in this process take place. You will want to watch for the steps as you read.

How a Cell Gets Energy

To live, a cell must have energy. To produce energy, a cell must have food. Tiny animals of only one cell can take food directly from the outside world. But the billions of cells in a larger animal, such as a human, have food brought to them.

When you feel hungry or thirsty, the cells in your body need more food or water. How do the cells get the food and water you eat and drink? First, your body breaks down the food into extremely small particles, including a simple sugar called glucose. (Glucose is *not* like the refined sugar you buy at the store.) The tiny glucose molecules are carried by the bloodstream and pass through the thin membranes of cells into the cytoplasm. From there they enter the power plants of the cells, the mitochondria.

Sample Warm-up Answer
Some molecules can move in and out of a cell through spaces between the molecules in the cell's membrane. Others enter the cell through a process similar to a revolving door. Molecules in the membrane carry out the revolving-door action.

In each mitochondrion, oxygen helps break down the glucose molecules even further. It's like burning fuel. The process releases water and a gas called carbon dioxide. These wastes leave the cell and eventually the body. When you breathe out, your body is getting rid of the carbon dioxide.

In addition to carbon dioxide and water, each mitochondrion also produces a substance called ATP. ATP is loaded with energy. Whenever any living thing—a one-celled animal, a tree, an elephant, or a human—breaks down substances to produce energy, we say that **respiration** has occurred.

After respiration, particles of ATP leave the mitochondrion and provide energy for such things as making proteins and moving molecules into and out of the cell. Some energy is stored for future use. You use the energy produced in cells every time you move.

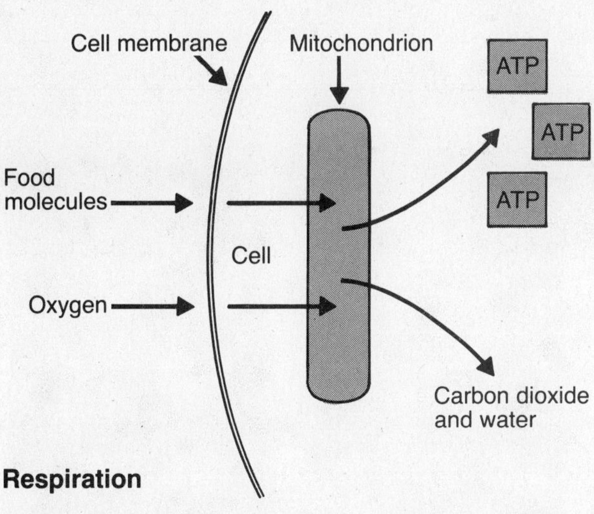

Respiration

Coming to Terms

respiration the act of breaking down a substance to produce energy. Carbon dioxide and water are given off during respiration.

Warm-up

Below are three steps involved in respiration. Write them in the order in which they take place.

Food molecules are broken down to produce energy.
Oxygen enters the cell.
Carbon dioxide leaves the cell.

____

____

____

____

Now you'll read about the way a cell makes a copy of itself. Living things would not be able to grow if cells couldn't copy themselves. The Warm-up will give you a clue to a substance that plays an important role in this copying, or reproducing.

How a Cell Divides

When a one-celled animal reproduces itself, or when a cell in a larger animal reproduces itself, the cell simply divides. One cell becomes two, each one just like the "parent." But before a cell can divide, there must be a way to give *both* of the two new "daughter" cells all the information they need to live. A substance called **DNA** carries this information. The DNA is on **chromosomes** in the nucleus of the cell. So before a cell can divide, each chromosome has to make a copy of itself. Then there will be two sets of information, one for each new cell. The diagrams on the next page show you what happens when a cell divides.

Warm-up Answer
Oxygen enters the cell. Food molecules are broken down to produce energy. Carbon dioxide leaves the cell.

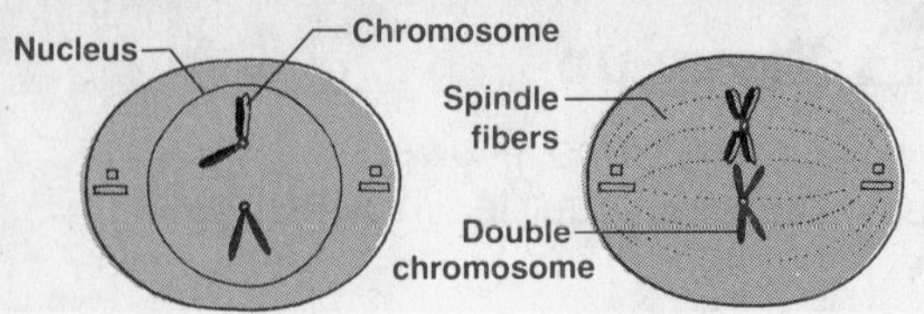

1. An animal cell with two chromosomes is about to divide. First, each chromosome will duplicate, or make a copy of, itself.

2. Each chromosome has duplicated itself. A spindle of fibers has formed, and the double chromosomes have moved to the middle of it.

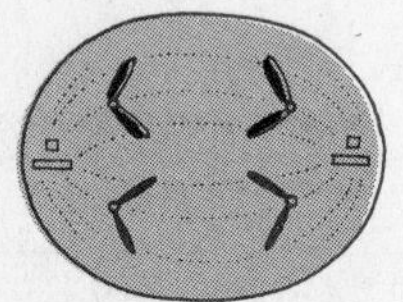

3. The double chromosomes separate. They move along the spindle fibers to opposite ends of the cell.

4. The cell splits in two. The new "daughter" cells are identical to each other and have the same number and kind of chromosomes as the "parent."

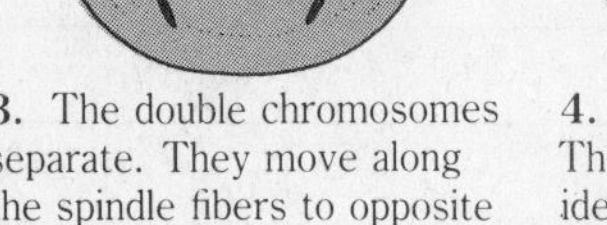

The photographs below show an actual cell dividing. Can you see how they resemble the diagrams above?

1.

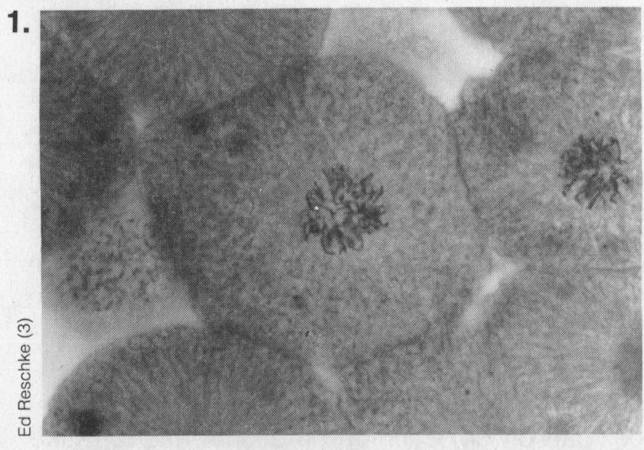

Ed Reschke (3)

2.

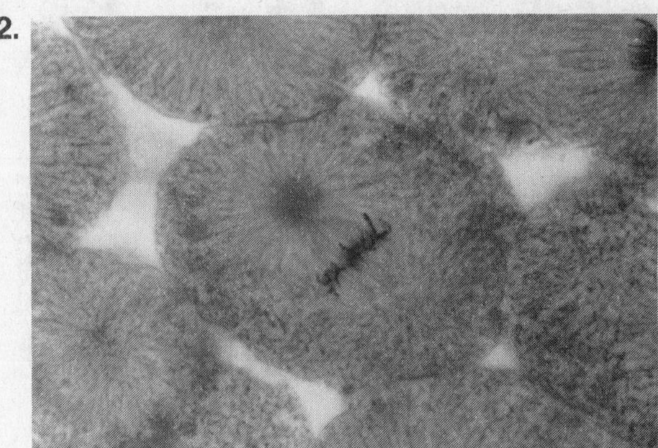

3.

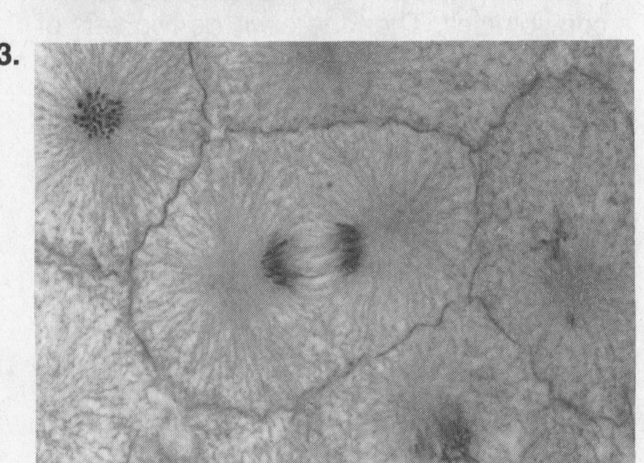

4.

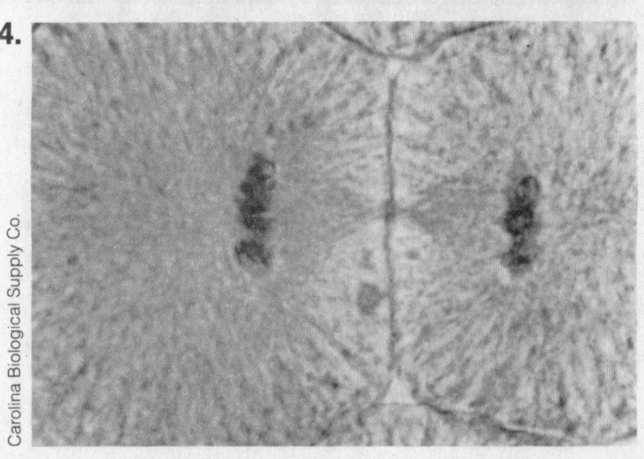

Carolina Biological Supply Co.

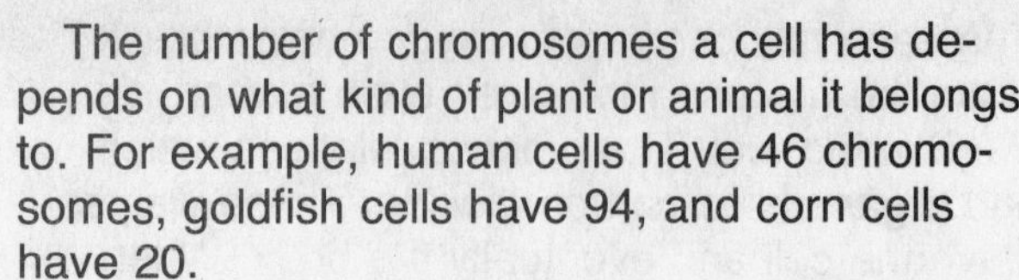

The number of chromosomes a cell has depends on what kind of plant or animal it belongs to. For example, human cells have 46 chromosomes, goldfish cells have 94, and corn cells have 20.

Coming to Terms

DNA a substance that has the information needed for reproduction and life

chromosome a structure in the nucleus of a cell that contains DNA

Warm-up

What is DNA and why is it important to living things? Write your answer in two or three sentences.

____

____

Sample Warm-up Answer

DNA is a substance found on chromosomes in the nucleus of a cell. It carries all the information that cells must have to live.

Inferring the Main Idea

What's Inference?

What is happening in this cartoon?

You can use the details in the picture to figure out what is happening. The "Deer Crossing" sign reveals that wild deer often try to cross the road at that point in the woods. The bumper-to-bumper traffic, though, has presented a problem. What is this deer's solution to the problem? The vaulting pole and his running position tell you that he's planning to vault over the traffic. Even without an explanation in words, you can **infer** the meaning of the cartoon. In other words, you can make a good guess based on the information given. To infer, or to use inference, means to make an educated guess.

Just as you used inference to tell the message of the cartoon, you may need to use inference to figure out the main idea of some scientific information. You know that often a single sentence in a paragraph states its main idea. But there's another kind of paragraph, one in which the author chooses not to state the main idea at all. Such a paragraph gives you all the details you need to *infer* the main idea.

Coming to Terms

Here are two words that are often confused.

imply to suggest or hint at an idea without actually stating it

infer to make a good guess based on information that has been given

Remember that an author implies an idea, while you, the reader, infer it.

Determining the Topic

To infer the main idea of a paragraph, you first need to figure out what the topic is. That means deciding what the paragraph is mainly about. The topic can be a person, a place, an object, or an idea.

Here's an Example

Read the brief passage below. It discusses a specific topic in biology.

■ Organisms grow larger by increasing the number of their cells. In order for the number of cells to increase, new cells must form from the cells that are already present. After a new cell forms, it grows to about twice its original size. As it grows, it doubles all of its parts. Then this doubly-large cell splits into two, forming two new cells from one.

The paragraph is mainly about living cells. It gives information about different aspects of cell growth, preparation to duplicate, and the duplication process. So the topic of the paragraph is cell duplication.

Try It Yourself

See if you can figure out the topic of this paragraph.

■ Some scientists think the key to aging and death lies in cells. Research shows that cells can reproduce only a limited number of times. Human cells, for example, divide about fifty times before dying. Chicken cells and rat cells divide even fewer times before death. After a set number of divisions, chromosomes seem to lose the ability to duplicate themselves. Cell division cannot occur. When the cells of an organism then begin to die, it is believed that the organism itself begins to age and die.

What is the paragraph about? It mentions a number of things: aging and death, human cells, chicken and rat cells, and so on. But almost every sentence gives some information about cell division and aging and death. That is the topic of the paragraph: how cell division is related to aging and death.

Topic + Details → Main Idea

Inferring the main idea is a simple two-step process. Just ask yourself these two questions.

What is the topic?
What point do the details make about the topic?

You have just read about the first step, finding the topic. From there you can go on to determine the point that the details make. When you have combined the answers to those two questions, you have inferred the main idea.

Here's an Example

Here is the same paragraph that was in the last example. You already know that the topic is cell duplication. Notice what the details in the sentences tell about that topic.

■ Organisms grow larger by increasing the number of their cells. In order for the number of cells to increase, new cells must form from the cells that are already present. After a new cell forms, it grows to about twice its original size. As it grows, it doubles all its parts. Then this doubly-large cell splits into two, forming two new cells from one.

Each sentence helps explain *how* an organism grows in size by detailing *how* the organism's cells grow in number. That is the main point, or main idea, of the paragraph. An organism grows in size as its cells double in size and then divide.

Try It Yourself

Here again is the passage from the last Try It Yourself. Remember that the topic is the relationship between cell division and aging and death. Infer the main idea by asking yourself this question as you read: What is the main point the details are making about the topic?

■ Some scientists think the key to aging and death lies in cells. Research shows that cells can reproduce only a limited number of times. Human cells, for example, divide about fifty times before dying. Chicken cells and rat cells divide even fewer times before death. After a set number of divisions, chromosomes seem to lose the ability to duplicate themselves. Cell division cannot occur. When the cells of an organism then begin to die, it is believed that the organism itself begins to age and die.

What do the sentences have to say about the relationship between cell division and aging and death? Some explain that cell division is limited. Others give examples of those limits. The last sentence relates this limited ability to the death of the cells and then to the aging and death of the organism. Those details should have helped you infer this main idea of the paragraph: The aging and death of the organism may be caused by the inability of its cells to divide any longer.

You can use the same method to infer the main idea of a scientific passage composed of more than one paragraph. See if you can use the same two steps to infer the main idea of this passage.

■ Although there are many kinds of cancer, they all have one thing in common: uncontrolled growth of cells.

Instead of dividing in an orderly way, a cell may go wild and multiply without stopping. One cell becomes two, two become four, four become eight, and so on until the wildly dividing cells have formed a tumor. If cells in the tumor begin to invade other body tissues, a cancer has developed.

One possible way to stop cancer is with a group of compounds called chalones. Some chalones prevent the duplication of chromosomes between periods of cell division. Other chalones prevent double chromosomes from separating during cell division. If each new daughter cell of a cancerous cell does not receive a complete set of chromosomes, it cannot survive. Biologists are trying to find out more about the way chalones work. If they succeed, they may be able to slow down the growth of cancer cells.

What is the topic of that entire passage? If you answered cancer, you were correct.

What is the main idea of the first paragraph? It states the one main characteristic of all cancers: uncontrolled cell growth.

What does the second paragraph tell you about cancer? Did you see that it details how uncontrolled growth may occur and develop into cancer?

What about the third paragraph? Each sentence in that paragraph helps explain how substances called chalones affect the growth of cancer cells.

You should have put those three ideas together to come up with a main idea for the entire passage that sounded something like this: Chalones may prove to be a way of treating cancer because they slow the growth of cancer cells by affecting cell division.

☑ A Test-Taking Tip

Some questions on the GED Science Test may ask you which of five statements best *summarizes* information given in a passage. A summary is a short statement of the main idea, often with some of the most important details. So to answer such a question, just note the topic and important details of the passage and infer its main idea from them. Then choose the statement that is most like your answer.

Coming to Terms

summary a short statement that gives the main idea and possibly the most important details

On the Springboard

Items 1–2 refer to the following passage. Note the topic and what the details say about the topic as you read.

When the concentration of a certain type of particle is greater inside a cell than outside, the crowded particles move through the cell membrane to the less crowded area outside in a process called diffusion. The same process works in reverse. If the concentration of certain particles outside the cell is greater than inside, some of those particles diffuse inside.

For example, human cells continually use sugar in the form of glucose. Blood must bring new supplies of sugar to the cells. The sugar molecules diffuse in through the cell membrane because there are fewer sugar molecules on the inside of the cell than on the outside.

Cells also continually produce wastes such as carbon dioxide. The carbon dioxide diffuses out of the cell through the cell membrane because there are fewer molecules of carbon dioxide outside the cell than inside. As the blood carries the carbon dioxide away, more carbon dioxide can diffuse out of the cell.

Water is both required by a cell and a waste product. When water diffuses back and forth through the cell membrane, the process is called osmosis.

1. What is the topic of the passage above?

   (1) sugar
   (2) water
   (3) diffusion

   ① ② ③

2. Which of the following statements best summarizes the passage?

   (1) Blood must constantly bring sugar to cells because they continually use it.
   (2) Carbon dioxide can flow out of a cell, but water can also flow into it.
   (3) Needed particles diffuse into a cell and waste particles diffuse out of it.

   ① ② ③

Turn to page 103 to check your answers to On the Springboard.

Were you able to identify the topic and main idea correctly? If so, congratulations! Read the tip that follows and then move along to "The Real Thing." If you need more help, read these pages on inferring the main idea again and then practice by rereading the material on cell activities at the beginning of the lesson.

☑ A Test-Taking Tip

A question on the GED Science Test may ask you to summarize a visual such as a diagram or graph. If so, look at the title of the visual. That should give its topic. Then study what the diagram shows or the relationship the graph reveals. Treat that information the same way you treat the details in the sentences of a paragraph. It will help you see the main point that the visual is making.

"The Real Thing"

Item 1 refers to the following diagram.

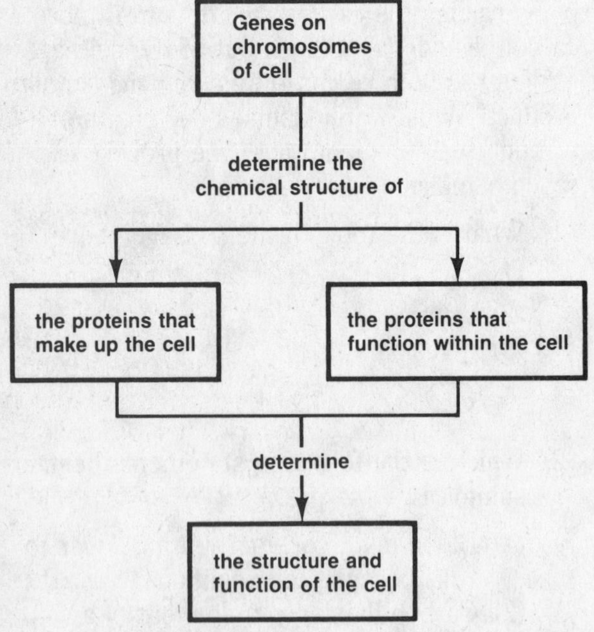

How Genes Determine a Cell's Characteristics

1. Which of the following statements best summarizes the diagram?

(1) Genes are found on the chromosomes of cells.
(2) Cells have both a particular structure and function.
(3) Proteins make up the structure of a cell.
(4) The nature of a cell is controlled by genes because they determine its proteins.
(5) Two kinds of proteins exist in a cell.

Items 2–4 refer to the following passage.

"If you were to break open a human cell and a yeast cell and compare them under a microscope, you'd have a terrible time telling the two apart," says Ron Davis, a Stanford molecular geneticist. Like us, yeast has two genders and reproduces with cells similar to eggs and sperm. It is a true eukaryote: each cell has a nucleus that separates its DNA from the viscous body of the cytoplasm (bacteria and other lowly organisms are prokaryotes, lacking a nucleus). Its 17 pairs of chromosomes behave remarkably like our 23 pairs, and can make the same mistakes during reproduction that in humans lead to such chromosomal disorders as Down syndrome. It manufactures enzymes similar to ours, and ferries them around inside itself and releases them in much the same way—and for much the same reasons—that our pancreatic, liver, or brain cells do. Most surprising, it harbors the oncogenes that are thought to trigger cancer, as well as versions of the viruses responsible for leukemia and AIDS. . . .

From a scientific standpoint, yeast cells have numerous advantages. . . . Unlike normal human tissue, yeast thrives in a petri dish. It divides once every two hours or so—whereas some human and mouse cells take twelve hours or more. This means that experiments can be completed more quickly. Yeast has only about 10,000 genes, less than three percent of the 400,000 found in human cells, and so can be more easily mapped and analyzed in fine detail.

2. The information in this passage can best be summarized by saying that yeast cells are

   (1) thought to be responsible for spreading AIDS and cancer
   (2) useless in studies of genetic disorders because of their seventeen chromosomes
   (3) good for research because they are like human cells, with added advantages
   (4) identical to human cells such as pancreatic, liver, and brain cells
   (5) true eukaryotes with two genders

   (1) (2) (3) (4) (5)

3. Which of the following is one way in which yeast cells and human cells are similar?

   (1) rate of reproduction
   (2) number of chromosomes
   (3) percentage of genes
   (4) ability to cause cancer
   (5) chromosomal behavior

   (1) (2) (3) (4) (5)

4. According to the article, yeast's ability to reproduce every two hours is an advantage because

   (1) yeast can then be grown and marketed very inexpensively
   (2) experiments with yeast take much less time than with other cells
   (3) yeast cells can be analyzed more easily
   (4) yeast can be used to make certain food products
   (5) quick cell division leads to disorders that can be researched

   (1) (2) (3) (4) (5)

Check your answers and record your score on page 105.

LESSON 5

Genetics

You've probably noticed how members of the same family tend to resemble each other. Yet no two people are ever exactly alike. In this section and the following one, you will learn about genetics, the biological processes that help make an organism unique. Previewing the Warm-up questions at the end of this section will help you focus on important information.

Sex Cell Production

You know that DNA, a material found in chromosomes, contains information in a cell. This information includes biological characteristics of the whole organism. You read in the last lesson that each type of organism has a specific number of chromosomes. You saw how—in regular cell division—the chromosomes duplicate and then separate so that the two new cells are just like the parent cell.

That system works fine to enable an organism to grow. But when a *new* organism is created, when biological **traits** such as hair texture and eye color are to be passed from one generation to the next, regular cell division will not work. Cells must combine to produce a new organism. Yet if two regular cells combined, the new organism would have *twice* as many chromosomes as it needs. So when traits are to be passed to the next generation of certain organisms, a special kind of cell division called meiosis takes place. Meiosis produces **sex cells.** Each sex cell carries only *half* the information from the parent cell.

The diagram on this page shows that meiosis is like regular cell division only in some ways. (In humans, meiosis takes place in cells with 23 pairs of chromosomes. To make the diagram easier to read, only one pair is shown.) Notice that in the third step of the process, some of the DNA of one chromosome may break off and cross over to the other chromosome. This crossing over creates new DNA patterns and helps cause the differences between parents and their offspring.

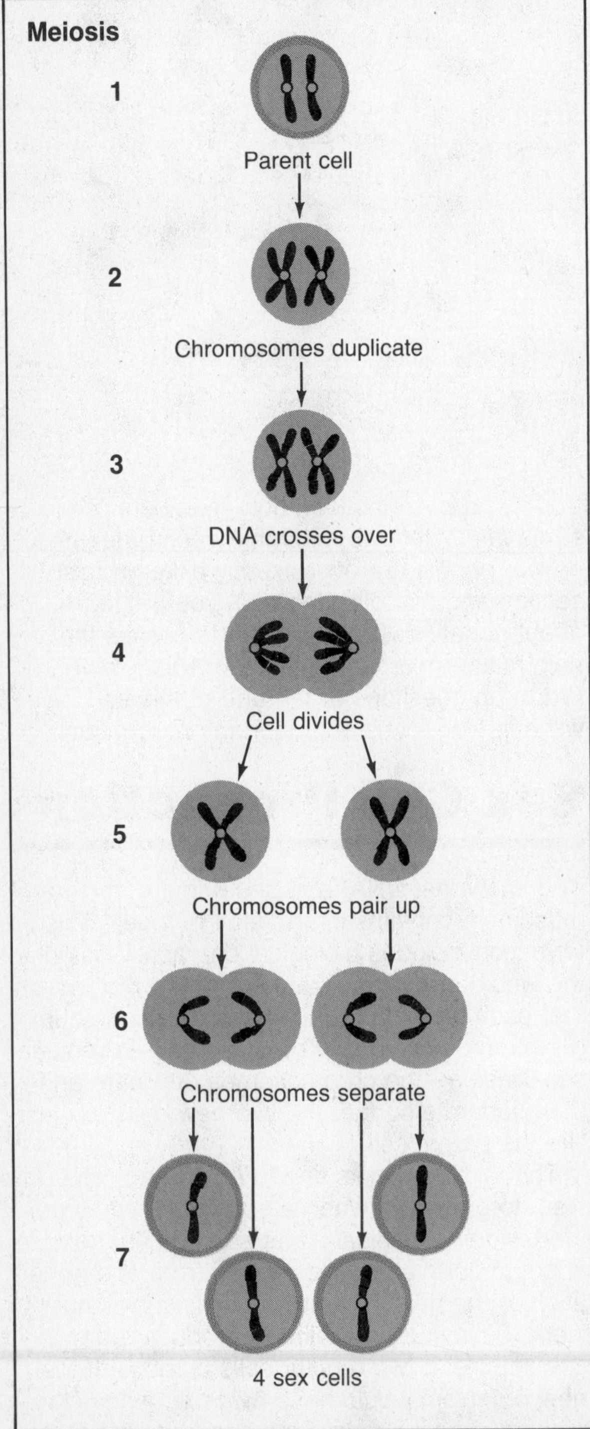

Notice also that meiosis ends with four sex cells rather than two "daughter" cells. Each sex cell differs from the parent cell in two important ways: It has only half as many chromosomes, and its DNA has changed patterns.

Fertilization occurs when a sex cell from a father joins with a sex cell from a mother. A new single cell is formed. This new organism has the correct number of chromosomes as well as its own individual pattern of DNA. Half the DNA information came from the father and half from the mother.

Coming to Terms

trait a biological characteristic

sex cells cells resulting from meiosis; cells that pass on biological characteristics from one generation to the next

fertilization the joining of a sperm with an egg

Warm-up

Write your answer to each question in a sentence or two.

1. Why is the pattern of DNA in sex cells important?

____

____

2. Compare the number of new cells resulting from regular cell division with the number resulting from meiosis.

____

____

Sample Warm-up Answers
1. The individual pattern of DNA in sex cell chromosomes helps make offspring different from their parents. **2.** Regular cell division produces two new cells. Meiosis produces four new cells.

The next section gives you an idea of how specific traits pass from one generation to another. It explains why children may look somewhat but not exactly like their parents. Before you read the section, first check the Warm-up activity. Keep it in mind as you read.

Inheritance of Traits

To understand how children inherit traits from their parents, you need to look again at the DNA in cells. Sections of DNA called **genes** are located along the chromosomes. Each gene carries a coded message something like a blueprint. The new organism, or offspring, inherits at least one gene for a certain trait from each parent. But if an equal number of genes are inherited from each parent, why do some children look more like one parent than the other?

The answer is that some genes are dominant. A **dominant gene** overrides or cancels out the effects of another. Genes that can be overriden are called **recessive genes.**

For example, consider the color of people's eyes. The gene for brown eyes, a dominant gene, overrides the gene for blue eyes, a recessive gene. What happens when a brown-eyed parent, with two dominant brown genes, and a blue-eyed parent, with two recessive blue genes, have children? All their children will have brown eyes. Each child receives one blue gene and one brown gene, which always overrides the blue gene. The blue gene is present, but the brown one is in control.

Now suppose that two brown-eyed people have children. Each parent has a dominant gene for brown eyes and a recessive gene for blue eyes. What color will the children's eyes be? The children could have either brown eyes or blue eyes, depending on which gene they inherit from each parent. A child will have brown eyes if he or she—

1. inherits a brown gene from each parent
2. inherits a brown gene from one parent and a blue gene from the other parent

Only the child who inherits a recessive blue gene from each parent will have blue eyes.

Sometimes the two forms of a gene for a certain trait are neither dominant nor recessive. Offspring will show a blend of the traits of their parents. Human skin color, for example, comes from more than one gene. Among plants, the offspring of a red petunia and a white petunia will be pink.

Two special chromosomes are the **X chromosome** and the **Y chromosome.** They determine an individual's sex. Females produce egg sex cells that *always* contain an X chromosome. Males produce sperm sex cells that have either an X chromosome or a Y chromosome. If an egg joins a sperm containing an X chromosome, the offspring will have two X chromosomes and be female (XX). However, if an egg joins a sperm containing a Y chromosome, the offspring will be male (XY). Therefore, the kind of sperm, X or Y, that joins with the X egg determines whether the baby will be male or female.

Coming to Terms

gene a small part of a chromosome that carries information about a trait

dominant gene a gene that overrides the effect of another gene for the same trait

recessive gene a gene that does not show its trait when a dominant gene is present

X chromosome a female chromosome

Y chromosome a male chromosome

Warm-up

In your own words, describe how the sex of an offspring is determined. Write your answer in complete sentences.

____

____

____

____

____

Sample Warm-up Answer
All egg cells contain X chromosomes. If a sperm with an X chromosome joins with an egg, a female (XX) will result. If a sperm containing a Y chromosome joins with the egg, the offspring will be male (XY).

The earth is home to many different kinds of plants and animals. Living organisms have not always had exactly the same traits that they have today. In the next section, you will read about how changes in the traits of organisms have taken place over long periods of time. Look at the Warm-up activity and then watch for clues to the answer as you read.

Natural Selection and Evolution

Scientific evidence shows that both the numbers and kinds of organisms have changed over time. Some organisms, such as saber-toothed tigers and woolly mammoths, have disappeared altogether and are considered **extinct.**

Scientists use the **theory of evolution** to help explain how organisms could have changed in number and traits. Evolution refers to the biological changes that take place in a group of organisms over a period of time. Horses, for example, would make up one group of organisms that has changed biologically over a long period of time. In forming the theory of evolution, scientists have relied on evidence from ancient fossils, on their own observations of living organisms, and on chemical tests in laboratories.

In the mid-1800s, the English scientist Charles Darwin tried to explain how evolution takes place. According to Darwin, organisms that are well suited to their natural environment tend to survive and reproduce. They pass along the traits that help them survive to their offspring. Organisms poorly suited to their natural environment are less likely to survive and reproduce.

Darwin called the process by which better-suited organisms are more likely to survive and reproduce **natural selection.** For example, if the climate suddenly became much colder, animals with thick fur would be more likely to survive than animals of the same kind with little body covering. Offspring of animals with thick fur would also have thick fur. After many generations, animals with thick fur would far outnumber those with little body covering. Those with little body covering might even have become extinct.

Darwin's ideas form the basis of modern biology. There is another way that the traits of organisms can change, however. Scientists have since found that the DNA in chromosomes can go through changes. They call such changes **mutations.** Mutations occur in the genes of an organism.

Mutations can cause a trait to change or become lost. Think of the difference between a peach and a nectarine. Because of a mutation, a certain type of peach lost the trait for fuzzy skin. The result was a smooth-skinned peach—a nectarine. Mutations can be either dominant or recessive. They pass from one generation to the next. Some mutations work to the advantage of an organism, but others decrease its chances for survival.

Coming to Terms

extinct no longer in existence

theory of evolution the scientific belief that inherited traits passed from one generation of an organism to the next change over a long period of time

natural selection the process by which those organisms best suited to the environment tend to survive, reproduce, and pass on their traits to the next generation

mutation a change in chromosomes that causes a change or a loss of a trait

Warm-up

Why is the term *natural selection* a good name for the process Darwin described? Write your answer in a sentence or two.

____

____

____

____

____

Sample Warm-up Answer
According to natural selection, organisms best suited to their environment will survive and produce the most offspring. Nature, then, helps select which organisms will prosper and which will have trouble surviving.

Seeing Relationships Between Ideas

Think for a moment about the different types of relationships between people you know. Some common relationships are the ones between husband and wife, parent and child, employer and worker, customer and businessperson, and neighbor and neighbor. In each case, the relationship involves some type of interaction—some way in which the people concerned influence each other.

As you read science materials, you will often find that facts and ideas relate to each other in certain ways also. Sometimes a fact is a specific example of a more general idea. Sometimes important similarities or differences between things are noted. At other times, the order of events is the most important relationship to understand. The next few pages will give you a chance to sharpen your skills at recognizing these relationships in the science material you read.

Here's an Example

As you read this passage, notice how the first sentence makes a general statement about genetic errors. Then see how the next two sentences give specific examples of such errors.

■ Errors sometimes occur in the transfer of the genetic information on a cell's chromosomes. Mutations may be caused by radiation or chemicals. Viruses may also produce mistakes.

The following passage uses the similarity between DNA and a familiar household item to help you understand what DNA is like.

■ Genes are composed of a complicated chemical called deoxyribonucleic acid, or DNA. Sugar, phosphoric acid and what are called four bases—adenine, cytosine, guanine, and thymine—are the ingredients of DNA. The molecules of these substances arrange themselves rather like a spiral ladder within each gene. The bases, linked in special combinations, as though they were the rungs of the ladder, are the factors that actually hold the key to our whole appearance and personality.

Did you see how the passage uses the *similarities* between a ladder and DNA to help you get a picture of the molecules in DNA? The next paragraph points out *differences* between two things to explain a concept.

■ Like identical twins, fraternal twins are two individuals produced at the same birth. However, identical twins develop from the same fertilized egg. Fraternal twins develop from two separate eggs fertilized by two different sperm. Therefore, they do not look exactly alike or share precisely the same inherited traits.

Another way in which ideas and events relate to each other is in time. Recognizing the order in which events take place will help you see how they relate to one another.

■ More than two thousand years ago, the Greek philosopher Aristotle taught that living beings could grow from nonliving matter. That theory prevailed for centuries. Then in the 1600s, Englishman William Harvey suggested that living beings grew from tiny, unseen eggs. No one was able to prove or disprove Harvey's theory with evidence. Other scientists of Harvey's time insisted that a tiny, perfectly formed person lay curled up in the head of each human sperm cell. Advanced laboratory equipment and years of careful study and research have given us the detailed information we have today about reproduction and inheritance.

Were you able to follow a sequence of events in the paragraph? First was the belief that living things grew out of nonliving material. Change came in the 1600s with William Harvey's theory and then went even further when modern science entered the laboratory.

Try It Yourself

A single passage of scientific writing often includes several different types of relationships between ideas. As you read the next selection, notice how the ideas and examples relate to each other.

■ Science fiction has suggested that researchers can produce a clone from the single cell of a living human being. The clone is an exact reproduction of the person. But that fantasy differs vastly from the truth. Clones *have* been successfully produced in laboratories, but not clones of human beings. And cloning does not always involve growth from a single cell. In a process called vegetative reproduction, a part of a plant can eventually produce a clone of the plant.

One such clone is a carrot. To clone a carrot, a scientist first prepares a dish of nutrients, made up of agar (a substance that looks and feels like gelatin), vitamins, and other materials that will support life and growth. Then, using a carefully sterilized razor or scalpel, the scientist cuts a small section from a carrot seedling and places it in the nutrients. Gradually, a group of cells called the callus tissue emerges. From each of these cells will grow a carrot that is genetically identical to the original—a clone.

What sorts of relationships between ideas did you find? If you detected a difference described early in the passage, you were right. The first paragraph tells how the concept of cloning in science fiction differs from reality.

In the second paragraph, did the phrase "One such clone" alert you to a relationship between the general group—clones—and a specific example of a clone—a carrot?

Where does the passage develop a time sequence? You are correct if you found one in the second paragraph. The paragraph describes a series of steps, one by one, used to clone a carrot in a laboratory.

On the Springboard

Items 1–2 refer to the following diagram and information. Be alert for different types of relationships in both. They will help you answer the questions that follow.

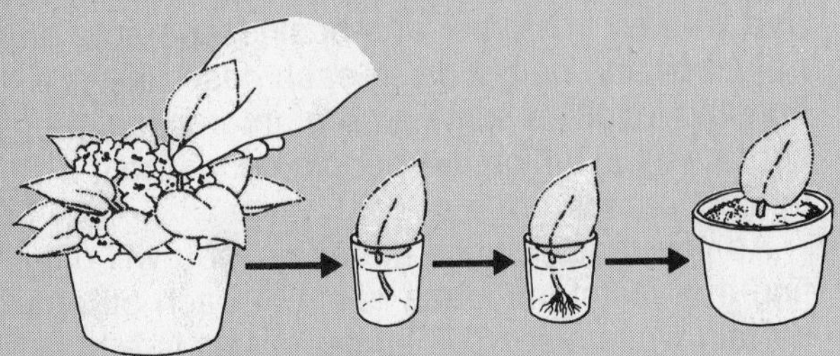

Cloning some plants is quite simple. Anyone who has ever taken a leaf from an African violet and put it in water to grow has done it. Cloning a plant is simply growing a new plant from a cutting that will have genes identical to those of its parent. No seed is used; no fertilizer is applied; no male or female takes part.

1. According to the information given, a cloned plant is similar to its parent in that the clone has

   (1) no male or female parts
   (2) the same number of leaves as the parent
   (3) the same number and kinds of genes as the parent

2. An African violet leaf cutting will grow roots after it has been

   (1) transferred to another pot
   (2) placed in water
   (3) fertilized

   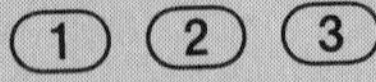

Turn to page 103 for the Springboard answers.

Understanding Cause-and-Effect Relationships

One very important relationship that can exist between ideas in scientific material is a cause-and-effect relationship. A **cause** is a thing or an event that makes something else happen. The **effect,** or the result, is the thing that is made to happen.

You deal with causes and effects every day. Turning on the oven (a cause) helps produce a cooked meal (the effect). A sudden rainfall (a cause) results in a ruined hairstyle (the effect). Hours of hard work (a cause) lead to a paycheck (the effect). The whole world is an ongoing stream of causes and their effects. That is why this kind of relationship is studied in science.

Coming to Terms

cause a thing or an event that makes something happen

effect the result that is produced by a cause

Here's an Example

Read this short paragraph, which contains *two* cause-and-effect relationships.

■ A Japanese scientist has found that a roadside weed, called a spiderwort, is sensitive to radiation. When exposed to even small amounts of radiation, the hairs on the plant's stamen change color. The color change *is due to* mutations in the plant's cells *caused by* radiation. Spiderworts are now being planted near nuclear facilities to detect radiation leaks.

The *italic* type helps you spot the cause-and-effect relationships. The color change (one effect) *is due to* mutations in the plant's cells (its cause). In turn the mutations are an effect; they are *caused by* radiation.

☑ A Test-Taking Tip

When you take the GED Science Test, you will find a number of questions that ask you *why* something happened (a cause) or what happened *because* of something else (an effect). Sometimes an author will use a key word to point out a cause-and-effect relationship. Here are some examples: *because, since, as a result, consequently, so, therefore, due to,* and *causing.* When you need to find cause-and-effect relationships, look for key words like those first.

Try It Yourself

Here is another passage that deals with causes and effects. See if you can determine what causes baldness.

■ A trait that is determined by genes on the sex chromosomes is a sex-linked trait. The human X chromosome carries many genes, but the human Y chromosome carries very few. One sex-linked gene determines baldness. The gene for normal hair growth is dominant over the gene for baldness.

Females are seldom bald. Each of their two X chromosomes has one gene that influences the trait for baldness. Usually, at least one of the two genes is for normal hair growth, so baldness among women is rare.

The male Y chromosome, on the other hand, has no gene that affects hair growth. If a male has inherited from his mother an X chromosome that has the recessive gene for baldness, he will have no dominant gene for normal hair growth. That is why far more males than females go bald. Women have *two* chances to receive the gene for normal hair growth; men have only one.

Now answer this question: What causes baldness? If you understood the relationship that was discussed in the first paragraph, you should be able to see that the cause of baldness is a sex-linked recessive gene on the female X chromosome.

Now try this question: Why do few women go bald? If you understood the information in the second paragraph, you could see that women usually have at least one dominant gene for normal growth that overrides the recessive gene for baldness, if it is even present. The word *so* in the last sentence of the paragraph is a clue to that cause-and-effect relationship.

Finally, why do more men than women go bald? The answer can be found in the last two sentences, beginning with "That is why. . . ." Women have two chances to receive the dominant gene, while men have only one.

On the Springboard

Item 3 refers to the following chart and information. Focus on understanding the causes and effects that are explained.

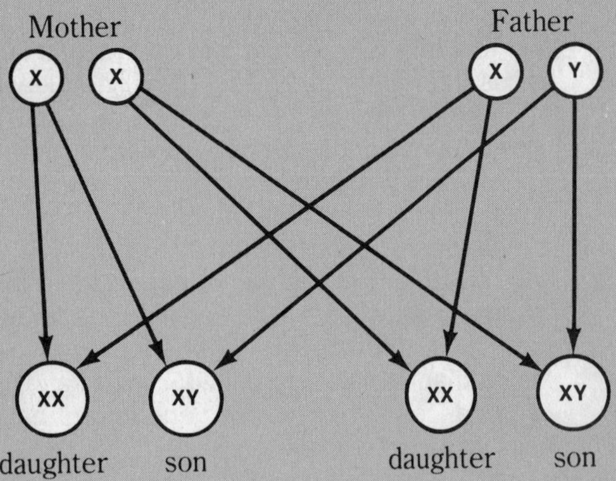

The chart above shows the possible combinations of X and Y chromosomes when two humans produce a child. Half of the male's sperm contain the X chromosome, and half contain the Y. Since sperm with X and Y chromosomes have nearly equal chances of fertilizing the female's egg, which is always X, there is nearly an equal chance that the offspring will be male or female.

3. Why are the chances of two humans having a son nearly the same as they are for having a daughter?

(1) because the male has both X and Y chromosomes
(2) because the different sperm have equal chances of fertilizing the egg
(3) because the female's X chromosomes will split apart

You can check the last On the Springboard answer on page 103.

Are you now clear on seeing relationships in scientific material in general and seeing cause-and-effect relationships in particular? If so, go on to the GED-level "Real Thing" to concentrate on the relationships found in that passage. If not, review these last two skills sections and then practice seeing the relationships discussed in the first part of the lesson.

“The Real Thing”

Items 1–3 refer to the following graph and information.

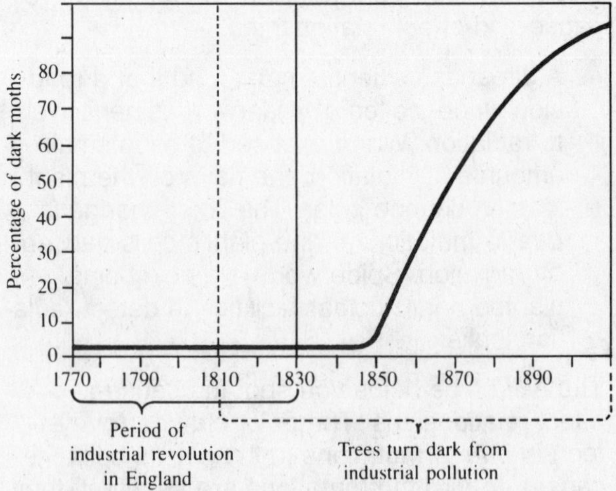

The peppered moth is commonly found in wooded areas of England. Before 1848, most of the peppered moths were light gray with dark markings on their wings. Black peppered moths were rare. As England built more factories, soot began to blacken trees, leaves, and rocks. The light-colored moths were easy to see against these darker backgrounds and became easy prey for hungry birds.

Because the dark-colored moths now had better camouflage, more survived and produced offspring like themselves. By 1898 about 98 percent of the peppered moths in some parts of England were black. The rapid shift toward darker coloration in the peppered moth is an example of industrial melanism. In unpolluted areas the moths are mostly light; in polluted areas they are dark.

1. How did the growth of industry affect the environment in industrial areas of England?

   (1) Soot blackened tree trunks and rocks.
   (2) Heat from factories killed many moths.
   (3) Soot in the air blackened moths' wings.
   (4) Poisons in factory smoke killed many moths.
   (5) Pollution caused light-colored moths to migrate.

2. Why did the dark-colored moths begin to increase in population?

   (1) The pollution killed off their natural predators.
   (2) There was better vegetation for them to feed on.
   (3) They began to feed on the light-colored moths.
   (4) They were healthier than the light-colored moths.
   (5) Fewer of them were eaten by birds.

① ② ③ ④ ⑤

3. Industrial melanism occurs when

   (1) a type of animal becomes too abundant
   (2) a changed environment favors one color
   (3) a change occurs in an animal's genetic material
   (4) pollution changes the color of animals
   (5) an animal changes its eating habits

① ② ③ ④ ⑤

Check your answers and record your score on page 105.

LESSON 6

The Variety of Life

Individual cells make up an amazing variety of living things. In the following section, you'll learn how scientists arrange living things into orderly groups. Before you begin, read the Warm-up question at the end of the section. It will help you focus on the main ideas as you read.

Classifying Living Things

Suppose a man writes a letter to a relative overseas. When addressing the envelope, however, he draws only a sketch of his relative and writes a description. He includes no name, no address, no street, city, or country. His letter would have little chance of reaching his relative. If everyone addressed letters in that way, the postal service could never deliver mail.

For centuries, scientists faced a similar jumble when they tried to classify living things. Often the best that early scientists could do was draw a picture of an organism and describe the way it looked or behaved. Then in the 1730s, a Swedish scientist named Carolus Linnaeus developed a logical system of classifying that people still use today.

Linnaeus looked at the way organisms were built. He then used similarities in their structures as the basis for classifying organisms. His first step was to classify broadly similar organisms into one of two huge groups called **kingdoms.** These were the plant and the animal kingdoms.

The next step was to find strong enough similarities among members of a kingdom to create somewhat smaller groups, called phyla (the singular is phylum). Members of a phylum were then divided into smaller groups called classes. Classes were divided into orders, and orders were broken down into families. Family members with strong likenesses formed genera (singular: genus). Within each genus several different **species** could be identified. Linnaeus identified the species as the basic, fundamental group. Members of a species can reproduce; that is, they can become parents of offspring like themselves. Members of different species cannot produce offspring that can themselves reproduce.

This system of classifying life is something like the process of sorting overseas mail when it is correctly addressed. First the mail is grouped into the largest possible category—the country it is going to. Then letters going to the same city are grouped together. Within that city, letters are grouped by street, and finally by address. Through this system, a single letter out of a group of thousands reaches the right person.

Over time, scientists have improved and expanded Linnaeus's system. For example, they have added three more kingdoms to account for "in-between" life forms visible under the microscope. But the idea of the species still plays a basic role in scientific study and research. And the idea of creating smaller and still smaller groupings has produced a clear, understandable order. About one-fourth of the earth's five million different kinds of living things have now been classified.

Coming to Terms

kingdom the largest group of living things

species the smallest, most basic group of similar organisms

Warm-up

Linnaeus spent five months studying living things in the wilds of northern Sweden and Norway. When he found a living thing he had not seen before, how would he classify it in his system? Write your answer in two or three sentences.

___

___

___

___

Sample Warm-up Answer
First he would look at the structure of the organism and place it in the proper kingdom. Then he would place the organism into smaller and smaller groups based on how similar it was to others.

In the next section, you will read about one-celled organisms that make up one of the five kingdoms of life. Read the Warm-up questions at the end of this section before you start. As you read, look for answers to those questions.

Monerans

Under the microscope are swarming organisms that do not fall neatly into the plant or animal kingdom. Monerans are one such group. Monerans are single-celled organisms that are more often called **bacteria** (singular: bacterium). Many scientists place them in a kingdom of their own.

Monerans differ from other organisms in several important ways. First, a bacterium cell lacks a clearly defined nucleus. Such a cell is called prokaryotic. It also lacks mitochondria, which produce energy, and other internal structures. A sticky layer surrounds a bacterium cell. It keeps the cell attached to a food supply. Besides a cell membrane, a bacterium has a cell wall.

Shapes of Bacteria

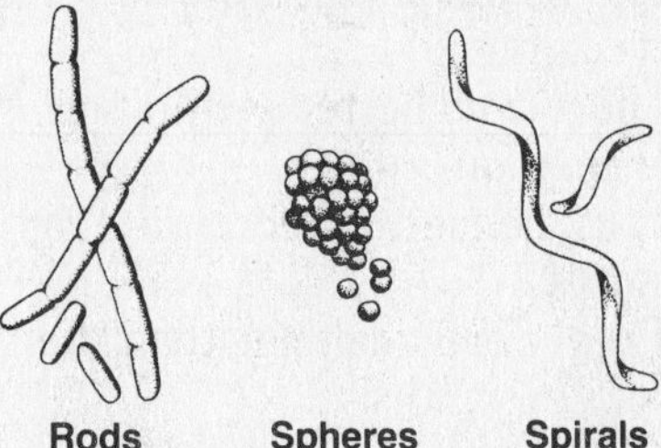

Monerans, or bacteria, show a great variety of forms and types. They can be shaped as rods, spheres, or spirals. Some bacteria can move on their own, like animals. They use flagella, which are whiplike tails or hairs, to propel themselves.

Some bacteria, like plants, are "producers." They use the energy of the sun to make food. Most, however, are "consumers." They get their food from outside living and dead things. Without bacteria, the world would be blanketed in a thick layer of dead bodies. Bacteria use dead organisms as food by decomposing them, or breaking them down into reusable products. Bacteria are the most abundant organisms on earth.

Bacteria serve other useful purposes as well. They keep soil supplied with nitrates, which green plants must have. Bacteria are essential in making cheese, pickles, and sauerkraut. They also improve the flavor of coffee, vanilla, and cocoa. They are used in some vitamins and certain industrial chemicals as well.

Some bacteria are harmful. You probably already know that they can cause certain common infections. Diphtheria, tuberculosis, cholera, tetanus, botulism, typhoid, scarlet fever, and bubonic plague are some of the other diseases caused by bacteria. The last one, called the Black Death, wiped out about a fourth of the population of Europe in the fourteenth century.

Viruses are other organisms that cause disease. Unlike bacteria, viruses are *not* distinct cells. They contain only genetic material and perhaps some protein. They cannot reproduce outside a living organism. For this reason, some scientists classify them among the nonliving things of the world. Others place them somewhere between nonliving things and members of the monerans kingdom.

Coming to Terms

bacteria simple cells with no distinct nucleus or other structures. Such a cell is a prokaryotic cell.

virus an organism that can reproduce only in the living cells of another organism

Warm-up

Write complete sentences to answer these questions.

1. How are monerans different from other organisms?

____

____

2. How do bacteria improve as well as harm life?

____

____

Sample Warm-up Answers
1. Monerans lack a distinct nucleus and other cell structures, including ones that produce energy. **2.** They improve life by clearing away waste materials and by helping make cheese and other good foods. They harm life by causing disease.

Monerans are the simplest form of life. Next, you will read about somewhat more complex organisms. Pay special attention to the differences between these organisms and monerans. Previewing the Warm-up questions at the end will help guide your reading.

Protists

If you want to look deep into the past, pick up a piece of chalk. It is made in part from the hard shells of certain protists that lived in the sea millions of years ago.

You do not need to look into the past to see protists, however. Go to any still pond. The scum that builds up on top is made up of great numbers of protists.

Like monerans, protists are single-celled organisms. Unlike monerans, however, protists are cells with definite nuclei and other defined parts, including mitochondria. Cells with these structures are called eukaryotic.

The way protists are classified depends on the way they move around. One main type of protist moves through the use of pseudopedia—"false feet." The ameba is an example of this type. A jellylike substance inside the cell membrane is always flowing. It presses on the membrane, forcing out footlike extensions. These move the cell over a leaf or the slimy bottom of a pond. New "false feet" form all the time while old ones return into the jellylike blob.

The ameba is one of the simpler kinds of protists. One of its special structures acts like a pump to squeeze out excess water in the cell. Without such a pump, the ameba would take in so much water that it would burst its membrane.

Ameba

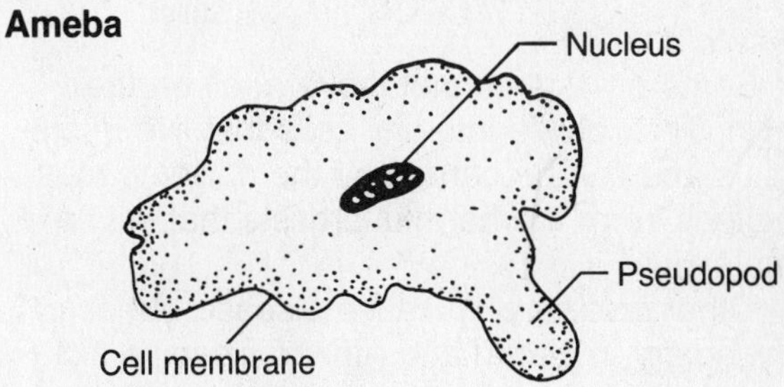

A second main type of protist moves by the action of flagella. One or more whirling tails propel these protists through water.

Euglenas are this kind of protist. They are more complex than amebas. A thick cell membrane surrounds them and gives them a definite shape. They also have plantlike structures that can convert sunlight into chemical energy. An eye spot, sensitive to light, helps this tiny organism move toward sunlight.

Euglena

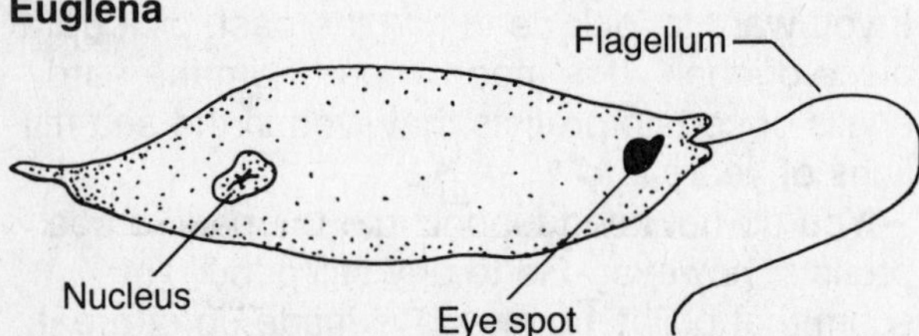

A third type of protist depends on hairlike structures called cilia for movement. Like tiny oars, cilia beat the water to move the cell forward or back.

Paramecia are slipper-shaped protists that move with cilia. They are among the most complex of the protists. One of their special features is an oral groove lined with beating cilia. The cilia brush food particles through the oral groove into a mouth pore. From there the food particles move to the gullet. Notice the other special features of a paramecium.

Paramecium

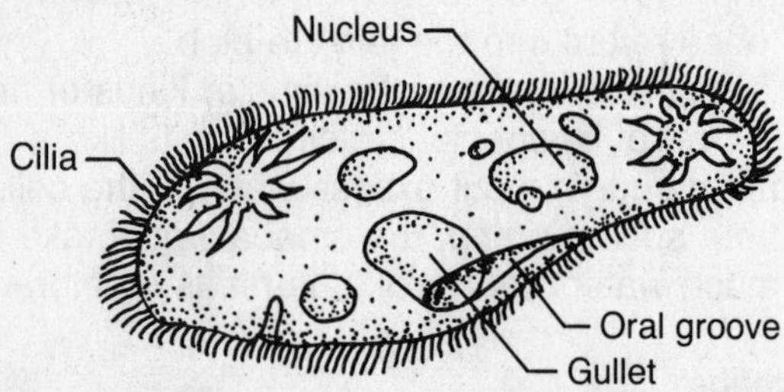

Some protists cannot move at all on their own. They divide into tiny cells that live in animals and can be carried by them. Some mosquitoes carry the harmful protists that cause malaria.

Other protists also cause disease. Amebic dysentery, malaria, and African sleeping sickness—carried by the tsetse fly—range from serious to deadly. On the other hand, some protists are valuable. Protist skeletons are the raw materials for limestone and flint as well as chalk. Some protists live in the intestines of cattle, where they help rather than hurt the animals by aiding digestion.

Warm-up

Answer each question in a sentence or two.

1. In what way are protists like monerans?

____

____

2. How are protists different from monerans?

____

____

In the section that follows, you'll learn about the third kingdom of life—the fungi. To help focus your thoughts on the main idea, read the Warm-up question at the end of the section first. Keep it in mind as you read.

Fungi

If you've ever had athlete's foot, you know from experience how hardy a fungus can be. Farmers know the same thing, for other forms of fungi plague crops and other plants. Yet these same kinds of organisms produce some of the tastiest foods and drinks—blue cheese, yeasty breads, mushrooms, wine, and beer.

A fungus can be made up of one cell or many cells. Fungi cannot move on their own like animals. Nor can they produce their own food as green plants do. Fungi feed on dead organisms or on other living organisms. In the process, they first release substances called enzymes into their food supply. The enzymes digest the food outside the fungi. The fungi then absorb the nutrients through stringlike tubes.

Fungi reproduce by forming **spores.** These cells float through the air and water. If they land in a suitable place to live—a damp piece of bread, for example—they grow and produce more spores.

Like many bacteria, most fungi are decomposers. Some feed on the dead leaves on the forest floor. In the process they bring about decay, which returns useful nutrients to the ground.

Other fungi are **parasites,** living entirely off another plant or animal called a **host.** In most cases the host is seriously harmed by the fungus.

Sample Warm-up Answers

1. Both protists and monerans are organisms that have only one cell. **2.** Protists have definite nuclei and other special cell parts. Monerans do not have such features.

Unlike monerans and protists, many fungi are household names. Molds are especially familiar to anyone who has left bread in the refrigerator too long or noticed a bluish fuzz on the skin of an orange. Penicillin, made by the same type of mold that grows on the orange, is a widely used germ killer.

Yeasts are common one-celled fungi. A favorite food for yeasts is sugar. As the fungi break down the sugar for use, carbon dioxide and alcohol are formed. In bread making, the carbon dioxide cannot escape from the gooey dough. Bubbles of the trapped carbon dioxide gas make the dough rise. Baking removes the alcohol. In wine making, of course, alcohol is the desired product. Yeast turns the sugar in grape juice into alcohol.

Certainly the best known fungi are mushrooms. Even though they may look like the variety you order on a pizza or slice in a salad, many mushrooms are very poisonous. Close relatives of the mushroom are bracket fungi, which you might have seen growing in horizontal "shelves" on trees. Puffballs are other mushroom cousins.

Coming to Terms

spore a reproductive cell from a fungus

parasite an organism that needs the living tissue of a host cell to grow

host an organism from which another organism, a parasite, takes food or finds shelter and protection

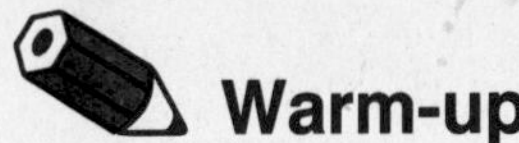

Warm-up

Fungi cannot move or make their own food. How do they get food? Explain your answer in complete sentences.

____

____

____

____

Classifying

Do you remember how the first section in this lesson talked about the ways scientists sort, or classify, living things into certain groups? Linnaeus and scientists since him have classified organisms based on similarities in their structures. Organisms could also be classified according to their behavior, the relationships between them, the places where they live, and other areas.

Classifying is not useful just in science. Just think of what shopping in a grocery store would be like if the items weren't classified and shelved according to what kind of food each is. Or imagine looking for a job in the want ads—the "classified" section of the newspaper—if similar jobs weren't grouped and alphabetized.

Classifying, therefore, is a useful skill in science and in everyday life. It's also an important skill to have for the GED Science Test.

☑ A Test-Taking Tip

A special item set appears on the GED Science Test. This item set first gives a set of categories that describe different kinds of animals, plants, relationships, behavior, or some other idea in science. Following these categories are specific examples of them. You'll be asked to classify each example. In other words, you'll need to decide which category the example belongs to. These items are not as challenging as they might appear. You may even find that they are actually fun—rather like a puzzle.

Sample Warm-up Answer
Fungi give off enzymes that digest the food outside the fungi. Then they absorb the digested food through tubes.

Here's an Example

Read these two descriptions of the causes of illness. Then go on to see how the specific example that follows can be classified using them.

■ virus = invades a living cell, where it can reproduce, eventually kill the cell, and spread to other cells. The body's own defenses eventually defeat most viruses.

bacteria = may damage cells by either reproducing in large numbers or producing poisonous substances. Some disease-causing bacteria can be killed by antibiotic drugs, which prevent the development of the protective cell walls in new bacteria.

Now read this specific situation.

■ The flu infects someone through the nose or mouth and then enters a lung or throat cell. Once inside, the flu takes over the cell and begins to multiply, in effect making the cell a "flu factory." The cell dies, and the flu spreads to other cells. After three days, the person recovers.

What causes the flu—a virus or bacteria?

If you match up the characteristics of the infection given in the example with the general characteristics of viral and bacterial infections, you can see that the flu is caused by a virus. It invades a living throat or lung cell, begins to multiply (reproduce), kills the cell, and then spreads. No antibiotic can be given to kill the virus; instead, the person recovers only after his or her body has taken three days to defeat the flu virus.

Try It Yourself

Read the descriptions of two types of fungi given below. The questions that follow will ask you to classify examples of fungi using the two categories.

■ parasite = a fungus that lives and feeds on living tissue

saprophyte = a fungus that feeds on dead or dying material

Now read this situation and determine what kind of fungus is involved.

■ A man finds a pair of old leather shoes in the back of his closet. They have a blue-green mold growing on them.

What kind of fungus is the mold—a parasite or a saprophyte?

To answer that question, first determine what distinguishes a parasite from a saprophyte. From the definitions given, the difference is that one feeds on living matter and the other feeds on dead or dying matter. Now look at what the fungus in the example is feeding on. Since it is growing on old leather, it is feeding on dead matter. Therefore, the blue-green mold must be a saprophyte. Is that what you said?

Try one more example.

■ A hiker walking through the woods notices some shelf fungus, a mushroom-type fungus, growing on the otherwise-healthy tree trunks.

What kind of fungus is the shelf fungus—a parasite or a saprophyte?

Since you know from the definition that a parasite feeds on living matter and that the trunks of the trees are living, you should have been able to classify shelf fungus as a parasite.

On the Springboard

Items 1–2 refer to the information below. You will be asked to classify some organisms.

Organisms can be classified according to the way in which they reproduce. Lower organisms, such as monerans, protists, and many fungi, reproduce asexually. That means that only one parent is involved in producing offspring. Here are three methods of asexual reproduction.

(1) **spore forming** = Tiny reproductive cells are formed by the parent organism. Some grow in a saclike cell and burst out when the cell pops open.
(2) **budding** = A bud grows out of the membrane, or wall, of the original cell. The bud swells, grows larger, and finally separates from the original cell.
(3) **cell dividing** = The parent cell grows to twice its original size. Then the DNA duplicates, and the cell splits into two new cells.

Each of the following items describes a process that refers to one of the three categories defined above. For each item, choose the one category that best describes the process. Each of the categories may be used more than once.

1. A biology student is studying cells under a microscope. She notices that some cells are twice as large as most of the others. Some of these large cells are splitting apart.

   The cells are reproducing by means of

   (1) spore forming
   (2) budding
   (3) cell dividing

2. A large brown puffball has popped open. On the ground beneath it lies a scattered, dustlike powder. The puffball is reproducing by means of

   (1) spore forming
   (2) budding
   (3) cell dividing

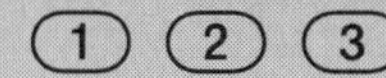

Check your answers to On the Springboard on page 103.

Were you able to place the two examples in the appropriate categories? If so, go on to "The Real Thing." If not, review this section on classifying before going on.

66 The Real Thing 99

Items 1–3 refer to the following information.

The five categories that follow describe different types of protists. The types are classified according to the different ways in which they can obtain food.

(1) **producers** = Some protists have dark green structures like those of plants and are able to use sunlight to produce their own food.
(2) **flagellates** = These protists move about to find food by the motions of whiplike tails called flagella.
(3) **ciliates** = These protists move about to find food by the action of many short hairlike cilia, which stick out through the cell membrane.
(4) **sarcodines** = Some protists have bodies so flexible that they can form small temporary feet, which they use to push forward and back as they move around to find food.
(5) **sporozoans** = These protists must obtain food from outside sources. However, they carry no visible means of movement.

Each of the following items describes an organism that belongs to one of the five categories defined above. For each item, choose the one category that best describes the organism. Each of the categories may be used more than once.

1. The organism that causes malaria is injected into a person's bloodstream by a mosquito. It floats in the blood and cannot direct its own movement.

   Such malaria-causing organisms would be classified as

   (1) producers (2) flagellates
   (3) ciliates (4) sarcodines
   (5) sporozoans

   1 2 3 4 5

2. Tiny projections cover the surface of the paramecium and allow it to move around and direct food into its "mouth."

   The paramecium falls into the classification of

   (1) producers (2) flagellates
   (3) ciliates (4) sarcodines
   (5) sporozoans

   1 2 3 4 5

3. An ameba can move its body to form small extensions. When an ameba finds a tiny alga or other piece of food, it extends its membrane to surround the alga on all sides.

   Amebas would be classified as

   (1) producers (2) flagellates
   (3) ciliates (4) sarcodines
   (5) sporozoans

   1 2 3 4 5

Check your answers and record your score on page 106.

LESSON 7

Plants

In the last lesson you read about three kingdoms of living organisms. The organisms you are probably most familiar with fall into the last two kingdoms: plants and animals. In this lesson you will learn about some of the special features of plants. Before you read the first section, look ahead to the Warm-up activity. It can help you pick out important information as you go along.

Plant Cells

You probably already have some idea of the great variety among plants. Plants come in many different sizes and shapes. On the one hand, some are so small that they can be seen only under a microscope. On the other, the giant redwood trees of California are so huge that people can carve spaces large enough for a car to pass through the bases of their trunks. Despite their many differences, plants have the same basic unit of life as all organisms—the cell. But as in other organisms, not all plant cells are alike.

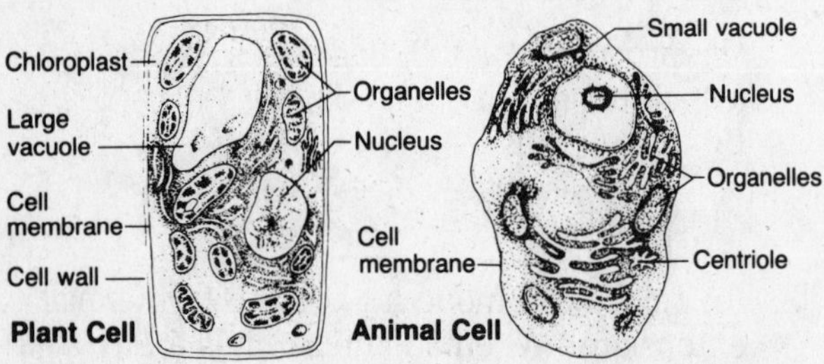

Plant Cell **Animal Cell**

The diagram helps you compare the similarities and differences between a typical animal cell and a typical plant cell. Most cells in all organisms contain droplets that hold water and other substances. These droplets are called vacuoles. Most plant cells have very large vacuoles. But animal cells usually have only a few small vacuoles.

You learned in earlier lessons that a thin membrane surrounds every living cell. In plants, a stiff, hardened **cell wall** surrounds the membrane. The cell wall is what makes the plant rigid, or stiff and firm. The stems of flowers you pick or stalks of celery you eat, for example, are often quite rigid and crisp. In a living plant cell, the cell membrane and the cell wall are pressed close together. It is usually difficult to tell one from another under a microscope.

Did you notice the chloroplasts in the diagram of the plant cell? Not all plant cells have chloroplasts. Only green ones do. Chloroplasts contain a substance called **chlorophyll.** Chlorophyll is what gives plants their green color and makes it possible for them to manufacture their own food. In the next section, you'll see how they do this.

Coming to Terms

cell wall a thin, hardened layer that surrounds the membrane of a plant cell

chlorophyll a substance contained in the cells of plants that gives them their green color and makes it possible for them to manufacture their own food

Warm-up

In a sentence of your own, explain why the trunk of a tree is rigid.

____

____

Now you'll read about the work that plants do that enables you and other animals to live. Before you read this section, preview the Warm-up activity. Watch for the information you will need to answer the question.

Photosynthesis

You see food-producing shops and factories all around you, in every part of the country. There are bakeries, dairies, and canning factories. Many large companies provide a great variety of foods for stores and their customers. But all the

Sample Warm-up Answer
The trunk of a tree is rigid because hardened cell walls surround the membranes of its many cells.

factories, shops, and companies put together cannot equal the food-producing work that green plants do. Green plants are the world's basic and most important food-producing factories.

Plants make their own food through a process called **photosynthesis.** *Photo* comes from a Greek word meaning "light." *Synthesis* means "to put together." *Photosynthesis,* then, means "to put together by light." The green parts of plants, usually the leaves, carry on photosynthesis.

For photosynthesis to take place, a green leaf must have energy. It gets that energy from light, usually sunlight. Most of a leaf's chlorophyll, which you learned earlier makes photosynthesis possible, is in its upper surface. So a leaf usually turns its upper surface toward the sun.

The lower surface of a leaf has tiny openings called stomata. During photosynthesis, carbon dioxide from the air enters the leaf through its stomata. At the same time, the plant's roots take in water from the soil. The water travels up the stem and into the leaf. The leaf then has all the things it needs to manufacture food: chlorophyll, light energy, carbon dioxide, and water.

Light energy allows molecules of carbon dioxide to combine with molecules of water. This change produces one new molecule of a simple sugar called glucose and six new molecules of oxygen.

The plant makes use of the glucose it manufactures in several ways. It uses some of the glucose immediately for food. It turns some of the glucose into starch and fat, which are stored as reserve foods. It changes still more of the glucose into the cellulose that stiffens its cell walls. And some of the glucose turns into sucrose, another kind of sugar—the kind you usually use in your kitchen. The plant sugars, cellulose, and starch are all **carbohydrates.** Some of the carbohydrates combine with other substances to form proteins that the plant needs.

The plant releases some of the oxygen it produces during photosynthesis through the stomata in its leaves. This oxygen adds to the supply needed by humans and other animals all over the earth.

Coming to Terms

photosynthesis the process by which a green plant produces its own food using chlorophyll along with light energy, carbon dioxide, and water

carbohydrates the sugars, cellulose, and starch produced in plants. Carbohydrates contain carbon, hydrogen, and oxygen.

Warm-up

What would happen to the process of photosynthesis if you covered both the upper and lower surfaces of a green leaf with cardboard? Explain your answer in a sentence or two.

___

___

___

In the next section, you'll learn how the full-grown plants of some species produce new generations of plants like themselves. Check the Warm-up activity before you begin. Keep it in mind as you read the section.

Reproduction of Flowering Plants

One of the most beautiful sights in nature is a fully developed flower with its special shape, color, and fragrance. There are more than 250,000 different kinds of flowers among the

Sample Warm-up Answer
Photosynthesis would stop because the leaf would not be able to get the light it needed. It also might not be able to take in carbon dioxide through its stomata.

earth's many plant species. Not all kinds of plants produce flowers, of course. But those that do would not survive as a species without their flowers. For flowers contain the reproductive organs of the plant.

To understand a flower's role in plant reproduction, you need to be familiar with its parts. Take a moment to study the diagram of a flower. Notice the pistil and its three different parts. The pistil is the female reproductive organ. Now look at the stamen and its two parts. The stamen is the flower's male reproductive organ.

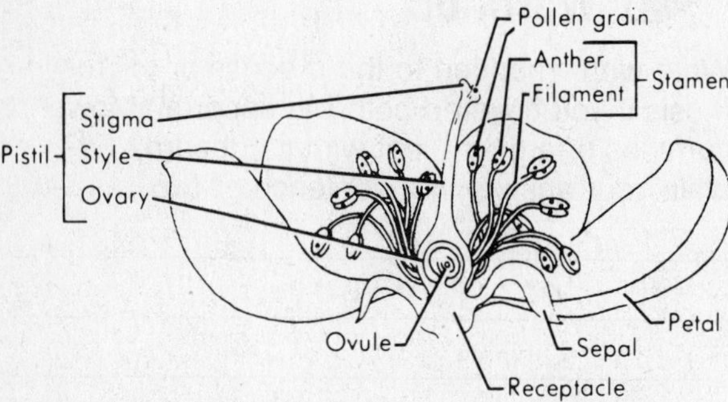

The process of reproduction begins when a seed is planted in the ground and ends when the adult plant produces a new seed. The ovary of a flower contains ovules, which are the parts that develop into new seeds. But first the ovules must be fertilized by pollen from the anther. Bees, butterflies, and other insects often help fertilization take place. As they move about on a flower, their legs and wings may carry tiny grains of pollen from an anther to the stigma of the pistil. This transfer is called **pollination.** Once placed on the stigma, the grain of pollen begins to grow a long tube that reaches down the style and into the ovary. There a male cell joins with a female cell. Fertilization is complete. A new seed forms and begins to grow.

While the new seed is growing, other parts of the flower change into food surrounding the seed. The growing seed and the food that surrounds it become the fruit of the plant. People eat some fruit, such as tomatoes, peaches, and pears. Birds and insects eat many more kinds of fruit. Some of the seeds, of course, fall into the soil to grow new plants.

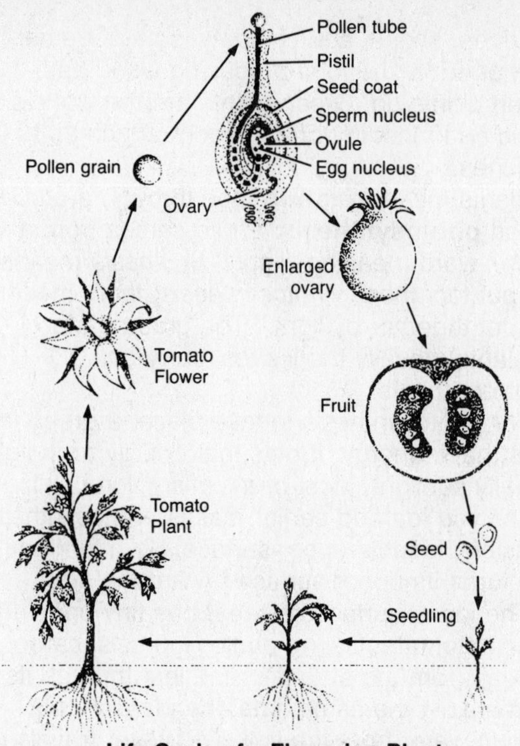

Life Cycle of a Flowering Plant

Coming to Terms

pollination the movement of pollen from a flower's stamen to its pistil. Insects, wind, and rain help transfer the pollen grains.

Warm-up

Look at the diagram showing the life cycle of the tomato plant. Then describe how a new tomato plant can be grown after the ovule is fertilized. Write your answer in two or three sentences.

____

____

____

____

Sample Warm-up Answer
The ovary grows larger and becomes fruit. The fruit contains seeds. When a seed is planted, a seedling begins to grow and finally becomes a full-grown tomato plant.

Recognizing Conclusions

"Warning: the Surgeon General has determined that use of this product could be hazardous to your health." You have probably seen warnings like this on certain products. It means that after careful study, public health officials have drawn the **conclusion** that the product could have dangerous side effects.

Drawing a conclusion means reaching a decision after considering all the appropriate factors. To arrive at the answer to a question or problem in science, scientists consider all the evidence they can collect. The evidence comes from their own observations, from different kinds of experiments, and from data gathered by other scientists. After examining all the evidence, a scientist draws a conclusion based on that evidence.

You will find that many of the materials you read in science deal with evidence and conclusions. An author may list a number of facts as evidence and give one or more conclusions that the facts support. Just as supporting details reinforce the main idea of a passage, factual evidence supports a scientific conclusion. Authors of scientific materials sometimes alert you to a conclusion by using such terms as "from conclusive evidence," "therefore," "concluded that," "determined that," or "established that."

Coming to Terms

conclusion an explanatory statement reached after weighing all the supporting statements, or evidence

Here's an Example

A laboratory assistant kept the following record of scientific observations he made. The last paragraph states his conclusion.

■ On Monday, I began to observe a pothos plant that had two dark green, waxy leaves. I watered it and placed it on a window sill.

By Wednesday, I noticed that both leaves faced southwest, directly toward the sun. I turned the plant so the leaves faced away from the sun.

By the following Monday, a new leaf was unfolding. All three leaves now faced the sun. The new leaf had opened toward the sun; the old leaves had grown so that they, too, faced the sun.

Over the next two weeks, I repeated the process of turning the plant away from the sun, only to find that later the leaves were again facing the sun.

I have concluded that plant leaves will gradually grow in the direction of the sun in order to get the greatest amount of light.

After a process of experimenting and observing, the laboratory assistant drew a conclusion. The last sentence states the conclusion. The three paragraphs that precede it make up the evidence supporting the conclusion.

Try It Yourself

In the following passage, where does the author state a conclusion about the age of some bristle-cone pine trees? On what evidence is the conclusion based?

■ The age of trees can easily be calculated if they grow in an environment where there are distinct seasons. In summer, when there is plenty of sunshine and moisture, they grow quickly and produce large wood cells; in winter when growth is slow, the wood is much more dense. This produces annual rings in the trunk. Counting those in the bristle-cone pine establishes that some of these gnarled and twisted trees germinated over five thousand years ago at a time when man in the Middle East was just beginning to invent writing, and have remained alive throughout the entire duration of civilisation.

If you look at the last sentence, you'll find that it contains the phrase "establishes that." This is a clue that the author is about to state a conclusion. And the conclusion is that some bristlecone pine trees are over five thousand years old. On what evidence is this conclusion based? The first part of the same sentence tells you. Scientists count the rings in the trees' trunks to see how many winters they have survived.

On the Springboard

Items 1–3 refer to the following paragraph. You will be asked to identify conclusions and supporting statements about a plant called chlorella.

Faced with an ever-increasing world population, many scientists in the second half of this century agree that we need to improve our methods of food production to avoid a future of worldwide hunger. In the 1970s, groups of researchers in Japan tried to find out whether it would be practical to cultivate a species of algae, called chlorella, as a food crop. For a number of years, several universities participated in research to determine whether these plants, which are grown in fresh water, would be easy to grow and would provide nutritious food. Eventually, the researchers concluded that it is possible to grow chlorella in large quantities and that it has value as food. However, chlorella also proved to be unpopular with Japanese consumers. As long as other food products are readily available, it is unlikely that chlorella will be able to compete with the familiar products now on store shelves.

1. Research done during the 1970s led scientists to the conclusion that chlorella
   (1) can grow in both fresh water and salt water
   (2) could be grown and used as food
   (3) is too low in nutrition to be useful

   (1) (2) (3)

2. Which of the following is a conclusion reached by the author of the passage?
   (1) Consumers will not eat chlorella if given a choice.
   (2) We must avoid a future of worldwide hunger.
   (3) Several universities cooperated in researching the plant chlorella.

   (1) (2) (3)

3. Which of the following statements did the author use to support her conclusion?
   (1) Chlorella is easy to grow in large quantities.
   (2) Chlorella has good nutritional food value.
   (3) Japanese consumers did not seem to like chlorella.

You can check your answers to On the Springboard on page 104.

Did you recognize the stated conclusions in the Springboard items correctly? Did you pick the right supporting statement? If your answers were correct, do "The Real Thing." If you need a little review, reread "Recognizing Conclusions" before moving on.

❝ The Real Thing ❞

Items 1–4 refer to the following passage.

Observant gardeners have long noticed that different flowers open and close their petals at different times of the day. So precise are these floral rhythms that the eighteenth-century naturalist Carolus Linnaeus used them to devise an ingenious circular clock garden. He planted each of 12 wedge-shaped areas with flower varieties that blossomed at different predictable hours, from 6 A.M. to 6 P.M. Linnaeus could tell the time of day simply by looking out his window at the garden.

The opening of a flower's petals is an example of a biological rhythm—an activity that regularly repeats itself or fluctuates in time with a natural cycle of the environment. . . . In the quest to discover the source of this chronological canniness, a simple experiment performed by the French astronomer Jean Jacques d'Ortous de Mairan in 1729 suggested a startling mechanism. He placed a mimosa plant in his perpetually dark cellar and found that it continued to open and close its leaves on approximately the same schedule as before. Without receiving any obvious cues about whether the outside world was experiencing light or darkness, the plant seemed to "know" the time of day.

Though crude, de Mairan's experiment was remarkable; it suggested the existence of a living timekeeper somewhere within the plant. In hundreds of variations of this experiment, scientists have come to the same conclusion. Even rhythms that cycle just once a year can persist in the constant conditions of a laboratory.

1. Which of the following conclusions does the author draw from the work of Linnaeus and de Mairan?

    (1) Artificial light is best for plants.
    (2) Plants have inborn biological clocks.
    (3) Flowers open at sunrise and close at sunset.
    (4) Flowers stay open longest on sunny days.
    (5) Biological rhythms change with changes in the environment.

    (1) (2) (3) (4) (5)

2. Linnaeus could tell the time of day by looking at the different flowers in his garden because

    (1) shadows fell on different sections of the garden at different hours of the day
    (2) different varieties of his flowers bloomed at each hour of the day
    (3) different varieties of his flowers bloomed during each month of the summer
    (4) Linnaeus knew how to estimate time from the position of the sun
    (5) Linnaeus carefully placed a sundial in the center of his floral clock

    (1) (2) (3) (4) (5)

3. Which of the following is an example of biological rhythm?

    (1) Watering a plant weekly helps it grow.
    (2) A cut rosebud will still open its petals.
    (3) An afternoon thunderstorm often occurs in higher elevations.
    (4) In northern areas, deciduous trees lose their leaves every autumn.
    (5) When the spring is moist, a greater than usual number of mosquitoes will hatch throughout the summer.

    (1) (2) (3) (4) (5)

4. Which of the following statements agrees with information in the article?

    (1) Plants' biological clocks are disrupted under laboratory conditions.
    (2) Scientists doubted de Mairan's finding because his experiment was too simple.
    (3) Scientists have repeated de Mairan's experiments many times with the same results.
    (4) De Mairan never understood how important his experiments were.
    (5) De Mairan proved that plants need sunlight in order to open their petals.

    (1) (2) (3) (4) (5)

Check your answers on page 106.

Drawing Your Own Conclusions

When you read scientific information, you can often form your own conclusions. In fact, the GED Science Test may ask you to do just that. This information may be given in a reading passage, in a graph, chart, or other visual, or in a combination of the two.

Here's an Example

The picture below shows four plants, all the same type and age. All have been given the same amount of water and plant food. The only difference is in the amount of sunlight they have received. The number under each drawing indicates how many hours of sunlight the plant has received each day.

Amount of Sunlight Received

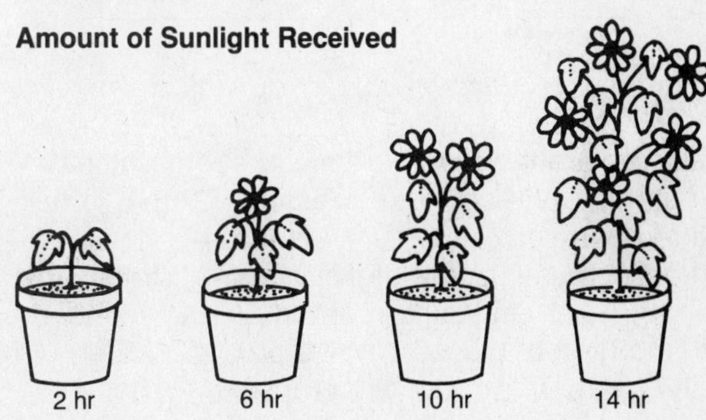

You can see how the amount of sunlight affects the growth of each plant. Notice that the plant that receives little light is shortest, has small leaves, and has no blossoms. As the amount of sunlight is increased, the numbers of leaves increase. Plants with six, ten, and fourteen hours of daily sunlight have blossoms too.

From this information, you can conclude that the amount of sunlight a plant receives daily affects its growth and production of blossoms.

Try It Yourself

Think about the items in the list below. Can you conclude what purpose they serve?

- spines on a cactus
  thorns on a rosebush
  bitter-tasting leaves
  skin-irritating liquid on poison oak
  blossoms that resemble a large wasp

What conclusion did you draw about this group of plant features? How is each useful? You are right if you concluded that some plants have developed characteristics that they can use to defend themselves against animals and insects that would feed on them. Each feature above would support that conclusion.

Now try drawing another conclusion. Study the following diagram and read the explanation that follows it.

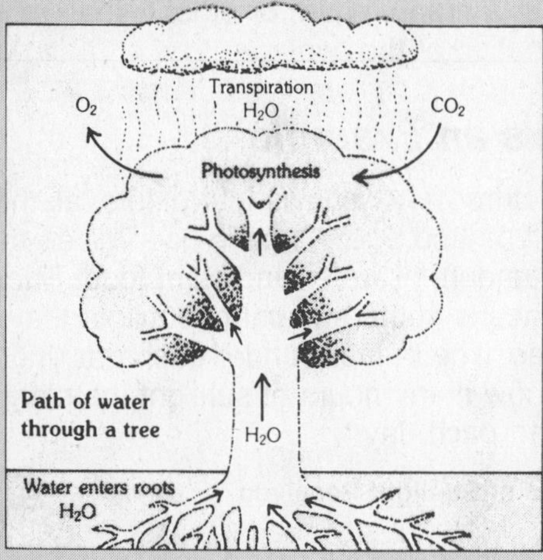

Leaves are the major organs of photosynthesis. In photosynthesis, molecules of chlorophyll capture energy from the sun. A series of chemical reactions uses some of this energy to transform water (H_2O) and carbon dioxide (CO_2) into food in the form of glucose. In the process, water and oxygen (O_2) are also produced.

Now answer this question: Based on the information and the diagram, what function do branches probably serve in a tree?

Think of how leaves produce food for the entire tree. Then picture how branches enable there to be more leaves on a tree. In addition, branches help join the roots and trunk with the leaves; in that way, they help transport the water from the roots that the leaves need to photosynthesize. Therefore, if you drew the conclusion that branches are needed to bring water to the many leaves they make possible, you were correct.

☑ A Test-Taking Tip

For GED Test items that ask you to draw your own conclusions, decide which of five options you are given most nearly agrees with the conclusion you've formed. You may find that the best way to decide on an answer is to use the process of elimination. Eliminate the three that seem most likely to be incorrect. You will then have just two options to consider, which makes selecting the final answer a little easier.

On the Springboard

Item 4 refers to the following information.

The seeds of a red maple tree are small and shaped in a way that enables them to catch and glide on the wind.

4. Southeast of three large red maples in a park are a number of red maple seedlings. Which of the following is the best conclusion about how they appeared there?

   (1) The wind has been blowing from the northwest.
   (2) The wind blew the seeds down beneath the trees, where they were collected and planted elsewhere.
   (3) The weather has been particularly calm.

Item 5 refers to the following passage.

Millions of years ago the earth was warmer than it is today. Dinosaurs cast huge shadows across the land, while smaller strange-looking creatures roamed through forests of giant ferns.

Most of the plants and animals that lived in those days are extinct now, but one type of tree still survives: the redwood tree. Redwoods grow naturally today in three places: California, a small section of Oregon, and one area of China.

Although living redwoods are not found elsewhere, geologists have found fossils of as many as twelve species of redwoods in different places around the globe. Redwood fossils have been found across Canada from the west coast to the east, in Greenland, on some Arctic islands, and from western Europe as far east as Japan.

5. From evidence in the passage, it can be concluded that redwood trees once

   (1) grew throughout much of the Northern Hemisphere
   (2) grew wherever the climate was warm
   (3) were more numerous than dinosaurs

You can check your Springboard answers on page 104.

Were you able to draw an accurate conclusion from the evidence given in each item? If so, go on now to "The Real Thing." If you had trouble with the Springboard items, reread Here's an Example and the Test-Taking Tip in this lesson first.

❝ The Real Thing ❞

Items 5–7 refer to the following passage.

Red clovers contain many small, tubelike flowers. Each flower's nectar is deep within the base of the tube. To feed on the nectar, an insect must be heavy enough to force open the flower. It must also have a long, tonguelike proboscis to reach the food. The bumblebee meets both of those requirements.

The location of the clover's pistil and stigma—parts of its female reproductive organ—is equally important. As the bumblebee moves into the clover, the pistil springs up against the bee's head. If the bee is carrying pollen, the pollen grains are brushed onto the stigma of the flower. As the bee plunges deeper into the flower, the stamens—the clover's male reproductive organs—shed their pollen onto the bee's head. These pollen grains are then carried to the next flower.

Other insects cannot pollinate red clover. In fact, when red clovers were introduced in Australia, they produced no seeds until bumblebees were brought in to pollinate them.

5. Which of the following conclusions is supported by evidence in the passage?

   (1) Red clovers have difficulty surviving due to their tubelike flowers.
   (2) The bumblebee's weight helps it collect more nectar than other insects.
   (3) Without red clovers, bumblebees would eventually become extinct.
   (4) The bumblebee's long, tonguelike proboscis often damages red clover flowers.
   (5) Bumblebees and red clovers are well suited to meet each other's needs.

6. As a bumblebee moves from clover to clover, it is most likely

   (1) cross-pollinating each clover with pollen from other clovers
   (2) taking away too much nectar from the flowers
   (3) damaging the flowers with its heavy body
   (4) shaking each flower's stamen onto its own stigma
   (5) preventing other insects from pollinating clover

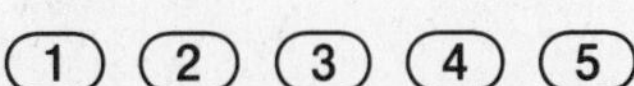

7. If pesticides eliminated all the bumblebees in a certain area, the red clovers in the area would most likely

   (1) stop producing nectar
   (2) begin to attract other insects
   (3) decrease in number
   (4) produce white flowers
   (5) grow larger

Item 8 refers to the diagram and information below.

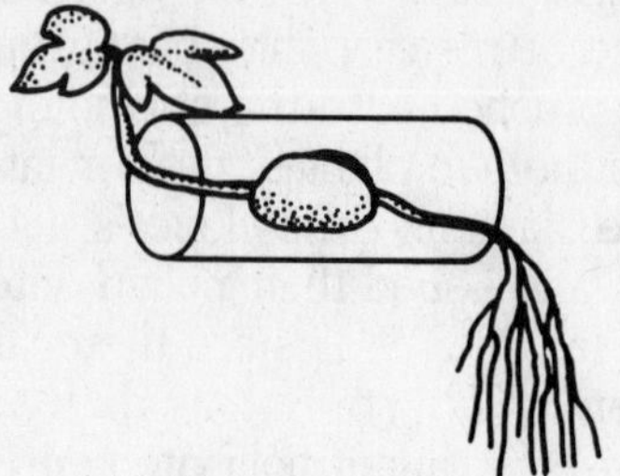

Plants respond to light, gravity, and sometimes even touch by growing toward or away from them. If a plant is suspended in air without light, its stem will still grow up, and its roots will always grow down.

8. From that information, one could draw the conclusion that

 (1) parts of a plant respond differently to gravity
 (2) the stem of a plant always seeks light
 (3) a plant's growth will be uneven and crooked if not planted properly
 (4) the roots of a plant become diseased and droop
 (5) the touch of a tube turns roots downward and stems up

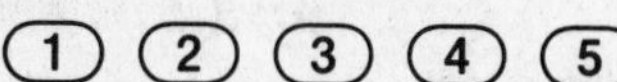

Check your answers and record your score for the entire lesson on page 106.

LESSON 8

Lower Animals

In this lesson you'll move from the plant kingdom to the fifth and final kingdom: the animals. You'll look at some of their outstanding traits and see how scientists group them. As you read the next section, keep in mind the special trait that all the animals mentioned have in common. But you may want to look at the Warm-up activity first. It can also help guide you to important information.

Invertebrates

Have you ever used a sponge to wash a car or do some household scrubbing? Did you know that you were using the skeleton of an animal? A sponge is an animal, usually found in the sea, whose skeleton is a rubberlike substance called spongin. Sponges are good examples of the many animals that are **invertebrates,** or ones with no backbone.

All animals are either invertebrates or **vertebrates,** ones that do have backbones. Scientists go on to classify vertebrates and invertebrates into smaller groups. But it is interesting to note that about 95 percent of all animals belong to the groups in the invertebrate category.

Invertebrates, which include animals such as sponges, sea anemones, jellyfish, and coral animals, have many cells. These invertebrates usually have tentacles covered with stinging cells. Stinging helps the animals protect themselves from larger animals and enables them to capture small organisms for food.

Worms belong to another group of invertebrates. Some flatworms are parasites and so get their food from other organisms. Earthworms, on the other hand, live in the soil and, from a human standpoint, improve it.

Some invertebrates, such as oysters, clams, and scallops, have soft bodies protected by hard shell coverings. You may already know that many of these shell-covered sea animals are good food sources for humans.

The group of animals known as arthropods, however, form the largest category of invertebrates. In fact, arthropods are the largest group in the entire animal kingdom. All arthropods have jointed legs. Some, like the crab and the lobster, live in water. Some land-dwelling arthropods look a little like worms. But they are not worms because they have jointed legs. The millipede and the centipede fall into this group. If you have ever watched one of these arthropods, you know how many legs these creatures have.

Insects make up by far the largest group of arthropods. An insect has three distinct body parts—the head, the thorax, and the abdomen. It also has six legs and usually two pairs of wings attached to its thorax.

Spiders, scorpions, and ticks fall into another group of arthropods. These animals have eight legs. Because the head and the thorax are fused together, each of these arthropods has only two distinct body parts.

Coming to Terms

invertebrate an animal with no backbone

vertebrate an animal with a backbone

Warm-up

This short exercise will help sharpen your classification skills as well as your ability to pick supporting statements for a conclusion. Use information from the section to complete it.

Write two or three sentences that support the following statement: A spider is an arthropod but not an insect.

____

____

____

Sample Warm-up Answer

Like all arthropods, a spider is an invertebrate with jointed legs. Unlike insects, though, spiders have eight legs and just two main body parts. Insects have six legs and three body parts.

The next section introduces you to the first group of vertebrates that you will read about. It would be a good idea to glance at the Warm-up questions before you read. They can focus your attention on important points of information.

Fish

You have probably eaten fish. You may also like to catch them or watch them in an aquarium. Fish come in many sizes, shapes, and colors.

All fish fall into two major groups according to their skeletons: those made of cartilage and those made of bone. The shark has a skeleton made up of cartilage. Cartilage is softer than bone; it can be both stiff and flexible. The tiny guppy and the large tuna have skeletons made up mostly of bones.

Nearly all kinds of fish breathe through gills, which are located on the sides of their heads. A flap covers each gill. When a fish breathes, it first takes in water through its mouth. The water runs across its gills, where blood flows close to the body surface. The blood of the gills removes oxygen from the water. The gills also release carbon dioxide from the blood of the fish into the water around it.

Fish are **cold-blooded animals.** The body temperatures of cold-blooded animals are about the same as the substances that surround them. The body temperature of a fish tends to equal the temperature of the water surrounding it.

Coming to Terms

cold-blooded animal an animal with a body temperature about equal to the air, water, ground, or other substance that surrounds it

Warm-up

Write a sentence or two to answer each question below.

1. How is the skeleton of a guppy different from a shark's skeleton?

2. How do fish get the oxygen they need to live?

Many people do not think snakes, frogs, and some other animals are very handsome or appealing. But snakes help control the populations of rats, mice, and insects by eating them. And frog legs are a food delicacy for many people. Before you read this section about frogs, snakes, and other such animals, look ahead to the Warm-up activity. Keep it in mind as you read.

Amphibians and Reptiles

You may have heard of amphibious vehicles—one that can travel on both land and water. In the animal world, **amphibians** are vertebrate animals that spend part of their lives in water and part on land. There are two main groups of amphibians. Animals in one group, which includes salamanders, newts, and mud puppies, have tails. Animals in the other group, which takes in frogs and toads, have no tails.

Amphibians are cold-blooded all their lives. But while they are young, most amphibians live entirely in lakes, ponds, or streams. Like fish, young amphibians use gills to breathe. As they grow up, most amphibians develop lungs and go to live at least part of the time on land.

Amphibians must return to the water to reproduce. Adult females lay eggs, and adult males fertilize them in the water. The eggs would dry out if they were not in water. Have you ever seen tadpoles—young frogs—in ponds or ditches in the springtime? Use the diagram below to see where the tadpole fits in the life cycle of the frog.

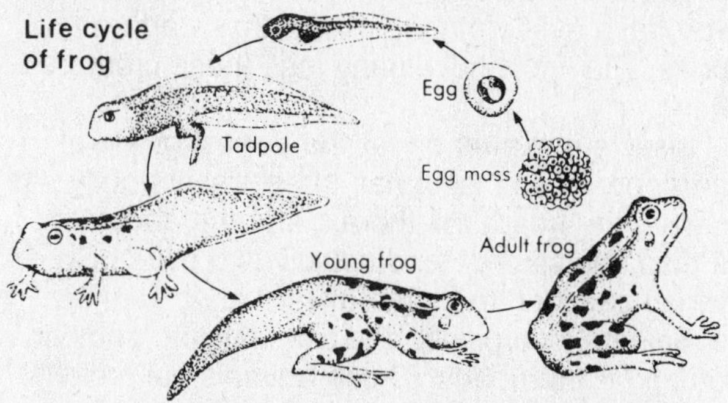

Turtles, lizards, snakes, and a group that includes both crocodiles and alligators are all in the **reptile** class. While some reptiles may spend a great deal of time in the water, they do not depend on water the way amphibians do. Some snakes, turtles, and lizards may spend their entire lives on land. Reptiles do not have to lay their eggs in water to reproduce, and they have lungs for breathing air throughout their life cycles.

The skin of reptiles is dry and covered with scales. Because of this, their bodies do not dry out as fast as fish or amphibians. But because they are cold-blooded, they must move often to control their body temperatures. If a reptile gets too warm in the sun, it will move to a cooler spot in the shade.

Coming to Terms

amphibian a cold-blooded vertebrate that lives part of its life in water and part of its life on land

reptile a cold-blooded vertebrate that uses lungs to breathe throughout its whole life

Sample Warm-up Answers
1. A guppy's skeleton is made of bones, but a shark's is made of cartilage. **2.** A fish takes in water through its mouth. The water flows across the gills, where blood removes oxygen from the water.

Warm-up

Answer the questions that follow with sentences of your own.

1. Why is water important to amphibians?

____

____

2. Why might a snake crawl onto a rock in the sun on an early spring day?

____

____

Distinguishing Facts from Opinions

A **fact** is a statement that can be proved true by means of experimenting, observing, or referring to a reliable authority. An **opinion** is a statement of belief or personal preference. Although some opinions are so commonly held that nearly everyone agrees with them, they cannot be called facts. There is no way to test and prove them.

Most scientific reading is a mixture of facts and opinions. Opinions, as long as they are based on facts, help people interpret the information that comes from scientific research. Sometimes, however, people mistake an opinion for a fact. The key to recognizing an opinion is that you can agree or disagree with it, but you cannot prove it.

Coming to Terms

fact a statement that can be proved with evidence

opinion a statement of belief or preference that cannot be proved

Sample Warm-up Answers
1. Amphibians must lay their eggs in water to keep them from drying out. Young amphibians must live in water. **2.** The snake would be trying to raise its body temperature on a cool day. The rock would be a good, warm place for it to do so.

Here's an Example

The paragraph below is a mixture of facts and opinions. The opinions are *italicized* so you can find them easily. As you read, think about how each of the facts could be tested and proved.

■ *Sponges are among the most fascinating animals you will ever study.* Many people are surprised to discover that sponges are animals because they have a number of plantlike qualities. The adult sponge attaches itself to a rock or other object on the ocean floor. Because it does not move from place to place, it looks like a plant that has rooted there. Most animals have wings, legs, or a head. Sponges, however, do not. Finally, like flowers, *sponges often have rich, beautifully bright colors.*

The first statement in the paragraph is an opinion. The second is a fact. You could test it by asking a number of people whether they think a sponge is a plant or animal. If many of them are surprised to learn that a sponge is an animal, you could see that the statement is proved true. The remaining statements of fact in the paragraph could be tested by observing live sponges or by examining photographs of them.

The first and last statements in the passage cannot be tested because they involve personal opinions. What is fascinating or beautiful to one person is not necessarily so to other people.

Try It Yourself

Can you find the opinions expressed in the paragraph below?

■ Some flatworms are parasites. The tapeworm is one example. It is a particularly disgusting invertebrate that lives in the intestines of larger animals. The tapeworm derives its nourishment from the animal in which it lives. It can grow to as long as nine meters in humans. Nothing about the tapeworm is appealing.

You are correct if you identified part of the third sentence and the final sentence as opinions. They cannot be tested. Now look back at the other statements in the passage. They are all facts. How could each be tested? All of them could be tested by observing tapeworms or referring to a reliable authority such as an encyclopedia.

On the Springboard

Item 1 refers to the passage below and the statements that follow it. As you read, be alert for expressions of personal opinion.

This terrible creature has eight long arm-feet, radiating out from around a hideous mouth. . . . The strength of these arms is almost unnatural, and their swift flexible movements are precisely those of an active snake. When the creature climbs swiftly up over a cliff like a spider, or creeps under an overhanging reef, he is horribly, squirmingly, frighteningly alive. And then suddenly he'll stop and be as horribly dead. Lying in wait for his prey, he'll turn to any color to match his background—pink, red, purple, blue. I've even seen him break out with dark stripes.

Below are five statements from the passage above.

A. The octopus has eight arms.
B. The mouth of the octopus is hideous.
C. The octopus lies in wait for prey.
D. A live octopus is frightening.
E. An octopus can change colors.

1. Which of the statements above could be tested in a laboratory or by referring to an expert?

   (1) B and D
   (2) A, C, and E
   (3) A and B

   (1) (2) (3)

Check your answer to On the Springboard on page 104.

Were you able to tell which statements were facts and which were opinions? If you were, go on to "The Real Thing" now. If not, it would be a good idea to review this section before you go on.

“The Real Thing”

Item 1 refers to the following statements.

A. Lobsters are crustaceans.
B. Blue lobsters grow larger than green ones.
C. Blue lobsters taste better than green ones.
D. Lobster meat contains cholesterol.
E. Lobsters are strange looking.

1. Which of the statements above could be proved true or false in laboratory tests?

   (1) A, B, and E (2) B and E
   (3) B and C (4) A, B, and D
   (5) B, D, and E

   (1) (2) (3) (4) (5)

Items 2–3 are based on the passage below.

The crayfish is a crustacean—an invertebrate with jointed legs and a soft body covered by a hard, protective coat. This exoskeleton gives shape to the animal and protects it from injury.

Crayfish live in lakes and rivers, usually in burrows or under rocks. They come out at night to eat small fish, snails, and insects.

Crayfish seldom grow to be more than six inches in length. They vary in color from white to pink or orange or from green to blue. The crayfish is considered good food in Europe and parts of the United States.

2. Which of the following states an opinion about crayfish?

   (1) Crayfish live in fresh water.
   (2) Crayfish are valuable animals.
   (3) Crayfish have no backbones.
   (4) Crayfish rely on small animals for food.
   (5) Many Europeans like to eat crayfish.

   (1) (2) (3) (4) (5)

3. A fisherman would like to catch a dozen crayfish to use as bait. Where should he probably look to obtain the best results?

   (1) under stones on a shore
   (2) in burrows in open fields
   (3) with schools of small fish in the ocean
   (4) with other crustaceans in open water
   (5) near rocks in a lake at night

   (1) (2) (3) (4) (5)

Check your answers on page 106.

Distinguishing Facts from Hypotheses

As you read earlier, a fact is a statement that can be proved true by experimenting, observing, or referring to a qualified authority. In contrast, a **hypothesis** is a statement that appears to be correct on the basis of known facts, but it has not yet been tested and proved. When you read scientific materials, you will often learn about different hypotheses that scientists work with. In this part of the lesson, you will have a chance to identify some hypotheses developed by biologists.

Coming to Terms

hypothesis a statement that tries to explain something, appears to be true, but has yet to be proved by experiment or research

Here's an Example

The following passage describes a problem and then discusses two hypotheses that scientists have suggested to explain what causes the problem.

■ The Great Barrier Reef off the eastern coast of Australia is a large natural ridge of living coral. It protects the coastal cities of Australia from the pounding of ocean waves. It is also the home of millions of plants and animals.

In recent years, however, the Barrier Reef has been damaged by the population explosion of a sea animal that eats coral: the crown-of-thorns starfish. This ocean animal normally feeds on living coral. But when the number of sea stars began to increase abnormally, they began to eat corals faster than the coral animals could reproduce.

Why have the sea stars become so numerous? Some people hypothesize that shell hunters have killed too many of the sea stars' natural enemies, animals that feed on the sea stars and keep them from multiplying too fast. Others assert that holes made for ships to pass through the Great Barrier Reef have shifted the balance of nature, allowing sea stars to live and reproduce in abnormal numbers. No hypothesis has been studied long enough to produce conclusive evidence.

The two different possible explanations, or hypotheses, for the sharp increase in the number of crown-of-thorns starfish are mentioned in the final paragraph. One is that the animals that eat the sea stars have been killed by humans, so there is no check on the sea stars. The other is that holes blasted through the reef have upset the balance of nature. Neither explanation has been proved. Each is still a hypothesis, not a fact.

Try It Yourself

Read the following passage to discover how a medical mystery was solved. What problem did Dr. Finlay face? What hypothesis did he form about the cause of the problem?

■ In the late 1800s, a disease known as yellow fever spread through Cuba and other Caribbean areas. A Cuban physician, Dr. Carlos Finlay, noticed that new cases of yellow fever increased dramatically when mosquitoes were especially plentiful. The number of new cases dropped off when dry weather conditions reduced the number of mosquitoes. Dr. Finlay also noticed that yellow fever victims had one thing in common: mosquito bites. Finlay guessed that the bite of a local insect, the stegomyia mosquito, might be responsible for spreading yellow fever.

After twenty years of observing the insects and stricken patients, Finlay convinced U.S. authorities that his hypothesis should be carefully investigated. A team of volunteer doctors and soldiers, with Dr. Walter Reed as their director, allowed themselves to be bitten by the stegomyia mosquito to test Finlay's hypothesis. The experiments eventually proved that Finlay's hypothesis was correct. The study also led to methods of controlling and treating yellow fever.

Did you identify Dr. Finlay's hypothesis? You are right if you said Dr. Finlay hypothesized that the stegomyia mosquito might be responsible for spreading yellow fever. The last sentence of the first paragraph states Finlay's hypothesis.

Was Finlay's hypothesis accepted immediately? No; doctors and soldiers tested it. The experiments proved the hypothesis correct and then led to the control and treatment of yellow fever.

On the Springboard

Item 2 refers to the following paragraph. The paragraph states a number of facts and one hypothesis. You will be asked to pick out the hypothesis.

Researchers at the University of Miami observed that the males among some species of fish make certain noises by drumming on their swim bladders with strong muscles. From what they had seen and heard, the researchers believed that the noises were part of the mating process among those fish. They set up a number of experiments to see if they were correct. The experiments showed that the noises made by the males did actually attract female fish—but not all female fish. Females responded only to the noises made by males of their own species.

2. Which of the following states the hypothesis tested by researchers at the University of Miami?

   (1) Certain fish make noises that are part of the mating process.
   (2) Some males make drumming noises that come from their swim bladders.
   (3) Female fish are attracted to males of their own species only.

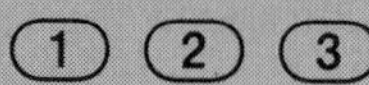

You can check your Springboard answer on page 104.

Were you able to tell the difference between the facts and the hypothesis in the paragraph? If so, you are ready to try "The Real Thing." If you had trouble with the Springboard item, take time to review this section first.

“The Real Thing”

Items 4–6 refer to the following passage.

Fossils show that dinosaurs had many traits similar to those of reptiles. For this reason, scientists long held that dinosaurs—like reptiles of today—were cold-blooded. But recently some scientists have pointed out facts that suggest otherwise. These scientists hypothesize, for one thing, that dinosaurs may have moved more swiftly than reptiles and other cold-blooded animals do. They base this hypothesis on the fact that dinosaurs had long, straight legs that extended downward from their bodies. Reptiles, however, have short legs that extend outward from their bodies and are ill-suited for speed. Generally speaking, cold-blooded animals cannot move swiftly for any period of time, as dinosaurs may have done.

Scientists also note that some dinosaurs had certain body parts that appear suited to regulating body temperature. Stegosaurs, for example, had two rows of bony plates down their backs. These plates could have been an efficient system for releasing the excess body heat that a warm-blooded animal would produce.

Dinosaurs, of course, are extinct. Without live animals to observe, scientists may never know for sure whether dinosaurs were cold-blooded animals.

4. Which of the following is a hypothesis suggested in the passage that might explain the purpose of the bony plates on the backs of stegosaurs?

   (1) Stegosaurs probably lived in cold environments.
   (2) Cold-blooded animals produce no body heat.
   (3) The appearance of the bony plates could have frightened off dangerous animals.
   (4) Stegosaurs may have released body heat through the bony plates.
   (5) Stegosaurs may have lived off reptiles with smooth backs.

5. Which of the following is a fact supporting the idea that dinosaurs may have moved swiftly?

(1) Dinosaurs had long, upright legs.
(2) Cold-blooded animals have to move swiftly to maintain body heat.
(3) Dinosaurs resemble reptiles in some ways.
(4) Legs of dinosaurs extended outward.
(5) Stegosaurs had sturdy bones in their legs and backs.

(1) (2) (3) (4) (5)

6. The reason for the extinction of the dinosaur has long been a topic of research and discussion among scientists.

Which of the following could be an example of one hypothesis about the reason?

(1) Scientists agree that dinosaurs became extinct about 65 million years ago.
(2) Dinosaurs may have become extinct when a heavy cloud blocked the sun's rays.
(3) Scientists need live animals to research dinosaurs.
(4) What we know about dinosaurs is from fossil evidence.
(5) Fossil dinosaur eggs have been found in the western United States.

(1) (2) (3) (4) (5)

Check your answers and record your score for the entire lesson on page 106.

LESSON 9

Higher Animals

In this lesson you'll read about some of the more complex members of the animal kingdom. The first section talks about birds. Before you go on, take a moment to preview the Warm-up. Let it guide your reading of the section.

Birds

Suppose someone said that you ate like a bird. The person probably would mean that you eat very little. But birds are actually very heavy eaters. Many birds eat enough food every day to equal their own weight. Imagine a 150-pound man eating 150 pounds of food a day!

Unlike fish and reptiles, birds are **warm-blooded animals**. The temperature of their blood stays the same regardless of how cold or warm their surroundings are. And as you know, birds have feathers, which help insulate their bodies against heat and cold. Feathers make birds unique among all the animals.

Have you ever stopped for a moment just to enjoy watching a bird in flight? A few birds, such as the penguin, cannot fly, but most can. A bird's body has several features that enable it to fly. The shape of its beak, neck, feathers, and tail give it a streamlined body, something like that of a jet airplane. Birds also have strong, lightweight skeletons and hollow bones.

Flying takes a great deal of energy. So does maintaining an even body temperature. If you guessed that birds get this energy from the tremendous amounts of food they eat, you're right.

Birds have lungs for breathing. Their lungs connect with storage sacs. When a bird inhales, some of the incoming air moves through the lungs. It travels into the storage sacs. When the bird exhales, fresh air in the storage sacs passes into the lungs again. So the bird's lungs receive oxygen both times—when the bird inhales and again when it exhales.

Coming to Terms

warm-blooded animal an animal whose blood temperature stays the same regardless of the temperature of the air or water surrounding it

Warm-up

Answer each question in a sentence or two.

1. In what ways is a bird's body well suited for flight?

2. Why do birds require a lot of food?

Not all the animals that swim in the sea are fish, and not all animals that fly in the air are birds. The next section tells you why this is true. Take time now to look at the Warm-up activity at the end. It can help guide you to other important information as you read.

Mammals

The tiny field mouse is only a few centimeters long. The giant blue whale's length would stretch across a third of a football field. Yet both animals have one important thing in common: they are both mammals.

Sample Warm-up Answers
1. Birds have lightweight skeletons and hollow bones. Their beaks, feathers, necks, and tails give them streamlined bodies.
2. Birds require much energy from food in order to fly and keep their bodies warm, in addition to carrying on all life activities.

Animals that fall into the group known as mammals actually have quite a number of things in common. All mammals have hair, though some kinds of whales have hair only before they are born. All mammals are warm-blooded, and hair can help keep body heat from escaping. It can also help protect the animal from some kinds of injuries.

Mammals have hearts with four chambers. Scientists think there may be a direct connection between the trait of the four-chambered heart and the trait of being warm-blooded. Mammals also have well-developed lungs.

A couple of small groups of mammals living in and near Australia hatch their young from eggs. Kangaroos and a few other Australian animals carry their newborn in pouches for a time. Aside from such rare exceptions, however, young mammals are born alive.

A young mammal feeds on milk from its mother's mammary gland or glands. Only female mammary glands secrete milk. But male mammals also have mammary glands, at least in the early stages of their development. Before venturing out on its own, a young mammal receives care, protection, and education from its parents.

Despite their many similar traits, mammals differ widely in their body shapes, limbs, and habits. Picture a giraffe for a moment. Then picture a seal, and finally a bat. All are mammals, yet how different they look and how differently they behave. Now think for a moment about the different types of body hair among mammals.

Rabbits, cats, and dogs may have thick, furry body coverings. But the hair of a scaly anteater appears as flattened plates. A sheep's hair takes the form of wool, and a porcupine's comes in sharp, pointed quills.

Most mammals live on land. A few, including the whale, porpoise, and dolphin, live in water. Bats and some squirrels can fly or glide through the air.

Warm-up

Answer the following question in one or two sentences of your own.

How do young mammals differ from the young of other animals?

____

____

In scientific terms, human beings are among the mammals of the animal kingdom. The next section tells you about some of the physical characteristics that make humans special and in some cases unique. Before you read, look ahead to the Warm-up activity. It can help you focus on important points of information as you read.

Humans as Mammals

You may have already known, or you may have concluded from what you've just read, that humans are mammals. Like other mammals, humans have hair, though not very much compared with most land mammals. Compared with whales, on the other hand, humans have quite a lot of hair. And like other mammals, humans are warm-blooded, are born live, and nurse their young with milk.

Humans stand and walk on two feet. This characteristic makes them unusual among mammals but not entirely unique. Kangaroos, for example, generally stand on two feet. Humans are also **primates,** or mammals that have well-developed fingers and toes. Primates can use their fingers and toes for holding and climbing. While this ability also makes humans special, again it does not make them unique. Monkeys and apes are also primates.

What are some things that do make humans unique among mammals? Intelligence is probably the first thing that comes to your mind. Humans are far more intelligent than any other animal. Human brain size is very large. The volume of the brain case in the human is about 1,200 to 1,500 milliliters. The volume of the brain case of the chimpanzee, one of the most intelligent animals, is only 350 to 450 milliliters.

Another thing that makes humans unique is the ability to do a great many physical activities. In addition to the many different things humans do with their fingers and hands, humans also swim, run, jump, ski, and perform dozens of other feats with their bodies. No animal can do so many different things. When it comes to any single physical ability, however, one or more animals can always far surpass humans. The cheetah, for example, can run at speeds of about sixty-five miles per hour. The best a human runner can do is about twenty-two miles per hour. There are many good human swimmers, but the swordfish can outdo them all by swimming ten times faster.

Coming to Terms

primate the type of mammal that has well-developed fingers and toes for climbing and grasping. Humans, monkeys, and apes are all primates.

Warm-up

Write one or more factual sentences to support the following statement.

A human being is unique among animals in some ways.

____

____

____

Sample Warm-up Answer
Most young mammals are born alive. They feed on milk from their mothers' mammary glands.

Sample Warm-up Answer
A human being can do a great many more things with his or her body than other animals can. The human being also has a large brain and much greater intelligence.

Recognizing Assumptions

Detecting Stated Assumptions

"I'D ALWAYS THOUGHT A BIRD BAND WAS A LITTLE METAL BRACELET WITH NUMBERS ON IT."

The man in the cartoon is stating an assumption. He says he has always thought, or assumed, that a bird band is the small metal identification tag that wildlife researchers sometimes place on a bird's leg. Of course, that assumption *is* correct. The cartoonist has playfully used the double meaning of the word *band* to produce a smile. But the cartoon helps point out how important assumptions can be.

An assumption is an idea that is taken for granted. People often speak and write without checking to see whether the ideas they assume to be factual are truly correct. Sometimes they are; sometimes they are not.

Coming to Terms

assumption an idea that is taken for granted

Here's an Example

In the statement below, the author has assumed something about birds. Do you think the assumption is correct?

■ Assuming that all birds migrate for the winter, we can also assume that all birds must be capable of flight.

In the first part of the statement, the author assumed that all birds migrate for the winter. Is that true? A little checking in an encyclopedia or reference book about birds would show that assumption is false. In fact, in many cases people would know simply from personal observation that some birds do not migrate for the winter. They may have even spread crumbs on snow-covered ground to feed birds that have stayed through the winter.

Since the first assumption is incorrect, do you think that the second part of the statement is reliable? You probably would want to check that statement in a reference book or with an authority on birds. If you did, you would find that a number of birds are *not* capable of flight, including the ostrich, penguin, and kiwi bird.

Try It Yourself

Sometimes an author of scientific material may ask you to assume—or accept—an idea that would be too difficult to investigate thoroughly. In the passage below, what does the author ask you to assume? Do you agree that it would be useless and too difficult to try to check the truth of the assumption?

■ Let us assume that nearly everyone has, at some point in his or her life, seen birds making a nest—either from first-hand observation or by seeing pictures of nest-building. These experiences could easily lead someone into thinking that all birds construct their nests of twigs, straw, and bits of paper, the way robins and other common birds do. But that is far from the truth. Certain species of sea birds make their nests out of pebbles. Some land birds place moss and grass inside a hollow tree. Still others create a home out of mud and prairie grasses. One of the most unusual nesting places is created by the male penguin. This father puts the egg on top of his feet and then covers it with a soft, feathery flap of abdominal skin to keep it safe and warm.

The author assumes that nearly everybody has seen birds making a nest at some time or other. The author asks the reader to share this assumption because it would be nearly impossible to find out whether "nearly everyone" has actually watched a bird building a nest.

Did you notice that another assumption follows immediately? In the second sentence, the author goes on to say that one could easily assume that all birds, like robins and other common birds, build nests from twigs, straw, and bits of paper. In the second sentence, the author is pointing out an assumption that is not accurate. The remainder of the paragraph explains why it is not. But in both instances, the author has clearly stated the assumptions you are to examine.

☑ A Test-Taking Tip

Sometimes authors use the terms *I think* or *I believe* to mean "I assume." To determine whether a statement on the GED Science Test is an assumption, ask yourself whether the author has given any evidence to show that the statement has been checked or investigated.

On the Springboard

Items 1–2 refer to the following passage. Read carefully to find any assumptions the author states.

Because dolphins live in water, and because they are shaped like fish, many people assume that they *are* fish. In fact, dolphins are mammals. Unlike fish, they are warm-blooded. Dolphins have lungs rather than gills, and they must rise out of the water regularly to breathe, usually about once or twice a minute. Young dolphins are nourished on their mothers' milk.

It is commonly thought that dolphins are among the best-loved animals on earth. We know that people have been attracted to dolphins for thousands of years because images of dolphins decorate many pieces of ancient pottery and old coins. Today zoos and amusement parks offer shows in which trained dolphins jump through hoops, leap high out of the water, and scoot backward on their tails. The performing dolphins seem to enjoy the companionship and attention of people as much as we enjoy them.

1. According to the passage above, many people incorrectly assume that dolphins
   (1) live in water
   (2) look like fish
   (3) are a species of fish

   (1) (2) (3)

2. The author of the passage above attempts to prove the assumption that dolphins are
   (1) the easiest animals to train
   (2) animals that have always appealed to humans
   (3) being abused by zoos and amusement parks

   (1) (2) (3)

Now check your answers to On the Springboard on page 104.

Were you able to pick out the assumptions stated in the passage? If so, go on to study unstated assumptions. If you had difficulty with this tricky subject, reread the section on recognizing stated assumptions first.

Identifying Unstated Assumptions

An unstated assumption, like the assumptions you studied in the last section, is an idea that an author or someone else has taken for granted. In the passages you have read so far, the authors have identified assumptions and stated them outright. But sometimes authors and others make assumptions that they do not point out. It is left up to you, the reader, to infer an assumption that's been made.

Here's an Example

In the following passage, the snowmobilers make an assumption about what is important in a wildlife refuge.

■ A group of snowmobilers asked permission to make a trail for their snowmobiles through a wildlife refuge. They stated that the trail would not change the appearance of the land. They promised, in fact, that once the snow was gone, the forest would look exactly as it had before they made the trail.

The game warden considered the request carefully, and then refused. He went on to explain that the noise of the snowmobiles in late winter and early spring could disturb many animals during their nesting and mating season.

The snowmobilers thought that it was only the appearance of the refuge that was important. They didn't state that idea, but the assumption was evident because they mentioned only the appearance, not the animals themselves.

Try It Yourself

In the following example, pet owners base their actions on a certain assumption. See if you can identify that assumption.

■ Many people think it is fashionable to own exotic pets such as large cats or monkeys. Sometimes such pets are obtained through illegal means. The owners simply do not know how to care for the pets. In the case of a monkey, for example, often an owner will provide merely a large, comfortable cage and all the bananas the monkey can eat.

As the monkey grows older, the owner realizes that its health is failing. By the time he or she finally finds a doctor who can help, the monkey has become blind—from malnutrition.

Did you recognize the assumption that owners of pet monkeys often make? They assume that a diet of bananas gives the monkey proper nutrition. That assumption is obviously faulty. Monkeys need a variety of different foods to stay healthy.

The following passage describes an experiment researchers conducted with bats. See if you can identify an implied assumption the researchers made regarding bat sounds and human hearing.

■ For years people puzzled over the ability of bats, who have poor eyesight, to fly safely around trees and other obstacles. Then two scientists formed the hypothesis that bats use sound echoes from their own voices to guide them around obstacles when they are flying.

To test their hypothesis, the researchers stretched wires about a room and then released a number of bats in the room. The bats easily flew around without striking or becoming tangled in the wires.

Next, the researchers covered the bats' ears so they could not hear. This time, the bats bumped into the wires and fell. The same thing happened when they covered the bats' mouths.

The researchers concluded that the experiment proved their hypothesis. Even though the researchers themselves heard no echoes, they were sure the bats were using sound echoes from their own voices to guide them around obstacles. Today this process is called echolocation.

Were you able to recognize the unstated assumption the researchers made about human hearing? They knew that they themselves could not hear the echoes, yet the bats seemed to be able to. They assumed that bats made sounds that were inaudible to the human ear. Did you notice that in this case the unstated assumption happened to be correct?

On the Springboard

Item 3 is based on the following information and graph. You will be asked to infer an unstated assumption.

Rabies is a virus disease that has spread among wild animals in many parts of the United States. In some areas of the Midwest, many skunks and raccoons have fallen victim to rabies. Because rabies can also affect pets and humans who are bitten by an infected animal, public health officials try to keep a record of the number of rabies cases discovered in wild animals.

Here are the records kept by officials in one northern county over a four-year period.

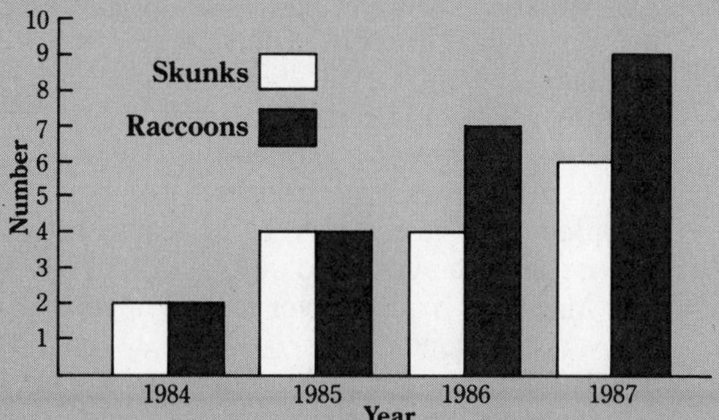

Rabies in Wild Animals: Haliburton County

3. According to the information given, it would be correct to assume that the figures in the chart represent only
   (1) the skunks and raccoons that officials caught and examined
   (2) what neighbors told county officials about their affected pets
   (3) the animal populations that are increasing in size

Item 4 refers to the following passage.

They live in Africa, near the equator. They live together in groups, needing companionship and social interaction with others like themselves. They travel about from place to place, seeking leaves, buds, and bark to feed on. In the wild, they never eat meat. They are quiet and usually timid of intruders. It will most likely surprise you to discover that these gentle animals are gorillas.

4. The author of the passage assumes that humans tend to
   (1) fear gorillas
   (2) feel scorn for gorillas
   (3) think of gorillas as humans

Check your answers to the Springboard questions on page 104.

Did you pick out the unstated assumptions correctly in the Springboard items? If so, congratulations. It is not an easy skill. You're ready to try "The Real Thing." If you had problems with the Springboard questions, review the pages on both stated and unstated assumptions before you go on.

☑ A Test-Taking Tip

On the GED Science Test, your skill in recognizing assumptions will help you in two ways. First, you want to watch for ideas in reading passages that could be based on unstated assumptions. Second, being able to recognize assumptions will help you answer one type of test item. In this type of item, a particular experiment or process is described, but one important idea is left out. In other words, it is assumed in the explanation. Your task is to picture the process being explained and then figure out what important piece of information has been taken for granted. In a way it is rather like finding the missing piece that will complete a jigsaw puzzle.

“The Real Thing”

Item 1 refers to the chart below.

Types of Mammals

	Monotreme	Marsupial	Placental
Habitat	Australia, New Guinea, Tasmania	Australia, N. America	Europe, Asia, the Americas, Africa
Special Trait	Young hatch from egg.	Young develop in pouch.	Young remain longer in mother's body.
Members in Group	Only two: Spiny anteater, duck-billed platypus	Examples: Kangaroo, opossum, wombat	Examples: Humans, dogs, horses, bats, whales, sheep

1. A scientist is trying to classify a mammal. If he is to classify the animal correctly, which of the following characteristics must it be assumed he will take into account?
   (1) where the animal is found
   (2) whether the animal is of use to humans
   (3) how many animals belong to the group
   (4) how the young are born
   (5) how old the animal grows to be

Items 2–5 refer to the following passage.

For two centuries beginning in the early 1600s, the word "beaver" was synonymous with "hat" in fashionable Europe. Beaver pelts lured Europeans to most of North America's wild reaches. . . . Between 1853 and 1877, the Hudson's Bay Company alone shipped three million pelts to Europe. But the nineteenth century invention of machines that could produce top-quality felt led to a change in fashion.

By then, beavers were a devastated species: there had been as many as 400 million beavers in North America before the Europeans came, but by 1890, only small populations survived, predominately in the Midwest. Today, the animals have made a slow comeback: there are now thought to be more than two million in the United States.

Unfortunately, civilization hasn't left the creatures much room. Conflicts between beavers and people today concern culverts blocked by beaver dams, or flooded hay fields, or stands of trees gnawed down at night. When their instinctive drive to impound running water runs afoul of civilization, the creatures are labeled a "nuisance" and destroyed or deported.

2. The age of machinery saved the beaver species.

   Given the information in the passage, for that statement to be true it would have to be assumed that

   (1) scientists would not have stepped in to protect the beaver with their technology
   (2) more humane traps would not have been produced
   (3) new uses would have been found for beaver fur
   (4) the beavers would have been hunted into extinction without machine-made felt
   (5) industry in the Midwest turned people's attention away from beavers

   (1) (2) (3) (4) (5)

3. According to the passage above, why did beavers become less desirable goods in Europe?

   (1) When felt hats became available, Europeans bought them instead of beaver hats.
   (2) Beaver hats became unpopular in Europe when it was learned they came from the American frontier.
   (3) Beavers became scarce, so beaver hats became too costly to buy.
   (4) Machines made beaver hats in unpopular styles and sizes.
   (5) Europeans eventually grew tired of wearing heavy beaver hats.

   (1) (2) (3) (4) (5)

4. When left on their own, beavers will

   (1) reproduce too much
   (2) construct dams that stop the flow of water
   (3) decrease in population
   (4) chew wood to sharpen their teeth
   (5) eat farmers' hay and grain

   (1) (2) (3) (4) (5)

5. Which of the following people would be most likely to consider beavers a "nuisance"?

   (1) a fisherman
   (2) a scientist studying pond life
   (3) a farmer who irrigates with a small stream
   (4) campers hiking through a woodland area
   (5) a cattle rancher in a dry area

   (1) (2) (3) (4) (5)

Check your answers and record your score on page 107.

LESSON 10

Animal Behavior

So far in your studies of animals, you have read mostly about the physical traits of various species. In this lesson you'll look at special ways animals behave and why they do so. Before you read the first section, look ahead to the Warm-up activity. Use it as a guide to important information.

Learning vs. Instinct

You can know how to pass the GED Test, repair an auto, operate a computer, or build a cabinet because you can *learn* how to do such things. But how does a spider know how to build an intricate web? It doesn't learn how to do it from books or from other spiders. It does it automatically—by **instinct.** You probably already have a good idea of what is meant by instinct. You've seen examples of it as you watched a squirrel gather acorns or a dog bury a bone. Animal instincts are complex behaviors based on an animal's heredity. Instinctive behavior requires no previous learning or experience.

Many times an animal's behavior involves both instinct and learning. Consider a bird building a nest. Instinct triggers its drive to construct a shelter. But conditions of its particular environment modify its actions: the final nest itself depends as much on the availability of a good site and appropriate materials as it does on the bird's instincts.

Not all **innate behavior** (*innate* means "inborn" or "inherited") is as complex as instincts such as web weaving or nest building. For example, a male moth just emerging from its cocoon will immediately fly toward a female of its species. The odor of the female attracts the male. Scientists would not call the male moth's behavior *instinct*. Although it is innate rather than learned behavior, the male moth demonstrates only a very simple response.

Learning depends on experience. Obviously, some species can learn more than others. And it appears that animals within the same species differ in their abilities to learn. You can see this among humans. Some people can easily learn communication skills, for example, but may have difficulty learning mathematics.

The more intelligent mammals learn much from their parents, from other members of their species, and from their own trial-and-error actions in new situations.

Coming to Terms

instinct complex, hereditary behavior among animals; behavior that does not depend on experience

innate behavior actions animals take because of their heredity rather than experience. Innate behavior can be complex instincts or very simple acts.

Warm-up

Use two or three examples from this section or of your own to support the statement below. Describe the examples in sentences of your own.

Instinct guides some animal behavior, but most behavior is modified or even learned from experience.

___

___

___

___

Sample Warm-up Answer
Spiders spin their webs by instinct. Birds modify their nest building according to the site and materials available. Humans can learn many things.

How many people have you interacted with today? You've probably cooperated and worked in a number of different ways with others in your family or at work. In the next section, you will read about the complex ways in which some animals interact. Before you read, glance at the Warm-up activity. Keep it in mind as you read the section.

Social Behavior and Communication

Scientists refer to the interaction among organisms of the same species as social behavior. If you've ever gazed at a flock of geese flying in formation, you've observed social behavior. If you've noticed cattle gather in herds or minnows dart quickly together in schools, you've seen social behavior. And, of course, whenever you interact with another person, you yourself are exhibiting social behavior.

Ants are social insects. The ones you see most often are ones that live and work together in ant colonies underground. Bees also have a complex social system based on a division of labor; honeybees even have a communication system using intricate movements that signal where and in which type of flower nectar can be found.

Such communication is an important way organisms have of behaving with one another. As with the bee's dance, animals often use visual means to communicate. A dog bares its teeth to indicate aggression, and a peacock spreads his colorful tail feathers to attract a mate. Can you think of ways in which humans change their appearance to show they are angry or to attract the opposite sex?

Sound is another way to communicate. The rattling and hissing of a rattlesnake are certainly effective in communicating its ability to defend itself. Bird songs help establish home territory and attract mates. It isn't too difficult to think of how human beings use sound to communicate.

Some animals even communicate by secreting chemicals that leave certain messages to others of their species.

Finally, actual physical contact may be used to communicate caring, hunger, dominance, or aggression. However, organisms other than humans seldom fight other members of their species to the death. They usually use some sort of physical contact until one animal indicates submission or flees.

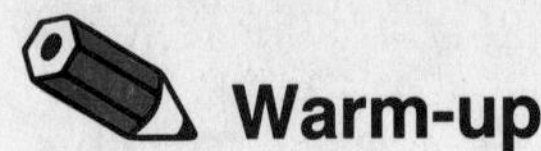

Warm-up

In one or two sentences, tell some of the general messages animals need to communicate to one another.

____

____

____

Assessing Supporting Data

To assess something means to determine its worth or value. To a jeweler, that could mean deciding the price of a diamond. To a surgeon, it could mean deciding whether a donor organ is right for a patient who needs a transplant. To a scientist, it often means deciding whether the data, or evidence, support a certain conclusion. When making this decision, the scientist must answer three questions:

1. Has enough information been gathered?
2. Was the information gathered in a scientific manner?
3. Does the information support the conclusion?

The remainder of this lesson will help you build your own skills in assessing data. Try to keep the three questions in mind as you read the following pages.

Here's an Example

A group of veterinary students were studying instinctive behavior in domestic, or tamed, animals. For one study, they chose a female dog who was about to give birth to her first litter of puppies. As you read one observer's notes—listed on the next page—notice which points would be appropriate in the study of instinctive behaviors. They are *italicized*.

Sample Warm-up Answer
Animals need to communicate such things as aggression, location of food, and affection to each other. They also need to attract mates and signal the area that is their home territory.

■ A few hours before the puppies were born, the mother dog took soft cloths from her bed and *created a "nest"* in a protected corner of the room.

As each puppy was born, the mother *bit off the umbilical cord and licked the puppy* to clean off the membrane.

The puppies *searched for the mother's teat to nurse*, almost immediately.

Later, the owner called, "Dinner!" At that signal, the mother dog rose from the floor and trotted over to her feeding dish.

Remember that instinct is behavior that is inherited, not learned. In this case, the mother dog had not had any prior experience with puppies, and there was no one to teach her how to care for them. Her nesting behavior and washing of the puppies *were* instinctive. In addition, the puppies themselves knew instinctively how to nurse. Each of those observations could be used to support the idea that dogs exhibit instinctive behavior.

Coming to the feeding dish on signal, however, was learned behavior. It would not apply to a study of instinctive behavior.

Notice that the researcher who took notes did *not* attempt to assist the mother or the puppies in any way. In fact, he stayed well in the background. Suppose, however, that he had stepped forward and placed the puppies in a position to nurse. Would he have changed the evidence at all? Of course, such interference would have prevented him from seeing whether the puppies could instinctively find their way to their first meal. Tampering with the evidence in this way would have made it unscientific and unreliable.

Another point to consider is whether watching one mother dog and her puppies would offer enough experience to form any conclusions. The researchers would want to watch many other mothers and litters of puppies before drawing any firm conclusions about dogs' instinctive behavior.

Try It Yourself

Read the passage below to understand the idea it is discussing. Then you'll deal with supporting evidence.

■ Imprinting in birds is a process in which the newly hatched young of some species looks on the first moving object it sees as its parent. The little hatchling behaves as if the animal (or even person) is a parent, seeing it as a role model and helper. The imprint may last even after the bird is full grown.

Now decide which of the following observations could be used as evidence to support the information in the paragraph.

A. A newly hatched chick instinctively pecks the ground around its mother for food.
B. A young goose constantly follows a dog that had been walking by when the bird was born.
C. A young robin waits in a nest for its mother to return with food.

The idea in the paragraph is that some young birds see the first moving object after they are born as their parent and act toward it accordingly. To support that idea, the example of the young goose could be given because it fits the characteristics of imprinting.

Now consider again the information in the paragraph and the observation that a young goose is mistaking a dog for its mother. Which of the following conclusions is there enough evidence to support?

A. Birds cannot learn once they have gotten past a certain age.
B. Innate behavior plays a role in some birds' development.

There is certainly evidence to support the idea that some birds' behavior is innately programmed. However, even if imprinting *can* last throughout a bird's life, that is not enough evidence to support the conclusion that a bird cannot learn anything past a certain age. So there is adequate data for the second conclusion but not the first. Is that what you had decided?

On the Springboard

Item 1 asks you to select appropriate supporting evidence for a stated conclusion.

1. Scientists have determined that bees have methods for communicating certain kinds of information to other bees in their colony. Which one of the following statements of evidence supports their conclusion?

   (1) Normally the queen bee grows and develops in a certain type of cell.
   (2) Bees store honey to eat during the winter, when there are no flowers.
   (3) A worker bee indicates the location of nectar by flying in a certain pattern.

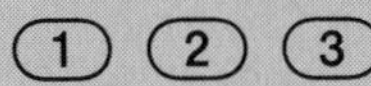

Item 2 refers to the paragraph and lettered statements below. Look for evidence and possible conclusions as you read.

Dolphins communicate with each other underwater by making series of noises. To humans, the sounds resemble clicks and whistles. Dolphins seem to use certain patterns of sounds at particular times. For instance, one certain pattern indicates that the dolphin is in danger or distress. However, different dolphins use different sound patterns. Researchers continue to study dolphins, hoping to learn how to interpret their communication system.

Here are two characteristics of dolphins' sounds.

A. the range of pitches that a dolphin can produce and hear
B. the distance in water that a dolphin's sounds travel

2. If a scientist wanted to reproduce dolphin sounds to see if a dolphin in a tank would respond to them, which of the characteristics would he need to take into account?

   (1) A only
   (2) B only
   (3) A and B

① ② ③

You can check your answers to On the Springboard on page 104.

How did you do? Were you able to assess the kinds of data that are needed to support conclusions? If you were, move ahead to "The Real Thing." If you need more help, reread these pages first.

"The Real Thing"

Item 1 refers to the map and information below.

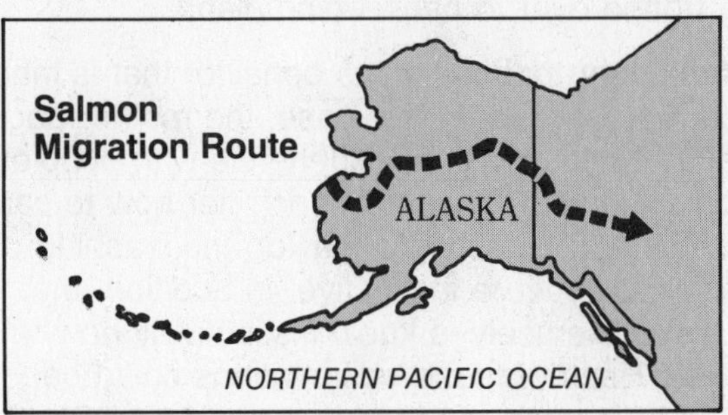

Salmon in the northern Pacific Ocean migrate. Young salmon swim out to sea from the freshwater tributaries of the Yukon River where they are born. After they have become adults, they migrate about 2,000 miles back up the Yukon to their birthplaces. There they mate, lay eggs, and die.

1. There is enough evidence given above to suggest that salmon migration is behavior that is

   (1) harmful
   (2) learned from parents
   (3) unnecessary
   (4) instinctive
   (5) communicative

<u>Item 2</u> refers to the statements below.

A. Coyotes can teach themselves how to spring hunters' traps.
B. Coyotes know how to howl from birth.
C. Coyotes' howling sounds lonely and sad.
D. Coyotes are wild members of the dog family.

2. Which of the following conclusions could be drawn on the basis of the observations above?

   (1) Coyotes experience emotions.
   (2) Both instinct and learning affect coyote behavior.
   (3) Coyotes are dogs that became wild.
   (4) Coyotes are more intelligent than humans.
   (5) Howling is a succesful method of communication among coyotes.

3. Which of the following statements could be used to support the conclusion that some species of wasps display social behavior?

   (1) Wasps destroy many insects and caterpillars that are harmful to humans.
   (2) Some wasps build their nests under porches or eaves.
   (3) A group of wasps builds a nest that all of them will occupy.
   (4) Wasps sometimes damage fruit crops.
   (5) Wasps build their nests out of "paper," which they make by chewing wood and plant fiber.

(1) (2) (3) (4) (5)

4. Which of the following is evidence that some animals learn?

   (1) A newly hatched sea turtle crawls directly from its egg shell to the sea.
   (2) A two-month-old eaglet watches its father dive for a fish and then repeats his actions.
   (3) Monarch butterflies migrate from the eastern United States to Mexico every year.
   (4) A newborn kangaroo crawls immediately to its mother's pouch.
   (5) A tadpole grows legs and sheds its tail.

(1) (2) (3) (4) (5)

Check your answers and record your score on page 107.

LESSON 11

Relationships

The materials you've read in biology have shown you a number of close-ups and details about plants and animals. Now, in the last biology lesson, you'll step back a little. You'll look at the earth and groups of organisms that make their home on the planet. Before you read the first section, check its Warm-up activity. Let it help you focus on important information.

Populations and Communities

When you say that the population of Chicago exceeds 3 million, you mean that more than 3 million people live in that city. You are using the term *population* to refer to the number of people who live in a particular area—the city of Chicago. Government and business leaders often use population figures to help them plan for the future of their cities, counties, or states.

Scientists too use the word **population.** They use it to refer to a group of organisms that live and reproduce in a given area. When discussing a population, a scientist is interested in the type of organism, the time and location of its existence, and usually the numbers of individual organisms. A researcher, then, who stated the number of armadillos living in Texas in 1988 would be describing a "population."

When scientists are working with populations, they are usually interested in learning the **population density.** Population density refers specifically to the number of organisms in a particular amount of *space* at a particular time. With regard to humans, you might say that New Jersey has a high population density. The average number of people per square mile in New Jersey is high. New Jersey is densely populated. Utah, on the other hand, has a low population density. The average number of people per square mile is low. Utah is a sparsely populated state.

Many different species of organisms may live in any given space. In other words, many populations may live in the same area. The whole group of populations in an area makes up a **community.** Some communities have hundreds of different populations.

A freshwater pond is a good example of a community. It has many populations of both plants and animals. The kinds of life found in it will vary with the physical conditions. The amount of oxygen dissolved in the water, seasonal temperature changes, and whether or not the pond dries up in the summer all help determine what organisms will live there. If conditions in the environment are stable, the pond will support a very large community.

Coming to Terms

population the number of a certain kind of organism living in a particular area at a given time

population density the number of organisms in relation to the amount of space they occupy at a particular time

community a group made up of all the populations in a particular area

Warm-up

Use the information listed below to describe a population of organisms. Write your answer in a complete sentence.

Place: Chickasaw County
Time: May 1987
Organism: Coyotes
Number: 600

____

____

____

____

Sample Warm-up Answer
In May 1987, the coyote population of Chickasaw County was 600.

If someone asked you what your most reliable source of food was, you'd probably name your favorite supermarket. You'd be correct, of course, but there's much more to the story. You'll see why in the next section. Before you read it, look ahead to the Warm-up questions. Use them as a guide to important information.

Food Chains

Grass in a green pasture provides food for a cow. The cow, in turn, provides you with food—a glass of milk or perhaps a steak from a steer. In this sequence, a transfer of food energy and nutrients from one organism to another takes place. Such transfers occur all th time. And each series of transfers makes up a **food chain.**

Where did the food chain begin in the paragraph you just read? With the grass in a pasture. *All* food chains begin with plants of one kind or another. That is because only plants can photosynthesize, or trap the light energy from the sun to make food. Some of this food is used by the plant, but much is stored in the leaves and stem. It can be used by animals that eat the plant. So all animals, either directly or indirectly, obtain their food from plants. When you eat an orange, you get food directly from a plant. When you drink a glass of milk or eat a hamburger patty, you get food indirectly from plants.

Some animals eat nothing but plants. These animals are said to be herbivorous. Other animals eat only the flesh, or meat, of other animals. They are carnivorous animals, or ones that eat only meat. And then there are omnivorous animals, or ones that eat both meat and plants. Humans are omnivorous.

A cow is herbivorous. You can see how the plants it eats go indirectly to you through the food chain.

plants → cow → human

A rabbit is also an herbivorous animal. Suppose a wildcat eats a rabbit. The food chain would look like this.

plants → rabbit → wildcat

Now look at this food chain. The hawk gets its food from plants even more indirectly.

plants → grasshopper → lizard → hawk

Coming to Terms

food chain the series of transfers of energy and nutrients from one organism to another

Warm-up

Write your own sentence to answer each question below.

1. Why would animals be unable to live without plants?

____

____

2. Tell which animal is herbivorous and which is carnivorous in this food chain.

plants → deer → wolf

____

____

In the following section, you'll read about the relationships between organisms and their environment. Take a moment to preview the Warm-up before you read. It can direct your thoughts to important points of information.

Ecosystems

You have read that a community is a group of populations all living in the same area. Every community has a physical environment made up of its surroundings: soil, water, air, rocks, and so on. A community and its environment make up an **ecosystem.** Organisms in an ecosystem interact with each other and with their environment.

Ecosystems occur in many varieties and sizes. A small aquarium, a large pond, and the seaside are all ecosystems. A terrarium, a prairie, and a city are also ecosystems. The largest ecosystem takes in the earth and all its communities. It extends above and below the surface of the earth. Scientists call this huge ecosystem the biosphere.

Sample Warm-up Answers
1. All animals get their food either directly or indirectly from plants. **2.** The deer is the herbivorous animal, and the wolf is the carnivorous one.

Every organism's environment in an ecosystem consists of two parts. First there is the environment made up of living things and things that were recently alive. This part of the organism's environment is called the biotic environment.

Think about your own ecosystem. Family members, coworkers, store clerks—any persons with whom you interact are part of your biotic environment. So are the flowers you may smell or pick, the trees that shade you, and the ants you may accidentally step on.

The other part of an organism's environment is called the abiotic environment. It consists of things that are not alive and never were. The soil, the air, and the rain are all parts of your abiotic environment.

Within an ecosystem, an organism is related to anything that affects it. There could be a direct relationship between you and a tomato, for instance. A tomato is food. You are a consumer of food. But suppose a fungus attacks the tomato. Then there would also be a relationship between you and the fungus. The fungus may destroy the food and deprive you of a tomato to eat.

The tomato and the fungus are both alive, so in that instance you would have interacted with parts of your biotic environment. But your abiotic environment also affects you. For example, an abnormally high amount of rainfall could destroy food crops. Air contains oxygen, which you need to live, yet it can also carry pollutants that harm you.

Coming to Terms

ecosystem a community combined with its environment. Organisms interact with each other and with the environment of their ecosystem.

Warm-up

Answer each question in a sentence or two.

1. How does the biosphere differ from all other ecosystems?

____

____

2. Give three examples of members of the biotic environment where you live.

____

____

Faulty Logic

High-powered microscopes, lasers, computers—these are just a few of the marvelous high-tech tools scientists use today. Yet none of these is more valuable to modern science than the human mind. It is human reasoning that interprets the results obtained with special equipment. Without human reasoning and logic, the information would be useless.

Of course, just as machines and tools sometimes don't work properly, people can make mistakes in reasoning. Sometimes they use irrelevant information to reach a conclusion. Sometimes they overlook evidence. Or they may mistakenly see a cause-and-effect relationship when there is none. Detecting such faulty logic in others' reasoning takes careful reasoning of your own.

Here's an Example

Sometimes people assume that when two events occur close together in time, the first one necessarily causes the second. In other words, they confuse a time sequence with a cause-and-effect relationship. There is such faulty logic in the following account.

■ A small inland lake had a large population of mussels, which are animals with a hinged shell and a soft, white body inside. In the year 1910, a dam was built at a river flowing into the north end of the lake to help control its water level. Soon it was noticed that the large population of lake mussels had decreased sharply.

The rumor spread that the dam had affected the mussel population. Since the dam came first and the decline in mussels was noticed soon after, many people were convinced that the dam must have killed the mussels.

Only much later, when hikers came upon the camp of the workers who had built the dam, was the truth discovered. In the woods behind the camp cooking shed, the hikers found large hills of mussel shells. And nearby was a pot that the cook had used to steam mussels for the hungry crew every night for several months.

The people thought the dam itself caused the mussels to disappear. They mistakenly believed that because the two events—the construction of the dam and the decline in mussels—occurred about the same time, the first must have caused the second.

Try It Yourself

Irrelevant means "beside the point." In the newspaper report below, someone is using information that is irrelevant to the point being argued. See if you can find the faulty logic.

■ The village council met last night to review complaints that Chandler's Dry Cleaners is polluting the air with chemical fumes that endanger the health of residents. Several nearby residents have complained of frequent headaches and nausea during the hours when Chandler's operates its cleaning equipment. They insist that Chandler's machinery and ventilating system must be checked by public health officials. A spokesperson for Chandler's listened to the complaints and then replied that they were unfounded because Chandler's uses only the finest, most expensive chemicals in its cleaning processes.

Did you see that Chandler's spokesperson used irrelevant evidence? What he said about the chemicals may be true, but it is beside the point and does not help solve the problem at all. The residents feel that the company is polluting the air. Even if it is polluted with fine, expensive

---

Sample Warm-up Answers
1. The biosphere is the largest of all ecosystems. It takes in the whole earth and all its communities. **2.** Your answer will depend on where you live, but it should name living persons, plants, or animals—or possibly things that were recently alive, such as leaves that have fallen from trees.

chemicals, it is still being polluted. The problem is not solved.

In this next account, someone mistakenly overlooks some important information in conducting research. Can you detect the faulty logic in the study described below?

■ A highway-expansion project was under consideration. It would extend a major road through the southern edge of a park, where a small wooded area, a pond, and a field could be found. Plans called for the pond to be dredged and a thirty-foot strip of the field to be paved, but the woods would not be directly touched.

To begin to determine the impact of such a road on the entire community of that section of the park, a team of researchers was sent to study all the different populations of plants and animals that would be affected. The team carefully observed and catalogued all the ground animals they could see in the field. They listed the grasses, mosses, and other plants. They even stripped small sections of topsoil to reveal earthworms and ant colonies. Then they reported to the highway commission the effects such a road would have on the park organisms.

Can you see what the researchers missed in their study? Think of everything that lives in and around a pond—fish, plants, waterfowl, and so on. A pond is a complex community. Yet the researchers didn't even bother to study the organisms that are part of the pond community, even though the pond was going to be dredged. And even though the woods were not scheduled to be touched, think of the organisms that live in such an area. Animals and birds most likely come out into the field and may even use the pond as a source of water. They would probably be affected by the noise and the car exhaust even if they always remained in the woods.

Did you see, then, all the important data that the researchers forgot to include in their study? Their report was nowhere near complete. The impact on the park community would be far more than they could predict with their limited information.

On the Springboard

Item 1 refers to the following passage.

The members of a community organization became concerned about the quality of the air in their inner-city neighborhood. They decided to investigate how clean the air really was. They covered twelve clean glass slides with a thick but even coat of petroleum jelly to collect particles from the air. They wanted to set the slides outside to find out how much particle matter from the air the slides would attract.

1. Which of the following would probably cause the greatest amount of error in the experiment?

   (1) applying an extra thick layer of petroleum jelly to the slides
   (2) placing all the slides in sheltered spots away from wind and traffic
   (3) leaving the slides outside for three days with average weather conditions

You can check your Springboard answer on page 104.

Were you able to pick out what the organization should do to avoid faulty logic in the Springboard item? If so, now try "The Real Thing." If not, it would be a good idea to review this section on faulty logic.

❝ The Real Thing ❞

Item 1 refers to the following statements.

A. Starlings are bigger than some birds native to North America.
B. Starlings nest in trees and eat fruits and berries.
C. Starlings have few natural enemies in North America.

1. The starling is not native to North America, yet these birds now form large populations in many parts of the United States. The people who brought starlings to New York from the British Isles in 1890 probably did not consider which of the facts given above?

(1) A only (2) B only (3) C only
(4) A and B (5) B and C

① ② ③ ④ ⑤

Items 2–4 refer to the diagram and passage that follow.

Food Web

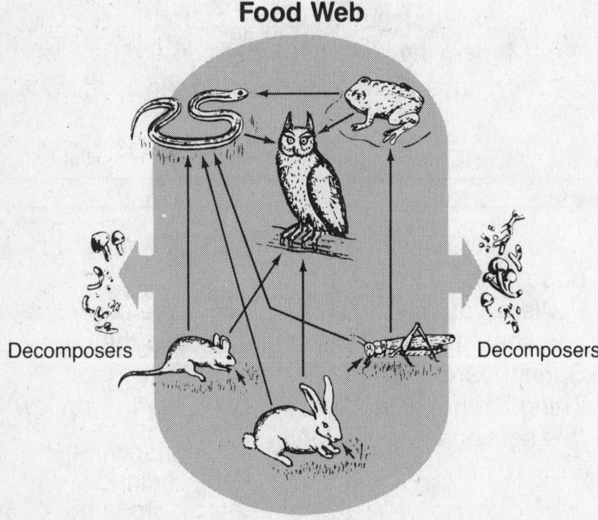

A food web is a network of the transfer of energy in food. In the food web shown above, the mouse, rabbit, and grasshopper are herbivores, which eat grass and other green plants. The other animals are carnivores, which eat meat. The decomposers at the beginning and end of the web eat dead plants and animals. As these dead organisms decompose, the energy and nutrients they contain are released into the environment and become usable once more by green plants.

A change in the feeding habits of one population can affect other populations in its food web. For example, when a population of tree beetles that feed on leaves increases, the tree population suffers damaged leaves. At the same time, the population of birds that feed on the beetles benefits from the larger food supply.

2. Based on the information given above, which of the following statements is illogical?

(1) Plants derive nutrients from the soil.
(2) Energy from plants is passed on to herbivores when they eat plants.
(3) Energy and nutrients are passed on to carnivores when they eat herbivores.
(4) A food web would eventually break down without decomposers.
(5) Herbivores would die but carnivores would survive if fire destroyed the plants in their community.

① ② ③ ④ ⑤

3. A rabbit is nourished directly by the plants it eats. However, a plant does not gain nourishment from a dead animal without the help of

(1) carnivores
(2) herbivores
(3) decomposers
(4) other plants
(5) the environment

① ② ③ ④ ⑤

4. Which of the following conclusions is supported by evidence in the diagram and passage?

(1) A severe drought would have no effect on decomposers.
(2) A long-lasting chemical pesticide, if eaten by a mouse, could harm an owl.
(3) If the grasshopper population decreased, the snake population would increase.
(4) Decomposers aid plants but harm plant-eaters.
(5) Herbivores are not a necessary part of a food web.

① ② ③ ④ ⑤

Check your answers and record your score on page 107.

Answers: On the Springboard

1 The Human Body: Input and Output
Understanding the Vocabulary of Science

Using Context Clues
(page 33)

1. (2) The word *renal* refers to the kidneys. A context clue appears in the passage: the first sentence begins, "Kidney failure. . . ." Then the next sentence begins, "Renal failure may also occur. . . ." The similar structure of these two sentences is a clue that kidney failure is the same as renal failure.

2. (2) A word-part clue can help you figure out the meaning of *transplant*. The word part *trans-* means "from one to another." So in the context of the passage, *transplant* means "to move an organ from one person's body to another."

2 The Human Body: Control and Movement
Restating Information
(page 40)

1. (1) The specific information you need to answer this question is found in the second and third sentences.

2. (2) Option (2) gives the same information as the last two sentences in the paragraph, without adding or omitting any details.

3 Cells
Finding the Main Idea
(page 44)

1. (3) The single most important idea contained in the paragraph is found in the first sentence. The appearance of a plant tells you whether its cells have enough water.

Seeing Patterns of Details
(page 46)

2. (1) The information contrasts, or shows the difference between, normal *round* red blood cells and *sickle-shaped* red blood cells. The difference is in their shapes.

3. (3) This answer restates the information in the last two sentences: sickle cells get caught in the very small blood vessels, causing poor circulation.

4 Cell Activities
Inferring the Main Idea

Topic + Details → Main Idea
(page 53)

1. (3) *Each* paragraph in the passage tells something about a substance diffusing through a cell membrane, so diffusion is the topic.

2. (3) The first paragraph discusses diffusion in general terms. The second paragraph tells how a needed substance diffuses into a cell. The third paragraph tells how a substance diffuses out of a cell. The last paragraph tells how water does both. Option (3) best summarizes all those ideas.

5 Genetics
Seeing Relationships Between Ideas
(page 60)

1. (3) The cloned offspring has exactly the same genetic makeup as its parent; its genes are identical. That is how it is similar.

2. (2) The diagram gives you the answer to this time-order relationship. The second drawing shows the leaf cutting placed in water. The third shows the cutting has grown roots.

Understanding Cause-and-Effect Relationships
(page 62)

3. (2) This reason is given in the explanation after the diagram. Reread the sentence beginning with, "Since sperm with X and Y chromosomes . . . "

6 The Variety of Life
Classifying
(pages 68–69)

1. (3) The cells are twice their normal size and splitting. Those are the characteristics of a cell dividing.

2. (1) This item describes what can be seen after a spore sac has burst open, sending tiny spores all over the ground.

7 Plants
Recognizing Conclusions
(page 74)

1. (2) The passage states that after their research the scientists concluded that it is possible to grow chlorella and that it has food value.

2. (1) The very last line of the passage states this conclusion. The author doesn't give you a clue with a word or phrase such as "I conclude." You must realize that she is drawing a conclusion. Option (2) is an opinion that the author may or may not hold. Option (3) states a fact given in the passage.

3. (3) The author concluded that people would not eat chlorella if given a choice. She reached that conclusion based on the fact that Japanese consumers did not choose to eat it.

Drawing Your Own Conclusions
(pages 76–77)

4. (1) For the seeds to be picked up and blown southeast, the wind would need to blow from the northwest.

5. (1) The fossils show that redwoods once existed across North America and northern Europe.

8 Lower Animals
Distinguishing Facts from Opinions
(page 82)

1. (2) Statements A, C, and E are all capable of being tested and proved; they are facts.

Distinguishing Facts from Hypotheses
(page 84)

2. (1) Notice that options (2) and (3) are facts observed by the research team before and during their experiment. They are evidence that helps support the hypothesis.

9 Higher Animals
Recognizing Assumptions
Detecting Stated Assumptions
(page 89)

1. (3) The assumption is stated in the first sentence of the passage.

2. (2) The information needed to answer this item is found in the second paragraph of the passage.

Identifying Unstated Assumptions
(pages 90–91)

3. (1) It is reasonable to assume that wildlife officials do not find every wild skunk and raccoon in a county to check it for rabies. The figures in the chart represent the animals that *were* caught and examined, possibly only a small portion of the actual population.

4. (1) The author assumes that most people think gorillas are fierce or frightening. That assumption is implied because she details gentle characteristics and then says, "It will most likely surprise you. . . ."

10 Animal Behavior
Assessing Supporting Data
(page 96)

1. (3) Only option (3) describes a way in which one bee shares information, or communicates, with others.

2. (3) To reproduce a dolphin's sounds, the scientist would need to take into account A. To be certain that the dolphin in the tank could hear the sounds, he would also need to take into account B. The dolphin can't react to sounds it cannot hear.

11 Relationships
Faulty Logic
(page 101)

1. (2) The plan behind the experiment is to collect particles from the air in the sticky surface of petroleum jelly. If the slides were placed in sheltered spots, where no or few particles could reach them, the slides would not give an accurate idea of how much matter was in the air.

Answers: "The Real Thing"

As you check your answers, you may notice that some question numbers are in color. This shows that those questions pertain to the skill taught in the lesson. The skill in each lesson is labeled with a heading that is in color. You'll probably want to go back and review the skills you had difficulty with before you complete the lessons in this section.

1 The Human Body: Input and Output

Understanding the Vocabulary of Science

Using Context Clues
(page 33)

1. (3) A context clue in the passage will help you select the correct answer. The second and third sentences mention that heart attacks occur when vessels are clogged and are not able to bring blood to the heart. This suggests that vessels must be tubes that conduct blood.

2. (4) *Sebaceous* means "made of or like fat." The third sentence gives a short definition of *sebaceous*: "such fatty deposits."

KEEPING TRACK
Top Score = 2

Your Score = ☐

2 The Human Body: Control and Movement

Restating Information
(pages 40–41)

1. (5) This answer restates information from the first two sentences of the second paragraph.

2. (2) The information needed to answer this question is in the final sentence of the passage.

KEEPING TRACK
Top Score = 2

Your Score = ☐

3 Cells

Seeing Patterns of Details
(pages 46–47)

1. (1) If you understand the way the information was written, understanding the answer to this question is easier. Cells are classified as being simple or complex. Simple cells, described first, have no nucleus. Complex cells, described last, do.

2. (4) The first paragraph compares plant and animal cells by listing the structures that they have in common.

3. (5) The second paragraph tells how plant and animal cells differ. It begins by pointing out that plant cells have a cell wall.

KEEPING TRACK
Top Score = 3

Your Score = ☐

4 Cell Activities

Inferring the Main Idea

Topic + Details → Main Idea
(pages 54–55)

1. (4) Each of the other options is true, but they are all supporting details from the chart that should be taken into account to produce the summary statement found in option (4). Reading the title of the chart should help you see that.

2. (3) This option takes into account the main idea of the first paragraph (that yeast cells are similar to human cells) and the main idea of the second paragraph (that yeast is good to use in research).

3. (5) Knowing that the first paragraph compared yeast with human cells could have led you back to this answer. Notice the sentence that begins, "Its 17 pairs of chromosomes behave remarkably like our 23 pairs. . . ."

4. (2) Combine and restate the meaning of the third and fourth sentences of the last paragraph, and you have this answer.

KEEPING TRACK
Top Score = 4

Your Score = ☐

5 Genetics

Understanding Cause-and-Effect Relationships
(pages 62–63)

1. (1) The effect of increased industry in England was that soot from factories darkened tree trunks and rocks.

2. (5) The last sentence of the first paragraph and the first sentence of the second paragraph help explain this cause-and-effect relationship. The black moths could not be so easily seen on the blackened trees, so fewer birds could see and eat them. More survived to produce offspring.

3. (2) The moths' shift from lighter to darker coloring is called industrial melanism. It occurred because the change in environment allowed darker moths to remain hidden from predators, while lighter moths were more easily seen and eaten.

KEEPING TRACK
Top Score = 3

Your Score = ☐

6 The Variety of Life Classifying
(page 69)

1. (5) The type of protist that is carried about by another organism's bloodstream is the sporozoan.

2. (3) The type of protist that moves about through the use of fine hairs or whiskers is called a ciliate.

3. (4) Protists that are flexible enough to extend their bodies to help move and even surround food are sarcodines.

KEEPING TRACK
Top Score = 3

Your Score = ☐

7 Plants Recognizing Conclusions
(pages 74–75)

1. (2) After considering the evidence of Linnaeus and de Mairan, the author concludes that plants must have a built-in timing mechanism.

2. (2) Linnaeus planted species that bloomed at 6 A.M. in one section of his garden, those that bloomed at 7 A.M. in the next section, and so on, around the clock. At any hour of the day, he could see which variety had bloomed most recently and discover from that what hour of the day it was.

3. (4) The term *biological rhythm* describes an event that naturally occurs at regular intervals. In northern climates, deciduous trees lose their leaves each year during autumn.

4. (3) According to the article, many studies similar to de Mairan's have yielded the same results. If an experiment can be repeated many times by different researchers, it is accepted as part of the body of scientific knowledge.

Drawing Your Own Conclusions
(pages 77–78)

5. (5) The evidence shows that the bee's body is perfectly shaped to obtain the clover's nectar, while the flower's design assures that the bee will pollinate it. Each seems to fit the other.

6. (1) The passage describes how one flower's pollen grains are likely to fall onto the bee's head and be carried to the next flower. There, they brush up against the stigma of the other flower. In other words, the bee is pollinating one flower with the pollen of another flower rather than its own.

7. (3) The bumblebee pollinates the clover flower. That allows the clover to reproduce. If there were no bees to pollinate the clover, there would be fewer plants.

8. (1) Since no light is present, and the tube is not touching either the roots or the stem, they must be responding to gravity. And since the stems grow *up* and the roots grow *down*, the two parts of the plant are responding differently.

KEEPING TRACK
Top Score = 8

Your Score = ☐

8 Lower Animals Distinguishing Facts from Opinions
(page 82)

1. (4) Statements A, B, and D could all be proved true by means of observing, experimenting, or consulting an authority. The other options state personal opinions.

2. (2) Option (2) is based on individual opinion because value is a personal judgment. Note that option (5), which appears to be based on opinion, actually states the *fact* that many people enjoy crayfish.

3. (5) Crayfish come out at night, so night would be the best time to find them. They live in rivers or lakes. They often burrow under rocks.

Distinguising Facts from Hypotheses
(pages 84–85)

4. (4) A hypothesis is a possible explanation for something. In the second paragraph you'll find the statement "These plates could have been an efficient system for releasing the excess body heat . . . ."

5. (1) The passage mentions that the short, extended legs of reptiles are not well suited for speed. The dinosaurs' long, upright legs may have been much better suited for speed.

6. (2) Option (2) gives a possible explanation for a scientific problem, so it is a hypothesis. The other options either are facts or they are statements contradicted in the passage.

KEEPING TRACK
Top Score = 6

Your Score = ☐

9 Higher Animals
Recognizing Assumptions
Identifying Unstated Assumptions
(pages 91–92)

1. (4) If you study the chart carefully, you'll see that the one distinguishing feature that separates one type of mammal from another is the "special trait"—the way the young are born. You have to assume that the scientist will use that characteristic to classify the mammal.

2. (4) The passage tells how, by the time machine-produced felt became available, the beaver population was "devastated"; only small populations existed. To say a machine saved the beaver is to assume that the beaver would have continued to be hunted if the machine hadn't been invented.

3. (1) Up until felt hats were available, beaver hats were considered fashionable. Machines that could make felt hats led to a change in fashion. In other words, many people stopped wearing beaver hats and began wearing felt hats.

4. (2) The final sentence in the passage suggests that it is a beaver's nature to make dams that will stop running water.

5. (3) A beaver dam might prevent the farmer from irrigating the land by stopping the flow of water from upstream.

KEEPING TRACK
Top Score = 5
Your Score = ☐

10 Animal Behavior
Assessing Supporting Data
(pages 96–97)

1. (4) All salmon perform this almost ritual act of migrating a long distance. It cannot be learned because the parents have died when the young salmon swim back to the ocean and then return as adults. The complex behavior of migration must be instinctive, then.

2. (2) Statement A shows that coyotes can learn, and statement B reveals instinctive behavior.

3. (3) Option (3) is the only one that gives an example of wasps working and living together. Such behavior is social.

4. (2) Many animals learn by imitating the actions of others. In this case, the eaglet is learning how to get food by watching its father and then imitating him.

KEEPING TRACK
Top Score = 4
Your Score = ☐

11 Relationships
Faulty Logic
(page 102)

1. (3) If the settlers had realized that the starling had few natural enemies on the continent, they would have realized that its numbers would probably grow too large. That situation has occurred because they didn't consider all the information they should have.

2. (5) Since carnivores depend on herbivores for food, an event that endangered the plant-eating animals would affect the meat-eaters, too.

3. (3) Decomposers such as bacteria and fungi break down the bodies of dead animals into nutrients that can be used by plants.

4. (2) When an owl eats a mouse, any chemical that is in the mouse's body enters the owl's body. If another animal killed and ate the owl, the pesticide would remain in its body, and so on through the food chain.

KEEPING TRACK
Top Score = 4
Your Score = ☐

Keeping Track

Now enter all your scores from the Keeping Track boxes on the lines below. Compare your scores with the top scores for the lessons.

Lesson	Top Score	Your Score
Lesson 1 Understanding the Vocabulary of Science	2	______
Lesson 2 Restating Information	2	______
Lesson 3 Seeing Patterns of Details	3	______
Lesson 4 Inferring the Main Idea	4	______
Lesson 5 Understanding Cause-and-Effect Relationships	3	______
Lesson 6 Classifying	3	______
Lesson 7 Conclusions	8	______
Lesson 8 Distinguishing Facts from Opinions and Hypotheses	6	______
Lesson 9 Recognizing Assumptions	5	______
Lesson 10 Assessing Supporting Data	4	______
Lesson 11 Faulty Logic	4	______
TOTAL	44	______

In which of the lessons did you get a top score? Are there any that you didn't do so well in? If so, now is your chance to review those lessons. Then you can sharpen your skills with the Extra Practice in Biology that follows.

Extra Practice in Biology

Directions: Choose the one best answer for each item.

Items 1–5 refer to the following article.

Any exercise that requires the use of many muscles continuously over a period of time can be used to increase the amount of oxygen available to the body's cells. Such exercise is considered aerobic. However, human muscles, like certain kinds of bacteria, can also work without oxygen, at least for a minute or two. This can happen when, for example, a runner is in a long race.

At the beginning of the race, the runner's muscle cells are using the available oxygen to produce energy. Despite the runner's increased breathing and heart rate, however, oxygen sometimes cannot be transported fast enough to meet all the muscle cells' needs. The cells begin to break down the simple sugar called glucose anaerobically, or without oxygen. Energy is still produced, but so is lactic acid, which is harmful to cells.

If allowed to build up, lactic acid interferes with the functioning of the muscles. The muscle cramps felt by the runner (or anyone who exercises too hard or too long) are a sign of excess lactic acid in the cells.

Once the muscle is allowed to rest, the lactic acid is carried away by the blood to the liver, where it is changed back to glucose. The runner's panting after the race helps speed this change because it increases the oxygen available for the process.

1. Which of the following recreational activities is an example of aerobic exercise?

   (1) bowling
   (2) golfing
   (3) bird watching
   (4) swimming
   (5) motorcycling

   (1) (2) (3) (4) (5)

2. On a wintry day, a cross-country skier is following a long trail. About halfway along the trail, he begins to feel cramping in both legs. To avoid further pain and cramping, he should

   (1) remove his jacket and boots to cool off
   (2) apply warm, moist cloths on his legs
   (3) stop and rest for a while
   (4) exercise his leg muscles
   (5) eat food that contains large amounts of protein

   (1) (2) (3) (4) (5)

3. Which of the following statements could not be tested scientifically?

   (1) the liver changes lactic acid to glucose.
   (2) Skiing is more rewarding exercise than running.
   (3) Muscles can function without oxygen.
   (4) Panting is a way of getting oxygen.
   (5) Many people think aerobic exercise is beneficial.

   (1) (2) (3) (4) (5)

4. Human cells function anaerobically when

   (1) lactic acid builds up
   (2) breathing and the heart rate increase
   (3) a lack of available oxygen exists
   (4) bacteria are present
   (5) the muscles are given rest

   (1) (2) (3) (4) (5)

5. Which of the following conclusions is supported by evidence in the article?

   (1) Aerobic exercises are more valuable than any other kind of exercise.
   (2) Some bacteria are structured very much like human muscle cells.
   (3) Running is harmful to many muscle cells.
   (4) Running is a good way to build up muscle strength.
   (5) Long-distance swimming makes oxygen available to body cells.

   (1) (2) (3) (4) (5)

6. Homeostasis is a state of balance. Every living thing tries to achieve homeostasis by regulating its processes. To achieve homeostasis, a cell that has taken in food would also need to do which of the following?

(1) use less energy
(2) take in still more food
(3) stop its other functions
(4) release waste materials
(5) divide into two cells

1 2 3 4 5

Items 7–9 are based on the chart below.

Kingdom	Characteristics
Monerans	Most are simple, one-celled organisms Some produce own food; others take it from outside sources
Protists	One-celled organisms More complex cell structure than monerans Some produce own food; others take it from outside sources
Fungi	Most made up of many cells Obtain food by absorbing it from living or dead plants and animals Cannot move about
Plants	Made up of many cells Have specialized cells for different tasks Can produce own food Cannot move about
Animals	Made up of many cells Have specialized cells for different purposes Most can move themselves about Obtain food from outside sources (ultimately, plants)

7. According to the chart, which of the following characteristics distinguishes fungi from plants?

(1) number of cells
(2) complexity of cells
(3) ability to move about
(4) method of getting food
(5) size

1 2 3 4 5

8. Foraminiferans are organisms with one complex cell. They surround themselves with a hard shell of lime. The shell has tiny holes in it. Through these holes the organism can extend "false feet" to move itself about.

In which kingdom do foraminiferans belong?

(1) monerans
(2) protists
(3) fungi
(4) plants
(5) animals

1 2 3 4 5

9. Monerans, protists, and plants could each survive in a world without animals, but animals and fungi could not survive in a world by themselves.

Which of the following statements would justify this conclusion, given the information provided?

(1) Animals and fungi must depend on food from other sources.
(2) Fungi and some animals cannot move about.
(3) Many-celled organisms require single-celled organisms to live.
(4) The cells of fungi and animals are susceptible to disease.
(5) The intelligence of animals has enabled them to find uses for fungi.

1 2 3 4 5

Items 10–12 refer to the following diagram and article.

Flu Virus Infection

Virus attaches to a lung or throat cell
Virus enters cell
Viruses enter nose or mouth
Virus takes over cell's metabolism
New viruses form and spread to other cells

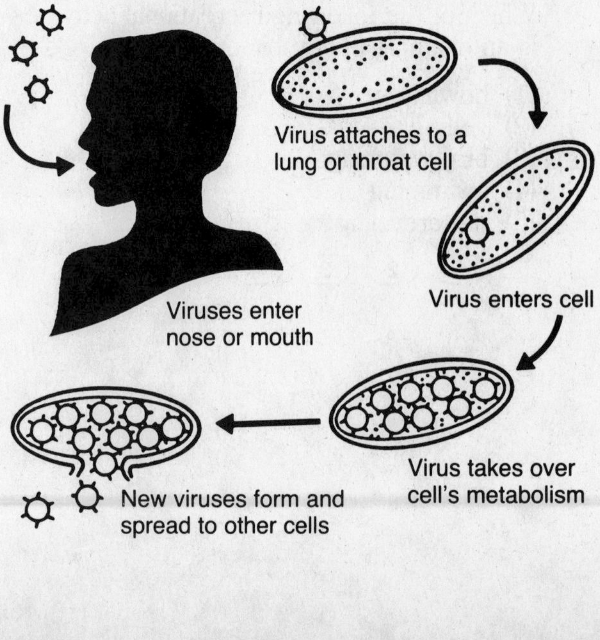

Viruses are not cells and are not made of cells. Scientists do not even consider them living organisms because by themselves viruses do not reproduce, respond to changes, use energy, or grow. However, when a virus enters a living host cell, the virus is able to reproduce. It uses the host's cell parts to reproduce itself.

When a person infected with the flu virus sneezes, coughs, or breathes, for example, viruses from that person may spread to another. A cell of the second person then becomes a host cell to the flu virus.

After thousands of flu viruses have formed within a host cell, it often dies. The new flu viruses spread and invade other cells. As the process continues, over and over again, many throat and lung cells are destroyed. The infected person then begins to feel ill.

Different viruses attack different parts of the body. Chicken pox and measles viruses attack cells of the skin, for example. Cold viruses invade cells that line the nose and throat.

10. Based on information in the passage and the diagram, the flu virus could enter the body in all of the following ways except

(1) eating food that has been prepared by a person who is beginning to feel sick with flu
(2) breathing after an infected person has just coughed or sneezed nearby
(3) absorbing the virus through the skin after shaking hands with someone infected with flu
(4) receiving dental treatment from someone who is infected with the flu virus
(5) putting hands to the mouth after having touched the mouth of a flu patient

① ② ③ ④ ⑤

11. In the early 1980s, the practice of vaccinating children against the viral disease of smallpox ended. Which of the following would justify this change in policy?

(1) Children do not like to be vaccinated.
(2) People are now more concerned about other illnesses, such as cancer.
(3) The World Health Organization found that there have been no cases of smallpox for many years.
(4) The vaccine caused illness in a very small number of cases.
(5) Some people were unable to pay for the vaccine.

① ② ③ ④ ⑤

12. Penicillin and other antibiotics cure illnesses by killing bacteria. Why are antibiotics useless for treating viral diseases?

(1) A virus takes over its host's cell metabolism.
(2) Viruses cannot be killed because they do not have the life processes that bacteria do.
(3) Flu viruses can kill living cells.
(4) Antibiotics cannot cure skin diseases or nose and throat ailments.
(5) Viral diseases are spread too easily from one person to another.

① ② ③ ④ ⑤

Item 13 refers to the following paragraph.

A scientist set up an experiment to see what happens when plant leaves cannot obtain carbon dioxide from the air. He covered some of the leaves of a healthy house plant with a thick oil and left the other leaves uncovered. He then placed the plant in a warm, well-lighted spot and gave it water and nutrients. After several days, the covered leaves darkened, wilted, and dropped off. The uncovered leaves remained healthy.

13. Which of the following would most likely cause the greatest amount of error in an experiment like the one above?

(1) selecting a plant with broad, pointed leaves
(2) covering the leaves on one side of the plant but not the other
(3) placing the plant in a plastic pot
(4) neglecting to use a plant with more than one stem
(5) failing to cover the bottoms of the test leaves

① ② ③ ④ ⑤

Items 14–18 are based on the information given below.

Every living thing depends on some living and nonliving things around it. The branch of science called ecology deals with the different ways in which living things relate to their surroundings. Below are listed five different groupings that ecologists study.

(1) population = all the organisms of one kind that live together in a certain area

(2) community = a group of populations that live in the same area and depend on each other for food

(3) ecosystem = a distinct community of species and the nonliving environment with which the community interacts

(4) biome = a large group of ecosystems with similar types of climate and communities

(5) biosphere = all communities on earth taken as a whole

Each of the following items describes an example that fits one of the five ecological categories listed above. For each item, choose the one category that best applies to the example. Each of the categories above may be used more than once in the following set.

14. In a laboratory's aquarium, rocks and sand anchor the plants and provide homes for the fish. The workers in the laboratory keep the rocks and sand clean so that they will not collect dead plant material and wastes from the fish. If allowed to accumulate, these wastes would eventually cause diseases and upset the balance of the aquarium.

    The aquarium is an example of

    (1) a population (2) a community
    (3) an ecosystem (4) a biome
    (5) a biosphere

    ① ② ③ ④ ⑤

15. Lemmings, a species of small mammals that live in the Arctic, appear to follow a three- or four-year cycle. Each year they increase steadily in number until they reach a peak. Then they experience a sharp decrease in number, only to repeat the same pattern.

    Lemmings are an example of

    (1) a population (2) a community
    (3) an ecosystem (4) a biome
    (5) a biosphere

    ① ② ③ ④ ⑤

16. Some scientists have reported that the earth is experiencing a gradual warming trend. This warming trend, ecologists warn, could eventually affect all living things above and below the earth's surface as well as those on the surface.

    The group of living things that will be affected are an example of

    (1) a population (2) a community
    (3) an ecosystem (4) a biome
    (5) a biosphere

    ① ② ③ ④ ⑤

17. In general, deserts receive less than twenty-five centimeters of rainfall each year. Plants and animals of the desert must be able to survive the dry, harsh climate.

    Deserts are one example of

    (1) a population (2) a community
    (3) an ecosystem (4) a biome
    (5) a biosphere

    ① ② ③ ④ ⑤

18. The animals and plants that live near the shore of a forest preserve's pond interact with one another in many ways. Some of the animals depend on fish for food. The fish, in turn, depend on small water plants for their food.

    The animals and plants in the pond are an example of

    (1) a population (2) a community
    (3) an ecosystem (4) a biome
    (5) a biosphere

Answers to Extra Practice in Biology begin on page 231. Record your score on the Progress Chart on the inside back cover.

Earth Science

"The forecast for today is cool and mostly sunny, with a slight chance for an afternoon shower." If you're like many people, you watch or listen to a weather report almost every day. Weather is one aspect of life on earth that affects everyone. And because it *is* an aspect of life on earth, weather is studied by earth scientists.

Weather isn't the only area of earth science that relates to people's everyday lives. The climate you live in, for example, affects the clothes you buy, the jobs you can have, even the food you eat. Some aspects of earth science may seem a little obscure and distant from you. The slow changes of the continents drifting and the mountains eroding are certainly not evident to most of us, yet the sudden and violent changes of earthquakes and volcanoes are. The formation of oil on the earth beginning millions of years ago may not seem particularly important, but its price at the gas pump or high heating bills are of concern to almost everyone.

Earth science on the GED Science Test deals with both the practical aspects as well as the more general concerns of this field of science. About one-fourth of the items will deal with earth science topics.

As with biology, you won't need to know dozens of facts about the earth to answer the earth science items. Instead, you'll need to read scientific information and work with it. Some items on the test will give you a little information and then ask you a question about it. Here is such a test item.

Scientists try to produce rain in dry areas using a method called cloud seeding. They spray chemicals into clouds that cause the moisture in the clouds to condense and fall as precipitation. In order for cloud seeding to succeed, which of the following factors must be assumed?

(1) The area must be excessively dry.
(2) The air must be warmer than the land.
(3) There must already be enough moisture to fall as rain.
(4) The wind must be gusting.
(5) There must be rivers and lakes to catch the falling rain.

(1) (2) (3) (4) (5)

All the information you need to answer that question is given to you; you need only read and think about it. Since cloud seeding does not actually produce moisture—it just makes it condense and fall—there must already be moisture present in the sky for cloud seeding to succeed. If you chose option (3) as the answer, you found an unstated assumption in an earth science test item without knowing all there is to know about earth science.

Many questions on the GED Science Test will be based on a longer written article or on a visual such as a diagram or table. Sometimes the visual will be accompanied by an explanation. Look at the example below.

Energy Use in the United States

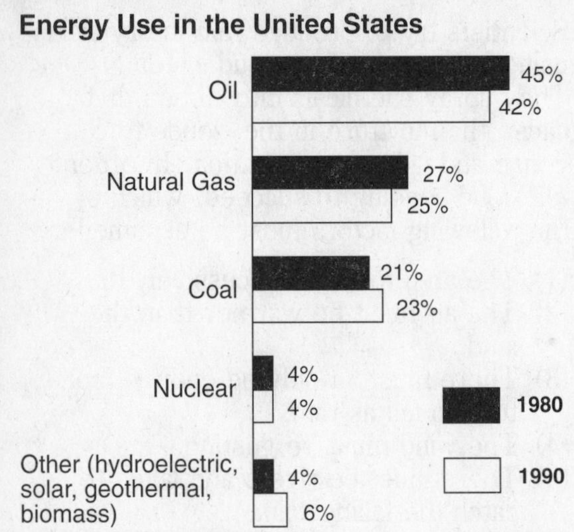

Four factors help determine which energy source or sources are used. The first is availability, which directly affects the cost. Location is the second factor. As an example, solar power would not be practical in the northwestern United States, where a cloud cover is common. Third, the effect on the environment must be considered. Certain energy sources polute or produce dangerous wastes. Fourth, use is a factor. Some sources are practical only for certain uses; for example, powering cars with nuclear fuel would be impractical.

The paragraph below the graph gives added information that can be used to answer questions. At the top of the next column is an example of the kind of question that could be asked about that material on the GED Science Test.

Oil use remained about the same between 1980 and 1990. Economists, however, had thought it would decrease. In which of the factors do you think economists expected a change?

(1) availability
(2) location
(3) effect on the environment
(4) tendency to pollute
(5) possible uses

You can use the information in the paragraph as well as your own practical knowledge to answer that question. The location, effect on the environment and tendency to pollute (which are actually one factor together), and possible uses for oil cannot really change. However, its availability can change. Therefore, the prediction must have been based on the expectation that oil would be less available in 1990 than it was in 1980. Since oil use actually changed very little, it is most likely that its availability also changed very little.

Now look at one more question related to the graph and paragraph.

In which area of the United States is it most likely that an increase in the use of solar power took place?

(1) the Northeast
(2) the Northwest
(3) the Midwest
(4) the Southwest
(5) Alaska

The paragraph explains that solar power is *not* practical in areas with cloudy weather. The graph indicates that the predicted increase in solar power (under the category "Other") will be quite small. With that information, you could reasonably guess that the warm, dry, sunny Southwest is the place most likely to begin using more solar power.

You can see that answering GED earth science questions demands good reading and thinking skills along with a practical knowledge of the world that you've gained as an adult. By reading the content and practicing the skills in the lessons that follow, you'll become more comfortable and skillful with both.

LESSON 12
The Universe

You live in the space age. Newspapers, magazines, and TV reports remind you of this frequently. Scientists are constantly making new discoveries about the universe—the parts of space that we know about and the parts that we can only imagine. The first section of this lesson explores our solar system—the sun, planets, and other heavenly bodies that are closest to us. Before you begin to read, look over the Warm-up activity for clues to important information in the section.

The Solar System

Imagine a huge cloud of gas and dust spinning in space. Scientists think that our solar system formed billions of years ago from just such a cloud. As the swirling cloud spun around, it gained speed and eventually took the shape of a large pancake. The force of **gravity** pulled some of the bits together into small clumps. The largest clump formed our sun; the smaller clumps became the nine planets.

The sun is a star made up of hydrogen and helium gases. These gases burn and produce huge amounts of energy that spread through the solar system. Energy from the sun reaches Earth and other planets in the form of heat and light.

The sun is the center of the solar system. All nine planets revolve around, or travel around, the sun in oval-shaped paths called **orbits.** Mercury, Venus, Earth, and Mars are closest to the sun. They receive more energy from the sun than the other planets do.

You may have seen Mercury low in the sky just before sunrise or for a short time after sunset. Because it is closest to the sun, Mercury is very hot. Its surface has many craters and cliffs. Venus is the next planet out from the sun and Earth's closest neighboring planet. Venus, too, is very hot. A thick layer of clouds surrounds it.

Earth is the third planet closest to the sun. You are familiar, of course, with Earth's moon. The moon is a natural satellite, a body that revolves around another body in space. Gravity holds the moon in its orbit around the earth. Mars, the other planet closest to Earth, is called the red planet. It looks reddish in the night sky. Mars is cooler than Earth and has many canyons and volcanoes.

The remaining five planets are much farther from the sun and from Earth as well. Take a moment to find them in the illustration of the solar system.

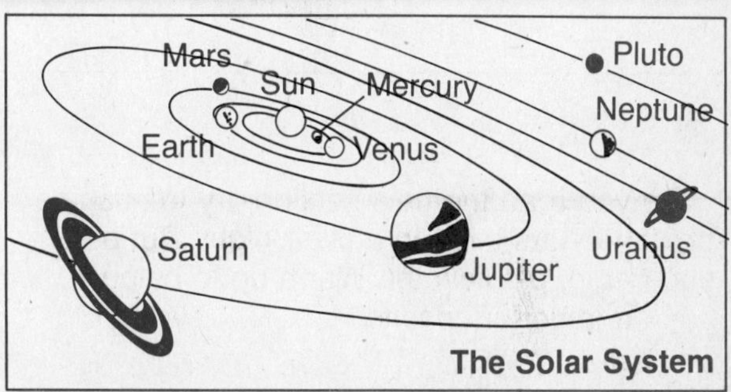

The Solar System

Some of the five outer planets have moons. Jupiter, the largest of all nine planets, has sixteen moons. Rings surround Uranus and Saturn. Pluto, the smallest planet, is also the farthest out. Unmanned U.S. spacecraft missions have increased our knowledge of all the planets, but much remains to be learned. Scientists would also like to know more about the **asteroids,** small rocky objects that orbit the sun in addition to the planets. Most asteroids are located in orbits between those of Mars and Jupiter.

Coming to Terms

gravity the natural force that attracts two bodies to each other because of their mass

orbit a fixed path in which one object travels around another.

asteroid a small rocky object that orbits the sun as the planets do.

Warm-up

Answer each question in a sentence or two of your own.

1. How are the planets of the solar system related to the sun?

____

____

____

2. How does the sun produce energy?

____

____

As you read the next section, try to imagine how the stars look on a clear night. But before you begin, preview the Warm-up to help you focus on important points.

Stars, Galaxies, and Quasars

"Twinkle, twinkle, Little Star
How I wonder what you are."

People have always watched and wondered about the stars. Recent technology has helped us answer many of the questions that people once only wondered about.

Stars are born, mature, and die in regular life cycles. A star forms when gravity pulls gas and dust particles in space together. As the particles come together, they begin to move faster and faster in all directions, and the gas heats up. The heat and motion cause energy to build up. Then the star gives off waves of energy called **radiant energy.** Stars shine because of the energy built up inside them. Remember from the last section that the sun is a star that formed in this way and gives off radiant energy in the form of heat and light.

The stars you see at night are much farther away from us than the sun. Great distances called **light-years** separate the earth from these stars. A light-year is the distance light can travel in one year, which equals about 5.8 trillion miles.

When you look up at the stars directly overhead, you see individual stars. But each star is actually part of a mass of stars. Each mass of stars is a **galaxy,** a group of billions of stars, gases, and dust. Some of these stars have planets revolving around them; they are the centers of other solar systems.

There are countless galaxies and groups of galaxies in the universe. We call our galaxy the Milky Way. The Milky Way is spiral shaped, like a pinwheel. Our solar system is near the outer edge of the Milky Way. Other galaxies have more unusual shapes than the Milky Way or no regular shape at all.

Scientists use telescopes, computers, and other advanced equipment to study the light reaching us from distant objects in the universe. They have found that light from an object moving toward the earth has a bluish tint. Light from an object moving away from the earth shifts slightly to a more reddish color. All distant galaxies show this red color shift. The more distant a galaxy is, the redder its shift is. Based on this evidence, scientists believe that the universe is expanding. The objects in it are moving away from each other.

Quasars are incredibly distant objects in space that have the largest red color shifts. Quasars look like stars but give off enormous amounts of energy in the form of light and radio waves. Scientists think that quasars may actually be galaxies in early stages of development. The light from them that is reaching the earth today left the quasars billions of years ago; we are seeing the light sources—the quasars—as they looked billions of years ago.

Coming to Terms

radiant energy energy that travels through space in waves

light-year the distance light travels in one year

galaxy a group of billions of stars, gases, and dust relatively close to each other in space

quasar a distant object in space with the largest known red color shift

Sample Warm-up Answers
1. The nine planets all revolve around the sun in orbits. They all receive heat and light energy from the sun. **2.** Hydrogen and helium in the sun burn and release huge amounts of energy.

Warm-up

Write a sentence to answer each question.

1. Where is our solar system located in the universe?

____

____

2. What have the red color shifts in light from distant objects led scientists to believe?

____

____

Restating Information

When you can restate an idea clearly and correctly in your own words, you can be sure that you understand that idea. Remember that the restated information must always mean the same thing as what you have just read or seen or heard.

> ### ☑ A Test-Taking Tip
>
> When you take the GED Science Test, you will not have to restate information in your own words, but you will have to recognize information—in both questions and answers—that has been said in a different way from the original.

Here's an Example

The paragraph below gives some interesting information about stars. Read it carefully.

■ Stars appear to the human eye in different colors. Betelgeuse and Barnard's Star, for example, are red stars; our sun is yellow; Sirius, Vega, and Rigel are blue or bluish white. Actually, all stars emit every color of light in the spectrum, but the hottest stars emit more blue light, while cooler stars emit more light at the red end of the spectrum. The same effect is produced by heating an iron or a steel bar. As its temperature rises, the bar will change from red to orange, yellow, white, and then blue.

If someone asked you, "What makes some stars appear blue?" you could answer the question by restating part of the third sentence. Hotter stars give off more blue light than cooler stars, so very hot stars appear blue. That is a good restatement of information.

Sample Warm-up Answers
1. Our solar system is on the outer edge of the Milky Way galaxy. **2.** Scientists think the red color shifts mean that the universe is expanding, or spreading apart.

Try It Yourself

Read the following passage. Keep in mind that you'll be asked a question for which you'll need to restate information.

■ The sun can damage your eyes if you look at it directly. The intense radiation can burn a hole in the retina of the eye very quickly, resulting in a permanent blind spot. People are most tempted to look at the sun during eclipses. Knowledgeable people use cameras, special filters, or viewing boxes to observe the sun during an eclipse.

Now try to answer this question: Which can happen if you look at the sun directly during an eclipse—intense pain or partial blindness?

Those exact phrases are not used in the passage, but "resulting in a permanent blind spot" is. A person with a permanent blind spot is partially blind, so the answer to the question is partial blindness.

Now read the next passage and study the illustration that goes with it. Then see if you can restate two points of information:

1. What happens during a total eclipse of the sun?
2. What happens during a partial eclipse of the sun?

■ About once every 18 months, the moon comes directly between the earth and the sun. A total eclipse of the sun takes place when the moon completely blocks the sunlight from certain places on the earth. When this happens, the sky becomes almost as dark as night in the middle of the day. The darkness of a total eclipse can last a few seconds or for almost eight minutes. Before and after the total part of an eclipse, the moon blocks only portions of the sun's surface. These phases of an eclipse may last for several hours.

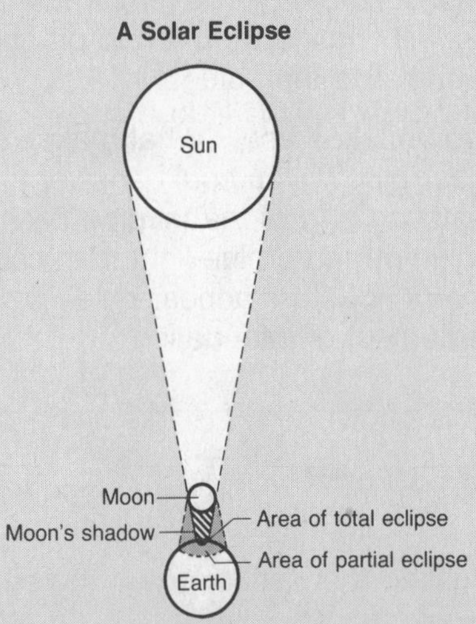

Did you find the illustration helpful in forming the restatements you were asked to make about total and partial eclipses of the sun? If so, your restatements might have read something like these: (1) During a total solar eclipse, the darkest part of the moon's shadow completely blocks a portion of the earth from the sun's light. (2) During a partial solar eclipse, lighter portions of the moon's shadow hide portions of the earth from only part of the sun's light.

On the Springboard

Item 1 refers to the following description of the planet Venus.

The temperature of the surface of Venus is 475°C. The weight of its atmosphere is one hundred times greater than that of Earth. Venus is covered with dense clouds of sulfuric acid that make its surface invisible to scientists on Earth. Carbon dioxide and other gases in Venus's atmosphere trap sunlight. This "greenhouse effect" makes the planet's surface extremely hot.

1. Which of the following statements best describes Venus?

   (1) Though hidden from view, Venus has many features similar to Earth.
   (2) Trapped sunlight spreads over the surface of Venus.
   (3) Because of its dense atmosphere and heavy cloud cover, Venus is hot.

Items 2–3 refer to the graph and paragraph below. You will be asked to identify restatements of information they contain.

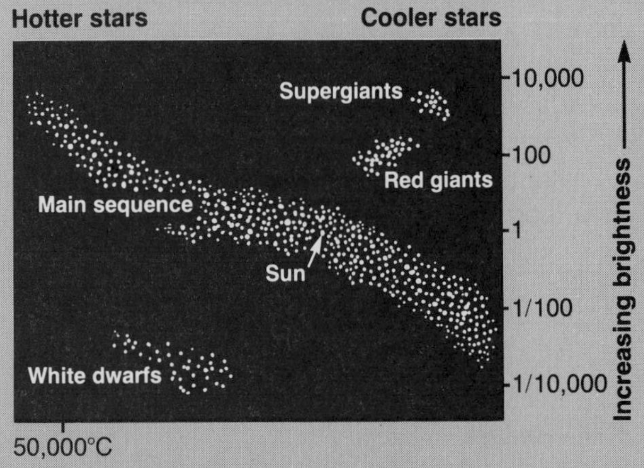

Scientists group stars by placing them on a graph like the one above. Most stars are in the main sequence. The sun is almost in the middle of the graph, among the main-sequence stars. The brightness of other stars on the graph can be compared with the sun's brightness, which has been set at 1, on the right-hand side of the graph. The surface temperature of the sun is about 5,500°C. The line below the graph shows how surface temperatures of other stars compare with the sun's.

2. How does the brightness of the sun compare with that of other stars?

   (1) The main sequence of stars hides the sun from view.
   (2) The brightness of the sun is much greater than that of red stars.
   (3) The sun is a star of about average brightness in the main sequence.

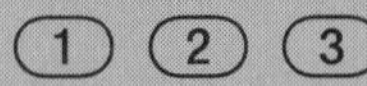

3. According to information given on the graph, which of the following statements is correct?

   (1) White dwarf stars are hotter and thus brighter than other stars.
   (2) Super giants are cool, bright stars.
   (3) Red giants are hotter than our sun.

☑ A Test-Taking Tip

Often a wrong option on the GED Science Test merely picks up words that were used somewhere in the passage. The people who write GED test questions know that poor or careless readers probably won't realize when information has been restated. Such test takers will pick an answer just because it uses words they recognize from the passage. Keep in mind that usually the right option will restate the information that answers the question; it won't use the exact words from the passage.

You can check your answers to the On the Springboard questions on page 155.

If you answered all three questions correctly, go on to "The Real Thing." If you had trouble, review this section on restating information before you go on.

“The Real Thing”

Items 1–2 refer to the passage below.

Sunspots are dark, relatively cool (4,500°C) areas on the sun's surface that are regions of intense magnetic activity. The number of sunspots increases and decreases at fairly regular intervals. Whenever the number of sunspots is highest, solar flares erupt on the sun's surface and shoot out particles and radiation that can reach the earth's atmosphere and interfere with radio transmissions and electrical power.

1. What happens when solar flares erupt on the surface of the sun?
   (1) The number of sunspots decreases.
   (2) Solar matter and radiation are sent into space.
   (3) Sunspots become cooler and smaller.
   (4) The sun becomes even hotter than normal.
   (5) The sun loses some of its magnetism.

   (1) (2) (3) (4) (5)

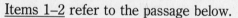

2. According to the passage, radio broadcasts are likely to be interrupted by static when
   (1) sunspots become cool
   (2) the sunspot cycle is at its highest
   (3) magnetic activity on the sun decreases
   (4) flares explode on the earth
   (5) the sun darkens

    (3)  

Item 3 refers to the diagram below.

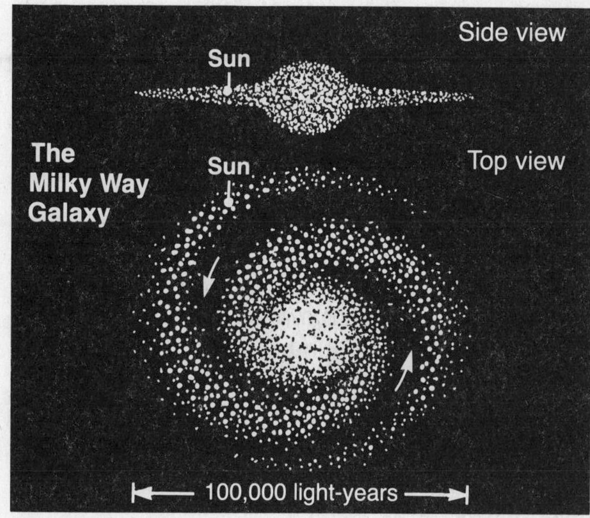

3. Which of the following statements best describes the Milky Way?
   (1) The Milky Way has two distinct groups of stars.
   (2) Stars in the Milky Way are an equal distance away from each other.
   (3) The star cluster at the center of the Milky Way is denser and brighter than any around the edges.
   (4) Stars at the edges of the Milky Way are spinning away from those in the center.
   (5) The Milky Way is a group of stars that revolve around the sun.

   (1) (2) (3) (4) (5)

Check your answers and record your score on page 156.

LESSON 13

The Earth

Most sections of the country experience four seasons. In the next section, you'll learn what the earth does that causes the changes in the seasons. Before you read, take a moment to glance at the Warm-up activity. It can help you pick out important information.

Tilt, Rotation, Revolution, and Seasons

You've read that the earth, like all planets, orbits the sun. The earth makes one complete orbit, or **revolution,** around the sun each year. Now imagine a straight line running through the earth from the North Pole to the South Pole. This imaginary line is the earth's **axis.** Look at the illustration to see how the earth tilts on its axis as it revolves around the sun.

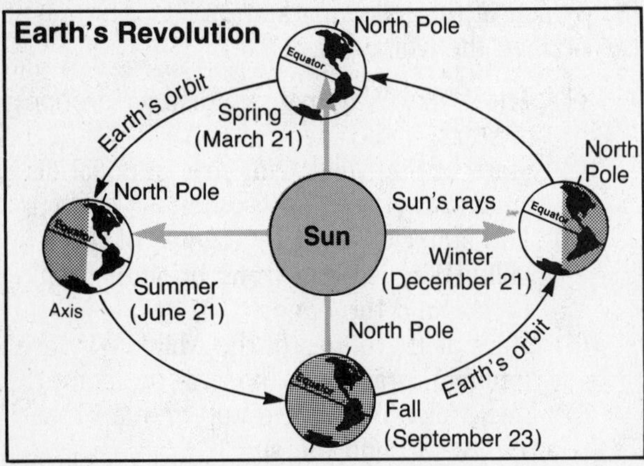

You live in the Northern Hemisphere, which is that portion of the earth between the equator and the North Pole. The earth's tilt on its axis combined with its location in its revolution causes the seasons.

Now look at the diagram to find the earth's location in its orbit on December 21, the first day of winter. Notice that the sun's rays—its radiant energy—are shining most directly south of the equator. The North Pole is pointed away from the sun. Winter comes to the Northern Hemisphere because only indirect rays from the sun reach it. Days are short, and temperatures are cool or cold. The first day of winter, the winter solstice, is the shortest day of the year.

Now follow the earth to its spring position. The North Pole is pointed neither toward the sun nor away from it. The sun's rays hit the equator most directly. More energy from the sun is beginning to reach the Northern Hemisphere, and temperatures are getting warmer. On what date does spring usually begin? On March 21—the spring equinox—all places on earth have twelve hours of sunlight and twelve hours of darkness.

Now notice what happens on June 21, the first day of summer—the summer solstice. The sun's rays hit the Northern Hemisphere directly, so more heat and light spread over this part of the earth. Summer days are longer than summer nights, and temperatures are generally the warmest of the year.

The earth's position in its revolution on September 23 marks the fall equinox. As on the spring equinox, the sun shines directly on the equator, and places all over the earth have twelve hours of daylight and darkness. Temperatures have begun to cool down in the Northern Hemisphere.

All the time the earth is revolving around the sun, it is also spinning around on its axis. It makes one complete turn about every twenty-four hours. This spinning is the earth's **rotation.** Rotation causes day and night. The side of the earth turned toward the sun has daylight; the side turned away from the sun has night, or darkness. You can understand that better by studying the diagram.

Coming to Terms

revolution The earth's revolution is the orbit that the earth makes around the sun every year—or every 365¼ days. Other planets revolve too.

axis The earth's axis is the imaginary line running through the center of the earth from the North Pole to the South Pole.

rotation The earth's rotation is the spinning of the earth on its axis. The earth makes one complete rotation about every twenty-four hours. Other planets rotate too.

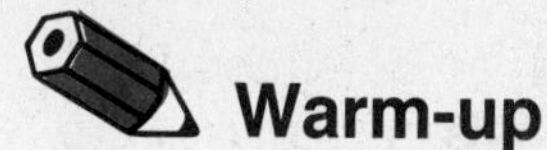

Warm-up

Write a brief paragraph describing why summer days are longer and warmer than winter days where you live. Mention the tilt of the earth's axis in your paragraph.

Have you ever used a compass in your car or on a camping trip? The next section will help you understand what makes a compass work. Glance at the Warm-up before you read to help you focus on important information.

Magnetism

To understand how a compass works, you need to know something about magnets. Magnets are objects that attract certain other objects by a force called **magnetism.** A magnet has two poles—a north pole and a south pole. The force of magnetism is strongest at a magnet's poles. The area around a magnet in which its force will act is its **magnetic field.**

Imagine that you have suspended a bar magnet on a string. Now suppose you place the north pole of another magnet near the north pole of the suspended magnet. The suspended magnet will turn away. But if you place the south pole of your magnet near the north pole of the suspended magnet, it will move toward your magnet. Poles of magnets that are like each other always repel; unlike poles attract.

If left unbothered, the suspended magnet will always point in the same direction. The reason is that the earth itself acts as a huge magnet. A compass is like the suspended magnet. Its free-spinning needle is actually a magnet. One end of the needle always swings to point toward the earth's magnetic north pole, located in the far north of the Northern Hemisphere.

The earth's magnetic north pole is not the same as the geographic North Pole. A compass needle, therefore, does not point *true* north, which is toward the North Pole. The two poles are close enough together on earth, however, to make a compass very helpful when you need to know general directions. Modern ships and airplanes use a kind of compass that doesn't depend on the earth's magnetism. This kind of compass does point true north. It is called a gyrocompass.

Earth's Magnetic Field

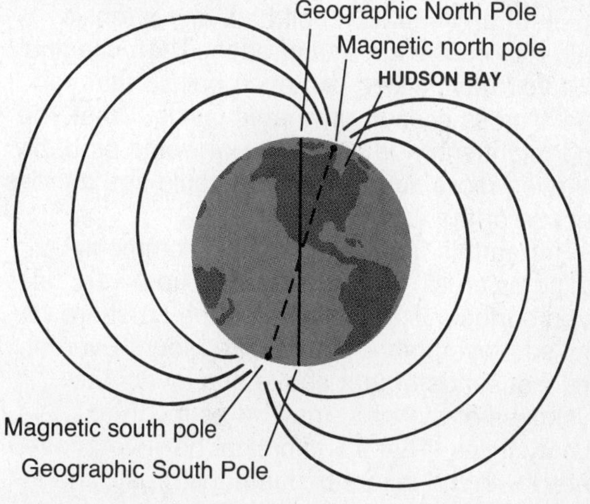

Coming to Terms

magnetism a force by which an object attracts certain other objects. Objects that exert this force are magnets.

magnetic field the area surrounding a magnet in which other magnetic materials are attracted or repelled

---

Sample Warm-up Answer
During the summer, the North Pole tilts toward the sun. The sun's rays shine more directly on the Northern Hemisphere. They bring more heat and light than during the winter.

Warm-up

Write your answers to the following questions in a sentence or two.

1. What rule of magnetism explains why two bar magnets will snap together if you place the south pole of one near the north pole of the other?

____

____

2. What is the difference between true north and magnetic north?

____

____

In the next section, you'll take a look around the inside and the surface of the earth. Glance ahead to the Warm-up before you read. Keep the points it mentions in mind.

The Structure of the Earth

Think of a baseball, a golf ball, and a tennis ball. Picture the surface of each. Then imagine that you have sliced into each ball so that you see a cross section of what is inside. What you find might surprise you. But you would probably be even more surprised if you could see a cross section of the earth.

The earth's firm, outer shell is commonly called its crust. This crust makes up a very uneven surface. Some places on the crust are below sea level; other places, like Mount Everest, are thousands of feet above sea level. The thickness of the crust may be as much as twenty miles. That's a thin skin, however, compared with the layers beneath the crust. The inside layers average a thousand or more miles. Each layer gradually blends into the next.

The layer immediately under the crust is the mantle. The upper part of the mantle seems to be made up of melted materials on which the crust "floats." The lower part of the mantle is probably made up of rocks, ones much heavier than those found in the crust.

Just below the mantle is the outer core. Scientists think that the materials in this layer are hot and flowing. They may contain liquid iron, nickel, chromium, and some silicates. Scientists believe that the inner core is made of the same materials in a solid form.

Another way to look at the structure of the outer part of the earth is to divide it into air, water, and rock. The air that surrounds the earth is called the **atmosphere.** People live at the bottom of this ocean of air. Then there are the waters of the planet. All the water and ice on earth and the water vapor in the air make up the hydrosphere. Finally, there is the solid rock that makes up the earth's surface; this is the lithosphere. The lithosphere is the crust and part of the mantle.

The Earth's Structure

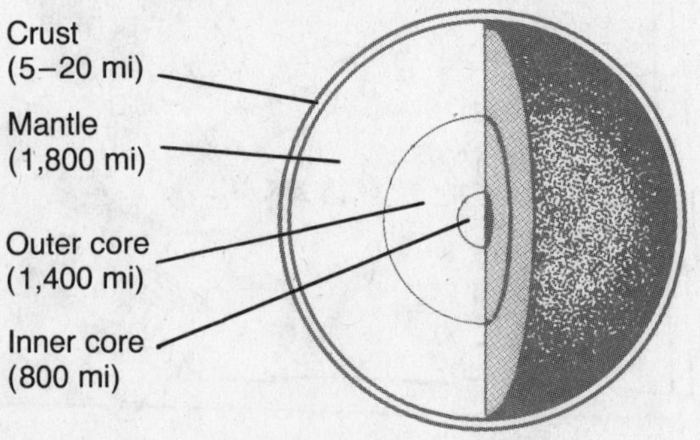

Coming to Terms

atmosphere the layer of air surrounding the earth

Warm-up

Answer each question in a complete sentence.

1. Is the Atlantic Ocean a part of the earth's atmosphere, hydrosphere, or lithosphere?

____

____

2. The structure of the earth includes four main parts. On which of these four parts do people live?

____

Sample Warm-up Answers
1. Like poles of magnets repel each other; unlike poles attract each other. **2.** True north is the direction toward the North Pole on the earth. Magnetic north is toward the earth's magnetic north pole.

Sample Warm-up Answers
1. The Atlantic Ocean belongs to the hydrosphere. **2.** People live on the earth's crust.

Inferring the Main Idea

You've already had some practice in the skill of inferring the main idea of biology material. In Lesson 4, you saw that an author sometimes presents a number of facts in a written article or even a visual without ever stating his or her main point directly. The main idea is only implied, or suggested. Remember that, as a reader, you can infer the main idea by examining the information you're given and then summarizing the point that it makes.

☑ A Test-Taking Tip

A good way to approach items that deal with main ideas on the GED Science Test is to decide how you would word the main idea or summarize the passage yourself. Then look at the choices you are given in the test item. Select the answer that is closest to your own. This method will help you avoid confusion between the best answer and those that may be only partially correct.

Here's an Example

The following passage tells you a number of facts about people and magnets.

■ Early people found that certain rocks were magnetic, or attracted to iron. When iron needles were rubbed on these rocks, they became magnetized and had poles that attracted or repelled one another. Because the earth is like a giant magnet, these needles pointed toward the earth's magnetic poles. Early travelers, especially sailors, used free-swinging magnets in compasses to find their way when stars were not visible.

If you skim this passage, you will see that some form of the word *magnet* is in every sentence. You can infer that the general topic of the passage is magnetism. The passage also refers to people's learning about magnetism and using it to their advantage. You could state the main idea this way: When early people learned about magnets, they began using them in compasses.

Try It Yourself

When you read this passage, look for the topic and what information is given about the topic. State the main idea in your own words.

■ The word *year* refers to the time a planet takes to revolve around the sun. An earth year has an uneven number of earth days—a little more than 365¼. For three of every four years, calendars ignore that one fourth of a day. By the fourth year, a full day has accumulated, so a day is added to the shortest month, February. Even this does not make calendars correspond exactly to the actual revolution of the earth. Periodically other changes have to be made to keep calendars accurate.

Did you notice that the passage in general dealt with the length of a year on earth? Two specific points were made about that topic: (1) The earth's revolution time and earth calendars do not match exactly. (2) Calendars have to be adjusted so that they correspond with the earth's rate of revolution.

Were you able to combine those two ideas so that they state one main idea? If so, you might have said something like this: Calendars have to be adjusted at regular intervals to account for the uneven time of the earth's revolution around the sun.

Now study the visual and read the longer passage below. Watch for the topic. When you have finished reading, pause for a moment to see how you would state the main idea. Then try summarizing the information.

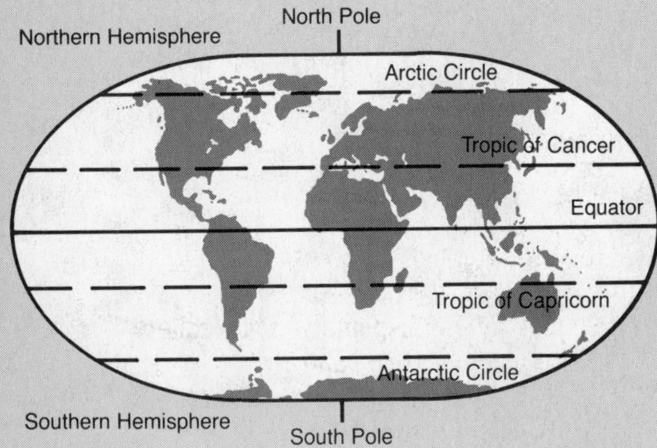

■ By far the largest portion of the earth's lithosphere, or dry land area, lies in the Northern Hemisphere. Huge landmasses reach northward from the equator and extend beyond the Arctic Circle. Much of the Southern Hemisphere's land, by contrast, extends south from the equator only as far as the Tropic of Capricorn. It follows, then, that most of the earth's hydrosphere, or water area, lies in the Southern Hemisphere.

This pattern of land and water distribution reverses itself in the polar areas. In the Northern Hemisphere, the Arctic Ocean covers the North Pole. But the South Pole lies in the Southern Hemisphere land of Antarctica.

Did you read both paragraphs before you tried to infer the main idea? Both paragraphs describe the distribution of land and water on the earth. What is the main point the passage makes about this distribution? Did you say something like this: "Land and water are distributed unevenly over the earth"? If so, you did a good job of inferring the main idea.

On the Springboard

Item 1 refers to the following passage. As you read, look for the main idea. Then think about how you would summarize it.

The sun's rays heat the earth most efficiently when they strike the earth directly, at a vertical angle. They heat the earth least efficiently when they strike at a wide slant. The sun's rays are most nearly vertical in the Northern Hemisphere during the month of June. Yet July and August are usually the hottest months in the Northern Hemisphere. Why is this so? Think for a moment about a pot of water on the stove. The stove's heating element gets red hot in just a few seconds. Yet the pot and the water take several minutes to heat up. The sun's heating effect acts in much the same way as the stove's heating effect. It takes a little time to warm up the earth. Some of the sun's heat is used to melt snow. Some escapes into space. Heavy cloud covers may sometimes keep the sun's rays from reaching the earth.

1. Which of the following statements best summarizes the information in the passage?
   (1) The angle of the sun's rays determines the temperature of the earth during June, July, and August.
   (2) A time lag exists between the sun's greatest heating effect and the warmest temperatures in a hemisphere.
   (3) The Northern Hemisphere enters its summer season after the sun's rays begin to strike there in wider and wider angles.

You will find the Springboard answer on page 155.

Were you able to pick out the best summary statement? If so, go ahead to "The Real Thing." If you had trouble with the Springboard item, review this section before you go on.

“ The Real Thing ”

Item 1 refers to the paragraph below.

Mountains make up the highest and most rugged lands in the earth's lithosphere. Most mountains are more than 6,000 feet above sea level. Hills are also raised areas, but they are more gentle than mountains. They reach heights from 1,600 feet to 6,000 feet above sea level. Plateaus, on the other hand, are flat areas located at heights covering about the same range as hills. Sprawling plains regions are flat or gently rolling lands. They lie at no more than 500 feet above sea level.

1. Which of the following statements best summarizes the passage?

   (1) The earth's hills, mountains, and plateaus are easy features to identify.
   (2) Although there are many areas that reach greater heights, plains regions make up most of the earth's lithosphere.
   (3) The earth's mountains and hills are located farther from the sea than plains and plateaus.
   (4) The earth has four major land features identified partly by their height above sea level.
   (5) There are great differences between land and sea areas across the surface of the earth.

Items 2–3 refer to the following diagram and information.

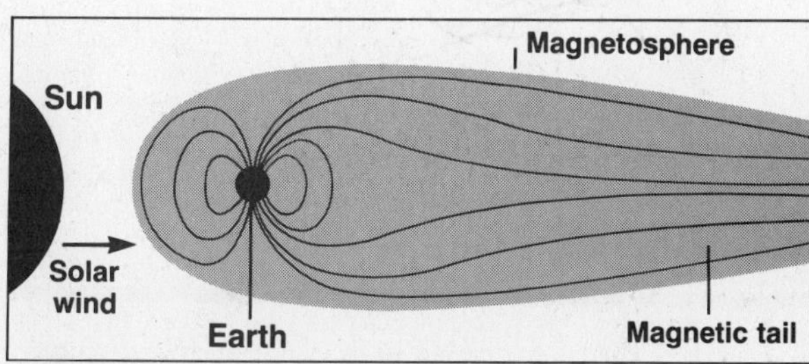

The magnetism of the earth is believed to come from electricity in the earth's core. The earth's magnetosphere is not symmetrical. Radiant energy from the sun acts like a wind and creates a long “tail” of magnetism extending from the side of the earth away from the sun.

The magnetic field protects life on earth by trapping particles from the sun and elsewhere in space. When disturbances on the sun create a great flow of particles, however, some of these electrically charged particles descend into the earth's atmosphere and cause brilliant glows of light. These auroras are most visible near the poles because the earth's magnetism guides the particles toward the poles.

2. Which of the following statements best summarizes the information in the diagram and article?

   (1) The earth's magnetosphere arises from the earth but interacts with the sun.
   (2) Beautiful displays of light called the auroras occur around the poles.
   (3) The sun creates magnetic fields around itself and the earth.
   (4) Magnetism comes from electricity.
   (5) The earth's magnetosphere is an oddly shaped magnetic field.

3. At which of the following spots would auroras be visible most often?

   A. the North Pole
   B. the South Pole
   C. halfway between the poles

   (1) A only
   (2) B only
   (3) C only
   (4) A and B only
   (5) A and C only

Check your answers and record your score on page 156.

LESSON 14

The Land

In this section you'll learn about some of the substances that make up and are stored in the earth's crust. Take a look at the Warm-up question at the end of the section before you start to read. The Warm-up will help you look for important information.

Minerals, Ores, and Rocks

Have you ever stopped to pick up a pretty rock along a path or on the beach? Perhaps the rock's color, shape, or sparkle attracted you. Earth scientists use these same characteristics along with some others to identify rocks on the earth.

Most rocks contain basic elements or combinations of elements called **minerals.** Gold, silver, copper, diamonds, sulfur, and iron are just a few of the minerals found in rocks. As you can see, many minerals are very useful and valuable. Most of the earth's minerals were never part of anything living. Rocks that contain deposits of minerals are called **ores.**

The most common mineral on earth is quartz. Sand, for example, is made up of tiny bits of quartz. If you were to look closely at a few grains of sand, you would see that they all have the same shape. Any basic earth substance that has a regular geometric shape is a **crystal.** Most minerals, like the quartz grains of sand, are crystals.

Scientists classify rocks according to how they were formed. Igneous rocks form when very hot liquid materials from deep below the earth's crust cool and become solid. Granite is an example of igneous rock.

Sedimentary rocks form when small particles fall to the ground or to the bottom of the sea and begin to pile up. Pressure on these sediments from sediments or water above them packs them together into rock. Sandstone, limestone, and shale are sedimentary rocks. You may have noticed that these kinds of rocks split easily into layers or that they come apart when rubbed. Sedimentary rocks are not as hard as igneous rocks.

Metamorphic rocks are the hardest rock of all. They are formed from igneous and sedimentary rocks. Heat and/or pressure help form metamorphic rock. Heat and pressure change limestone into marble, for example. People make chalkboards of metamorphic slate, which was once shale. Quartzite, the reddish rock you may have seen under railroad ties, was sandstone before heat and pressure changed it.

Coming to Terms

mineral a solid, nonliving substance made up of one or more elements

ore a rock that contains a mineral

crystal a mineral material that has a regular, geometric shape

Warm-up

What is the difference between an ore and a mineral?

____

____

____

The history of the earth is a long, fascinating story. In this section you'll learn about "chapters" in the earth's story and discover guideposts that scientists use to identify periods of the earth's past. Look ahead to the Warm-up question for clues to the important points in this section.

Geologic Eras and Fossils

Imagine a birthday cake with 4.5 billion candles on it. That is how many candles would be needed to celebrate the earth's birthday. Four-and-a-half-billion years is too long a period to consider in terms of a human life. So scientists

Sample Warm-up Answer
A mineral is a basic element like gold or silver, while an ore is a rock that contains a mineral.

divide the earth's history into extremely long time periods called **eras.**

Humans are very recent newcomers to the earth. Try to think about all of the earth's history as having taken place in a single twenty-four-hour time period. Human beings would be on earth for just the last few seconds before midnight. If people are so new to earth, what went on before they appeared?

The earliest period of earth's history is called Precambrian time. During Precambrian time the earth was formed, and enormous sheets of rock first gave shape to the earth's crust. The oceans and atmosphere developed, and simple life began in the form of algae and fungi.

The first land animals and plants developed during the Paleozoic era, which began about 600 million years ago. Snails, sponges, insects, early reptiles and amphibians, seed plants, and evergreen trees came into being. The Appalachian Mountains, coal, and some oil and natural gas formed in the Paleozoic era.

The Mesozoic era came next. The dinosaurs and many other large reptiles lived during this era. The Rocky Mountains formed, and more oil and gas deposits developed. If you could walk through a Mesozoic forest, you would recognize many of the hardwood and evergreen trees. You would also notice early small mammals.

You live in the current era, the Cenozoic era, which began "only" 65 million years ago. In this period many volcanoes have been active, and the Alps, Himalayas, and Cascade mountain ranges have formed. Gold, tin, silver, copper, and most oil and natural gas deposits have been laid down during this period. Human beings and other large mammals arrived during the Cenozoic era.

How do scientists know of these eras and their life forms? By determining the ages of rocks and studying **fossils.** Fossils are evidence of past life on earth. You may have noticed fossils of small sea animals or ferns in limestone or sandstone. Fossils reveal information about how life, the climate, and the earth's geography have changed over long periods of time.

Fossils are all we have left of dinosaurs and other early plants and animals. Most organisms die and are soon decomposed. Occasionally an animal or plant dies and is quickly covered by clay or silt. Over a long period of time minerals fill in the cells of the plant or animal. A permanent record of the organism remains as a fossil. The oldest fossils are of simple algae and fungi in Precambrian time.

Coming to Terms

era a major division of time in the earth's history

fossil evidence of past life on earth

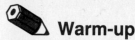

Warm-up

Using your own words, tell why fossils are important to earth scientists. Write your answer in complete sentences.

____

____

____

____

Sample Warm-up Answer
Fossils are records or evidence of past life. Scientists study fossils to find out how living things, the climate, and the geography of the earth have changed over time.

Drawing Conclusions

By now you've had a bit of practice in inferring main ideas from information given in scientific articles and illustrations. And as you learned in Lesson 7, you can also sometimes infer other ideas by drawing conclusions based on information.

You draw conclusions every day without even thinking about it. Suppose, for instance, that you are driving your car and the engine begins to sputter. The gas gauge reads half full, but you know it has gotten stuck in the past. You recall that you haven't bought gas in quite a while. Using your observations and memory, you conclude that your gas gauge is broken and your car is running out of fuel.

The ability to draw conclusions is obviously useful. You've done it in everyday life and with biology materials; you can draw conclusions about earth science information too.

Here's an Example

The following paragraph gives a number of facts. They suggest several conclusions.

■ The LaBrea tar pits are located in modern-day California. In past eras the tar pits were pools of asphalt. Asphalt is a thick, sticky substance that comes from the seepage of underground petroleum. When covered with water, the asphalt pools looked like ordinary watering holes. When covered with leaves and dust, they appeared to be solid ground. Thousands of animals from many different species died in these pools.

You probably noticed that the paragraph gives information about the nature and composition of asphalt, about the appearance of asphalt pools, and about animals that died there. From that information you could draw such conclusions as these:

Animals became mired in the sticky asphalt and could not get free.

Mired animals starved or suffocated in the pools.

Scientists have found the fossils of many animal species in the LaBrea tar pits.

Try It Yourself

Look at this small chart and the explanation below it.

■ Scale of Mineral Hardness

1. Talc	6. Orthoclase
2. Gypsum	7. Quartz
3. Calcite	8. Topaz
4. Fluorite	9. Corundum
5. Apatite	10. Diamond

On this scale 1 is the softest mineral, and 10 is the hardest. Each mineral will scratch any mineral that has the same number or lower. Each mineral can be scratched by a mineral with the same number or higher.

If you scratch a piece of gypsum with your fingernail, it will leave a mark. On the other hand, a piece of calcite will scratch your fingernail. What can you conclude about the mineral hardness of your fingernail?

To scratch gypsum, your fingernail must rank 2 or higher on the scale. And to be scratched by calcite, it must be 3 or lower. If you concluded that the hardness of your fingernail must be from 2 to 3, you concluded correctly. (Its hardness is 2.5.)

After you have read the following paragraph, see if you can reach a conclusion about ocean mining.

■ Very small quantities of metals occur almost everywhere over the earth. When relative amounts of a certain metallic mineral are higher than average in a given location, scientists and mining experts call it a mineral deposit. The concentration of the metal must be high to make mining profitable. In recent years, new and advanced mining methods have made it possible to mine deposits that were left untouched in the past. The ocean contains millions of tons of valuable metallic minerals. These metals, however, have never been mined.

Can you figure out why so many minerals in the ocean have not been mined? The passage states the concentration of a metal must be high, and the ocean has tons of metallic minerals. The passage also states that new mining methods have made mining certain deposits possible. If you concluded that a profitable method for mining many minerals from the ocean has not been found yet, you drew the correct conclusion.

☑ A Test-Taking Tip

When you are inferring or drawing conclusions on the GED Science Test, you will sometimes be expected to use your own everyday knowledge to help you form conclusions. Remember, your own observations from living in the world are also part of your scientific knowledge.

On the Springboard

Item 1 refers to the information below. Look for a conclusion that can be drawn.

The fossil of a giant fish was found in Kansas. A fossil skeleton of a smaller fish seemed to be lying where the stomach of the large fish must have been. The larger fish appears to have eaten the smaller fish. These and other fish fossils of the same age have been found throughout Kansas.

1. Based on the information above, what conclusion can you draw about Kansas?
   (1) People in Kansas often go fishing.
   (2) Kansas is a good place to look for dinosaur bones.
   (3) Kansas was once covered with water.

Item 2 refers to the paragraph and diagram that follow. You will be asked to draw a conclusion from the information.

The earth's crust has many layers of rock and soil that scientists think formed at different times in the earth's history. Generally, if the layers are left undisturbed, the deepest layers are the oldest. They formed at the earliest stages of the earth's past. Scientists have modern methods for determining the age of rocks. Often they can estimate the age of a fossil from the age of the rock layer in which the fossil lay when it was discovered.

Earth layers with fossils

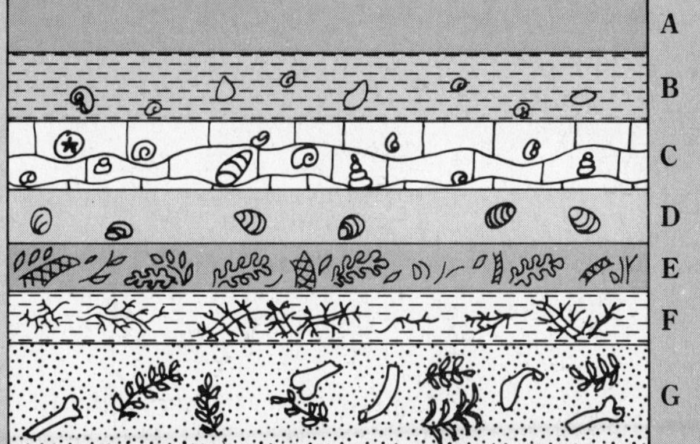

2. According to information in the passage, which of the following conclusions about the diagram above would be most accurate?
   (1) Animals whose fossils lie in layer E lived longer ago than animals whose fossils are found in layer B.
   (2) The fossils in layer G came from simpler life forms than those in layer D.
   (3) Scientists have disturbed the fossils in all the layers shown.

(1) (2) (3)

Check your answers to On the Springboard on page 155.

If you answered both Springboard items correctly, test your skill at drawing conclusions with the GED-level "Real Thing." If you had trouble with the Springboard items, review this section first. You might also want to review the pages on drawing conclusions in the *Biology* section.

66 The Real Thing 99

Item 1 refers to the following information.

Large, well-shaped crystals form when liquids that contain minerals cool slowly in uncrowded conditions. Geodes are small, round hollow balls of limestone. The inside of a geode is lined with sparkling quartz crystals.

1. Based on the information given, it can be concluded that geodes are formed when
   (1) liquids containing minerals are added to limestone
   (2) limestone balls filled with liquid cool slowly
   (3) water freezes and changes into sparkling ice crystals
   (4) volcanoes erupt and spill hot, melted rock on the earth
   (5) limestone is mixed with quartz in uncrowded conditions

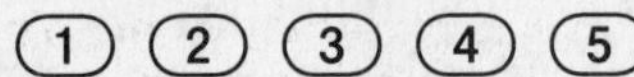

Items 2–4 are based on the article below.

Some minerals came from the remains of living matter. Sedimentary rocks, such as limestone and chalk, often hold bones and shells of sea creatures that were pressed together at the bottom of ancient seas. Oil deposits may have formed when ancient marine plants were exposed to great pressure over long periods of time.

Coal is one mineral that can still be found in varying stages of development. Coal in its earliest stage is peat. It is made up of partially decomposed plant matter. As lignite, it is harder and more solid. Lignite is often called brown coal.

"True" coal is older than peat and lignite and formed under greater pressure. It comes in two main grades. Bituminous coal is the softer grade of coal. Anthracite coal is very hard and gives off great heat when burned.

Scientists believe that the formation of coal requires several conditions. First, the climate must be warm, damp, and mostly unchanging. In addition, there must be lush plant life amid standing pools of water that contain little oxygen. Finally, dead and dying plant material needs to accumulate under the water and eventually under deep layers of the earth's crust, which apply intense pressure over long periods of time. The greater the pressure, the higher the grade of coal.

Though peat bogs still exist today, the conditions for turning the peat into true coal do not. Moving water, seasonal rains, and bodies of water fed by streams introduce too much oxygen. The plant life rots away before it can be transformed into coal.

2. Given the information in the article, which of the following is the best conclusion to draw about the availability of coal on earth?
   (1) There will be enough coal on earth to last as long as people want it.
   (2) Changing temperatures on the earth have caused peat bogs to expand.
   (3) Future generations may be able to mine coal on other planets.
   (4) Many factories and homes now depend on heat from lignite.
   (5) Scientists do not expect earth's existing supplies of coal to increase.

3. The information in the passage can best be summarized by which of the following statements?
   (1) Earth's minerals came from ancient animals trapped in standing water.
   (2) Studying earth's layers of rock has shown scientists how to produce certain minerals.
   (3) Changing living matter into minerals requires great pressure and long time periods.
   (4) Scientists are still developing theories to explain the origin of minerals.
   (5) In the future, scientists will develop new minerals unknown to people today.

4. In which of the following places did anthracite coal most likely form?
   (1) rocky seacoasts
   (2) stagnant, warm marshes
   (3) cold, flowing rivers
   (4) stream-fed swamps
   (5) areas with dry summers and rainy winters

Check your answers and record your score on page 156.

LESSON 15

The Water

Oceans cover more than half the earth's surface. Before you read about them in the next section, use the Warm-up to preview it.

The Oceans

"Water, Water everywhere,
Nor any drop to drink."

That is a line from a poem about an ocean voyage. Ocean water is undrinkable because it contains dissolved salts and other elements from the earth's crust. The **salinity,** or amount of salt, in ocean water varies from place to place. The Mediterranean Sea, for instance, is much saltier than the Atlantic Ocean. Salinity is comparatively low at places where rivers empty fresh water into the ocean and where melting ice from polar regions pours into the ocean.

Sunny ocean beaches attract many tourists all over the world. Sunlight also attracts life forms that live in the sea. Most ocean organisms live in the upper layers of the water, where sunlight can penetrate. Very small plant and animal organisms called **plankton** float near the ocean's surface. Plankton are the basis of the ocean's food chain. They also release huge amounts of oxygen into the air. Fish, sea mammals, and other ocean life forms abound in the sunlit upper regions of the oceans.

Fewer and fewer organisms live in the deeper layers of the ocean's waters, where sunlight does not penetrate. The pressure of the water above at the greater depths also discourages life. A gallon of milk weighs about the same as a gallon of saltwater. Imagine stacking thousands of one-gallon cartons of milk into a column. The cartons at the bottom would be under a great deal of pressure from the cartons above. In the same way, pressure in the ocean increases as the depth increases.

Coming to Terms

salinity the amount of salt dissolved in water

plankton small plant or animal organisms that live in the upper regions of the ocean

Warm-up

Answer the questions in sentences of your own.

1. Why is ocean water unfit to drink?

____

____

2. Why are plankton important organisms?

____

____

Have you ever tried to dock a boat? You may have found it to be a tricky job. The boat never wants to hold still. It keeps moving because the water under it is in constant motion. In this section, you'll read about the way the ocean moves with the tides. Look ahead to the Warm-up to help you identify main points in the section.

The Tides

Along most of the earth's coastlines, the ocean water rolls in over the shore twice each day. At these times the water is at **high tide.** Then the water moves back, or recedes, from the shore. At these times the water is at **low tide.** Low and high tides alternate about every six hours.

The gravity of the moon is the main cause of the tides. As the moon revolves around the earth, its gravity pulls on the earth. At the same time, the earth is spinning around on its axis once every twenty-four hours. The moon's gravity pulls the water on the side of the earth facing the moon into a bulge. At the same time, it actually pulls the earth away from its waters on the side of the earth turned away from the moon. So a bulge in the ocean's waters also occurs on the opposite side of the earth.

Sample Warm-up Answers
1. Dissolved salts and other elements in ocean water make it undrinkable. **2.** Plankton are the basis of the ocean food chain. They also release oxygen into the atmosphere.

Neap Tide

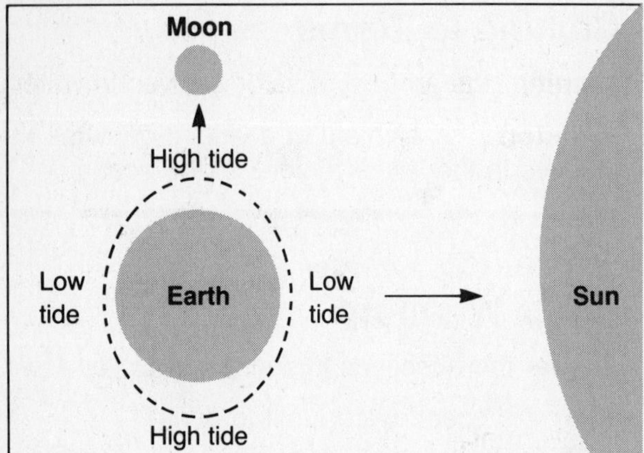

Spring Tide

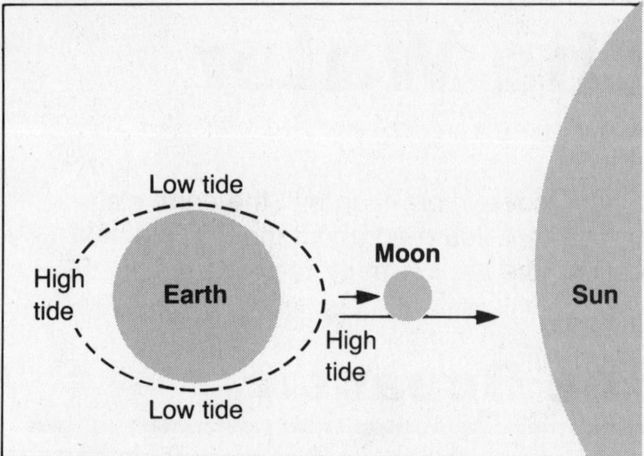

Because the moon is revolving around the earth and the earth is revolving around the sun, the positions of the three in relation to one another change. Depending on the moon's position, the sun's gravity can either help or hurt the moon's effect on the tides. The bulges shown in the first illustration on this page represent high tides. The narrower bands between the bulges show low tides. When the moon is in this position, the sun's gravity works against the moon's gravity. The differences between low tides and high tides are then least noticeable. At this time, coastlines are having neap tides.

Now notice the position of the moon in its orbit in the second illustration.

It takes the moon about a month to make one complete revolution around the earth. Twice each month, the moon lines up directly with the sun—either between the earth and sun, as shown, or on the other side of the earth. At these times, the moon's gravity and the sun's gravity have a combined effect. Differences between high tides and low tides are then at their peak. Coastlines have spring tides at these times.

Coming to Terms

high tide the higher ocean level that occurs twice each day, about every 12½ hours

low tide the lower ocean level that occurs twice each day, about every 12½ hours

Warm-up

In sentences of your own, explain why spring tides are higher than neap tides.

____

____

____

In the next section, you'll learn about another way in which the ocean waters are in motion. Before you read, glance at the Warm-up to pick up clues to important information.

Ocean Currents

You're probably familiar with rivers that cut through the land. But did you know that the ocean also has "rivers"? The ocean's "rivers" are actually streams of water that flow through it over fixed routes. Most are either warmer or colder than the waters through which they flow. These ocean streams are called **ocean currents.** Winds, the water's salinity, differences in water temperatures, shapes of the earth's land areas, and the earth's rotation and revolution all help cause ocean currents.

The Gulf Stream is a warm, swift current that flows in a regular path across the Atlantic Ocean between North America and Europe. The

Sample Warm-up Answer
When coastlines have spring tides, the moon is lined up with the sun. Gravity of both the sun and the moon combine to pull on the earth and its water.

Humboldt Current is a cold current that flows along the Pacific coast of South America. These currents both flow close to the surface of the ocean. Surface currents help sailors figure out efficient travel routes. They also help distribute nutrients among the ocean's life forms.

Some currents flow deep below the surface of the ocean, with greater up-and-down movements. Cold water is heavier than warm water. It also contains more oxygen. Because of its weight, colder water sinks below the warmer, lighter surface waters. It takes oxygen to the depths of the ocean and stirs up materials at the bottom. Deep **upwelling** occurs when currents of warmer water meet colder water. An upwelling pushes water from the bottom toward the surface. Upwelling locations are rich in living organisms because they contain nutrients brought up from the bottom of the ocean.

Very salty water is heavier than water with lesser salinity. As the saltier water sinks toward the bottom of the ocean, it sets up a current that flows in an opposite direction from lighter, less salty water. Rivers and streams on the land carry mud and sand into the ocean. Their muddy waters are also heavier than ocean water. These waters, too, create currents as they enter the ocean.

Coming to Terms

ocean current a stream of water that flows in a fixed path through the ocean. A current is usually warmer or colder than the water around it.

upwelling the process in which water from the bottom of the ocean is pushed upward, toward the surface

Warm-up

In a complete sentence or two, tell why currents and upwellings are important to life in the ocean.

___

___

___

Sample Warm-up Answer
Currents help distribute nutrients among the ocean's life forms. Upwellings bring nutrients up from the bottom of the ocean.

It's not hard to see how water moves in tides, currents, and waves. But water also moves constantly—in less obvious ways—between the land and bodies of water on the earth. You'll see how this happens as you read the next section. First, check the Warm-up so that you will be alert to important points.

The Water Cycle

Have you ever noticed a puddle disappear after a rainstorm? The puddle grows smaller and smaller until it becomes just a damp spot and then vanishes altogether. The puddle disappeared because the water changed into vapor and became part of the air. In other words, the water evaporated. **Evaporation** is the process in which a liquid changes to a gas.

Warm air can hold quite a bit of water vapor. However, when air is cooled, it can no longer hold as much water vapor. The vapor changes back into a liquid. Think of the times when you have noticed beads of water collecting on the outside of a glass of cold water. The cold water cooled the air surrounding the glass so that it could no longer hold all its vapor. **Condensation** is the change of a vapor back into a liquid. The water vapor in the air condensed and collected on the outside of the glass.

The same thing happens in the earth's atmosphere. When warm, moist air meets colder air, the warm air cools, and its water vapor condenses. Eventually, the condensed moisture falls to the earth as rain, snow, sleet, or some other form of precipitation.

Evaporation and condensation are always at work. Water from oceans, streams, rivers, ponds, and lakes evaporates into the air. It condenses and collects in clouds. When the air becomes cool enough, further condensation in the clouds brings on precipitation. The water that falls on the land eventually drains back into the bodies of water. This movement of water between the land, bodies of water, and the air is called the water cycle.

Coming to Terms

evaporation the process by which a liquid changes to a gas

condensation the process by which a gas changes into a liquid

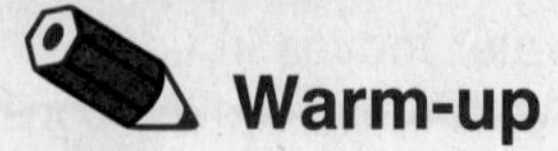

Warm-up

Answer each question with your own sentence.

1. What causes moisture to condense in the atmosphere?

____

____

2. What are the three major stops water makes as it constantly moves through the water cycle?

____

____

Inferring Cause-and-Effect Relationships

When the wind blows across the ocean, it creates currents on the surface. Wind action and surface currents show a direct cause-and-effect relationship. As you read earlier, a cause is something that makes something else happen. An effect is a result, or something that is made to happen.

Sometimes several causes work together to bring about a single effect, as when the combined forces of gravity from the sun and moon create spring tides. On the other hand, a single cause may produce several effects. Changes in air temperature can cause such different effects as thunderstorms, tornadoes, or high winds.

Some scientific materials you work with will present the cause first. Others will mention the effect first and then later state the cause. Sometimes causes and effects are left unstated. Then you have to infer the relationship. In most cases, you'll succeed best by looking for the cause first and then searching out the effects.

Here's an Example

■ One way to increase production of food taken from the sea is through sea farming. The number and size of fish living in a certain area would increase if their food supply were increased. For example, the minerals that plankton need for food could be brought up from deep waters. The supply of plankton would increase, and sea life that feeds on plankton would also grow in size and number.

The passage implies several cause-and-effect relationships; it doesn't directly state them. It begins by saying that sea farming (a general cause) could increase food production. Then, more specifically, it says that increasing the amount of minerals (cause) would lead to more plankton (effect); more plankton (cause) would lead to yet another effect—an increase in the size and numbers of larger sea life, which could provide food for people. Notice that the effect precedes the cause in the first two sentences. The last two sentences suggest the causes first and then the effects.

Try It Yourself

As you read, watch for a cause-and-effect relationship implied in the following passage.

■ A warm ocean current in the Pacific called El Niño has sometimes brought disaster to Peruvian fishers. The anchovies they catch for a living depend on the upwelling of cold water along the western coast of South America. But periodically, when southerly winds fail, the cold Humboldt Current turns west, away from land. Then the warm waters of El Niño move into the coastal area. Anchovies cannot live in these warm waters. The fishing boats come back empty, and many Peruvians go hungry.

Why do Peruvian fishing boats return empty when El Niño occurs?

As this question implies, there is a cause-and-effect relationship between El Niño and empty fishing boats. To answer the question, you must know what El Niño is and what happens when it comes. Look at the passage for clues.

El Niño is warm, and anchovies need cold water to live. The warmth of El Niño kills the anchovies, so there are none for the fishers to catch. You correctly identified the cause-and-effect relationship between El Niño and the empty boats if you noticed a series of causes and effects: Failing southerly winds produce changing ocean currents, which bring warmer waters, which destroy anchovies. The final result is empty fishing boats.

Sample Warm-up Answers

1. Moisture condenses in the atmosphere when the temperature of the air cools. **2.** In the water cycle, water stops on the land, in the air, and in bodies of water.

As you read this next passage, look for the answer to this question: What is the main cause of waves in sea water?

■ The movement of ocean waves is very different from that of currents. Currents move forward. Waves move up and down. The power of most waves depends on the strength of the wind blowing across the water. During storms at sea, waves may rise to heights of 40 feet or more. One very powerful kind of wave is set off by earthquakes and undersea volcanic eruptions. This is the dreaded tsunami. A tsunami is barely felt or seen on the open sea. Only when it touches land does a tsunami unleash the full force of the energy it carries. Then it becomes a killer wave.

Were you able to identify the main cause of waves? The passage gives several interesting points of information about waves. But only two sentences name some forces that can cause ocean waves. One force is wind, and that seems to be the main cause because the passage says, "The power of most waves depends on the strength of the wind. . . . " Earthquakes and volcanic eruptions also produce waves, but the "killer waves" they produce are obviously less common. Were you able to infer the relationship between ocean waves and wind?

On the Springboard

Item 1 refers to the paragraph below. Watch for a cause-and-effect relationship.

Precipitation falls to the earth as fresh water even though much of it comes from salty seawater. When evaporation occurs in ocean areas, water vapor rises into the air, while the salts remain behind.

1. Raindrops never taste salty because
   (1) freshwater lakes and rivers supply the water that moves through the water cycle
   (2) pollution has killed the taste of salt in seawater
   (3) evaporation turns salt water into fresh water

   (1) (2) (3)

Items 2–3 refer to the passage below.

Upwelling occurs in the ocean when warm currents meet denser, heavier water layers. The warmer, lighter currents rise toward the surface carrying material from the bottom upward. Upwelling waters teeming with life are found not only along some coasts but also under a variety of conditions in the open sea. Such waters are usually murky or tinged green or brown by vast numbers of plankton. The color of the water deepens when more life is present. Albacore, a kind of tuna, and other big fish have learned to seek out such waters. In turn, people who are deep-sea fishing have learned to watch for edges of green or brown bands at sea. A colored band of water is almost as reliable as a flock of seagulls as a sign of good fishing.

2. Why do fishers look for green or brown bands at sea?
   (1) They want to avoid dangerous currents.
   (2) Large game fish come to such areas to feed.
   (3) Sea gulls feed at the bands.

   (1) (2) (3)

3. Upwelling waters are often teeming with plankton because they
   (1) carry minerals and other foods up from the ocean bed
   (2) occur mainly along populated seacoasts
   (3) are warmer and less dense than the rest of the ocean

   (1) (2) (3)

☑ A Test-Taking Tip

When you look for causes and effects on the GED Science Test, the two most effective words to use are *if* and *then*. When you think you have found an example of a cause-and-effect relationship, ask yourself, "*If* **this** happens, *then* will **that** happen?" If the answer is yes, you have found a cause and its effect.

Take the time to check your answers to On the Springboard on page 155.

If you felt confident about answering the Springboard questions and were able to infer the cause-and-effect relationships, move on now to "The Real Thing." If you are still uncertain about recognizing causes and effects, take time to review these last few pages.

❝ The Real Thing ❞

Items 1–2 refer to the map and passage below.

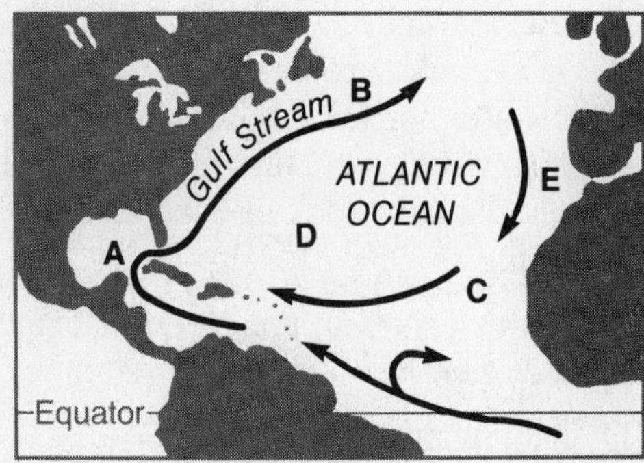

The powerful Gulf Stream and other currents encircle much of the North Atlantic Ocean. Within this area, away from prevailing winds, lies the nearly motionless Sargasso Sea. Large masses of sargassum seaweed accumulate on the surface and float on the remarkably clear blue water. Because there is almost no current here, no new water enters. The whole area remains warm under the sun's heat. No upwelling occurs in the motionless mass of water to bring nutrients up from the depths below. Other than the floating seaweed and the eels that spend part of their life cycle there, the Sargasso is a "dead sea."

1. What makes the Sargasso a "dead sea"?

   (1) No ships can sail through the mass of seaweed.
   (2) As in a desert, no rain falls on the Sargasso.
   (3) Its blue, warm water cannot support life.
   (4) Surface winds stir up violent storms.
   (5) It supports relatively little life because of the lack of nutrients.

   ① ② ③ ④ ⑤

2. Given the information in the passage, at what location on the map would you expect to find the calmest waters?

   (1) A
   (2) B
   (3) C
   (4) D
   (5) E

Item 3 refers to the diagram below.

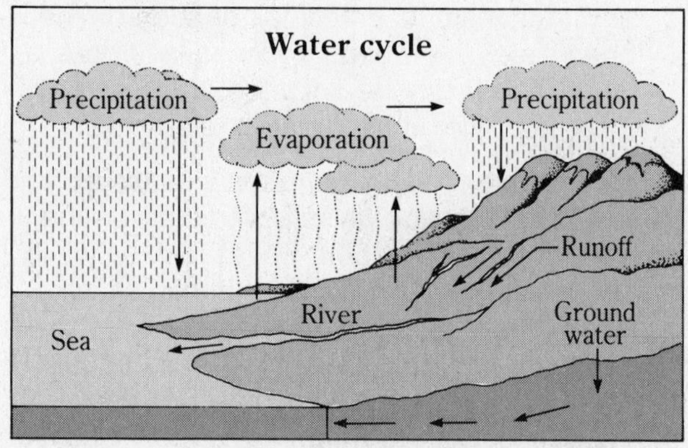

3. How might clouds formed over the sea reach the land?

   (1) Winds push the clouds toward land.
   (2) Ground water attracts low clouds.
   (3) The clouds evaporate over the land.
   (4) Runoff gathers clouds together.
   (5) Storms always move from left to right.

Check your answers and record your score on page 156.

LESSON 16

The Air

You're probably aware that the earth is a unique planet in our solar system because of its ability to support life as we know it. One of the many things that gives the earth this unique ability is its atmosphere. Before you read the following section about the earth's atmosphere, check the Warm-up question. Use it as a guide to important information.

Layers of the Atmosphere

You've just read about the ocean of water on the earth. The atmosphere makes up the ocean of air that we live in. This ocean of air covers the entire earth and extends many miles upward from the planet's surface. It is divided into a number of layers.

People live in the lowest layer of the atmosphere, called the troposphere. Here there is plenty of oxygen. The pressure that the air exerts on the surface of the earth is also suitable for many different life forms. Approximately three-fourths of the weight of the air is in the troposphere. Like water in the ocean, air in the troposphere is never still. The earth's rotation and revolution cause it to move in great currents. The troposphere is the layer where weather occurs.

While the thickness of the troposphere varies, it averages 7.5 miles thick. That is more than 39,000 feet. So if you've ever flown in a jet, you probably flew up through the top of the troposphere. The top of the troposphere is very cold; the average temperature is about −50°F.

The layer of the atmosphere directly above the troposphere is called the stratosphere. Scientists have sent balloons and rockets into this layer to study temperature changes. They learned something interesting. A few miles into the stratosphere, the temperature of the air begins to rise. At a distance of 28 miles from the earth's surface, the average temperature is nearly 32°F. From that point to 50 miles, the temperature drops to about −90°F. Then it begins to rise again. Why does this happen?

About 30 miles above the earth is a high concentration of a substance called ozone. While the earth receives some ultraviolet radiation from the sun, the ozone shields us from much of it by absorbing it. That's why the temperature at this point is warmer. Ultraviolet radiation is very intense; most life forms would perish if they were exposed to sizable amounts of it for any period of time.

The next layer of the atmosphere is the ionosphere. This layer contains large numbers of electrically charged particles called ions. These particles absorb unshielded energy from the sun. About 100 miles from the surface of the earth, the temperature is extremely hot. In fact, it is 212°F—the temperature at which water boils. Radio waves from earth bounce off the ionosphere, making long-distance radio broadcasts possible.

Finally, there is the exosphere, the layer of the atmosphere that begins about 350 miles from the earth's surface. Here the air molecules are very far apart. Temperatures in the exosphere have been estimated at 3,000°F. Gradually the exosphere fades off into space; the atmosphere has no distinct end.

Warm-up

Use information from the section to support the statement below. Write your answer in a sentence or two.

The atmosphere's ozone layer is important to life on earth.

____

____

____

Sample Warm-up Answer
The ozone layer shields the earth from the sun's ultraviolet radiation. Too much ultraviolet radiation would be harmful to life forms on the earth.

You learned in the last section that weather takes place in the layer of the atmosphere called the troposphere. In this section you'll study a few more important points about weather. Preview the Warm-up exercise before you begin. It will help you focus on important information.

Weather

An airplane flight is canceled because of heavy fog. A bad freeze destroys a citrus crop. A torrential rain causes flooding in a residential area. These are all negative effects of weather. But there are also many positive effects. You go to a football game on a cool, sunshiny day. You have a beach party on a hot summer evening. A light snowfall gives you an opportunity to take beautiful photographs. What are the causes of the negative and positive effects of weather? Air and the water that is in it.

Air is heavy. The air in the atmosphere presses on the surface of the earth and on every object it touches. Air pressure can be a strong force. Think for a moment of the pressure the air inside the tires of a car puts on the inside walls of the tires. The inflated tires hold up the weight of the entire car. The pressure in the atmosphere is called **atmospheric pressure**, and it, too, is a strong force. At sea level, air exerts a force of 14.7 pounds per square inch on the earth's surface. An instrument called a barometer measures atmospheric pressure.

Cold air is heavier than warm air; in other words, it exerts greater atmospheric pressure. A mass of air with cool temperatures and high pressure is called a **high**. A mass of warmer air with low pressure is a low. Air tends to move from areas of high pressure to areas of low pressure. You feel that movement as the wind. When a strong high and a strong low meet, stormy weather with high winds can develop in an area.

Air contains varying amounts of water. The moisture, or wetness, held in air is the **humidity**. The average humidity in Phoenix, Arizona, is very low. The average humidity of New Orleans, Louisiana, is high. You would quickly feel the difference in humidity on a visit to these two cities.

You often hear or see weather reports that give the **relative humidity**. Relative humidity tells you the amount of moisture air holds compared with the amount of moisture it *could* hold at its particular temperature. Cold air holds less moisture than warm air. Suppose, for instance, a mass of air is holding only one-half the amount of water it is capable of holding at its temperature. Its relative humidity is 50 percent. If the temperature decreases, the moisture may condense and fall as rain or snow because the colder air cannot hold it.

Coming to Terms

atmospheric pressure the force with which air presses down on the earth

high a mass of air with high atmospheric pressure

low a mass of air with low atmospheric pressure

humidity the wetness, or moisture, in air

relative humidity the amount of moisture in the air compared with the maximum amount of moisture it could hold at its temperature

Warm-up

Answer each question in a sentence or two.

1. What atmospheric conditions could produce stormy weather in your area?

____

____

2. Describe the condition of the air if the relative humidity is 78 percent and the temperature is 80°.

____

____

Sample Warm-up Answer
1. Storms can develop when a high meets a low. **2.** With a relative humidity of 78 percent, the air holds 78 percent of the moisture it could hold at 80 degrees.

You've probably heard jokes about frequent or unusual changes in the weather. But when climates on the earth begin to show unusual changes, everyone takes a more serious look. You'll get an idea why in the next section. Take a minute to check the Warm-up activity now. Let it help focus your thoughts as you read.

Climate

Imagine this weather report: "Six inches of snow fall on San Antonio, Texas. The temperature drops to 20°F." Would such an announcement serve as proof that San Antonio has a cold **climate**? No, it would not. What the city experienced was a severe change in weather—not a change in its climate, which is known for long, warm summers.

Weather can change on a daily basis. It can change drastically during the same day. It would be possible for a city to experience sunshine, rain, sleet, and snow during the same day. Perhaps you have seen this happen. But when you think about climate, you must consider weather in a certain place over a long period of time. Climate involves average temperature and rainfall over many years. It considers extremes of weather. It also includes seasonal changes.

Over a year's time, regions near the equator receive more heat from the sun than northern or southern areas receive. If you remember how the earth's axis tilts toward and then away from the sun during the earth's yearly revolution, you understand why this is true. Regions near the equator receive much more direct radiant energy from the sun each year. Generally speaking, the closer a region is to the equator, the warmer its climate. The illustration in the next column shows how the earth can be divided into three different climate zones reaching north and south from the equator. Places in the temperate zones have climates with highly noticeable temperature changes from season to season. Places near the equator are mostly warm all year round. Places near the poles, where the sun's rays are always indirect, are cold all year round.

Nearness to the equator has the greatest influence on climate. But it is not the only influence. The height of land above sea level and its nearness to large bodies of water also help determine climate patterns.

In recent years, there has been much concern about the effect of human activities on climate. For example, exhaust from motor vehicles and the burning of fossil fuels by industry cause large amounts of carbon dioxide and other gases to be released into the air. These gases stay trapped in the atmosphere and form a kind of thermal blanket around the earth. The warming of the earth's climate that results from this thermal blanket is often referred to as the "greenhouse effect." Many scientists believe that the greenhouse effect could eventually cause a temperature rise significant enough to bring about dramatic changes in world climate.

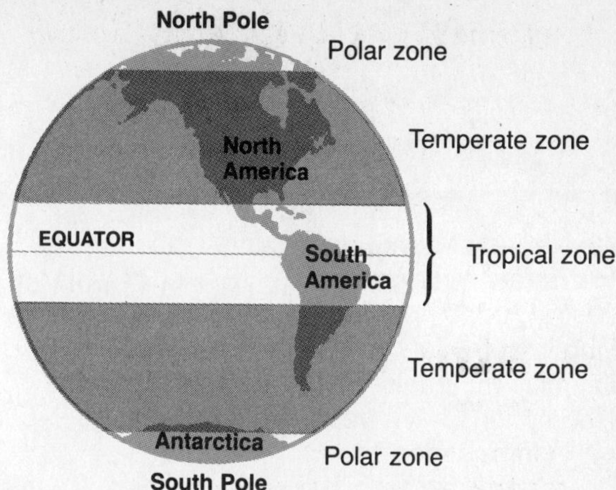

Coming to Terms

climate the average weather conditions in a certain place over a period of many years

Warm-up

Use a sentence or two to answer each question.

1. What are the names of the three climate zones on the earth?

____

____

2. Which of the three climate zones is the warmest? Why?

____

____

Sample Warm-up Answers
1. The three climate zones are polar, temperate, and tropical.
2. Tropical regions are usually the warmest because they receive the most direct radiant energy from the sun each year.

Recognizing Unstated Assumptions

You've learned that an assumption is an idea that is taken for granted. A speaker or writer or illustrator does not always describe an underlying assumption that he or she is making. In scientific materials, you have to realize what assumptions have been made or must be made from stated facts.

Here's an Example

Think for a moment about this scientific fact.

■ Air moves constantly from areas of high pressure to areas of low pressure. This movement of air causes winds.

Now suppose a breeze is blowing steadily across the shore along an ocean. Given the fact above, you can make an assumption about the pressure of the air over the ocean and the pressure of the air over the land. Since air moving from high-pressure zones to low-pressure zones creates winds, you can assume correctly that the air over the ocean has higher pressure than the air over the land. The breeze is blowing from the ocean toward the land.

The next passage describes some more facts. Look them over carefully.

■ The higher the altitude, or distance above sea level, the lower the air pressure will be. At lower air pressure levels, water takes longer to boil. Cooking temperatures and times required for cooking are different from those at lower altitudes, where air pressure is greater.

Given the information above, you can make an assumption about baking a cake, for instance, in mountain areas. Since mountains are located at high altitudes, you know that air pressure there is relatively low. And since water takes more time to boil under conditions of low air pressure, you can assume that a great-tasting cake must have been baked at a warmer oven temperature or for a longer period of time.

Try It Yourself

Read the passage below. Then see if you can identify an assumption that engineers made when they designed more modern airplanes.

■ The first airplanes could not fly nearly as fast as those of today. One reason was that some rather large parts of early airplanes protruded from the body of the craft. One way that modern designers increased air speed was to develop landing wheels that folded up into or against the body of the plane while it was in the air.

This is an instance where you might be able to draw on your own knowledge and experience. If you've ever put your arm out the window of a moving car, you know that you felt pressure against it. The fast forward motion of your arm met wind resistance, or pressure from the air it moved into. The same is true of airplanes. They meet wind resistance as they move through the air. Airplane designers assumed they could cut down on wind resistance by retracting the wheels of the plane. Less wind resistance meant that a plane could move faster. Were you able to see what the designers had in mind? If so, you identified an unstated assumption.

The passage below contains an unstated assumption about particles in the air and climate. See if you can figure out what it is.

■ At one time, scientists agreed that major climate changes on earth required periods of hundreds of thousands of years. New research has demonstrated otherwise. Scientists now know that a Little Ice Age occurred between the 1500s and the 1800s. Temperatures in the Northern Hemisphere averaged two to three degrees colder than they do now. Just this small difference caused crop failures and starvation in Europe and China.

Volcanic activity can bring widely felt climate changes by increasing the amount of dust in the air. Pollution from industries, like ash from volcanoes, can also increase the amount of dirt particles, as can certain types of farming practices. All these things can bring cooler temperatures because the particles block the sun's heat. Some people claim that, given our dependence on industry, we will create a new Little Ice Age.

The passage tells of certain people who believe we are headed for another Little Ice Age. What are those people assuming to be true about industrial pollution? They must think that industry will continue to pollute. They must also take it for granted that the amount of pollution is enough to absorb solar heat and reduce temperatures. Such people, therefore, are making *two* assumptions. Did you catch at least one of them?

On the Springboard

Item 1 refers to the weather map below. Study the map, and then find the correct unstated assumption about weather forecasting.

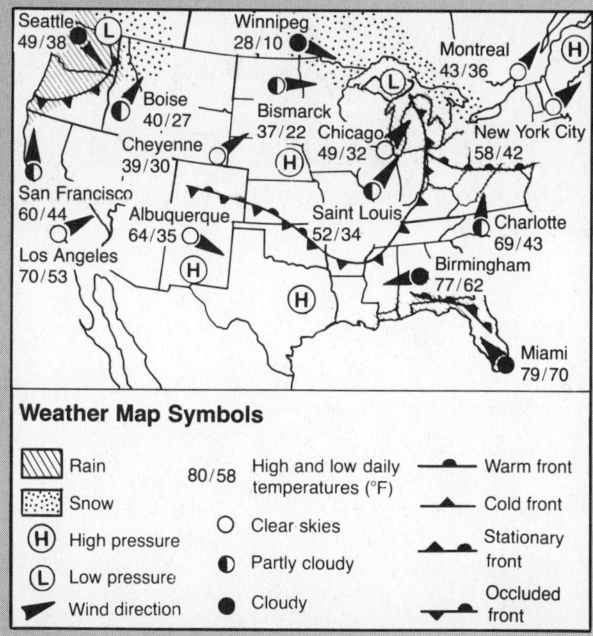

1. Weather forecasters predict that temperatures in Cheyenne will be in the thirties for the next several days. What are they assuming?

   (1) The high-pressure area over the center of the country will remain stationary.
   (2) Colder air will arrive from Bismarck.
   (3) The Rocky Mountains prevent warm air from moving in.

Item 2 refers to the paragraph below. You will be asked to identify an assumption.

When a barometer shows that air pressure is falling, it may mean that a storm is coming. The barometer inside Mr. Field's house showed a low reading an hour ago. Now it shows an even lower reading.

2. If Mr. Field correctly predicts that a storm is approaching, which of the following must be assumed?

   (1) The earth's climate is undergoing a steady change.
   (2) Weather in Mr. Field's city has been cooler than normal.
   (3) Air pressure inside Mr. Field's house is the same as the air pressure outside.

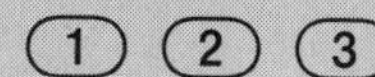

Check your answers to On the Springboard on page 155.

Did you choose the correct assumptions in the Springboard items? If you did, good for you. Now try "The Real Thing." If you had problems, take time to reread these pages. You can also review the pages on unstated assumptions in Lesson 9.

"The Real Thing"

1. A hot-air balloonist needs to increase his altitude to avoid some electrical wires. He quickly turns up the balloon's gas heater. What is the balloonist assuming?

   (1) The heated balloon will move to an area of high pressure.
   (2) Flames will force the surrounding air downward.
   (3) Warmer air in the balloon will be lighter than the surrounding air.
   (4) Electrical charges will repel the heated balloon away from the wires.
   (5) A heated balloon will increase wind resistance.

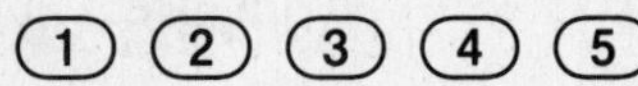

Items 2–3 refer to the following passage.

About 34 percent of the sun's energy entering the atmosphere is reflected back into space by clouds. About 19 percent is absorbed by the air and warms it. About 47 percent reaches the ground, where it warms land surfaces and bodies of water. Heat from land and water, in turn, warms the air further. The air absorbs some of this heat and keeps it from passing back into space. The retaining of the sun's heat in the atmosphere is called the greenhouse effect.

Carbon dioxide gas in the air helps create the greenhouse effect. Certain fuels that people burn increase the levels of carbon dioxide in the air. Some scientists believe that the burning of these fuels increases the greenhouse effect and warms the earth even more.

2. If it is true that a greater greenhouse effect is warming the earth, which of the following assumptions must be made?

   (1) The atmosphere is capable of holding more heat than it does now.
   (2) Energy from the sun decreases as carbon dioxide in the air decreases.
   (3) Fewer clouds are forming to reflect heat back into space.
   (4) Heat from land and water is rising farther and farther into the atmosphere.
   (5) More gardeners than ever before are growing plants indoors.

   (1) (2) (3) (4) (5)

3. Which of the following is a source of heat for the atmosphere?

   A. the sun
   B. land on earth
   C. water on earth

   (1) A only (2) B only
   (3) C only (4) A and B only
   (5) A, B, and C

Check your answers and record your score on page 156.

LESSON 17

Changes on the Earth

In this lesson you will learn about some forces that work constantly to shape and reshape the surface of the earth. Before you read the first section, look ahead to the Warm-up. It will help you pick out important ideas.

Continental Drift

Do you like to put jigsaw puzzles together? For many years, scientists thought they saw a jigsaw puzzle effect among the earth's seven largest landmasses, or continents. They saw that the edges of continents fit together like pieces of a puzzle, even though the continents are sometimes separated by thousands of miles of ocean. They wondered if the continents could have once been joined together in one huge landmass. But no one could explain how the continents might have separated.

In the 1940s, new instruments opened up research in the oceans. Scientists learned that the ocean floor has a number of long, narrow, deep trenches. In addition, they found that an underwater mountain chain—the Mid-Oceanic Ridge—circles through the ocean. Melted material from deep inside the earth rises to the surface along cracks in the middle of the Mid-Oceanic Ridge. This material hardens into new crust, and pushes the older crust back.

Scientists used the new data to develop a **theory**, an accepted idea, that explains how the continents drifted apart. The new idea was the theory of **plate tectonics**. It states that the earth's crust is broken into about twenty large sections, or plates. The plates are rigid. They move slowly on the softer layers below. The plates may slide past one another, bump into each other, or move away from each other.

Attached to separate plates, the continents moved away from each other. Continental drift, or the slowly changing position of the earth's landmasses, is still going on. New crust formed along the Mid-Oceanic Ridge continues to push plates apart. As plates collide, material from one plate slips under another, melts, and slips back into the inside of the earth. The map shows the earth's major plates and the tectonic action around their edges. Notice that most of the United States is on the North American Plate. A small part of the U.S. Pacific Coast, however, is on the Pacific Plate.

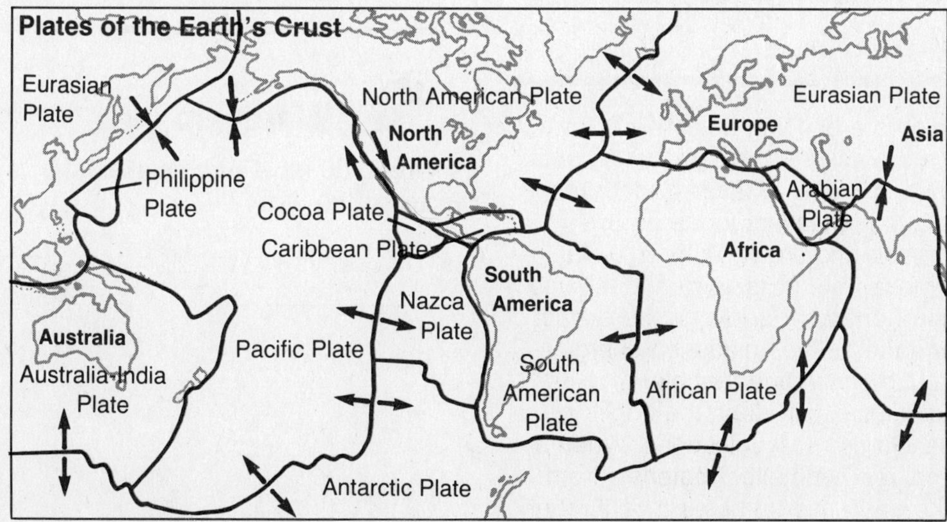

Coming to Terms

theory a generally accepted explanation

plate tectonics the widely accepted idea that the earth's crust is broken into about twenty large sections that float

Warm-up

Write a brief summary to explain what continental drift is and how it takes place.

___

___

___

___

Earthquakes and volcanoes often make the news. Each can bring sudden destruction, death, and changes in the earth's surface. In this section, you'll learn what causes such violence. Look ahead to the Warm-up to help you focus on important points as you read.

Earthquakes and Volcanoes

Imagine that you are bending a yardstick. As you increase the pressure, the stick bends until it finally snaps and breaks. Placed under pressures from below, rock layers in the earth's crust will also snap and break. When rock layers suddenly move, the rocks snap and release huge amounts of energy. People on the surface feel an **earthquake** as the unleashed energy makes the ground shake and tremble.

Most earthquakes occur along the edges of tectonic plates. So do most volcanoes. When a **volcano** erupts, red-hot melted materials from deep inside the earth rise to the surface through deep cracks. This molten material is called magma. When magma reaches the surface and spreads on the ground, it is called lava. As lava cools, it hardens into rock.

Think of what happens when you shake a bottle of soda and then take off the cap. Soda sprays everywhere! Pressure built up inside the bottle makes the soda shoot out. In a similar way, pressure builds up inside the earth. When it becomes strong enough, it sends water vapor, ash, rocks, gases, and magma to the surface. A volcano erupts. Some eruptions are violent. In others, the lava oozes slowly over the ground.

The shape a volcano takes on the surface depends on the way it erupts and the kind of materials that come to the surface. Gently sloping cinder cones form when the eruption contains mostly ash and rocks and very little magma. Quiet lava flows create shield cones. Composite cones have layers of ash and dust covered by lava. Volcanic domes build up when very thick lava bursts forth violently.

Coming to Terms

earthquake a trembling and shaking of the ground as moving rocks near the surface of the earth release great amounts of energy

volcano an opening in the surface of the earth through which magma, ashes, water vapor, and other materials escape

Warm-up

Where do most earthquakes and volcanoes occur on the earth?

___

___

Sample Warm-up Answer
Continental drift means that the earth's continents slowly move. It happens because the earth's crust is divided into plates that move on the earth's softer mantle. The continents move with the plates.

Sample Warm-up Answer
Most earthquakes and volcanoes are along the edges of the plates in the earth's crust.

In the next section you'll see how mountains, over a space of thousands of years, come into being. Read the Warm-up first to help you focus on important points.

Mountain Building

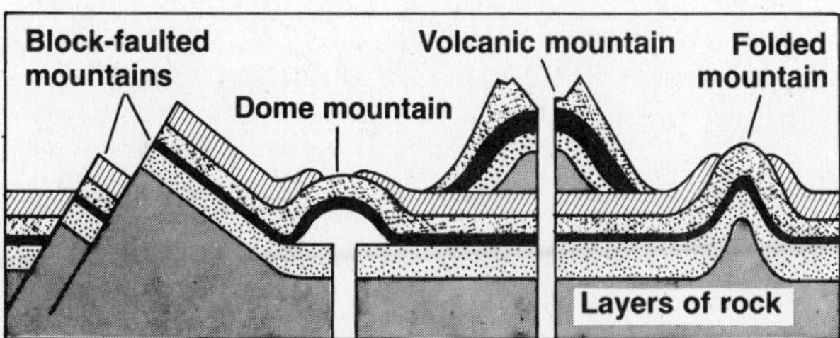

Volcanoes put out enormous quantities of lava, ash, cinders, and rock. The domes and cones they pile up often form volcanic mountains. Mount St. Helens is an active volcano in the volcanic Cascade Mountain range of the western United States. Perhaps you remember that it erupted in 1980. Volcanoes that occur underwater may build up so much material that their peaks eventually rise above the water's surface. The Hawaiian Islands formed like this. They are the tops of volcanic mountains rising from the ocean floor.

Now imagine a pillow under the bedcovers. You can't see the pillow, but you can see a lump. Dome mountains form when magma from the interior of the earth pushes up against rock layers near the surface. The rock layers bend over the lump, or dome, of magma. The Black Hills in South Dakota are dome mountains.

Rock movements along **faults**, or cracks in the earth's crust, may cause huge blocks of land to rise. The rock layers on one side of the fault may rise higher than those on the other side. This action forms block-faulted mountains. The Grand Tetons in Wyoming were raised by block-faulting.

Folded mountains take shape in yet another way. Sometimes colliding plates push up on rock layers near the surface of the earth. The rock layers bend and fold but they do not break. The Alps in Europe and the Himalayas in Asia are folded mountains. They are still growing higher because they occur along the boundaries of colliding plates.

Some mountains build up from a combination of several of the forces you have just read about. The Rockies are a good example.

Coming to Terms

fault a break in the earth's crust. Land on either side of the break has slid sideways along the break or has moved upward or downward.

Warm-up

Answer the following question in two or three of your own sentences.

Why are the Alps and Himalayas still increasing in height?

____

____

____

____

You've just read about ways that forces within the earth slowly build up portions of the earth's surface. Now you'll learn about forces at work *on* the earth's surface—and how they gradually wear it down again. Before you read this section, take a look at the Warm-up activity. Keep it in mind as you read.

Weathering and Erosion

The Appalachians in the eastern United States are very old and gently sloping mountains. But once, long ago, they were high and rugged. Over thousands of years, **weathering** and **erosion** have lowered and smoothed them down.

Sample Warm-up Answer
The Alps and Himalayas are along the edges of plates in the earth's crust. The plates are colliding. They are pushing, or folding, the mountains even higher.

Weathering, the process that breaks down rocks, takes place in two ways. Physical weathering breaks rocks into smaller and smaller chunks. For example, water trickles into cracks in rocks; when the water freezes, it expands and makes larger cracks in the rocks. Plant roots can also help crack rocks. When animals burrow in the ground, they bring rocks to the surface, where they are more easily weathered. Lightning and forest fires crack open rocks. People cause physical weathering when they build roads, cut up rocks for building materials, or move large amounts of land around.

Chemical weathering occurs when the chemicals that make up rocks mix with other chemicals. Smaller and softer rocks result from chemical weathering. Water, oxygen, and acid rain all bring about chemical weathering. In time, chemical and physical weathering turn rock into the fine particles that make up soil.

Once rocks have been broken down, the smaller chunks and particles can easily be moved. Erosion is the moving of weathered rock from one place to another. Gravity pulls materials down hillsides and so causes one kind of erosion. Running water causes a great deal of erosion as it carries along loose materials from the earth's surface. Water underground dissolves and carries away limestone. Huge, slowly moving sheets of ice, called **glaciers**, also move materials. As they grind over the earth's surface in mountains or cold climate regions, they carve, scour, and wear away other rock. Wind picks up and moves pieces of rock and soil in dust storms or sandstorms.

Through mountain building, weathering, and erosion, the earth's surface features constantly build up and wear down.

Coming to Terms

weathering the process that breaks rocks of all sizes into smaller and smaller pieces

erosion the moving of weathered rock from place to place

glacier a huge sheet of slowly moving ice on the earth's surface

Warm-up

Answer each of the following questions with a sentence of your own.

1. How can lightning and forest fires help change the earth's surface features?

____

____

2. How can running water change the earth's surface features?

____

____

Faulty Logic

Have you ever read or heard a statement that just didn't seem to make sense to you? You try to follow the reasoning behind the statement, but somehow something seems to be missing. In these cases, you're probably dealing with someone else's faulty logic.

You've already had some practice in identifying faulty logic. In Lesson 11, you saw that such logic can result from using irrelevant evidence, making errors in procedures, and seeing cause-and-effect relationships when there are none. Sometimes people "jump to conclusions" without sufficient evidence. Now you'll have the chance to sharpen your skill at spotting such faulty logic in earth science materials.

Here's an Example

The following passage illustrates some faulty reasoning. The author has overlooked some important points and so failed to think through the problem.

■ New Orleans and other towns in Louisiana are built on soft, muddy ground. The Mississippi River, over hundreds of years, has built up this soft earth with deposits of silt as it empties into the Gulf of Mexico. Each year, government and industry spend millions of dollars to save buildings, offices, and roads from sinking into the soft soil and to prevent

---

Sample Warm-up Answers
1. Lightning and forest fires can crack open rocks and so cause weathering. **2.** Running water causes erosion by carrying along rocks and soil particles.

flood damage. This money could be saved if laws prevented people from building on soft soil deposits.

The author of the passage is concerned with only one issue: the expense of maintaining structures built on the soft earth. The conclusion drawn from this thinking, then, is that people should not be allowed to build cities and roads in such areas. The author jumps to this conclusion without considering the benefits of cities and roads in these areas. New Orleans and other cities in the area are busy port cities that do a thriving trade with many other seaports all over the world. Business, government, and industry consider the advantages of their location well worth the expense of maintaining buildings and roads in the area.

Try It Yourself

See if you can tell the mistake in reasoning that the author of the following paragraph made.

■ I've seen the Grand Canyon in Arizona a number of times since I was a child. The Colorado River flows through the floor of the canyon. Although scientists say that the river is carving the canyon out of the rock layers, I know this could not be true. The canyon is still the same size as it was when I first saw it twenty years ago: two hundred miles long and a mile deep.

What did the visitor to the Grand Canyon not consider in reaching the conclusion that the Colorado River could not have created the Grand Canyon? Did you say time? If so, you're right. It took an extremely long time for the river to erode the Grand Canyon that we see today. The visitor jumped to a hasty and therefore faulty conclusion.

On the Springboard

Item 1 refers to the following diagram and passage. You'll read about a scientist who *did* reach a conclusion that had merit, yet other scientists rightfully said that he did not have enough evidence to justify his conclusion.

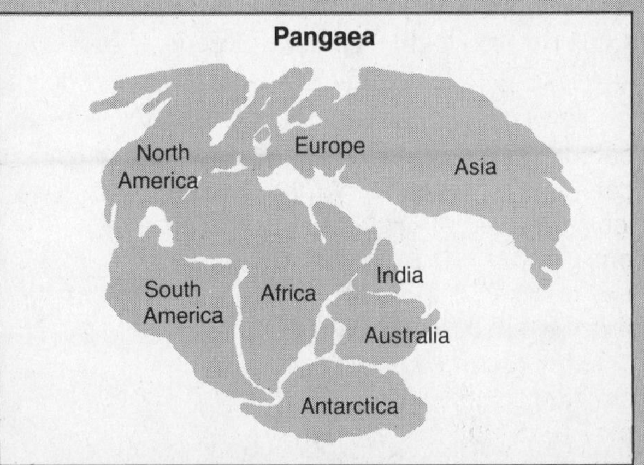

In 1912 Alfred Wegener, a German scientist, concluded that all the earth's continents were once joined together in a single continent, which he called Pangaea. Wegener claimed that the continents we know today broke off from Pangaea and "drifted" to their present locations. He based his conclusion on the fact that the edges of today's continents seem to fit together like pieces of a jigsaw puzzle. He also used ancient rock layers and animal fossils for evidence. Fossils and rocks along the east coast of South America matched many of those along the west coast of Africa. Fossils found in Greenland and Antarctica were of plants that grow near the equator. Wegener was convinced that the land had once been joined but later separated into pieces that drifted apart. Scientists of Wegener's day could not totally accept his conclusion, however. They needed further evidence.

1. To support his conclusion fully, Wegener needed evidence that showed how

   (1) the coasts of continents fit together
   (2) continents could drift apart
   (3) the same animals and plants lived on different continents

Item 2 refers to the following passage. You will be asked to identify the mistake in reasoning the passage contains.

In 1811 and 1812, violent earthquakes shook New Madrid, Missouri. New Madrid is located near the middle of the North American plate. The quakes that occurred there were strong enough to change the course of the Mississippi River. People as far away as Massachusetts felt the tremors. Records show that the greatest number of earthquakes occur along the edges of tectonic plates. The violent quakes in New Madrid, therefore, indicate that the North American plate is breaking into two new plates.

2. The author of the passage has mistakenly concluded that earthquakes must always occur

 (1) along plate boundaries
 (2) in the center of tectonic plates
 (3) near large rivers

Check your answers to On the Springboard on page 155.

How did you do? Were you able to evaluate the reasoning in each passage? If so, try "The Real Thing" now. If you had trouble with the On the Springboard questions, take a moment to review this section. You could also reread the section on faulty logic in Lesson 11 for additional help.

☑ A Test-Taking Tip

Remember that on the GED Science Test you don't get any points taken off for wrong answers. So if you have thought about a question carefully but still cannot choose an answer you are sure of, *don't be afraid to guess*!

❝ The Real Thing ❞

Item 1 refers to the following information.

Dunes are hills of windblown sand. They are just one effect of wind erosion. People cannot stop erosion by the wind. Once weathering has broken rocks into small pieces, the wind will act on them. Vegetation, however, can act as a windbreak. It can also hold soil together to protect it from the wind.

1. A farmer wants to increase his acreage, so he cuts down a small wooded area on the edge of his land and plants corn.

 What is wrong with the farmer's logic?

 (1) The wood would bring him more money than corn.
 (2) The corn plants will most likely be blown away.
 (3) A sand dune will cover his fields.
 (4) The topsoil in his fields may be eroded by the wind.
 (5) He shouldn't worry about wind erosion because there is nothing he can do to stop it.

Items 2–4 refer to the diagram and passage below.

A River System

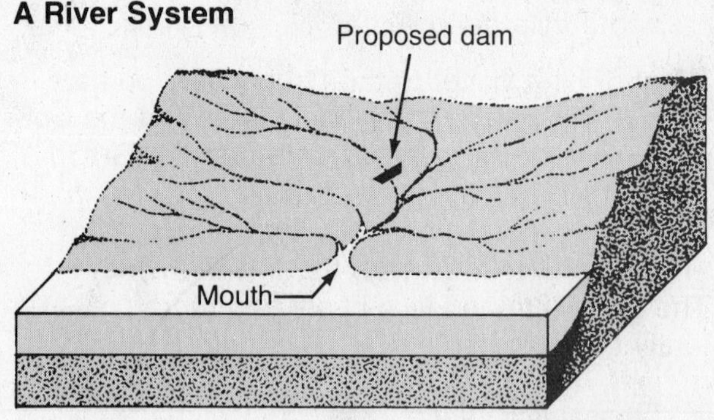

Rainwater that runs into rivers is one path of erosion. Also known as runoff, this moving water drains off the land into regular small streams and larger rivers. The runoff carries sediment from the land into the streams. Streams come together to become part of a river system. The river system drains all the land through which the connected rivers and streams flow. Eventually sediments from this land area move with the flowing water into a lake or ocean at the mouth of the largest river.

2. The state wants to build a dam at the site shown on the diagram to create a freshwater lake that would be used for recreation. Which of the following pieces of information is it neglecting to consider?

   (1) Only wealthier people will be able to use the lake.
   (2) Sediments will eventually build up behind the dam and in the lake.
   (3) The dam will stop a necessary step in the water cycle.
   (4) The dam will prevent all the water from reaching the end of the river system.
   (5) The water in the lake will not be fresh because it is too close to the ocean.

   (1) (2) (3) (4) (5)

3. According to the passage, rainwater causes erosion when it

   (1) falls into rivers and streams
   (2) floods an area after a heavy storm
   (3) breaks through dams
   (4) collects in lakes behind dams
   (5) carries soil into rivers

4. What would be the most likely effect of the movement of sediments to the mouth of a river?

   (1) Lakes and oceans at the mouth cause further runoff.
   (2) The river speeds up near its mouth.
   (3) The river system eventually dries up.
   (4) A large desert area is created upstream.
   (5) Land builds up at the mouth of the river.

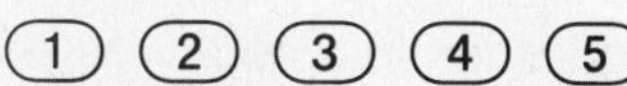

Check your answers and record your score on pages 156–157.

LESSON 18

Energy

People did not think much about the energy they used until the 1970s, when the first "energy crisis" occurred. In this lesson you'll read about where energy comes from and how people use it today or may use it in the future. Glance at the Warm-up before you read the first section. It can help you pick out important ideas.

Renewable Sources

People walk and jog. Cars move slowly on the freeway during rush hour. Big jets streak the sky at more than five hundred miles an hour. What do people, the cars, and the jets have in common? They all use energy.

People, of course, get their energy from the food they eat. Where do they get the energy to power their machines? It comes from many different sources. Some sources of energy will always be around; they can't really be used up. Such sources of energy are said to be **renewable sources.** The sun, the wind, water, and the earth's heat stored below its surface are all renewable sources of energy.

The sun's energy is solar energy. The earth receives a tremendous amount of energy from the sun every day. People have invented ways to collect and store some solar energy. They use the sun's heat to heat fluids or charge storage batteries. You may have seen homes and buildings that use solar energy to run heating and cooling systems.

People have used the wind's power for centuries. Wind energy moves sailing boats and turns windmills. The rotating shaft of a windmill can crush grain or raise water from a well.

People have also used waterpower for a long time. Falling or running water can turn waterwheels that drive machinery. The power produced by waterfalls and dams operates turbines; the turbines drive generators that produce electricity. This kind of power is hydroelectric power. *Hydro* means "water."

There is a great deal of heat energy inside the earth. This geothermal energy shows itself in volcanoes and spouting hot water, called geysers, on the earth's surface. At present, the country of Iceland, which has many geysers, relies entirely on geothermal energy.

Coming to Terms

renewable source a source of energy that cannot be used up

Warm-up

Write a sentence in which you name four examples of renewable energy sources.

____

____

In the next section you'll read about some of the more familiar sources of energy. Look at the Warm-up before you read to help you locate important points.

Nonrenewable Sources

It may seem strange that the remains of tiny plants and animals help run our cars. But it's true. The remains of past life formed the fossil fuel called "crude oil." Gasoline and many other petroleum products come from crude oil. The earth's crust contains only so many deposits of crude oil. Once people have used them up, there will be no more. Since crude oil cannot be replaced, it is a **nonrenewable source** of energy.

Coal is another nonrenewable fossil fuel. About 325 million years ago, during the Paleozoic era that you read about in Lesson 14, large ferns and trees with woody stems grew near shallow swamps. When these green plants died, they fell into the wet swamps. As the trees decayed, substances containing the element carbon broke down. Soft carbon was left. After millions of years, the decayed material thickened and hardened. Rock layers formed on top of it. Then the sea rose and created great pressure on the black, carbon substance. Eventually, the water receded, and the process began again: more trees, more sediment, more pressure. By the time the era ended, the large green trees had changed into the black coal that heats homes and provides energy for factories today.

The element uranium provides the fuel for nuclear energy. Uranium deposits are very scarce, so nuclear energy is also a nonrenewable source of energy. It does, however, produce huge amounts of power. Many places in the world use nuclear reactors, fueled by uranium, to generate power. Heat from the reactor boils water and produces steam. The steam drives a turbine that generates electricity.

The future of nuclear energy is uncertain. Besides being nonrenewable, nuclear power requires strong safety measures to keep heat and dangerous substances from escaping into the environment. Nuclear reactors also produce dangerous wastes. These must be stored for perhaps hundreds of years before they no longer threaten living organisms.

Coming to Terms

nonrenewable source a source of energy that cannot be replaced once it has been used up

Warm-up

Answer each question in a complete sentence.

1. Why are crude oil and coal called fossil fuels?

____

____

2. How do people use nuclear reactors today?

____

____

Sample Warm-up Answer
Solar energy, wind energy, waterpower, and geothermal energy are all renewable sources of energy.

Sample Warm-up Answers
1. Both crude oil and coal formed from the remains of ancient plant and animal life. **2.** Many nuclear reactors heat water and produce the steam that drives electric generators.

In this final earth science section, you'll look at people in relation to the earth's energy supplies—both renewable and nonrenewable. Before you read the section, preview the Warm-up for main points of information.

People and Energy

At times in the recent past, there have been shortages of crude oil—a fuel used in one form or another to run cars, produce plastics, and heat homes. What about the future? With more and more cars on streets and highways, will there always be enough crude oil to fuel them? As you learned in the last section, crude oil is a nonrenewable fossil fuel.

Now think about water. Water is a renewable source of energy. Waterfalls and swift rapids, however, are not always located where industries can easily draw upon their energy.

Recent concerns over possible shortages in gasoline and energy supplies in general are real. Even though there is much more coal stored in the earth than crude oil, it too is nonrenewable. How should people view their almost unlimited needs for energy with the limited supplies of energy resources?

Many people insist the answer is **conservation.** Conservation means using the earth's resources, including energy supplies, thoughtfully. It means protecting them from loss, damage, and especially waste.

Another way to deal with the need for energy is to develop new fuels or use old fuels in new ways. A combination of gasoline and alcohol, for example, produces a fuel called gasohol. Most cars in Brazil and some in our own country run on gasohol. Some experimental cars run on electric batteries. In some countries windfarms—acres of land with hundreds of windmills—help convert wind power to electrical power.

Scientists are also studying the possibility of using nuclear fusion—the energy that powers the sun itself—here on earth rather than nuclear fission. Nuclear fission is what most nuclear power plants currently use to produce energy.

The benefits of using a particular energy source—whether it is renewable or nonrenewable—must also be weighed against its possible drawbacks. Fossil fuels, for example, produce pollution. In addition, mining such fuels can erode the land and endanger the lives of the people who mine them. And the hazards that accompany nuclear power include handling the fuel itself and disposing of the by-products. Expense is still another factor that must be considered when making energy decisions.

Coming to Terms

conservation the protection of energy supplies and other natural resources on the earth through wise use

Warm-up

In what ways might you, as an individual, conserve energy? Write your answer in a sentence or two.

____

____

____

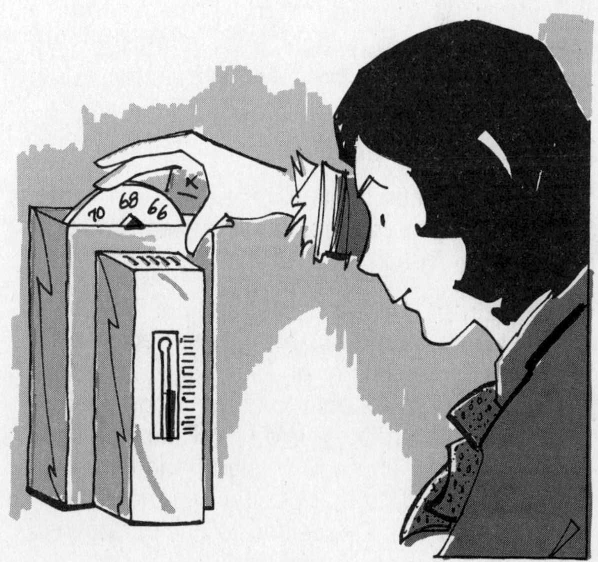

Sample Warm-up Answer
You could name dozens of ways to conserve energy—for example, cut down on unnecessary car trips, join a car pool, turn off unnecessary lights, use fewer electrical appliances, insulate your home, weatherstrip doors and windows, and set the thermostat lower in winter.

Values in Beliefs and Decision Making

Scientists try to be objective in their work. To be objective means to look at facts without allowing personal desires or values to alter conclusions or actions. Scientists are taught to view test results and data and to record exactly what they observe, not what they hope to see. They also learn to look at *all* the data, not just the data that support their own ideas.

All people, however, are more objective in some areas than in others. A scientist who is very objective with data concerning nuclear power, for example, might be much less objective when it comes to endangered species. That scientist's high regard, or value, for the environment may influence his or her conclusions and beliefs more than the facts do.

When you read science materials, you will sometimes find examples of personal values influencing conclusions or actions. For example, in early history, some scientists found evidence that the earth moves around the sun. Other equally famous scientists insisted that the earth was the center of the entire universe. They discounted the evidence because an earth-centered universe agreed with their religious beliefs.

Often the role such values play in scientific thought is not obvious, but it is possible and even necessary to recognize the effects of values on theories and conclusions.

Here's an Example

The paragraph below is part of a speech written by a person protesting against nuclear power plants.

■ We are told by the utilities people that we don't understand nuclear power because we are not scientists or professors. I say, "You don't have to be able to lay an egg to tell when one is rotten." We understand the implications of Three Mile Island and Chernobyl. They tell us that people can make mistakes and will. Opposition to nuclear power plants is a moral necessity.

That is clearly an opinion about a source of energy. According to the writer, the utilities people claim that one has to be highly educated about physics to decide if nuclear power is safe and desirable. The writer insists that non-scientists can recognize examples of danger and concludes that nuclear energy is not safe. The value behind this piece of writing might be stated like this: The first priority of energy production is safety. Notice that you do not have to agree with the values of the writer to identify them.

Now read the following passage on the same subject.

■ The antinuclear movement has become widespread and powerful. The only way to meet and understand it is to discuss in detail each argument that is raised against reactors. This may not convince professional objectors, but it is necessary for the general public, whose vital interest is at stake.

That passage appears to be less emotional and more objective than the previous one. However, you may have noticed that the statements imply several things. They imply that, given enough details, every argument against reactors can be silenced. The last sentence implies that some people object because they are "professional objectors." The author may mean that these objectors earn money by leading protests or that they protest because they enjoy doing it, not out of sincere belief. Either way, that is an opinion, not fact.

The writer of the second passage obviously values the good that nuclear energy can provide. He also values knowledge and assumes that people who disagree are not knowledgeable.

Those two passages may help you think about your own values related to this issue. However, neither one offers enough factual material for you to arrive at an informed decision. You can be most objective yourself when you are well informed about facts and when you can recognize implied values.

☑ A Test-Taking Tip

You may not always agree with the values given in passages used on the GED Science Test. Try to set aside your personal opinions and answer the questions according to what is stated or implied in the test item. Your ideas are not being challenged by the passages used in the test. Your ability to understand and recognize the influence of values is the point of such test items.

Try It Yourself

The following passage contains both factual information and opinions based on the values of the writer. As you read, remember that a *fact* is something that can be proved. An idea that depends totally on personal taste or values is an *opinion.*

■ There is still enough coal on earth to last for centuries. Some of this coal has a high sulfur content. The sulfur remains unburned and enters the air as pollution. Environmental groups have successfully fought the use of high-sulfur coal. Their actions have unnecessarily prevented the use of a readily accessible source of energy.

Were you able to sort out the factual material? The facts are the following: there is still coal on earth; some coal has high sulfur content; the sulfur pollutes the air. There is also an assumption that may be true: the statement that coal will last for centuries *may* be an informed idea, but the writer has not proved it.

Did you decide the last sentence was an opinion that revealed an underlying value? The idea that controls on high-sulfur coal are unnecessary is an opinion based on a value that the writer holds: filling an energy need is more important than clean air. Were you able to identify this underlying value in the author's remarks?

On the Springboard

Item 1 refers to the passage below. The writer holds a value that you can infer by reading carefully.

Some energy sources leave significant pollution and toxic wastes behind, while other sources are relatively clean. Coal, petroleum, and nuclear fuels are in the first group. Wind, water, geothermal power, and solar power are in the second group. Natural gas, which in the past has been relatively pure, is now becoming a dirtier source of energy.

Unfortunately, dirty power sources have been easy to develop. They are the ones that have brought the rapid growth of industry that our society desires. What are the possibilities for clean energy? Wind power can be used locally but is undependable. Solar power has been developed in areas where it is practical, but it is expensive when used on a large scale. Scientists have great hope for using the heat energy beneath the earth's crust and the energy of the tides and currents. These two energy sources offer the best hope for clean, plentiful power.

1. Which of the following sentences states a probable belief of the author?
   (1) Cost and simple production methods should determine which energy sources to develop.
   (2) Combining many kinds of energy sources is the ideal way to provide energy needs.
   (3) Great research and effort should be devoted to developing clean power sources.

Now check your answer to the Springboard item on page 155.

If you were able to answer this question correctly and easily, go on to "The Real Thing." If you had some difficulty, review the explanations and exercises in this section before you go on.

❝ The Real Thing ❞

Items 1–4 are based on the following passage.

Energy in the form of heat can be easily converted to electrical power. Geothermal heat is already an important source of energy in New Zealand, Iceland, and Italy. Areas where humans have greatest access to geothermal heat are particularly appropriate for development. The western United States, where two of the earth's crustal plates meet, is such a region.

Geothermal heat is most easily converted to usable power when underground water meets molten rock. High temperatures of the melted rock turn the water to steam. This steam is sometimes pure. In some areas, though, such as high-sulfur regions, the steam is contaminated and requires costly cleaning. Furthermore, geothermal plants along the edges of plates might speed up the loss of heat and water from deep inside the earth. This, in turn, could cause earthquakes.

1. Which of the following beliefs does the author of the passage probably have?

   (1) The western states should be working to develop their geothermal potential as rapidly as possible.
   (2) Other countries have been unfairly monopolizing geothermal energy sources.
   (3) Steam heat is too costly and impure to use for generating electricity.
   (4) More research is needed before the United States builds geothermal energy plants.
   (5) Geothermal energy is an unacceptable source of energy for modern society.

   ① ② ③ ④ ⑤

2. Natural steam occurs within the earth when

   (1) contaminants enter the groundwater
   (2) two plates in the earth's crust meet
   (3) earthquakes occur
   (4) high concentrations of sulfur are present
   (5) underground water encounters melted rock

   ① ② ③ ④ ⑤

3. According to the passage, three factors that help determine where development of geothermal energy is practical are safety from earthquakes, purity of the steam, and

   (1) nearness to the earth's surface
   (2) need of the population
   (3) temperature of the steam
   (4) accessibility to major cities
   (5) absence of melted rock

   ① ② ③ ④ ⑤

4. Geothermal heat can be a practical source of energy.

   Which of the following pieces of evidence from the passage could be used to support that statement?

   (1) Sulfur contaminates steam in some areas.
   (2) Two crustal plates meet in the western United States.
   (3) Geothermal heat is already being used in some countries.
   (4) Geothermal plants at the edges of plates could lead to earthquakes.
   (5) Geothermal energy can be expensive.

   ① ② ③ ④ ⑤

Check your answers and record your score on page 157.

Answers: On the Springboard

12 The Universe Restating Information
(page 118)

1. (3) The words *atmosphere, cloud,* and *hot* are key words in this description of Venus.

2. (3) The sun is roughly in the middle of the main sequence.

3. (2) Super giants are low on the temperature axis of the graph but high on the brightness axis.

13 The Earth Inferring the Main Idea
(page 124)

1. (2) Option (1) states only one supporting fact, and option (3) is incorrect. It is winter when the sun's rays hit at a wider slant. Most of the paragraph explains the time lag between the greatest heating effect and the hottest temperatures.

14 The Land Drawing Conclusions
(page 129)

1. (3) The fact that fossil fish of the same age have been found *throughout* Kansas indicates that a large amount of deep water must have been present when the fish lived there.

2. (1) An older layer does not necessarily contain simpler fossils. Simple one-celled animals are present even today. As the deepest layers are usually oldest, option (1) is most likely the accurate conclusion.

15 The Water Inferring Cause-and-Effect Relationships
(page 135)

1. (3) Because salts are left behind when seawater turns to vapor, evaporation is the reason that rainwater is fresh.

2. (2) Brown and green waters are signs of upwellings, which are full of minerals and rich in life. Therefore, fishers expect to find large fish feeding in these areas.

3. (1) Although upwellings are often warmer and less dense than other waters, that is not a reason for the presence of food. It is the action of the water as it rises that brings food to the area.

16 The Air Recognizing Unstated Assumptions
(page 141)

1. (1) If the high-pressure area stays where it is, the temperatures in Cheyenne will not change too much.

2. (3) Mr. Field's correct prediction would indicate that, even though his barometer was inside, the conditions were the same as on the outside.

17 Changes on the Earth Faulty Logic
(pages 147–148)

1. (2) Wegener showed how the coastlines fit together, and he used fossils from different continents as evidence. He never explained, however, how the continents could move. Evidence for such movement came long after Wegener's time.

2. (1) Note that the passage states "the greatest number of," not "all," earthquakes occur on edges of tectonic plates.

18 Energy Values in Beliefs and Decision Making
(page 153)

1. (3) The word *unfortunately* tells you how the writer feels about using cost and simplicity to determine which energy sources to use. Clean power is clearly mentioned as an important issue throughout the passage.

Answers: "The Real Thing"

As you check your answers, you may notice that some question numbers are in color. This shows that those questions pertain to the skill taught in the lesson. The skill in each lesson is labeled with a heading that is in color. You'll probably want to go back and review the skills you had difficulty with before you complete the lessons in this section.

12 The Universe
Restating Information
(page 119)

1. (2) This information is in the third sentence.

2. (2) According to the passage, when the number of sunspots is highest, solar flares shoot out particles that can interfere with radio transmission.

3. (3) This statement describes the dense, bright cluster of stars you can see in the diagram at the center of the Milky Way.

KEEPING TRACK
Top Score = 3
Your Score = ☐

13 The Earth
Inferring the Main Idea
(page 125)

1. (4) This statement summarizes the two key ideas: there are four types of land, and they are identified by their height.

2. (1) This statement summarizes the specific source of the magnetosphere and the specific ways in which it interacts with solar radiation.

3. (4) Since the solar particles are guided toward the poles by the magnetosphere, both the North and South Poles would be good spots to see the auroras.

KEEPING TRACK
Top Score = 3
Your Score = ☐

14 The Land
Drawing Conclusions
(page 130)

1. (2) Only option (2) contains the necessary condition that a liquid cools slowly in the uncrowded center of a limestone ball.

2. (5) The passage states that the conditions necessary for coal production no longer exist on earth. This fact supports the conclusion stated in option (5).

3. (3) The role of high pressure exerted over long periods of time is mentioned throughout the passage as necessary for oil, coal, and limestone to develop.

4. (2) Only stagnant (still), warm marshes provide the calm, low-oxygen environment that prevents plant matter from rotting or being disturbed.

KEEPING TRACK
Top Score = 4
Your Score = ☐

15 The Water
Inferring Cause-and-Effect Relationships
(page 136)

1. (5) The passage states that the lack of current and of new water in the Sargasso Sea means that no upwelling occurs to provide the nutrients that support life.

2. (4) D is the spot nearest to the Sargasso Sea, according to the description in the passage.

3. (1) The arrows help you infer that winds move evaporated seawater back toward land in the form of clouds.

KEEPING TRACK
Top Score = 3
Your Score = ☐

16 The Air
Recognizing Unstated Assumptions
(page 142)

1. (3) If the warm air is lighter, it will lift the balloon.

2. (1) If the earth's atmosphere held all the heat it could already, we wouldn't have to worry about increasing the greenhouse effect with more carbon dioxide.

3. (5) According to the information given, some heat from the sun is absorbed directly by the atmosphere. Additional heat hits the land and the water and then is given off to the atmosphere.

KEEPING TRACK
Top Score = 3
Your Score = ☐

17 Changes on the Earth
Faulty Logic
(pages 148–149)

1. (4) The farmer should leave the woods to act as a windbreak. Otherwise, his topsoil is exposed to the wind during the time the corn plants have yet to sprout.

2. (2) Sediments will run off into the small streams and the lake behind the dam; they will be blocked from moving into the main river by the dam.

3. (5) Erosion is the *movement* of particles, so rainwater erodes when it moves soil as it drains into rivers.

4. (5) The sediments are carried down the river system and settle at its mouth, where the river flows into a larger body of water. As they settle, land builds up.

KEEPING TRACK
Top Score = 4

Your Score = ☐

18 Energy
Values in Beliefs and Decision Making
(page 154)

1. (4) The writer names several pluses as well as several problems in using geothermal heat for energy. Therefore, option (4) most likely represents one of her beliefs.

2. (5) You can find this information in the first two sentences of the second paragraph.

3. (1) In the first paragraph, access is discussed. You can infer from the last sentence of that paragraph that it is not the nearness of geothermal energy to major cities but, in the western United States, nearness to the surface of the earth, where plates meet.

4. (3) The fact that geothermal energy is already being used in New Zealand, Iceland, and Italy helps show that it is a practical, workable source.

KEEPING TRACK
Top Score = 4

Your Score = ☐

Keeping Track

Now record your scores from the Keeping Track boxes on the lines below.

	Top Score	Your Score
Lesson 12 Restating Information	3	______
Lesson 13 Inferring the Main Idea	3	______
Lesson 14 Drawing Conclusions	4	______
Lesson 15 Inferring Cause-and-Effect Relationships	3	______
Lesson 16 Recognizing Unstated Assumptions	3	______
Lesson 17 Faulty Logic	4	______
Lesson 18 Values in Beliefs and Decision Making	4	______
TOTAL	24	______

How did you do in *Earth Science*? Now is the time to review any skills that you may have had problems with. Use your scores in the lessons to help you determine which lessons you may need to reread. Then sharpen all your reading and thinking skills on the Extra Practice in Earth Science that follows.

Extra Practice in Earth Science

Directions: Choose the one best answer for each item.

Items 1–2 are based on the following passage.

The earth's atmosphere contains billions of tons of air. At any given time it is swirling, mixing, and moving in countless directions. Air masses near the surface of the earth may be traveling from one to three miles per hour, while five miles up they may be rushing along at more than 250 miles per hour. The moisture content of the moving air varies as a result of changes in temperature and terrain. For that reason, perfect weather forecasting is not yet possible.

Errors in weather predicting occur for three main reasons. Weather forecasters, known as meteorologists, do not understand all the physical interactions that occur when different portions of the atmosphere mix together. More problems occur because of lack of data. For example, there are only five hundred weather stations operating in all of North America, so there are large areas of the continent where weather information is not available. Incomplete information results in error because a slight weather change in one location can drastically affect the conditions in an area near by. Since the 1960s, weather satellites have helped solve this problem, but even they do not cover the entire earth.

Surprisingly, computers used in forecasting weather also result in errors. Although the computers actually do their job very well, the necessary calculations are so complex and take so long that shortcuts must be used. These shortcuts are simplified programs that allow the calculations to be done more quickly, but the results seldom give a complete picture of the weather.

Despite these problems, most weather predictions are still very useful. Meteorologists can forecast temperature, wind direction, and wind speed fairly accurately. They usually cannot accurately predict the amount of rain to be expected. Weather predictions made one or two days ahead are usually accurate. Beyond seventy-two hours, though, they can be depended on only for general weather patterns.

1. Which of the following statements best summarizes the passage above?

   (1) Weather predicting is more accurate in some parts of the country than in others.
   (2) The main problem in predicting weather is the mixing of air that occurs in the atmosphere.
   (3) Current weather forecasting has little basis in scientific fact.
   (4) Limited data and understanding of the atmosphere make weather predictions inexact.
   (5) Atmospheric movement cannot be described by physical laws.

   (1) (2) (3) (4) (5)

2. The author implies that weather forecasting could become more reliable and accurate if there were more

   (1) weather satellites
   (2) staff at weather stations
   (3) computers
   (4) shortcuts in calculations
   (5) television weather forecasters

   (1) (2) (3) (4) (5)

---

3. Below are four statements about diamonds from a jewelry store advertisement.

   A. Diamond is the hardest mineral known.
   B. Many diamonds are yellow, blue, or pink because they contain impurities.
   C. Only about 20 percent of the diamonds mined each year are used in jewelry.
   D. Light reflecting from the cut surfaces of a diamond is what makes the stone beautiful.

   Which of the statements above represents an opinion rather than a fact?

   (1) A only
   (2) B only
   (3) C only
   (4) D only
   (5) B and D

   (1) (2) (3) (4) (5)

4. Color can indicate temperature. For example, if a metal is heated, it first becomes "red hot." If it is heated to higher temperatures, its color changes from red to orange to yellow to white to blue-white and finally to blue. A star radiates all colors, but its temperature determines which color it emits most strongly. Based on this information, the hottest stars appear to be

(1) red hot
(2) yellow
(3) white
(4) blue-white
(5) blue

(1) (2) (3) (4) (5)

Items 5–7 are based on the following graph and information.

Oil Use in the United States

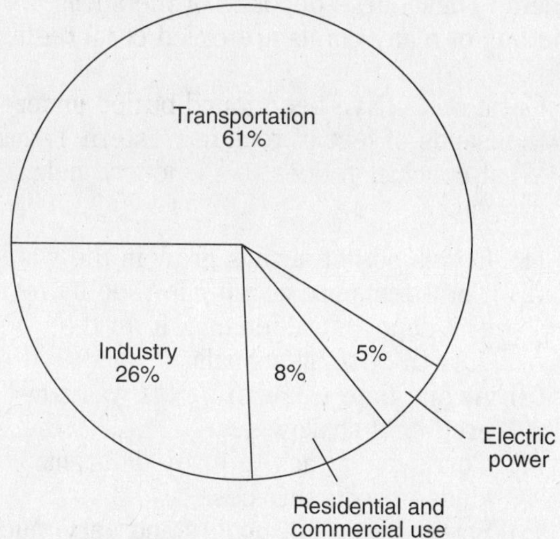

Liquid fossil fuel is called oil, or petroleum. When petroleum is brought up from beneath the earth's surface, it is called crude oil. Crude oil is refined to make usable products such as gasoline for automobiles, home-heating oils, and petrochemicals. Petrochemicals are used to make products such as plastics, medicines, fabrics, and building materials.

5. According to the graph, approximately how much oil in the United States is used for electricity and industry?

(1) one-tenth
(2) one-fifth
(3) one-fourth
(4) one-third
(5) one-half

(1) (2) (3) (4) (5)

6. A homeowner thinks that heating oil is expensive because only 8 percent of all the oil found can be used to produce heating oil. This person is misreading the graph because he thinks that it shows the percentages of

(1) oil remaining in the ground
(2) oil available on the world market
(3) the ways oil can be used
(4) the different uses people have for oil
(5) the relative cost of oil

(1) (2) (3) (4) (5)

7. A government worker predicts that the United States will suffer severe shortages of transportation fuels in the next twenty years because the oil-producing countries say they will reduce the amount of crude oil they produce. What is the worker assuming?

(1) The demand for transportation fuels will remain at least the same.
(2) Fewer people will be driving cars and taking airplane trips.
(3) New transportation fuels will be developed.
(4) More crude oil will be used to produce fuel.
(5) Fewer refineries will be working.

(1) (2) (3) (4) (5)

Items 8–9 refer to the diagram and information below.

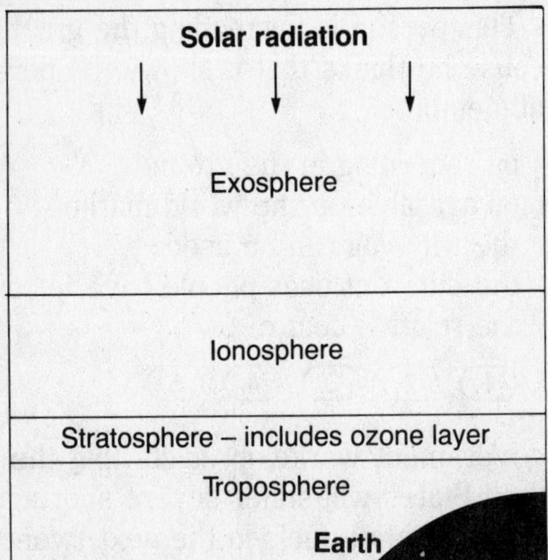

Ultraviolet light (UVL) in solar radiation can kill living organisms. However, not much UVL reaches the earth's surface because it is absorbed by the gases oxygen and ozone in the upper atmosphere. Scientists believe that oxygen absorbs a little UVL and in the process converts into ozone. The ozone then absorbs large amounts of UVL. There is evidence that the ozone in the atmosphere is disappearing, and some scientists believe that pollution may be stopping the reaction that converts oxygen into ozone. These scientists suggest that the chemical used in air conditioners, refrigerators, spray cans, and cleaning solutions may be the main pollutant.

8. What effect might occur if ozone disappears from the upper atmosphere?

(1) There will be less ultraviolet light in the atmosphere.
(2) More ultraviolet light will be absorbed by the atmosphere.
(3) The amount of ultraviolet light reaching the ground will increase.
(4) Pollutants in the atmosphere will increase.
(5) Less oxygen will form in the atmosphere.

① ② ③ ④ ⑤

9. Which of the following statements is a hypothesis suggested in the passage?

(1) Ultraviolet light can kill living organisms.
(2) Ozone absorbs ultraviolet light.
(3) Ozone is a form of oxygen.
(4) A chemical used on earth is decreasing the ozone.
(5) There is evidence that the ozone in the atmosphere is disappearing.

Item 10 is based on the information below.

Corals are tiny sea animals that live in colonies. They remain attached to rocky sea floors in clear seawater that is no deeper than 46 meters and has a temperature of 18–21°C. They make their shells from the chemicals in seawater. When corals die, their shells remain attached to the rocks, and new corals grow on top of them. These large deposits of the shells and skeletons of many corals are called coral reefs.

10. Coral reefs have been found buried under thousands of feet of rock in western Texas. What conclusion does this evidence help support?

(1) Corals do not always grow in the water.
(2) Coral reefs are actually formed by mineral deposits rather than from the growth of small animals.
(3) At one time western Texas was covered by a shallow sea.
(4) Corals can attach to many different kinds of rock surfaces.
(5) Scientists do not understand very much about coral reefs.

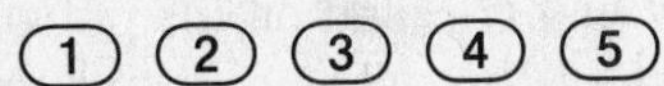

Items 11–14 refer to the following information.

Many physical and chemical processes change the surface of the earth. These processes involve the action of wind, water, ice, heat, and gravity on the earth's surface. Five of these processes are defined below.

(1) abrasion = wearing away of rock by the grinding of ice, soil, or other materials against it

(2) creep = very slow movement of soil downhill

(3) deposition = accumulation of substances that are no longer dissolved in water

(4) exfoliation = peeling or flaking of thin layers from the surface of rock

(5) leaching = the removal of minerals from the soil as water moves through it

Each item below demonstrates one of these processes. For each item, select the one process that is best illustrated. Any term may be used more than once or not at all.

11. A woman decided to replant her African violet because it was no longer growing well. When she removed the plant from its container, she found that the bottom and sides of the pot were lined with a thick layer of white salts.

    The layer of salts formed because of the process of

    (1) abrasion
    (2) creep
    (3) deposition
    (4) exfoliation
    (5) leaching

    ① ② ③ ④ ⑤

12. After a spring thaw, a homeowner swept many small pieces of rock from the surface of her stone patio.

    The small pieces of rock appeared as the result of

    (1) abrasion
    (2) creep
    (3) deposition
    (4) exfoliation
    (5) leaching

    ① ② ③ ④ ⑤

13. As Ice Age glaciers moved across mid-Europe, they scraped across solid rock and left behind a layer of rounded boulders, pebbles, and sand grains.

    The rocky debris formed through the process of

    (1) abrasion
    (2) creep
    (3) deposition
    (4) exfoliation
    (5) leaching

    ① ② ③ ④ ⑤

14. A rancher noticed that the fences he put up some years ago across the side of a hill now tip downhill rather than point upward.

    The fence posts now point downhill because of

    (1) abrasion
    (2) creep
    (3) deposition
    (4) exfoliation
    (5) leaching

    ① ② ③ ④ ⑤

Answers to Extra Practice in Earth Science begin on page 231. Record your score on the Progress Chart on the inside back cover.

Chemistry

To you, it may only be an ice cube to chill your drink, but to a chemist, it's H_2O in its solid state. To you, it's just an old rust spot on the car, but to a chemist, it's the result of a chemical reaction between iron and oxygen.

Chemistry may *seem* far removed from your everyday life, but appearances are deceiving. Everything around you—and you yourself—are made of matter, and matter is at the heart of chemistry. Chemists study matter, its properties, and the changes it goes through. The results of their work include synthetic fabrics such as polyester and nylon, plastic materials such as milk containers, hair curlers, and car bumpers, and medicines such as stomach antacids and aspirin or aspirin substitutes.

Chemistry on the GED Science Test deals with the general properties of matter that scientists have discovered *and* the method that they use to discover them. The items will be short pieces of information followed by one question or longer articles followed by several questions. Sometimes a visual aid such as a graph or diagram will be used. As with biology and earth science, the information you need to answer each question will be there on the test. You have to figure out what information you need to answer the question, find it in the written or visual material, and think about it to come up with the correct answer. In the next column is an example of a single chemistry item that might appear on the GED Science Test.

The atoms, ions, or molecules of some substances arrange themselves in definite patterns known as crystals. Diamonds, table salt, and sugar are crystals. Because of their shape, there is space between crystals. Think about a teaspoonful of sugar. Air fills the space between the crystals of sugar. When the crystals are dissolved, the particles making up the crystals fit together more closely than they did before they were dissolved.

In making lemonade, ½ cup of crystalline sugar is added to 4 cups of water. Which of the following amounts would the resulting sugar solution be?

(1) 8 cups
(2) 4¾ cups
(3) 4½ cups
(4) less than 4½
(5) less than 4 cups

(1) (2) (3) (4) (5)

That question is asking you to apply some general information about crystals to a specific situation involving sugar crystals. To answer it, you don't need to know the technical definition of *crystal* or *molecule*. The information you need is given to you: The air space between dissolving crystals disappears, so the molecules can fit closer together. That fact means that dissolved sugar takes up less space than sugar crystals. So one-half cup of sugar crystals will dissolve into *less than* one-half cup of sugar molecules. (You can't know for sure how much less, but you don't need to.) The resulting sugar solution will be four cups of water plus less than one-half cup of sugar molecules, or less than 4½ cups. The answer is option (4).

Some chemistry items on the GED Science Test will ask you to evaluate the accuracy of data used to make certain claims or to draw certain conclusions. This process is part of the scientific method. Look at this example.

The label on a package of a popular brand of ice cream makes these claims:

A. contains all-natural ingredients
B. has the flavors that everyone loves
C. only 100 calories per one-half cup serving
D. now richer and tastier than ever

Which of the statements above could be proved in a laboratory analysis of the advertised product?

(1) A and B only
(2) A and C only
(3) B and C only
(4) B and D only
(5) C and D only

① ② ③ ④ ⑤

Can you see that the correct answer would be option (2)? The presence of natural ingredients and the number of calories are statements that can be tested in a laboratory. The richness and tastiness of the ice cream are claims about the quality of the ice cream that cannot be tested. Such questions have to do with the scientific method and the kinds of data that chemists must use to come up with new facts and theories about the nature of matter.

The following section will help you sharpen your own skill at the scientific method using chemical information. That will sharpen your ability to succeed on the chemistry items on the GED Science Test.

LESSON 19

The States of Matter

This first lesson in chemistry will introduce you to the matter that makes up the world. Matter is anything that has weight and takes up space. But it does so in three different forms, or states. The following section tells you about matter in its solid state. Before you read it, look ahead to the Warm-up. It can help you focus on important points.

Solids

You've probably heard the old expression "It's as solid as a rock." Indeed, a rock is a solid. But what does being a solid mean? To answer this question, think about some common solids. Consider a pencil, a coin, and an ice cube. Think about a match, a cup, and this page of your book. They are all alike in two ways. The first way is that each takes up a definite amount of space. The second way is that each has a fixed shape.

All matter is made up of microscopic particles. A solid holds its shape because its particles are in a fairly fixed position. The particles in a solid vibrate rapidly, but they always vibrate around a certain point. They have little freedom to move away from that point.

Most solids that you see are crystalline solids. The molecules in this kind of solid are arranged in a definite pattern. Sugar, ice, and emerald are crystalline solids. But there are solids that are not crystals. Their molecules are arranged in random patterns. Most glass, tar, and gum, for example, do not form crystals.

Now think about different properties of solids that you can observe. You can stretch a rubber band. You can bend a metal coat hanger. You can shape a piece of putty.

Some solids have certain special properties. Copper, for one, does. Drawing heated copper through a small hole shapes it into a fine wire. A solid that has this property is a ductile substance. Copper can also be hammered into thin sheets. So can aluminum and gold. Such solids are malleable. China dishes and a drinking glass break easily. They are brittle. Peanut brittle gets its name because it is easily broken. Some solids are very hard. Diamond is the hardest of all. One solid is harder than another when it can scratch the other. A diamond can scratch all other solids.

Differences in the ways their particles behave and arrange themselves can cause some solids to do strange and interesting things. Particles in some solids actually escape into the air. You can observe this by leaving a mothball open to air. Particles of the mothball will pop free and jump into the air. In time, the solid mothball will disappear.

Sometimes particles of two different solids will move into each other. Researchers demonstrated this when they clamped a piece of gold and a piece of lead very close together. Over a period of time, traces of gold moved into the lead, and a minute amount of lead moved into the gold.

Warm-up

Answer each question in a complete sentence.

1. In what two ways are all solids alike?

____

____

2. What special property do malleable solids have?

____

____

Sample Warm-up Answers
1. Solids take up a definite amount of space and have fixed shapes. **2.** Malleable solids can be hammered into thin sheets.

In the next section you'll learn about the behavior of particles in liquid matter. Take time to preview the Warm-up to help you focus on important points as you read.

Liquids

You just learned how particles in solids behave. Vibrating rapidly about a fixed point, they have little freedom. But there is a way to give the particles more freedom. You can do that by applying heat. If you give the particles in a solid enough heat, the solid will change to a liquid.

If that process sounds like something done only in chemical laboratories, consider this example. Suppose someone leaves an ice cube tray out of the freezer. There is much more heat in the kitchen than in the freezer. The heat causes the particles of ice to move faster. Soon you have a tray of liquid water instead of solid ice cubes. The particles in the water remain at a somewhat fixed distance from each other, but they are not as tightly packed as they were in the solid ice cubes. They slide over, under, and around each other.

Those movements give a liquid its particular properties. The first property of a liquid is that it occupies a definite amount of space. The second is that it takes the shape of its container.

If you do the opposite process and cool a liquid, it will change into a solid. That's what you're doing when you put a water-filled ice cube tray into the freezer. Water happens to freeze at 32°F. Each substance turns into a solid, or freezes, at a particular temperature. That temperature is the substance's freezing point.

A liquid always seeks its own level. In other words, it tends to keep its upper surface as low as possible as it evens out in its container. (Just think of pouring water from a tall, narrow container into a wide shallow pan.) A liquid seeks its own level because gravity pulls each particle down until it can travel no lower.

Many liquids tend to be thin, or watery. Soda pop, orange juice, and milk are watery. But other liquids are not. Think about the ways in which molasses, chocolate syrup, and vegetable oil pour from their containers. They resist flow much more than watery liquids. They are viscous liquids.

One of the most unusual liquids is mercury, sometimes called quicksilver. It is the only common metal that is a liquid, not a solid, at room temperature. Mixed with silver, the shiny, heavy mercury forms silver amalgam. Dentists use this substance to fill teeth. Mercury is also used in certain types of barometers, thermometers, and light switches.

Warm-up

Describe the two properties of a liquid. Use complete sentences in your answer.

____

____

In this final section you'll learn about the behavior of particles in gases. Read the Warm-up exercise at the end of this section before you begin. It will guide you to the main ideas as you read.

Gases

You now understand how particles behave in solids and liquids. You also know that a sufficient amount of heat can change a solid into a liquid. Do you know what will happen when a liquid is heated? If the liquid is heated enough, it will change to a gas. A pot of boiling water will simply boil away, or evaporate, if the water receives enough heat. Water boils at 212°F. Other liquid substances begin to boil at different temperatures. Each substance, therefore, has its own boiling point.

Moving from a liquid to a gas is another change in the state of matter. Whenever matter changes its state, the behavior of its particles changes too. When going from a liquid to a gas, particles pick up speed because the heat gives them energy. They move about quickly, somewhat like a swarm of wasps. The particles of gas in a closed container are constantly bumping into each other. They also collide with the walls of the container. Even if the size of the container is made larger, the particles behave in the same way. They continue to speed about and collide with the walls of their container. But if the top of the container is opened, most of the particles will escape. (Think of taking the lid off a pan of boiling water.)

Sample Warm-up Answer
A liquid occupies a definite amount of space. Unlike a solid, it also takes the shape of its container.

Understanding the behavior of particles in a gas helps you pinpoint the single property that defines a gas. A gas takes the exact size and shape of its container.

Now you can probably figure out what happens when you blow up a tire on a bicycle or car. Adding air to the tire sends a stream of millions of particles into it. Each particle exerts a force as it strikes the inside wall of the tire. The sum of the forces of the millions of particles in the tire is the air pressure. Since there is a greater concentration of particles inside the tire than outside, the tire expands to an inflated position.

Warm-up

State the property of a gas. Use a complete sentence for your answer.

____

____

Applying Ideas

Whenever you transfer a skill or idea you've just learned to a new situation, you are *applying* it. For instance, suppose you read that fresh meat can be preserved for many months by storing it at a temperature below 30°F. You might then apply that principle by purchasing extra meat when it is at a low price and freezing it for use when prices are higher. Applying is a practical skill because you're using an idea in an everyday situation.

Applying principles from chemistry can help you keep a car or bicycle from rusting; it can help you know how to use household cleaners and appliances safely; it can help you make wise decisions in many situations.

Here's an Example

Many different cooking processes depend on the way in which matter can change from a solid state to a liquid state. Below is a principle you just read. It can be applied to some cooking processes.

- If you give the particles in a solid enough heat energy, the solid will change to a liquid.

You know that the sugar you buy in the store is in the form of a solid—tiny white crystals. But some recipes for desserts call for liquid sugar. How can you turn the crystals into a liquid? You can heat the sugar crystals in a heavy pan. As the temperature rises, the crystals reach their melting point and gradually turn into an amber-colored, syrupy liquid called caramel.

If you allow the caramel syrup to cool rather quickly, it will return to its solid state, but this time you will not be able to see the individual crystals. The rapid cooling will cause the syrup to harden in a glossy, brittle sheet. So if your recipe calls for liquid sugar, you will need to use the syrup while it is still hot.

Sample Warm-up Answer
A gas takes the exact size and shape of its container.

Try It Yourself

You know that if liquid is heated enough it will change into a gas. Can you see how that principle applies to the fact that firefighters often wear protective face masks?

■ Some synthetic (humanmade) materials, including many household plastics, are completely safe when they are solids. But they become poisonous in their liquid states. Even more dangerously, these substances, if heated to the point that they become gases, release toxic fumes.

Did you decide why firefighters need to wear protective masks when they enter a burning home or office building? Heat from the fire can melt the synthetic material in furniture, carpet backing, and other items into a liquid and then a gas. As toxic fumes spread in the burning building, they can become as much a hazard as the fire itself.

You also learned earlier in this lesson that the particles of some solids will escape into the air. After you read the paragraph below, try to decide how you are using this principle when you take a block of dry ice along to cool drinks at a picnic.

■ Dry ice is a solid made of carbon dioxide. It is very cold, so people frequently use it to cool other substances. When dry ice is exposed to room temperatures, it gradually warms up, and its particles enter the air around it. Instead of melting into drips and puddles, the dry ice turns into a gas.

What did you decide about dry ice as a cooling agent? Besides being very cold, dry ice is also more convenient than regular ice to take along in a truck or car. You applied a scientific principle if you decided that people sometimes use dry ice in order to avoid messy drips and pools of melted water.

On the Springboard

Item 1 refers to the illustration below. You'll have to apply a principle of chemistry that you have already learned.

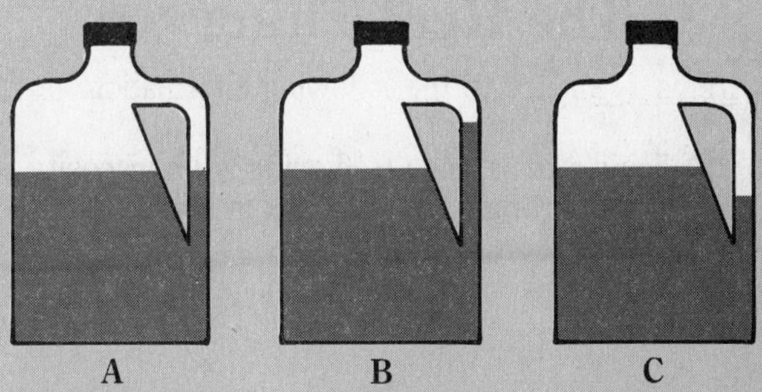

1. If water seeks its own level, which of the pictures above shows what will happen if you pour about three-fourths of a gallon of water into a gallon container with a hollow handle?

   (1) A
   (2) B
   (3) C

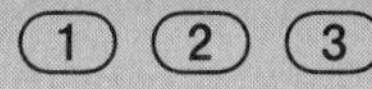

2. Water seeks its own level because gravity pulls down on its particles. Therefore, astronauts cannot drink liquids from a cup or glass while they are in gravity-free space because

   (1) the liquids become very thick and do not pour easily
   (2) the particles in the liquids cannot be made to drop into a person's mouth
   (3) unprotected liquids boil easily and turn into steam

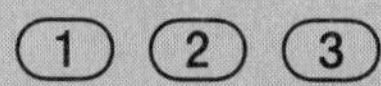

You can check your Springboard answers on page 192.

How did you do? Were you able to apply the principles from chemistry correctly? If you were, try "The Real Thing" next. If you had problems, reread the skills section of this lesson.

“The Real Thing”

Items 1–2 refer to the following information.

A liquid's resistance to flowing is its viscosity. The more strongly the particles in a liquid attract each other, the more viscous it is. Heat can reduce the viscosity of a liquid. Cold can increase it.

1. Motor oil is a viscous liquid that reduces heat from friction inside an engine and makes it run smoothly. The heavier the oil, the greater its viscosity and the less friction in the engine.

   A motorist might need to change to a heavier weight of oil when planning a trip from

   (1) a seacoast to a dry prairie
   (2) an inland region to a coastal region
   (3) a cool area to the other side of a hot desert
   (4) a city to the country in the fall
   (5) a warm southern state to a cold northern state

   (1) (2) (3) (4) (5)

2. As molten rock, or magma, rises from deep inside the earth, it often flows like water. When it spills over the ground, it becomes lava, which has greater viscosity.

   Which of the following conclusions is supported by the properties of magma and lava?

   (1) Lava sinks easily into the surface of the earth.
   (2) Hardened lava retains great amounts of heat.
   (3) Magma mixes easily with moisture in the atmosphere.
   (4) Temperatures inside the earth are extremely high.
   (5) Heat from volcanic eruptions turns magma into lava.

   (1) (2) (3) (4) (5)

3. When a gas is compressed and cooled to below −100°C or lower, it becomes a liquid.

   In a cryogenics laboratory, liquid oxygen is used in experiments and also to cool other substances. If a lab technician accidentally spilled open a container of liquid oxygen, the contents would most likely

   (1) remain in a large puddle, where it fell
   (2) remain in the container
   (3) burn any surface it touched
   (4) evaporate into the air
   (5) turn to ice

   (1) (2) (3) (4) (5)

Check your answers and record your score on page 193.

LESSON 20

The Structure of Matter

In the last lesson you learned about the three states of matter. You observed some of the properties of solids, liquids, and gases and saw that the arrangement and behavior of the particles in them can cause them to do seemingly unusual things. Now you're ready to look deeper into the makeup, or structure, of matter. Use the Warm-up at the end of this first section for an overview of important information.

Atomic Theory

Many centuries ago, people believed that matter was made up of particles. They were right, up to a point, but our knowledge of matter has greatly expanded since that time.

John Dalton, a British chemist and physicist, developed an atomic theory in the early 1800s. His work with matter led him to the idea that all elements are made up of tiny, indestructible particles called atoms. An **atom** is the smallest unit of an element.

Dalton's work paved the way for scientists to learn even more about atoms. We now know that every atom has a center, or **nucleus**. The nucleus is the heaviest part of an atom. Within this nucleus are particles called neutrons and protons. **Neutrons** have no electrical charge; **protons** have a positive charge. Revolving around the nucleus are lighter particles called **electrons.** These particles have a negative charge. Atoms of the same element always have the same atomic mass, or number of protons and neutrons.

In 1913 Neils Bohr, a Danish professor, developed a model of an atom. He believed that nearly the entire mass of an atom is in the nucleus and that the electrons of the atom revolve around the nucleus in shells, or energy levels. Bohr also believed that the electrons moved around the nucleus in definite circular orbits. We now know that the orbits of the electrons are not always perfect circles, and that the orbits are not all in the same plane.

In 1920, scientists learned more about the nucleus of an atom. They found that the nucleus contains tiny particles with positive electrical charges. These positively charged particles are **protons.** While the proton is a very light particle, it is still 1,840 times heavier than an electron. Later, scientists found another particle in the nucleus of an atom—the **neutron.** Neutrons are neutral; they have no electrical charge.

Coming to Terms

atom the tiniest particle of an element. It cannot be broken into smaller pieces and still be that element.

electron a tiny atomic particle with a negative electrical charge

nucleus the center of an atom, around which electrons revolve in fixed orbits

proton a positively charged particle in the nucleus of an atom

neutron a particle with no electrical charge found in the nucleus of an atom

Warm-up

Use two or three sentences of your own to explain why scientists no longer think of atoms as solid bits of matter.

____

____

____

____

Sample Warm-up Answer
Scientists have found that atoms contain electrons that revolve around the nucleus at the center of the atom. The nucleus itself is made up of separate particles.

Now you'll find out about the simplest substances that make up the many different kinds of matter. You may want to look at the Warm-up before you read the next section. You'll find that it will help you concentrate on important ideas.

The Elements

An ancient theory about the nature of matter was that all matter is made up of four basic substances—earth, air, water, and fire. These substances were called the "elements." Even though scientists know this theory is false, they still use the term *element* to refer to a substance that cannot be separated into simpler substances—it is all of one kind.

We now know of 106 different elements. Most occur naturally as solids, but others are liquids or gases. From this bank of elements, thousands of other substances can be made by combining certain elements in the right amounts. For example, two atoms of the element hydrogen combine with one atom of the element oxygen to form the smallest possible particle of water.

The simplest atom is the one for the element hydrogen. It has one proton in the nucleus and no neutron. It also has only one shell occupied by a single electron. The "shell" is a cloudlike layer formed by the electron orbiting the nucleus. An atom of helium, on the other hand, has two electrons, two protons, and also two neutrons. The diagrams below show how electrons, protons, and neutrons are arranged in hydrogen, helium, and oxygen. All three elements occur naturally as gases.

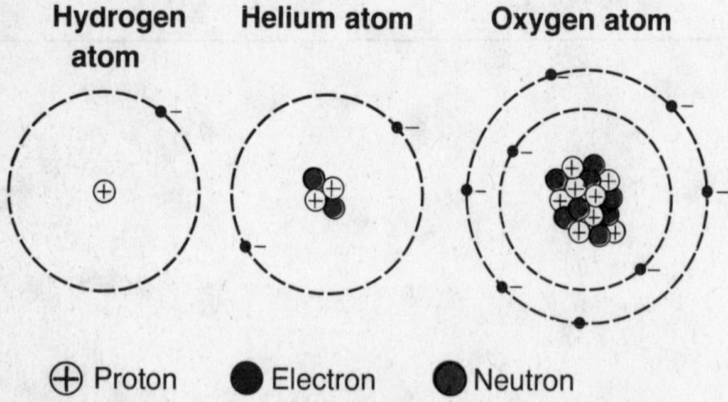

Notice that the hydrogen atom has no neutrons. The helium atom has one shell with two electrons. The oxygen atom has two shells and a total of eight electrons. It also has eight neutrons and eight protons in its nucleus. Each of the elements has its own numbers of shells, electrons, protons, and neutrons.

All the atoms of a certain element have the same number of protons. Still, they may not always have the same atomic weight. The reason is that some atoms of that element may have different numbers of neutrons in the nucleus. These elements, then, exist in several slightly different forms called **isotopes.** The diagram showed hydrogen in its most common form. Deuterium is an isotope of hydrogen with one neutron. Tritium is an isotope of hydrogen with two neutrons.

Scientists have long known that different elements can have similar chemical properties or makeup. They have arranged the 106 elements that we know about into a chart, called the periodic table of elements, to show how these similarities occur at regular intervals. Each element on the periodic table gets its own box. Each box gives the same kind of information for an element. Look at the box for gold. The labels show what each piece of information is.

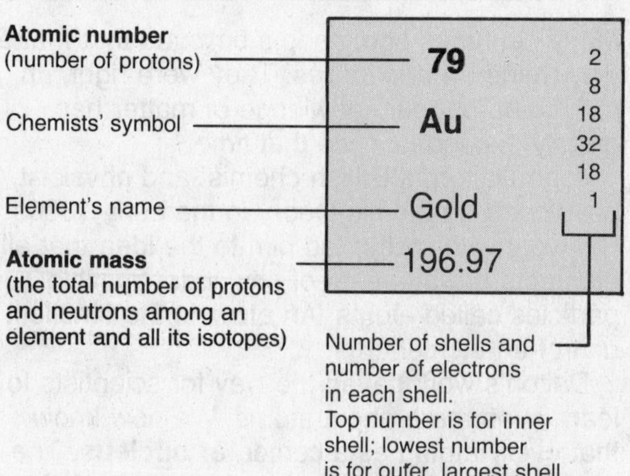

The next illustration shows a portion of the periodic table with boxes for a number of elements in their correct sequence on the table. Compare the numbers that show the electrons for each element. If you read a row from left to right, you see that each element in the row has the same number of electrons in its inner shell, while the number in the outer shell gradually increases for each element. If you read downward in a row, you see that every atom has the same number of electrons in the inner and outer shells, with varying numbers in between.

		2 **He** Helium 4.00 2
8 **O** Oxygen 16.00 2 6	9 **F** Fluorine 19.00 2 7	10 **Ne** Neon 20.17 2 8
16 **S** Sulfur 32.06 2 8 6	17 **Cl** Chlorine 35.45 2 8 7	18 **Ar** Argon 39.95 2 8 8
34 **Se** Selenium 78.96 2 8 18 6	35 **Br** Bromine 79.90 2 8 18 7	36 **Kr** Krypton 83.80 2 8 18 8
52 **Te** Tellurium 127.60 2 8 18 18 6	53 **I** Iodine 126.90 2 8 18 18 7	54 **Xe** Xenon 131.30 2 8 18 18 8

Solid Liquid Gas

Coming to Terms

isotope a form of an element with the same number of protons but a different number of neutrons

Warm-up

Look carefully at the illustrations in this section. Then answer each question in a complete sentence.

1. How many protons and how many electrons does an atom of sulfur have?

____

2. What does "Br" mean to a chemist, and in what state is this substance usually found?

____

Sample Warm-up Answers
1. Sulfur has sixteen protons and sixteen electrons. **2.** "Br" stands for the liquid element bromine.

Distinguishing Facts from Opinions and Hypotheses

You've already had some practice in sorting out facts from opinions and hypotheses with biological information. Now you'll be able to sharpen your skill with materials in chemistry.

Here's an Example

Read these three sentences about diamonds.

1. Diamonds are made of the element carbon.
2. Diamonds are more beautiful than other gems.
3. It may be possible to apply enough pressure and heat to other substances to produce materials that are as hard as diamonds.

If you remember that a fact is a statement that can be proved true by observing, by experimenting, or by consulting a reliable source, you'll recognize that the first sentence states a fact. Laboratory tests can prove that diamonds are made of the element carbon. But what about the second sentence? Would it be possible to *prove* that one jewel is more beautiful than another? No. Beauty is a matter of individual preference. The second sentence is based on opinion.

The third sentence states a hypothesis. Remember that a hypothesis offers a possible explanation or a suggestion that can be tested. Usually a hypothesis is the basis for study and research. It is not a fact itself, but it may lead to the discovery of facts.

Try It Yourself

Diamonds are a form of carbon. Carbon exists in many other forms too, including graphite, the "lead" in most ordinary pencils. You might be surprised to learn that you contain carbon also. Carbon is present in all living things.

As you read over the following statements about carbon, decide which of them are facts.

1. Carbon is a nonmetallic element.
2. Some forms of carbon are used in industry.
3. Everyone should learn about the many uses of carbon.
4. Carbonized cotton thread might work successfully as the filament in an electric light bulb.

Did you decide that the first and second sentences are facts? If so, you're right. Each could be proved by scientific means or by checking with a reliable source.

What about the third sentence? Could it be tested? No, it is an individual opinion. While some people may have this opinion, it still cannot be proved by scientific means.

Did you decide that the fourth sentence is a hypothesis? It is. It's a suggestion that might solve a problem. And, in fact, it *did.* Thomas Edison tested hundreds of other substances unsuccessfully. Finally, he hypothesized that if he covered an ordinary cotton thread with carbon from an oil lamp and then passed electricity through it, the carbonized thread might glow brightly enough to produce artificial light. As you may already know, Edison proved his own hypothesis correct.

On the Springboard

Items 1–2 are based on the following information. Look for facts, opinions, and hypotheses.

Copper is a metallic element that has many uses. Because copper is malleable, it can be made into sheets of various thicknesses. Because copper is ductile, it can be drawn into fine wires and used to conduct electricity. Copper pipes and tubes are used in plumbing. Copper is also used to make jewelry and household ornaments. Scientists believe that it may have first been used by people to make weapons.

1. A cooking wares salesman makes the following statements about some copper pans he is attempting to sell.

   A. They conduct heat evenly.
   B. Copper pans are used by the finest chefs.
   C. There is absolutely no lead in them.
   D. They are beautiful as well as useful.

   Which of the statements above are most likely based on facts rather than opinions?

   (1) A and B only
   (2) B and D only
   (3) A and C only

   ① ② ③

2. Which of the following is a hypothesis suggested in the passage rather than a fact?

   (1) People use copper pipes in plumbing.
   (2) People may have first used copper for weapons.
   (3) People make copper sheets of various thicknesses.

   ① ② ③

Turn to page 192 and check your answers to On the Springboard.

Do you feel confident that you can now separate facts from opinions and hypotheses? If so, go on to "The Real Thing." If you need a little review, reread these pages. You might also want to review the two skills sections in Lesson 8.

“The Real Thing”

Item 1 is based on the information below.

People in one Texas county had remarkably little incidence of tooth decay. If people from other areas moved into that county, their teeth seemed to grow stronger. Doctors suggested that some factor in the drinking water was protecting teeth against decay. It might be that fluorine, which occurred naturally in the water, protected teeth.

1. Based on observation, doctors hypothesized that fluorine

   (1) should be added to water
   (2) weakened teeth
   (3) occurred naturally
   (4) protected against tooth decay
   (5) was found in drinking water

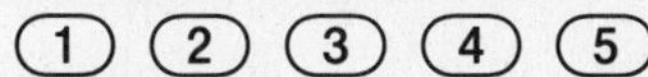

Items 2–4 refer to the following information.

Lead is a heavy, metallic element. For thousands of years, people have used lead in building construction, in pottery, and in paints and glazes. Today lead is also used in explosives, in insecticides, in equipment to shield people from X rays, and in many other ways.

While lead has proved useful, it has also presented some hazards. Lead is a poison, and small amounts have worked their way into some water supplies and into the air. Inside the body, lead interferes with the production of red blood cells and can damage the brain, kidneys, and other vital organs. Lead from water pipes may even have caused nervous disorders and shortened people's lives in ancient Rome.

2. An informational leaflet about the element lead and its uses contains the following statements.

   A. A mixture containing lead is put into some gasoline to improve engine performance.
   B. The burning of tetraethyl lead—the lead in gasoline—contributes to air pollution.
   C. Gasoline manufacturers should not put any lead at all into gasoline products.
   D. Industries that use lead must avoid releasing harmful fumes containing lead into the air.

   Which of the statements above is based on fact?

   (1) A only
   (2) A and B only
   (3) B and C only
   (4) B and D only
   (5) C and D only

   ① ② ③ ④ ⑤

3. Which of the following is a hypothesis about lead suggested in the passage?

   (1) Water supplies can become contaminated by lead.
   (2) Lead is a heavy metal.
   (3) People have found a variety of uses for lead.
   (4) Lead has damaging effects on human blood cells and organs.
   (5) Lead from water pipes was the cause of nervous disorders in ancient Rome.

   ① ② ③ ④ ⑤

4. Which of the following statements best summarizes the information in the passage?

   (1) Lead is both a useful and a dangerous element.
   (2) Lead is a heavy, metallic element.
   (3) Lead can damage the human body.
   (4) People should avoid using lead.
   (5) Lead can be used to protect against harmful X rays.

   ① ② ③ ④ ⑤

Check your answers and record your score on page 193.

LESSON 21

Changes in Matter

In the last lesson you learned about the *structure* of atoms. You saw that different kinds of atomic structures make up a total of 106 known elements, or basic substances. Now you'll learn something about the *behavior* of atoms. Before you read the first section, look ahead to the Warm-up. You'll find a useful guide to important information there.

Molecules, Compounds, and Mixtures

All the atoms of a given element are the same; every atom of hydrogen is the same as every other atom of hydrogen. Every atom of oxygen is identical to every other atom of oxygen. Generally atoms that are identical bond together to form an element. But sometimes atoms of different elements combine to form a new substance: a **compound.** In the case of hydrogen and oxygen, atoms from these two elements can bond in a definite proportion to make a new substance—water. The properties of the compound are usually unlike those of the original elements. For example, hydrogen and oxygen are gaseous elements, but when they combine in the proper proportion to form water, they form a liquid.

A **molecule** is the smallest particle of any compound that has all the properties, or characteristics, of that compound. In other words, a molecule of water is the smallest possible quantity of the compound water. The chemical formula of water is H_2O. The formula tells you that two atoms of hydrogen join one atom of oxygen to yield one molecule of water. If the molecule breaks up, you no longer have water; you have hydrogen and oxygen. The illustration below shows the bond that hydrogen and oxygen form to make one molecule of water.

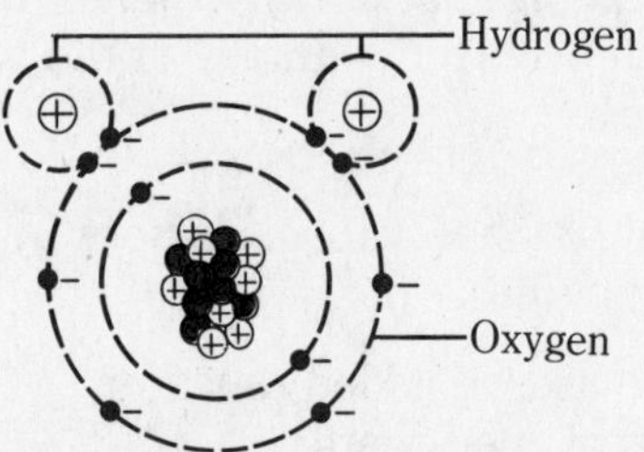

An H_2O Molecule

It is important to remember that both hydrogen and oxygen are gases. But when they bond to form H_2O, they form a liquid—water. They have undergone **chemical change** because they have formed a new substance. They have also lost their properties as gases.

Sometimes, however, a substance can change without giving up its chemical properties. For example, an ice cube can melt into the liquid water, and the water can change into a gas (steam) if you heat it. Ice, water, and steam are all H_2O, but each is matter in a different state. The changes the H_2O has undergone are **physical changes,** not chemical changes.

Now suppose that you pour some salad oil into a glass of water. What do you have? If you stir or shake them together, you have a mixture. A **mixture** is two or more substances joined together but not chemically bonded. The substances in a mixture can be either elements or compounds. In some mixtures, you can see the substances that make them up. You can see the sand, rock, and clay that mix together to make soil, for example. But you cannot see the water, fats, and other substances that make up the mixture milk.

Coming to Terms

compound a new substance formed when atoms from two or more elements combine

molecule the smallest particle of a compound

chemical change a change that alters the properties of the molecules that make up a substance

physical change a change in a substance that does not alter its chemical makeup or nature

mixture a combination of two or more substances that results in *no* chemical change

Warm-up

Write a brief summary describing the difference between a chemical change and a physical change.

In the next section you'll find out more about making different substances. Preview the Warm-up activity. It will help you focus on important points as you read.

Chemical Bonding

Iron, copper, and gold are elements. So are silver, zinc, and carbon. They can exist as single elements that you easily recognize. But not all forms of matter exist as single elements. The elements named above as well as others can combine, or bond, with others to form new substances. That is what happens when hydrogen bonds with oxygen to form water.

The elements are something like letters of the alphabet. People can combine the twenty-six letters of the alphabet in enough ways to produce a huge dictionary. The elements, too, can bond to form thousands of different substances.

The electrons in the outer shells of atoms are responsible for the bonding that produces chemical changes. They form two different kinds of bonds.

One kind of bonding between atoms is called ionic bonding. In ionic bonding, each atom either gains or loses an electron in its outer shell. Consider table salt. Its chemical name is sodium chloride. Using chemical abbreviations, it can be written like this: NaCl. The *Na* stands for sodium. The *Cl* stands for chlorine. These two elements combine to form sodium chloride.

Look at figure 1. It is a model of an atom of sodium. Its outermost shell has one electron. Look at figure 2. It is a model of an atom of chlorine. Its outermost shell has seven electrons. Note that the sodium atom is giving up an electron to the chlorine atom.

How an ionic bond forms

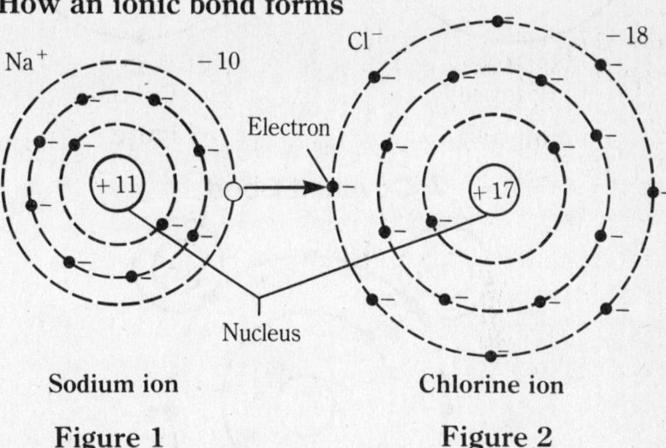

Figure 1 **Figure 2**

Remember that electrons have negative charges. The sodium atom becomes positively charged when it gives up an electron. The chlorine atom becomes negatively charged when it receives an electron. Such electrically charged atoms are **ions.** The positive and negative ions attract each other and ionically bond together.

Sample Warm-up Answer
In a chemical change, the properties of the molecules within the substances involved are altered. In a physical change, substances do not change their chemical makeup or properties.

The second kind of bonding is covalent bonding. In this type of bonding, no atom loses or gains an electron. Instead, atoms share electrons to form molecules.

Consider natural gas. Its chemical name is methane. Its formula is CH_4. The C stands for carbon. The H stands for hydrogen. One atom of carbon joins four atoms of hydrogen to form a molecule of methane.

Look at figure 3. It is a model of an atom of hydrogen. It has one electron in its outer shell. Look at figure 4. It is a model of an atom of carbon. It has four electrons in its outer shell. Now look at figure 5. It shows how the four hydrogen atoms share electrons with an atom of carbon to form a covalent bond.

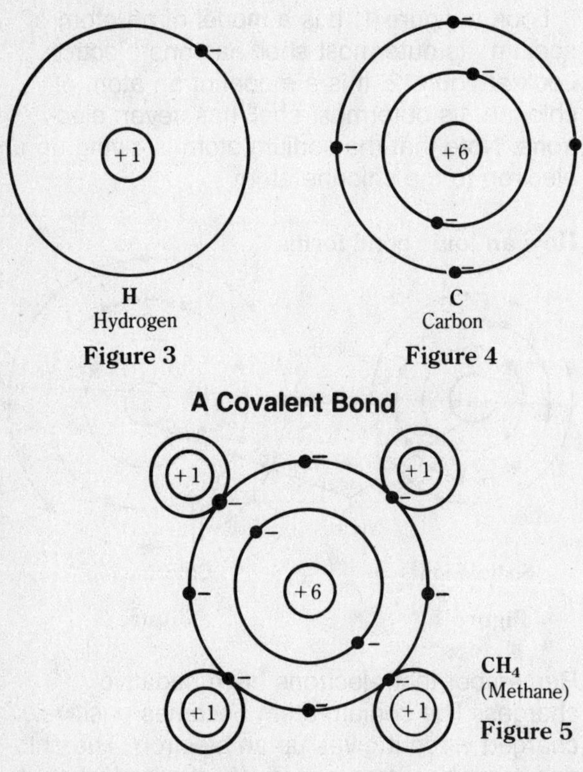

Figure 3

Figure 4

Figure 5

Coming to Terms

ion an atom with either a positive or a negative electrical charge

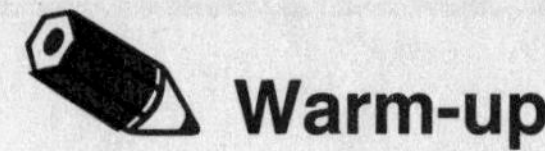

Warm-up

In your own words, tell how ionic chemical bonding differs from covalent chemical bonding.

____

____

____

When you bake a cake, you follow a recipe. Scientists follow a kind of recipe when they join elements and compounds to form new substances. You'll see how in the next section. Look at the Warm-up before you read. It will lead you to important points.

Chemical Reactions

When a substance undergoes a chemical change—such as when gaseous hydrogen and oxygen become liquid water—a series of chemical reactions occurs. You might describe this series of reactions in the following way: "Atoms of hydrogen bond with atoms of oxygen. The compound water is formed." Chemists, however, use equations to describe chemical reactions. A chemical equation tells how many atoms of each element or molecules of each compound interact to form a different substance or substances.

In any chemical equation, the arrow means "produces." The number in front of a symbol or formula tells the number of atoms or molecules. For example, look at the equation for the formation of water.

$$2H_2 + O_2 \rightarrow 2H_2O$$

Two molecules of hydrogen gas (H_2) join with one molecule of oxygen gas (O_2) to make two water molecules.

Here is how a chemist would show the chemical reaction between sodium and chloride to form sodium chloride—common table salt.

$$2Na + Cl_2 \rightarrow 2NaCl$$

Sample Warm-up Answer
In ionic bonding, an atom either gives an electron to another atom or receives one. In covalent bonding, atoms share electrons of their outer shells.

During a chemical reaction, atoms are regrouped, but the number of atoms always remains the same. This principle follows the **law of conservation of mass,** which states that matter cannot be created or destroyed.

Since the number of atoms cannot be increased or decreased during a chemical reaction, chemical equations must be balanced. The one below is.

C_3H_8	+	$5O_2$	→	$3CO_2$	+	$4H_2O$
propane		oxygen		carbon dioxide		water

Count the atoms of each substance on both sides of this equation. On the left side, you find 3 atoms of carbon (C) and 8 atoms of hydrogen (H). To find the number of oxygen atoms, multiply 5 times 2 for a total of 10. On the right side of the equation, you again find 3 atoms of carbon. To find the total number of oxygen atoms, multiply 3 times 2 and add 4 more from the water molecules. This makes 10. To find the number of hydrogen atoms on the right side of the equation, multiply 4 times 2 for a total of 8. The equation is balanced because each side has 3 carbon atoms, 8 hydrogen atoms, and 10 oxygen atoms.

Coming to Terms

law of conservation of mass a principle of science that says matter cannot be created or destroyed

Warm-up

Write a sentence to answer each question.

1. What does a chemical equation tell you?

____

____

2. Why must chemical equations always be balanced?

____

____

Sample Warm-up Answers

1. A chemical equation tells how many atoms or molecules of a substance interact to form one or more new substances.

2. Chemical equations must be balanced because matter cannot be created or destroyed.

Distinguishing a Conclusion from Supporting Statements

You've learned that a conclusion is a decision reached after evidence has been considered carefully. The facts, events, and other factors that back up the conclusion are the supporting evidence. You also have seen that a conclusion may not always be stated in the materials you read or illustrations you examine for information. Sometimes the writer states a conclusion; other times you draw the conclusion. Now you'll get more practice in looking for conclusions—stated and unstated—and finding the evidence that supports them in chemistry.

Here's an Example

The last sentence in the paragraph below is a stated conclusion. See how the information in the rest of the paragraph leads up to it.

■ Molecules of matter are too tiny to see without high-tech equipment, but they are present all about you. In fact, molecules make up every cell in your body. Water molecules make up a large part of each cell in the human body. Molecules of protein make most of the specialized structures within a cell. Carbohydrate molecules supply energy. Water, protein, and carbohydrates, therefore, are necessary ingredients in a person's diet.

The list of different types of molecules in each cell and their importance strengthen the final conclusion. Each piece of information is a piece of supporting evidence.

Try It Yourself

See if you can pick out a conclusion stated in this paragraph. Then try to identify the evidence supporting it.

■ A chemical reaction occurs when molecules of different substances combine. Fire is one very familiar chemical reaction. During this chemical reaction, oxygen unites very rapidly with some kind of fuel. The reaction produces heat and light. In order for the chemical reaction of fire to occur, there must be two things: oxygen and fuel heated to the kindling temperature. It follows, then, that one way to prevent or extinguish fires is to eliminate the oxygen. Many effective fire extinguishers do, in fact, use water, sand, carbon dioxide, or other substances that will keep oxygen away from fuel.

Did you find the conclusion? It is stated in the sentence that begins with the words "It follows, then. . . ." Since oxygen must be present for a fire to occur, the author of the paragraph concludes that taking away oxygen will prevent and eliminate fires. The need for oxygen is one piece of supporting evidence. Another strong piece of supporting evidence comes from the use of fire extinguishers that work precisely because they keep oxygen away from contact with fuel.

Now see if you can find supporting evidence to draw your own conclusion. This paragraph talks about another chemical reaction involving oxygen. Read it carefully and then answer the question that follows it.

■ Molecules of oxygen and molecules of iron can combine to form the red, powdery substance called rust. Reddish rust has pitted many old wrought-iron gates. It also attacks steel garage doors, bicycles, cars, and other objects made entirely or partially of iron. Homeowners can buy special paints and sealing agents that help protect their possessions from rust.

What conclusion can you draw about the reason sealing agents help protect against rust? Did you conclude that paints and sealers keep oxygen in the air away from the iron in articles that are apt to rust? If so, you're right. The first sentence supports the conclusion that oxygen must come into contact with iron if rust is to occur.

On the Springboard

Items 1–2 refer to the following passage. Be alert for both stated and unstated conclusions based on the facts.

Hydrogen peroxide, like water, is a compound containing the elements hydrogen and oxygen. Hydrogen peroxide even looks a good deal like water, but its chemical formula is different. The formula for water is H_2O: two atoms of hydrogen combined with one atom of oxygen. The formula for hydrogen peroxide is H_2O_2: two atoms of hydrogen combined with two atoms of oxygen.

Light encourages a chemical reaction in hydrogen peroxide, shown by this equation:

$$H_2O_2 \rightarrow H_2O + O$$

In other words, the hydrogen peroxide changes into water and oxygen. Therefore, manufacturers of hydrogen peroxide package their product in brown, opaque bottles that keep out light.

1. What conclusion did manufacturers of hydrogen peroxide reach?

   (1) Hydrogen peroxide contains the same elements as water.
   (2) Protecting their product from light would preserve it.
   (3) The best formula for their packages would be $H_2O + O$.

   (1) (2) (3)

2. Hydrogen peroxide is a bleach and an antiseptic. Based on the information given above, a person using hydrogen peroxide that has been exposed to light might correctly form which of the following conclusions?

   (1) The hydrogen peroxide may have lost some of its strength.
   (2) The hydrogen peroxide will be an especially good bleach.
   (3) The hydrogen peroxide should be put back into its brown bottle.

   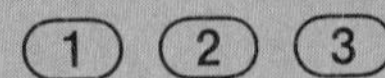

Check your answers to On the Springboard on page 192.

How did you do? Did you pick out the correct conclusions? Did you keep the supporting evidence separate from the conclusions? If so, you're ready for the GED-level "Real Thing." If you had trouble, take a little time to review this section first. Lesson 7 in *Biology* can also help you.

❝ The Real Thing ❞

<u>Items 1–3</u> refer to the following passage.

The ions in a solid ionic compound are arranged in an orderly way to form crystals. Ionic bonds are especially strong because they extend throughout an entire crystal. Ionic compounds have high melting points. For example, sodium chloride melts about 800°C.

In the solid form, ionic compounds do not conduct electricity. In a liquid state, or when dissolved in water, the ions separate and move about freely. In these cases, ionic compounds conduct electricity easily.

Ions do not exist only in solids and liquids, however. They also exist in gases. In gases ions are often too far apart to be attracted to other particles, so they may drift by themselves without forming compounds.

The Van Allen belts are areas of high concentrations of ions that surround the earth. These ions are attracted by the earth's magnetism, which then directs them toward either the north or south magnetic pole. As they approach either pole, they are bounced back away from the pole and begin moving toward the opposite pole. This process keeps them constantly in motion as they continue to move back and forth between the poles.

Activity from the sun occasionally interferes with the movement of the ions in the Van Allen belts, causing magnetic storms. These can interfere with radio reception and cause auroras such as the northern lights.

1. At room temperature, it can be concluded that sodium chloride will

   (1) melt into a liquid
   (2) be a solid
   (3) form a new ionic compound
   (4) have freely moving ions
   (5) change to a gas

   (1) (2) (3) (4) (5)

2. Because calcium chloride is an ionic compound, it can be concluded that a solution of water and calcium chloride will

   (1) group into patterns of crystals
   (2) have a low melting point
   (3) turn into a gas
   (4) conduct electricity
   (5) cause magnetic storms

3. What are the Van Allen belts?

   (1) areas of high concentrations of charged particles
   (2) sources of intense radiation
   (3) sources of auroras such as the Northern Lights
   (4) regions of magnetism
   (5) areas of sodium chloride gas

   (1) (2) (3) (4) (5)

Check your answers and record your score on page 193.

LESSON 22

The Behavior of Matter

You've learned how chemical reactions cause changes in matter. Now you'll read about some other kinds of changes that matter can make. As you read the first section in this lesson, pay special attention to the way molecules behave. But first look at the Warm-up. It can guide you to important points of information.

Solutions

When you put a teaspoonful of sugar into a glass of iced tea and stir it, the sugar seems to diappear. Yet you know the sugar is there because the tea tastes sweet. Chemically speaking, here's what happens. The sugar breaks up into molecules, which are so small you can't see them. The sugar molecules spread out and mix themselves evenly among the water molecules. Other than that, the molecules remain unchanged.

When free and separate molecules of two or more substances mix, usually in a liquid, a **solution** forms. The substance that dissolves other substances is a **solvent.** Substances dissolved in a solvent are **solutes.** In the sweetened iced tea, sugar was the solute, and the iced tea was the solvent. Do you think the unsweetened iced tea was a solution? What was dissolved in water to make the unsweetened iced tea? Tea, of course. So the glass of sweetened iced tea is actually a solution of tea and sugar as solutes and water as a solvent.

Water is the most common solvent. Most things will dissolve in water to some degree if given enough time. But some solvents work much better with specific solutes. For example, you might try to remove a spot of dried paint from a piece of lumber by rubbing it with a cloth dampened with water. Unless the paint is water soluble, you won't have any luck. But if you use turpentine instead of water, you'll probably remove the paint.

Many solutions consist of a solid dissolved in a liquid. Waffle syrup is an example of a solid (sugar) dissolved in a liquid (water). But a solute can be a gas or a liquid instead of a solid. Carbon dioxide gas forced into water forms the sparkling water used as a base for soda pop. This gas-in-water solution forms yet another solution when liquid flavoring is dissolved in it. Vinegar is a good example of a liquid dissolved in a liquid. It is a solution of acetic acid, a liquid, dissolved in water.

Some substances break down into ions when they go into solution. Table salt, sodium chloride, divides into ions when it forms a solution. An ionized solution conducts electricity well.

Coming to Terms

solution a mixture formed when atoms or molecules of a gas, liquid, or solid are dissolved in another gas, liquid, or solid. The particles are spread evenly throughout the solution.

solvent a substance that dissolves another substance

solute a substance that is dissolved in another substance

Warm-up

Write your answer to each question in a complete sentence.

1. What happens to sugar when it dissolves in water?

____

____

2. What happens to table salt when it dissolves in water?

____

____

You'll learn some important information about three special kinds of chemical substances in the next section. Take a moment to preview the section by reading the Warm-up.

Sample Warm-up Answers
1. Molecules of sugar spread themselves evenly among the water molecules. **2.** The salt breaks down into ions and forms a solution.

Acids, Bases, and Salts

Grapefruit, vinegar, and sour milk are alike in one way. How? Each contains an **acid.** Grapefruit contains citric acid. Vinegar is a weakened solution of acetic acid. Sour milk contains lactic acid.

Acids have a sour taste. But don't try to identify any unknown substance by tasting it. Many substances are poisonous. Chemists have a good method of testing a substance to see if it is acidic. They use a strip of blue paper containing litmus, which is a dye from a specific kind of plant. When the blue litmus paper makes contact with an acid, the paper turns red.

Practically all acids contain hydrogen. In solution, most hydrogen breaks down into hydrogen ions ($H+$). The $+$ shows that they are positively charged ions. But hydrogen gas is released when an acid reacts with certain metals, such as zinc (Zn). Look at the following chemical equation.

$$Zn + 2HCl \rightarrow ZnCl_2 + H_2 \uparrow$$

The equation shows that one atom of zinc combines with two molecules of hydrochloric acid (HCl) to yield one molecule of zinc chloride ($ZnCl_2$) and one molecule of hydrogen (H_2). The upward arrow indicates matter in its state as a gas. Note that two atoms of hydrogen form a molecule of the gas hydrogen.

Bases form another type of chemical. Every base is made of a metal and one or more hydroxyls. A hydroxyl is a unit of oxygen and hydrogen (OH). When a base dissolves in water, hydroxide ions (OH^-) form. Notice that they are negative ions. Milk of magnesia is a base. Its chemical name is magnesium hydroxide. Its chemical formula is $Mg(OH)_2$.

Bases have a bitter taste. But it is too dangerous to test for bases by tasting. To identify a base, chemists use a strip of red litmus paper. A base will turn the red litmus paper blue. Bases usually feel slippery to touch.

Something interesting happens when proper proportions of an acid and a base combine. They neutralize each other. The acid loses its properties. So does the base. The result is a salt—and water. Look at the following equation.

$$NaOH + HCl \rightarrow NaCl + H_2O$$

In that equation, a molecule of sodium hydroxide (NaOH), which is a base, combines with a molecule of hydrochloric acid (HCl). The result is a molecule of sodium chloride (NaCl), which you know is table salt, and a molecule of water (H_2O).

The table below shows some common salts and how people use them.

Salt	Formula	Common use
Copper sulfate	$CuSO_4$	Copper plating
Magnesium sulfate	$MgSO_4$	Medicine (Epsom salt)
Silver nitrate	$AgNO_3$	Medicine and photography
Sodium chloride	NaCl	Food seasoning

Coming to Terms

acid a sour-tasting substance that turns blue litmus paper red. Acids in solution give up positive hydrogen ions.

base a bitter-tasting substance that turns red litmus paper blue. Bases give up negative hydrogen-oxygen ions in solution.

Warm-up

In a sentence or two of your own, tell what happens when an acid and a base combine in proper amounts.

____

____

☑ A Test-Taking Tip

You won't need to know chemical formulas and equations when you take the GED Science Test. If a formula or equation is used on the test, it will also be explained to you in words, the way the formulas and equations were in this section. So you can become comfortable with such chemical information by practicing with the material in this *Chemistry* section.

Sample Warm-up Answer
The acid and the base neutralize each other. They lose their own properties because they form a salt and water.

In the following section you'll read about some chemical reactions involving oxygen. You'll want to pay close attention to the way electrons behave. Preview the Warm-up before you begin to help focus your thoughts.

Oxidation-Reduction Reactions

Sometimes elements lose or gain electrons in their outer shell. Such reactions are called oxidation-reduction reactions.

The following chemical reaction is an example of an oxidation-reduction process.

$$2Ca + O_2 \rightarrow 2CaO$$

The equation tells you that 2 atoms of calcium (Ca) combine with a molecule of oxygen (O_2) to yield two molecules of calcium oxide (CaO). Look at Figure 1. It shows a calcium atom with two electrons in its outer shell. (The electrons in the three inner shells are not shown.) Now note in Figure 2 that an oxygen atom has six electrons in its outer shell.

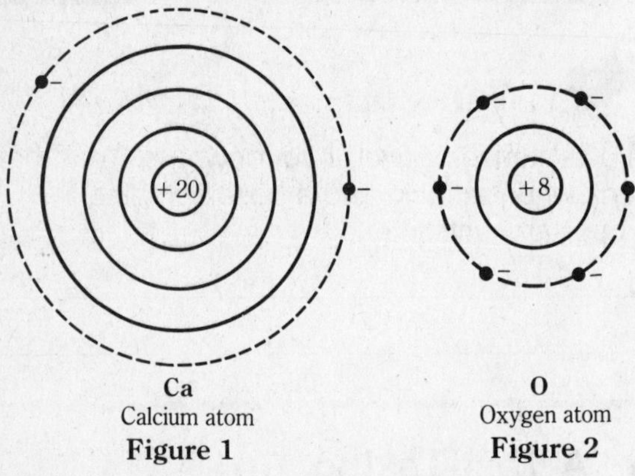

Figure 1 Figure 2

In this oxidation-reduction process, the calcium loses its two outer-shell electrons. The calcium has been *oxidized.* As part of the same process, each oxygen atom gains two electrons from each calcium atom. The oxygen has been *reduced.*

Oxidation-reduction reactions do not always involve oxygen. Look what happens when copper is combined with chlorine gas to form copper chloride.

$$Cu + Cl_2 \rightarrow CuCl_2$$

No oxygen was involved in this reaction, but the copper was oxidized because it lost two electrons. The chlorine gas gained electrons, so it was reduced.

When thinking about the oxidation-reduction process, remember that an oxidized element always loses electrons in its outer shell, and a reduced element always gains electrons in its outer shell. Oxidation and reduction always work together.

Warm-up

Answer each question in a sentence of your own.

1. What happens to the electrons in an element if it is oxidized?

____

____

2. What happens to the electrons in an element if it is reduced?

____

____

Assessing Supporting Data

A traveling medicine show was a form of entertainment to people in small towns a century ago. A "magic" man brought his brightly painted wagon to town and attracted customers with magic tricks or other spectacular performances. After each show, he sold bottles of his own special "medicine," which he claimed would cure many illnesses and complaints. His customers

Sample Warm-up Answers
1. An oxidized element loses electrons in its outer shell. **2.** A reduced element gains electrons in its outer shell.

had only his word to rely on. He gave them no evidence that his product was pure or would really cure any physical ailments.

Exactly what is evidence? Evidence is any type of information—facts, figures, examples, reasons—that helps demonstrate the truth of a statement or claim. You've already seen that scientists rely on evidence. Before scientists accept any statement as true, they make sure that there is adequate evidence to support it. They look to see if the evidence is accurate—if it was obtained scientifically. They also make sure that enough evidence was gathered and that it relates directly to the topic under study. Once they are certain of these factors, they probably will consider the evidence adequate enough to support a given statement.

Now you'll have opportunities to think like a scientist. You'll examine evidence in chemistry and decide if it adequately supports a conclusion.

Here's an Example

Read the following sentence.

■ Your kitchen is full of colloids.

How would you react if someone walked into your home and said this to you? Would you believe it? Would you be alarmed or perhaps wonder if you should call an exterminator? Probably you'd ask the speaker to prove his or her statement.

First the person would have to tell you what colloids are. Colloids are materials in which very fine particles of one substance are suspended—*not* dissolved—in another substance. Would that be enough evidence to help you decide if the statement was true? Probably not. You would ask for some specific examples of colloids before you accepted the fact that there are many of them in your kitchen. If you learned that milk, butter, whipped cream, and ketchup are all colloids, you'd probably agree that your kitchen does, indeed, contain many colloids. You've collected adequate evidence to support the statement.

Try It Yourself

Suppose you spilled a pan of soapy water on the carpet. Someone tells you that you can clean up the spot with vinegar. Before you reach for the bottle of vinegar, you think about the evidence given in the paragraph below. Read it and decide whether you would risk adding vinegar to the mess already on your carpet.

■ Vinegar contains chemicals that qualify it as an acid. Soapy water, on the other hand, is a base. Lye and baking soda in water are also bases. All make good household cleaners. When mixed, acids and bases neutralize each other.

Would you use the vinegar on your carpet? Probably you would—and with good results. Since the acid vinegar would neutralize the base soapy water, the stain on the carpet would most likely disappear. Many acids and bases make good household cleaners, even when used on each other. A knowledge of chemistry gives you the evidence you need to decide which one to use.

Now read the following sentence from an advertisement for a medicine.

■ Milk of magnesia takes away excess stomach acid.

Below are several pieces of evidence. Which of them would help convince you that the statement above is true?

1. Milk of magnesia comes in liquid or tablet form.
2. Milk of magnesia is recommended by doctors.
3. Milk of magnesia is a mild base.

How would you evaluate the three pieces of evidence? Would any of them convince you that milk of magnesia can be effective in curing acid-stomach problems?

The first piece of evidence may be true, but it is irrelevant; it discusses the product but does not say how the product will help. Is the second statement relevant? Not really. It doesn't say what doctors recommend milk of magnesia for. Does the third statement give evidence that supports the claim in the advertisement? Yes, it does. If you remember that a base will neutralize an acid, you'll see that a mild base such as milk of magnesia can eliminate excess stomach acid.

On the Springboard

Item 1 refers to the following article. As you read, ask yourself if the article convinces you that seawater can be made useful.

Fresh water is scarce in many parts of the world today. Oceans hold over 97 percent of the earth's water. Ocean water is too salty for drinking or for irrigating crops. Even some groundwater is too salty for those purposes.

The salt dissolved in water exists as ions of sodium and chlorine. The sodium ions have a positive charge. The chlorine ions have a negative charge. Electrodialysis removes the ions from the water. First the salt water enters a large tank with a positive electric pole at one end and a negative electric pole at the other end. Then an electric current is run through the water. The positively charged sodium ions move toward the negative pole, and the negatively charged chlorine ions move toward the positive pole. This movement leaves water in the middle that has no sodium or chlorine ions. In other words, it is salt free.

1. Which of the following conclusions is adequately supported by data in the passage?

   (1) About 3 percent of the earth's water lies underground.
   (2) Electrodialysis can be used to produce fresh water from salt water.
   (3) Electrodialysis will satisfy the world's need for fresh water.

   (1) (2) (3)

Item 2 refers to the advertisement below. An advertisement for bottled drinking water that has been desalinated makes these claims:

A. world's best-tasting water
B. makes terrific coffee
C. is sodium free
D. contains absolutely no pollutants

2. Which of the statements above could be supported by scientific evidence?

   (1) A and B only (2) B and C only
   (3) C and D only

   (1) (2) (3)

Take the time now to check your Springboard answers on page 192.

Did you correctly evaluate the evidence in the Springboard items? If so, congratulations. Go on now to "The Real Thing." If you had problems with the Springboard, be sure to review this section first. You might also want to go back and reread the skill section of Lesson 10.

“The Real Thing”

Items 1–3 refer to the following article.

Foods that are stored for a time may change color or develop bad odors as a result of chemical changes. For example, fats or oils exposed to air will take on oxygen. Such oxidation causes them to turn rancid and develop an unpleasant, stale taste. Other factors, too, can spoil foods. Bacteria form acids that cause some foods to turn sour; yeasts can cause some fruits and juices to ferment; molds often change the color and flavor of food.

Refrigeration and freezing can prevent or delay such chemical changes. Today many food product manufacturers rely on chemical preservatives to reduce food spoilage. The chemicals are easy to use and do help prevent food waste. Preservatives such as sodium nitrate, sodium benzoate, BHA, BHT, and calcium propionate are very effective in prolonging the freshness and purity of many foods. Many of these chemical preservatives maintain freshness by preventing the food from oxidizing. However, their use has become controversial because many also have unhealthy side effects. Researchers suspect that some even cause cancer or damage nerves.

1. Some chemical preservatives are natural and perfectly safe.

Which of the statements below supports this conclusion?

(1) Boxes, bags, and other packages in which food is sold often contain human-made materials.
(2) Some cereal products contain butylated hydroxytoluene.
(3) Citric acid (vitamin C) from lemon juice helps some foods keep their color and taste.
(4) Improperly processed rye flour may cause a disease of the central nervous system.
(5) Freezing prevents bacteria from growing in meat and other foods.

(1) (2) (3) (4) (5)

2. Even when butter is stored at temperatures cool enough to prevent it from melting, it can gradually turn rancid if it is in the presence of

(1) moisture
(2) darkness
(3) light
(4) oxygen
(5) BHA

(1) (2) (3) (4) (5)

3. Which of the following statements best summarizes what is known about chemical food preservatives?

(1) Chemicals keep food fresh only when combined with refrigeration or freezing.
(2) Chemical preservatives keep many foods fresh but may have undesirable side effects.
(3) Chemical preservatives should be used sparingly if at all.
(4) Chemicals are much more effective than refrigerating or freezing foods.
(5) Chemicals preserve food by speeding up the oxidation process.

(1) (2) (3) (4) (5)

Item 4 refers to the following graph and the information below it.

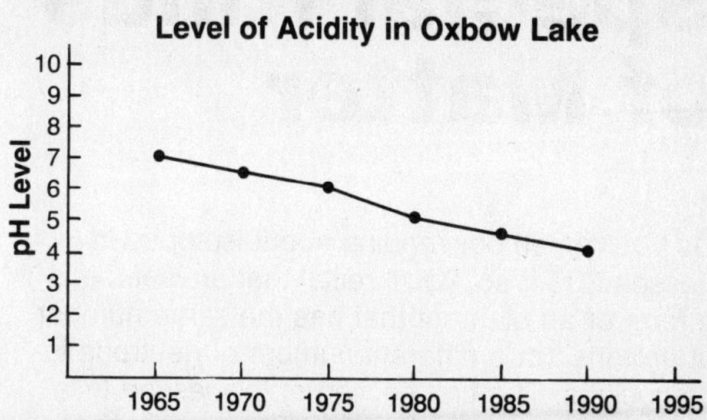

Some industrial pollutants and auto exhaust fumes collect in the atmosphere and eventually return to the ground in the form of acid rain or snow. The graph above shows how the acid level of one northern lake has changed. The pH scale is used for measuring acids. A rating of 7 means neutral; lower numbers mean increasing acidity; higher numbers mean less acidity.

4. Evidence in the graph supports the conclusion that Oxbow Lake will

(1) continue to be neutral
(2) become neutral in 1995
(3) become less acidic by 1995
(4) become more acidic by 1995
(5) make no change at all until after 1995

(1) (2) (3) (4) (5)

Check your answers and record your score on page 193.

LESSON 23

Special Kinds of Matter

Do you remember reading about isotopes in Lesson 20? If so, you'll recall that an isotope is a form of an element that has the same number of protons but a different number of neutrons in its nucleus. The first section of this lesson tells you what's so special about isotopes. Try reading the Warm-up first. It will clue you to some basic information.

Radioactive Elements

An interesting thing happens to certain isotopes of some elements. The nuclei of their atoms actually fall apart, or disintegrate. Uranium, plutonium, and thorium are examples of such elements. When the nucleus of such an isotope disintegrates, it emits charged particles and radiant energy. Elements that behave in this way are called radioactive. The isotopes are called radioisotopes.

There are three kinds of rays emitted during **radioactivity.** First there are the alpha rays. Alpha rays are particles with a positive charge. Each particle consists of two protons and two neutrons. It is actually the nucleus of a helium atom. Then there are the beta rays. They are particles with a negative charge. The beta ray is a stream of electrons. Sometimes scientific materials refer to the electrons as beta particles. Finally there is the gamma ray. This ray of energy is somewhat like invisible light.

Radioactive rays vary in their ability to go through other materials. A mere sheet of paper, for example, can stop an alpha ray. A piece of wood only an inch thick can stop a beta ray. But the gamma ray has tremendous penetrating power. It takes a thick lead shield to stop a gamma ray. Since all these rays are coming from the breakdown in the nucleus of an atom, the radiation is called nuclear radiation.

The rate at which different radioisotopes decay, or disintegrate, varies greatly. Scientists measure the rate of decay in a unit called a half-life. A half-life of a radioisotope is the time it takes for one-half of the nuclei of any amount of the substance to disintegrate. For example, a radioisotope named thorium-234 has a half-life of twenty-four days. In twenty-four days, one-half the atoms in a given amount of thorium-234 will decay. The list below shows the tremendous range of half-life among a few different radioisotopes.

Radioisotope	Half-life
Antimony-124	60 days
Calcium-45	152 days
Cobalt-60	5.2 years
Nickel-63	85 years
Potassium-40	1,400,000,000 years

Nuclear radiation is very dangerous to living things. It can cause radiation sickness, which can be fatal. On the other hand, if it is carefully controlled, nuclear radiation can bring many benefits. Doctors and medical technicians use it to kill diseased cells in some cancer patients. Technicians store radioisotopes in lead containers when they are not in use. When technicians are working with radioisotopes, they stay behind thick lead shielding to protect themselves from the radiation.

Coming to Terms

radioactivity the decay of an atom's nucleus, which results in a lighter nucleus, very tiny charged particles, and radiation

Warm-up

Write a sentence in which you name the three kinds of rays emitted during the decay of a radioisotope.

Radioisotopes, which you read about in the last section, are mostly rare elements on the earth. In the next section, you'll read about the most common element—carbon. But first look ahead to the Warm-up. It will help you focus on important information.

Organic Materials

Carbon is a nonmetallic element with some unusual properties. One of these properties is that carbon atoms can form four strong covalent bonds. The other is that carbon atoms can also bond with other carbon atoms. Because carbon atoms can bond in so many different ways, they form more than a million different carbon compounds! In fact, for every substance that does not contain carbon, there are about one hundred other substances that do contain it. The cells in your body consist of many different kinds of molecules. Yet almost every molecule contains carbon atoms. An alien from outer space might call you a carbon compound. Because so many earth substances are carbon compounds, there is a separate branch of chemistry given to their study. It is called **organic chemistry.**

Carbon compounds have many different properties. A diamond, the hardest natural substance known, is a compound of pure carbon. Carbon atoms bond in a regular pattern to form crystals of diamond. Graphite, on the other hand, is a soft, slippery substance. You may have used it to lubricate door locks. Yet graphite, like diamond, is pure carbon crystal; it merely has a different arrangement of bonded carbon atoms.

Sample Warm-up Answer
The rays emitted during the decay of a radioisotope are alpha rays, beta rays, and gamma rays.

When carbon atoms bond with hydrogen atoms, they form a cluster of materials known as **hydrocarbons.** The natural gas that a stove or furnace burns is a mixture of hydrocarbons. So are petroleum and all the gasoline, motor oils, and other substances manufactured from petroleum. Many useful chemicals, called hydrocarbon derivatives, come from hydrocarbons. Their molecules contain oxygen as well as carbon and hydrogen atoms. The alcohol used in many medical products is a hydrocarbon derivative.

Another important group of organic compounds contains carbon, hydrogen, oxygen, and nitrogen. These are amino acids—the building blocks of protein.

By now you can see that organic materials, or ones containing carbon, are in and all around you. The starches, sugars, and fats you eat are all organic materials. So are the fuel in cars and buses, the clothing you wear, the furniture in your home, and the plastic in credit cards. The paper in the book you are reading contains cellulose, yet another organic material.

Coming to Terms

organic chemistry the branch of chemistry dealing with carbon compounds

hydrocarbons a group of compounds containing carbon and hydrogen

Warm-up

Write the answers to the questions below in complete sentences of your own. Use information from the section you just read.

1. Why do you think some scientists specialize in the study of organic chemistry?

2. Give at least three examples of materials made from hydrocarbons and hydrocarbon derivatives.

Sample Warm-up Answers
1. There are so many different carbon compounds that a special branch of chemistry studies only organic materials.
2. Gasoline, motor oils, natural gas, and alcohol all come from hydrocarbons or hydrocarbon derivatives.

How many shirts, blouses, or slacks do you have that you can wash and wear without having to press? If you're like most people, you have a number of wash-and-wear clothing items. And you're probably grateful for the convenience they provide. In this section, you'll learn about some chemical principles that make modern synthetic fabrics possible. Take time to preview the section by reading the Warm-up.

Polymers

If you use a rubber eraser during your work with this book, you'll be using a **polymer.** A polymer is a giant molecule formed when many small molecules undergo a chemical change and join to make one long chain. The compounds made of such giant molecules are usually called polymers also. The rubber in your eraser is a polymer that comes from the milky fluid in rubber trees.

Cellulose is a polymer found in plants. Cotton and flax fibers are cellulose polymers that people use to make cotton and linen cloth. Wool and silk fibers are protein polymers. People have made clothing from cotton, linen, wool, and silk for several thousand years. But these were not wash-and-wear items. Wash-and-wear polymers are a product of our own twentieth century.

Early in the twentieth century, scientists in laboratories began making synthetic polymers. The first was rayon, made from cellulose molecules. Rayon was a cheap substitute for silk. Then came nylon. Nylon is as sheer and beautiful as silk, but it is much stronger than either silk or rayon. During World War II, the army made parachutes from nylon fabric. After the war, manufacturers used nylon to make many new products for homes and industries. Since then, science has produced even more synthetic polymeric fabrics. These fabrics often go by brand-name labels that appear in the clothing you buy. Many of them resist wrinkling, creasing, fading, and soiling.

Scientific work during World War II also led to the polymers that produced plastics and the thousands of items today that are made of plastics. Polyethylene, for example, is the compound used to make most plastic laundry and trash bags. The name *polyethylene* is a clue to the makeup of this common polymer. Ethylene is a hydrocarbon. *Poly* means "many." Manufacturers make polyethylene plastic by chemically joining many ethylene molecules into giant chainlike molecules. The substance that results is tough, flexible, and waterproof.

Coming to Terms

polymer a large, long, chainlike molecule formed from the joining of many identical small molecules

Warm-up

Write sentences of your own to answer each question.

1. What two kinds of natural polymers did people use to make fabrics before the twentieth century?

____

____

2. Explain the chemical makeup of the substance called polyethylene.

____

____

Sample Warm-up Answers

1. People made cloth from cellulose polymers (cotton and linen) and from protein polymers (wool and silk).

2. Polyethylene is made from many large ethylene molecules joined together in a large, chainlike molecule.

Values in Beliefs and Decision Making

How would you answer if someone asked you to name the three or four things in life that are most important to you? Perhaps you have certain memories that mean a lot to you. You might also list your religious faith, your skills, or certain possessions. As you learned earlier, all such things help make up a person's values. Whether you realize it or not, your values strongly influence the decisions you make and the courses of action that you choose to follow in your life. The fact that you are studying to take the GED Test shows that you value learning and believe that education can improve your life.

Values also influence the choices and decisions that scientists and others make. Sometimes political and economic values help them decide what topics they will research and in what way. At other times, personal values determine how individual scientists choose and conduct their areas of research. In the following activities, you'll have a chance to identify the roles that values play in chemistry.

Here's an Example

The following passage talks about two famous chemists of the last century, Pierre and Marie Curie. As you read, think about some of the values reflected in their lives and in their work.

■ In 1896, a French scientist named Antoine-Henri Becquerel discovered that some uranium ore he was working with gave off powerful invisible rays that could expose photographic film even more strongly than sunlight. These rays, the result of nuclear decay, were radioactive.

Two young scientists in Paris, Pierre and Marie Curie, learned of Becquerel's discovery. They decided that they wanted to investigate the subject of natural radioactivity. Pierre had recently completed a study of how magnetism affected metals. Marie had come to Paris from Poland in order to study science. Both were eager to learn and to add to scientists' knowledge of radiation.

As the Curies worked with large masses of pitchblende, a type of uranium ore, they hypothesized that something in the ore *besides* the uranium must be emitting radiation. After a long, hard period of study, sometimes under difficult physical conditions, they were able to isolate a new, highly radioactive element. They named it radium. Later, they also isolated a second element, polonium.

The Curies shared their findings because they believed that radium would benefit people in general. The years have proved that belief true. Radium is used now to treat certain forms of cancer and some skin diseases.

That account points out some of the things the Curies valued most: learning, discovery, and using new knowledge to aid people. How did these values affect their lives? Both were willing to dedicate long, patient hours to their research. They were willing to work under difficult physical conditions as well. Finally, they chose to give their discoveries freely to the world instead of insisting on payment in return for their discoveries.

Try It Yourself

Earlier in this lesson, you read about polymers and how manufacturers use them in many synthetic fabrics. What values might lead people to prefer those new synthetics over fabrics made from cotton, wool, silk, and other natural fibers?

The two advertisements below suggest some answers to that question. As you read them, try to pick out words that reveal what kinds of values each ad appeals to.

- Sportsbest jackets are ideal for Americans' active, outdoor life-style. The jackets are made of lightweight synthetic fabric that makes them almost entirely carefree. They resist stains, repel water, and never require ironing or special treatment.
- Somerset jackets reflect the tradition of using fine wool in distinctive clothing. They are made of warm, natural, long-wearing wool with soft leather patches on the elbows to give maximum comfort and durability.

What values does the first advertisement suggest? If you noticed the emphasis on practicality and easy care, you will probably agree that the ad is meant to appeal to a person who values an active life and convenience.

Does the second advertisement appeal to the same values? No. The emphasis there is on distinction, tradition, durability, and comfort.

On the Springboard

Item 1 is based on the following passage. As you read the information, think of how it could influence the values of homeowners.

Modern materials and efficient building techniques make it possible to build homes that are almost completely weather-tight. As a result, homeowners can enjoy comfortable indoor temperatures with low heating and cooling costs. The nation can conserve valuable fossil fuels and reduce air pollution by using less fuel for heating homes.

The process of sealing buildings against the weather has so many advantages that it is hard to believe there could be disadvantages. But there are some. As buildings are more tightly insulated and sealed, ventilation decreases. Toxic gases that come from some building materials are sometimes sealed inside living quarters. And in some areas radon gas, a natural product of the decay of radium, may seep into homes from underground sources. Radon frequently increases the risk of lung cancer. A lack of ventilation can seal radon into homes just as it does with other gases.

1. Given the information above, a homeowner who insulates his or her house probably places a high value on

   (1) traditional materials and building techniques
   (2) reducing fuel costs and conserving fossil fuels
   (3) avoiding risky situations

You can check your Springboard answer on page 192.

If you were able to answer the question correctly, go directly to "The Real Thing." If you need a little review, reread this section as well as the skills section of Lesson 18.

❝ The Real Thing ❞

Items 1–4 refer to the following passage.

Nuclear power plants currently provide about 10 percent of the electricity used in the United States. As the needs for power continue to grow, so do problems connected with nuclear power plants. A growing stock of nuclear wastes is one of the major problems.

At present, nuclear power companies are sealing and storing wastes directly on their power plant sites. But they agree that this is just a temporary solution. In the 1970s, plans got under way to reprocess nuclear assemblies so their parts could be reused to make more power. Then in 1977, the U.S. government banned the building of reprocessing plants. Political leaders feared that during the shipping and recycling of the nuclear wastes, someone might steal enough radioactive materials to manufacture an atomic bomb. In 1981, the government lifted the ban on reprocessing. Still, no companies have built reprocessing plants because they are so expensive.

1. What was the value behind public officials' decision to ban nuclear reprocessing centers?

(1) concern for national security
(2) interest in saving money
(3) concerns for public health
(4) determination to investigate radioactivity
(5) desire for speed and efficiency

① ② ③ ④ ⑤

2. Which of the following actions would be based on a value for operating nuclear power plants safely?

(1) Electric companies switch from hydroelectric power plants to nuclear plants.
(2) Protesters picket an electric power company's offices after a rate increase.
(3) Construction workers at a new power site go out on strike for more benefits.
(4) Power companies band together to finance research for new waste storage methods.
(5) Power companies using nuclear plants charge lower rates than companies that burn coal.

① ② ③ ④ ⑤

3. According to the passage, companies have not built and used reprocessing plants because

(1) people are now concerned about the safety of nuclear reprocessing plants
(2) officials are still concerned about nuclear theft
(3) the technology is now out of date
(4) reprocessing plants are too expensive to build and operate
(5) communities will not approve sites for building nuclear reprocessing plants

① ② ③ ④ ⑤

4. Which of the following statements best summarizes the passage?

(1) Nuclear power plants are our most efficient source of energy.
(2) Nuclear power plants provide only a small portion of the electricity used in the United States.
(3) The continued use of nuclear power causes a growing problem with radioactive wastes.
(4) Nuclear assemblies could be reprocessed for future use.
(5) Storage of nuclear waste on plant sites is just a temporary solution.

① ② ③ ④ ⑤

Check your answers and record your score on page 194.

Answers: On the Springboard

19 The States of Matter
Applying Ideas
(page 167)

1. (1) Liquids tend to seek their own level, or level themselves out. In containers such as those shown in the diagram, the liquid in the handle of the container would adjust to the level in the container itself.

2. (2) As astronauts move farther into space away from the earth, they are less influenced by the earth's gravity. Without the gravitational force that causes liquids to pour on earth, astronauts would not be able to drink from an open cup or glass in space.

20 The Structure of Matter
Distinguishing Facts from Opinions and Hypotheses
(page 172)

1. (3) Statements A and C could both be proved with experiments or even by consulting a reliable reference book. Statements B and D, on the other hand, are both statements of personal opinion.

2. (2) The test item asks for a hypothesis from the passage, which is a possible explanation for something or a statement that can be used as a basis for research. Option (2) fits the second description.

21 Changes in Matter
Distinguishing a Conclusion from Supporting Statements
(page 178)

1. (2) In the presence of light, hydrogen peroxide decomposes into water and oxygen. If the product is stored in bottles that protect it from light, it will stay fresh and effective longer. Naturally, manufacturers wish to keep their product fresh as long as possible.

2. (1) Since hydrogen peroxide does decompose in the presence of light, it is reasonable to assume that when some of it is exposed to light for a time, it might lose some effectiveness as a bleach or antiseptic.

22 The Behavior of Matter
Assessing Supporting Data
(page 184)

1. (2) The information in the passage explains how electrodialysis does produce fresh water from salt water.

2. (3) A and B are both value judgments; they cannot be proved. Statements C and D, however, could both be proved by chemical analysis.

23 Special Kinds of Matter
Values in Beliefs and Decision Making
(page 190)

1. (2) Insulation lowers the cost of heating and air conditioning. It also helps conserve fossil fuels. A homeowner who feels it is important to reduce heating and cooling costs and to conserve fossil fuels will probably insulate thoroughly.

Answers: "The Real Thing"

As you check your answers, you may notice that some question numbers are in color. Those questions pertain to the skill taught in the lesson. The skill in each lesson is labeled with a heading that is in color. You'll probably want to go back and review the skills you had difficulty with before you complete this section.

19 The States of Matter
Applying Ideas
(page 168)

1. (3) As the car travels from a cooler area (where less viscous oil is needed) to a very hot area, the motorist would need to change to a more viscous oil. The heavier oil will help reduce friction and therefore heat.

2. (4) Greater heat inside the earth makes the magma flow more easily. As it erupts from the volcano and meets with the cooler air of the atmosphere, it cools and becomes more viscous.

3. (4) Air is cooled and compressed to make liquid oxygen. Once the liquid oxygen is brought to room temperature, it would quickly warm up and turn back into a gas. Therefore, it would evaporate back into the air.

KEEPING TRACK
Top Score = 3
Your Score = ☐

20 The Structure of Matter
Distinguishing Facts from Opinions and Hypotheses
(page 173)

1. (4) The doctors suggested that a factor in the drinking water—fluorine—protected teeth against decay. That suggestion is a hypothesis because it talks about a possible cause of something.

2. (2) Statements A and B both are capable of being proved. Both are based on fact. Statements C and D are both opinions, statements of individual judgment.

3. (5) Options (1)–(4) can be eliminated because they are based on fact. Option (5) is a hypothesis; it states a possible explanation for the occurrence of nervous disorders in many Roman citizens.

4. (1) The main ideas in the two paragraphs of the passage are that lead has many practical uses and that lead can be a hazardous substance. Option (1) summarizes those ideas.

KEEPING TRACK
Top Score = 4
Your Score = ☐

21 Changes in Matter
Distinguishing a Conclusion from Supporting Statements
(page 179)

1. (2) Sodium chloride melts at a very high temperature—800°C. Since room temperature is much lower, sodium chloride cannot melt at room temperature. In other words, it remains a solid.

2. (4) The passage tells you that ionic compounds dissolved in water conduct electricity well. Since calcium chloride is an ionic compound, it will conduct electricity in water.

3. (1) The fourth paragraph states that the Van Allen belts are areas of high concentrations of ions, which are electrically charged particles.

KEEPING TRACK
Top Score = 3
Your Score = ☐

22 The Behavior of Matter
Assessing Supporting Data
(pages 184–185)

1. (3) Lemon juice, which is considered safe to eat or drink, actually preserves the color and taste of some foods. It is, therefore, an example proving that some preservatives are safe to use.

2. (4) The first paragraph explains that oxidation causes fats and oils to become rancid. Since butter is a fat, it follows that exposure to oxygen would cause butter to become rancid.

3. (2) This option details the key ideas from the entire passage.

4. (4) The more acidic a substance is, the lower the reading on the pH scale. Over the years, the measurement for Oxbow Lake has gradually followed a downward trend. In other words, the lake has been growing more acidic. If the trend continues, the lake will become more acidic by 1995.

KEEPING TRACK
Top Score = 4
Your Score = ☐

23 Special Kinds of Matter
Values in Beliefs and Decision Making
(page 191)

1. (1) According to the second paragraph, the U.S. government banned nuclear reprocessing plants because of fear that nuclear materials could be stolen while being transported. In other words, officials felt that transporting nuclear materials threatened national security. Their action was intended to keep the nation safe from such thefts.

2. (4) Since radioactive waste is highly dangerous, any action intended to promote safe disposal of such wastes would reflect a desire to operate nuclear plants safely.

3. (4) A concern for saving money is the value reflected here. The passage states that now reprocessing plants have not been put into operation because of their expense.

4. (3) Option (3) gives the important message of the passage without adding or omitting any key information.

KEEPING TRACK
Top Score = 4
Your Score = ☐

Keeping Track

Here's a chart for you to record your scores from the Keeping Track boxes.

Lesson	Top Score	Your Score
Lesson 19 Applying Ideas	3	_____
Lesson 20 Distinguishing Facts from Opinions and Hypotheses	4	_____
Lesson 21 Distinguishing a Conclusion from Supporting Statements	3	_____
Lesson 22 Assessing Supporting Data	4	_____
Lesson 23 Values in Beliefs and Decision Making	4	_____
TOTAL	18	_____

Look back now at how you did in *Chemistry.* Were there some lessons you did especially well in? Were there some for which you need a little more work? Now is the time to review those lessons. Then sharpen your skills on the Extra Practice that follows.

Extra Practice in Chemistry

Directions: Choose the one best answer for each item.

Items 1–2 refer to the following paragraph.

Bread is made from flour, water or milk, yeast, and salt. Sometimes sugar is added to the dough to sweeten the bread and to promote the growth of yeast. Yeast contains living organisms that break down sugar to produce carbon dioxide gas (CO_2) and alcohol. The carbon dioxide expands, causing the bread to rise. Later, high baking temperatures kill the yeast and evaporate the alcohol in the dough.

1. As bread bakes, it stops rising because

(1) alcohol evaporates at high temperatures
(2) heat kills the yeast that makes CO_2
(3) the dough begins to shrink
(4) heat eliminates the sugar
(5) moisture in the dough evaporates

(1) (2) (3) (4) (5)

2. The teacher of a bread-making class suggests that a student's first loaf should be sweetened bread because the extra sugar

(1) makes the bread bake faster
(2) gives the bread a better texture
(3) reacts with CO_2 to make the bread rise
(4) promotes the growth of yeast that makes CO_2
(5) makes it possible to use less CO_2

(1) (2) (3) (4) (5)

Items 3–4 refer to the following information.

The strong attraction of water molecules for each other along a surface is called surface tension. Surface tension causes water molecules to form a thick layer, or skin, strong enough to support a lightweight object.

3. Which of the following is possible because of surface tension?

(1) Water evaporates on a sunny day.
(2) Water reflects sunlight.
(3) A heavy object sinks into deep water.
(4) A small insect walks on water.
(5) Water pours from a container.

(1) (2) (3) (4) (5)

4. A bowl is filled to the brim with water, and a needle is gently placed on the surface. The needle remains there until two drops of liquid soap are added to the water; then the needle plunges to the bottom.

Which of the following explanations best describes the situation above?

(1) The needle has been magnetized.
(2) The water has been heated.
(3) Soap has reduced the surface tension.
(4) Soap has made the needle heavier.
(5) Soap has destroyed the needle.

(1) (2) (3) (4) (5)

5. Acids and bases neutralize each other. Most cleaning agents, soaps, and detergents are bases. Yet vinegar and some other mild acids can also make effective cleaning agents.

If a window washer attempts to make a double-strength cleaning solution by mixing vinegar with a detergent that is a base, the solution would probably

(1) clean twice as well
(2) explode
(3) evaporate
(4) not clean anything
(5) burn the window washer's hands

① ② ③ ④ ⑤

6. An advertisement for hand soaps makes the following claims.

A. contains no acids
B. is kind to your hands
C. removes bacteria from your skin
D. is pleasantly scented

Which of the above claims can be tested scientifically?

(1) A and B only
(2) B and C only
(3) C and D only
(4) A and C only
(5) B and D only

① ② ③ ④ ⑤

Items 7–8 refer to the following diagram and information.

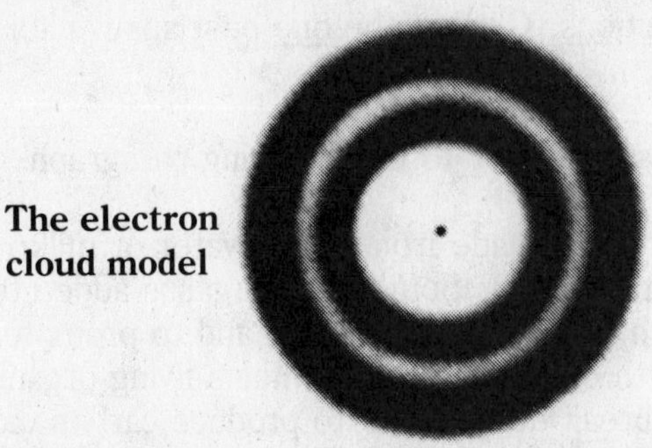

Various scientists have created models of the atom. The model that is used today is the electron cloud model, shown above. In this model, an electron moves rapidly through the atom. Its position is described as a cloud rather than a precise point. The darker areas show the distance from the nucleus where electrons are most likely to be.

7. According to the model, how do electrons move?

(1) along straight lines away from the nucleus
(2) around the nucleus in orbits
(3) in figure eights
(4) along straight lines toward the nucleus
(5) around each other in orbits

① ② ③ ④ ⑤

8. Which of the following conclusions about the scientific study of the structure of the atom is supported by evidence in the diagram and paragraph?

(1) Scientists use different atomic models depending on the reason for their study.
(2) Scientists now know exactly what an atom looks like.
(3) It is impossible for a scientist to know exactly where each electron is at any one time.
(4) Scientists do not know how the electrons produce clouds in an atom.
(5) Scientists cannot study the nucleus of an atom because it is surrounded by an electron cloud.

① ② ③ ④ ⑤

Items 9–12 are based on the information that follows.

Scientists sometimes group elements according to their properties. Below are descriptions of five physical properties that help identify different elements.

(1) luster = degree to which an element shines
(2) ductility = ability to be drawn into wire
(3) malleability = ability to be hammered, rolled, or shaped
(4) heat conductivity = ability to transfer heat
(5) electrical conductivity = ability to carry electricity

Each of the following items is a practical application of a physical property. For each item, identify the physical property described above that is most appropriate. Each of the categories may be used more than once.

9. A camper wraps aluminum foil around fresh fish to store it.

   The camper is making use of aluminum's

   (1) luster
   (2) ductility
   (3) malleability
   (4) heat conductivity
   (5) electrical conductivity

   (1) (2) (3) (4) (5)

10. Ancient Romans polished silver for use as mirrors.

    The Romans were making use of silver's

    (1) luster
    (2) ductility
    (3) malleability
    (4) heat conductivity
    (5) electrical conductivity

    (1) (2) (3) (4) (5)

11. A large cast-iron skillet cooks food quickly and evenly.

    The makers of the skillet are making use of iron's

    (1) luster
    (2) ductility
    (3) malleability
    (4) heat conductivity
    (5) electrical conductivity

    (1) (2) (3) (4) (5)

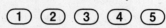

12. A jeweler makes a fine thin chain from platinum.

    The jeweler is making use of platinum's

    (1) luster
    (2) ductility
    (3) malleability
    (4) heat conductivity
    (5) electrical conductivity

Answers to Extra Practice in Chemistry are on page 232. Record your score on the Progress Chart on the inside back cover.

Physics

Every time you watch television, twist a screwdriver, cut with scissors, turn on a light switch, or recharge a battery, you're making use of a scientific principle from physics. Those tools, machines, and actions are all ways people have found to use the laws of nature that physicists have discovered.

Physicists study matter and energy and forces. Very often the results of their research find their way into people's everyday lives.

Physics on the GED Science Test will concentrate on just such practical applications of the general laws of physics. Fewer than half of the 66 items will involve physical laws, and, like the other areas of science on the test, most of the information you need to answer the items will be given to you right there. Many of the items will use visual materials. Here's an example of one such question.

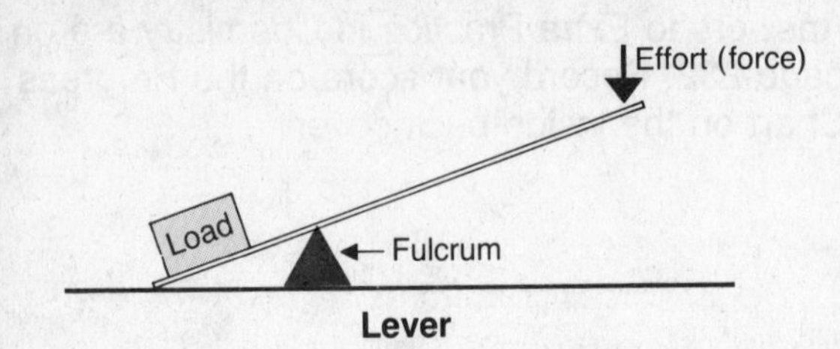

One of the oldest—and most effective—tools used to move heavy objects is a lever used over a fulcrum. The closer the fulcrum is to the object being lifted, the greater the force that is exerted on the object by pressing on the opposite end of the lever.

Do you understand the principle of the lever from that explanation and diagram? Now look at the question about that information.

A homeowner tries to pry loose a stump using a steel rod as a lever over a cement block. On the first try the stump will not move. What could be done to increase the chances of moving the stump?

(1) move the block away from the stump
(2) move the block closer to the stump
(3) replace the block with a large rock
(4) grasp the rod closer to the block
(5) reverse the position of the rod

The information below the diagram mentions that the closer the fulcrum is to the thing being lifted, the more force there will be. In the situation given, the cement block is acting as the fulcrum. Therefore, moving the cement block closer to the stump will result in greater force and a better chance of moving the stump. So the answer is option (2). Even if you've never seen the words *lever* and *fulcrum* before, do you see how all the information was given to you right with the question?

Some physics items on the test will be based on longer reading passages. Many of these passages will tell about interesting new developments in physics. On the next page is one such passage, along with a question that could be asked about it.

Late at night the lights at a train crossing flash as a car waits for the train to pass. The train silently appears, sweeps by with a swish of air, and is gone. The usual roar of the engine, shaking of the ground, and clanking of the steel wheels are absent. People sleeping in nearby houses are unaware that a train with two hundred passengers has come and gone.

Such a train is possible today because of the discovery years ago that electricity travels faster when a metal is cold than when it is warm. The train can move silently using electric currents and magnets that are supercooled by refrigeration units on the train. These cold magnets are superconductors and will stay powerful without a constant source of electricity.

An electric current turns the train track into an electromagnet. The magnets in the train repel the magnets in the track, so the train rises a short distance off the rails. The train rides this moving electromagnetic wave as if it were an electromagnetic surf. The faster the wave, the faster the train will go. Such trains should reach speeds of 250 kilometers per hour.

Electromagnetic trains can ease environmental problems in several ways. Besides making far less noise, they will not pollute the air with smoke. In metropolitan areas, more commuters may take the train rather than drive cars, thereby conserving fuel and further reducing air pollution.

One reason an electromagnetic train is quieter than a fuel-driven train is that the electromagnetic train

(1) moves above the track
(2) is not made of steel
(3) has an engine that is muffled by magnets
(4) travels faster
(5) does not pollute

If you understood the principle of how an electromagnetic train works, you could answer that question fairly easily. The passage tells you that the train "rises a short distance off the rails" and rides the electromagnetic wave, not on the tracks themselves. Also, no fuel-driven engine is needed. Think of your everyday experience and how noisy train engines usually are. Those aspects of an electromagnetic train would explain the quiet nature of the train.

Look at one more question that could be asked about that passage.

Electromagnetic trains may help improve the environment in all of the following ways except by

(1) reducing people's reliance on fuel
(2) making less noise
(3) not emitting smoke
(4) reducing the amount of pollution that comes from using automobiles
(5) reducing the need for electricity

① ② ③ ④ ⑤

The last paragraph in the passage gives you much of the information you need to answer that question. Using your logic will help too. An electromagnetic train doesn't need fuel or a loud engine or an exhaust system to release smoke. The one thing such a train *does* need is electricity. Option (5), therefore, names the one way in which such a train will not help improve the environment.

Did you understand the reasoning process that went into answering those sample GED test items? That is the same sort of thinking you will need to do to succeed on the GED Science Test. Working through the following section on physics will help you polish the thinking skills you've been practicing throughout this book.

LESSON 24

Basic Principles of Physics

As you read about some of the main concepts that scientists work with in physics, you may find that many of them are already familiar to you. Before you read the first section, glance at the Warm-up for clues to important points.

Motion and Forces

Motion occurred when you picked up this book. Motion occurs whenever an object is moved from one place to another. Look around the room. Do you observe any motion? Is someone turning on the TV, making a shopping list, or using a calculator? If so, motion is occurring.

If you throw a baseball, you put the ball in motion. Stop the baseball, and you have stopped motion. Both starting and stopping the motion require a force. A force is an influence that causes motion or prevents motion. A push or a pull upon an object is a force.

To understand motion and forces, you need to know the three laws of motion. Sir Isaac Newton, an English mathematician, first stated these laws about three hundred years ago.

The first law of motion says that a body that is not moving will remain at rest unless acted upon by some outside force. Likewise, a body in motion will remain in motion unless an outside force acts upon it. The body will travel at the same velocity, or rate of motion, and in the same straight line.

Use your imagination to picture a bowling alley that is several miles long. Imagine a bowling ball moving along the middle of the alley in a straight line. If no force acted on it, the ball would roll and roll without ever slowing down or stopping. But the forces of air and of friction with the wood in the alley gradually slow down and eventually stop the ball. This example shows Newton's first law of motion at work.

The first law of motion also explains **inertia.** The tendency of a body in motion to remain in motion or of a body at rest to remain at rest is the property of inertia. Have you ever been a backseat passenger in a car when the driver made a sudden stop? If so, you probably noticed that you continued to move forward for an instant or two. Inertia kept you moving even though the car had stopped.

Newton's second law states that the greater the mass of an object, the greater the force needed to accelerate the object, or set it in motion. (Mass refers simply to the amount of matter an object contains.) For example, you would have to throw a 16-ounce steel ball with twice the force you would use with an 8-ounce ball in order to accelerate it.

Newton's third law states that for every action there is an equal and opposite reaction. Have you ever fired a 12-gauge shotgun? If so, you saw Newton's third law of motion in action. The shot moves through the barrel toward the target with a powerful force. There is an equal force in the opposite direction. It's a heavy push against your shoulder. This push is referred to as a "kick." This law is also at work in the launching of rockets and the flying of jet planes.

Coming to Terms

inertia the tendency of a body in motion to remain in motion or the tendency of a body at rest to remain at rest

Warm-up

Answer each question below in a sentence or two.

1. What is a force?

____

____

2. According to the first law of motion, what would happen to an arrow if you shot it upward and there was no air or other force to act on it?

____

____

Sample Warm-up Answers

1. A force is any influence that causes or prevents motion.

2. The arrow would keep going in the same direction and never slow down or stop.

Scientists think of energy as the ability to do work. Electricity, sound, and light are all forms of energy. So is heat. Before you read this section on energy and heat, look ahead to the Warm-up. Focus your reading on the points it covers.

Energy and Heat

Energy comes in many different forms. In the last section you read about motion; the kind of energy that comes from motion is called **kinetic energy.** The light that comes in waves from the sun is an example of radiant energy. In biology, you learned how plants can change such radiant energy through photosynthesis. Energy stored in plants is an example of chemical energy. Nuclear energy is released when the atoms you studied in chemistry split or combine. Electrical energy is carried by electrically charged particles. These different forms of energy can change back and forth into each other.

Heat is one form of kinetic energy. It works like this: The molecules in all matter are always in motion. When an object gains heat, its molecules speed up. When it loses heat, its molecules slow down. You frequently speed up and slow down the molecules in substances right in your own kitchen. Suppose you heat a pan of water or skillet of potatoes on your stove. You speed up the motion of the molecules in the water, the potatoes, and cookware that you place on the burner. If you place food in the refrigerator, you slow down the molecules in the food and in the containers that hold the food.

Gases behave in special and interesting ways when they gain or lose heat energy. As a gas is heated, its molecules move faster and faster, just as they do in solids and liquids. But the volume, or amount of space, the gas occupies will also increase as the gas gains heat. If you increase the temperature of a liter of oxygen, for example, the volume of the oxygen will also increase. But this principle holds true only if the pressure on the gas remains the same.

If you keep the temperature of the gas the same but change the pressure, the gas will also change its volume. In this case the greater the pressure, the lower the volume. Go back for a moment to your liter of oxygen. You have kept the pressure, let's say, at 15 pounds per square inch. Then you increase the pressure to 30 pounds per square inch. The volume of the oxygen will decrease to one-half liter.

Your liter of oxygen has just demonstrated two laws of physics:

1. If the pressure on a gas is kept the same, the volume of the gas will increase or decrease as the temperature increases or decreases.

2. If the temperature of a gas is kept the same, the volume of the gas will increase as its pressure decreases, and vice versa.

Coming to Terms

kinetic energy the energy of motion

Warm-up

Answer each question in a sentence of your own.

1. What happens to the molecules in a substance when they gain or lose heat?

____

____

2. If the volume of a given mass of gas decreased when more pressure was applied, what was true of its temperature?

____

____

Sample Warm-up Answers

1. Molecules move faster when a substance is heated and slower when a substance is cooled. **2.** The temperature of the gas remained the same.

The next section tells you about some principles of physics that help make life a little easier for you and most other people in the world. Before you read it, glance at the Warm-up. Use it as a guide to some important points.

Work and Simple Machines

You perform many tasks every day, and you call your efforts work. Certainly they are. But scientists look at "work" in a special way. They define **work** as applying force to an object and causing it to move. They figure out the amount of work done by multiplying the force by the distance through which the force acts. For example, suppose you carry a 5-pound box of plastic bags a distance of 30 feet. The amount of work you perform would be 5 × 30, or 150 foot-pounds. How much work would you do if you carried a 10-pound bag of feed 55 feet? The answer is 550 foot-pounds, which is the same as 1 horsepower.

Fortunately, machines help us do much of our work. The machines that help people do physical work are based mostly on six different simple machines. Every day you use simple machines and combinations of simple machines working together.

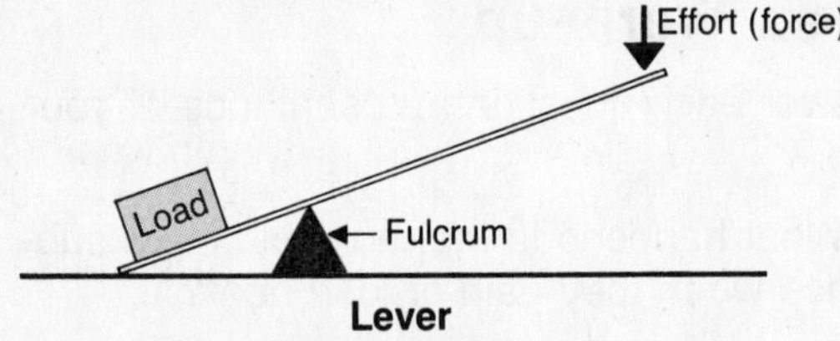

Lever

The lever is a simple machine, probably one of the first ever used. As you can see in the illustration above, a lever is a rigid bar that is free to turn about a fulcrum. Applying force to the bar on one side of the fulcrum will lift the load on the other end of the fulcrum. Have you ever used a crowbar? It is a lever.

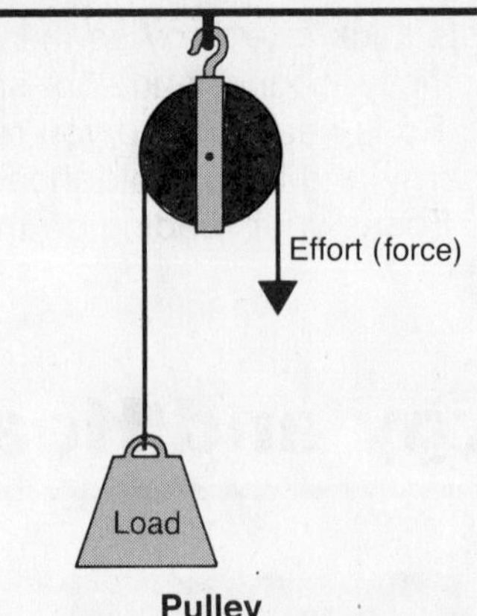

Pulley

Now look at the simple machine called the pulley. A pulley has a grooved wheel over which a rope passes. You could use a fixed pulley to change the direction of a force. In other words, if you pull down on the rope, the load will move up.

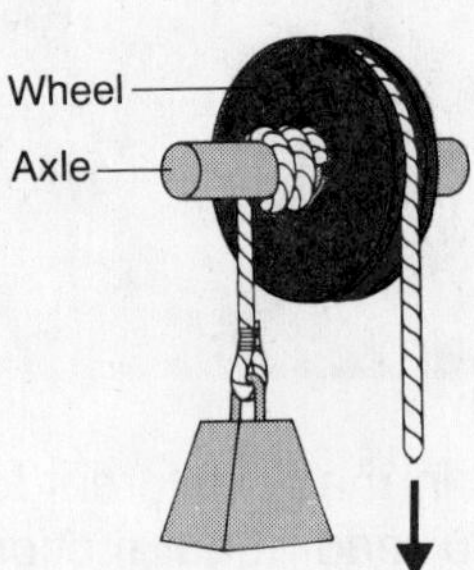

Wheel and Axle

A wheel and axle is made of a large wheel attached to a smaller circular rod. Look at the diagram to see how the wheel and axle always move together. A screwdriver is a commonly used type of wheel-and-axle simple machine.

Inclined Plane

Have you ever dragged or pushed something up a ramp? If so, you made your work easier by using the simple machine called the inclined plane.

Wedge

A wedge has either one or two inclined planes placed back to back, with their slanting sides out. Some of the everyday simple machines that use the principle of the wedge are an ax, scissors, and a knife.

Screw

A screw is an inclined plane that spirals around a cylinder. Notice how the grooves in the screw shown in the illustration slant as they wind upward or downward. Lids on jars also use this principle.

Coming to Terms

work the application of force on an object that causes the object to move

Warm-up

Name the six kinds of simple machines. Write your answer in a complete sentence.

___

___

___

Sample Warm-up Answer
The six simple machines are the lever, pulley, wheel and axle, inclined plane, wedge, and screw.

Predicting Outcomes

You predict outcomes every day. To do so, you use knowledge and rules of behavior that you have learned through life. When you cross a busy street, you make predictions based on your past experiences with traffic speed, direction, and braking distances. You don't step off the curb until you can safely predict that no car will try to occupy the same space as your body.

Predicting outcomes is an important part of scientific study. Scientists use what they have learned or observed in the past to predict what might happen in new circumstances. You can apply some of the rules and laws of physics to predict outcomes.

Here's an Example

You've learned that inertia is the tendency for a body at rest to resist motion or for a body in motion to resist any change in its motion. You can use that knowledge to predict an outcome based on the information below.

■ A couple of backyard mechanics removed the large eight-cylinder engine from a heavy luxury car. They fitted the luxury car with a four-cylinder engine taken from a small, subcompact auto. Then they switched on the ignition and drove the luxury car to test its acceleration.

Your knowledge of inertia tells you immediately how the car reacted. Its acceleration was very slow and sluggish. The heavy luxury car had so much inertia that a small, light engine could hardly get it to move.

The same principle of inertia would work the other way around too. If the mechanics had installed brakes from the subcompact on the heavy car, the greater inertia of the heavier car would make it harder to slow down.

Try it Yourself

Read the passage below. Then think about the predictions you would make to answer two questions: In what direction did the passengers in the car move when the driver braked? In what direction did they feel they were moving when the driver suddenly accelerated again?

■ A woman was driving down the street with her two children in the back seat and a bag of groceries beside her on the front seat. Suddenly a cat shot into the street in front of her with a dog in close pursuit. The woman braked hard to miss the darting animals and then accelerated quickly to avoid being rear-ended by a car coming up behind her. Then she swung sharply to the right down Hardy Avenue to get out of the stream of traffic and recover her breath.

What predictions did you make? Did you think that the children moved forward at the same speed they had been traveling when their mother braked? That would be the correct prediction. When the mother quickly accelerated again, her children *felt* that they were moving backward. They were not actually moving backward, but the car seat was overtaking them. Its pressure on their backs made them feel for an instant that they were going backward. Did you apply the principle of inertia to figure that out?

☑ A Test-Taking Tip

On the GED Science Test, you could get a wrong idea about the meaning of a test item if you miss a word by reading too fast or only once. Reading every question twice, word by word, is a good precaution to take.

On the Springboard

Items 1–2 refer to the two drawings below. Each shows a common kind of lever. In each drawing, *E* stands for effort, or force; *L* stands for load; and *F* stands for fulcrum. You will be asked to predict how the levers behave.

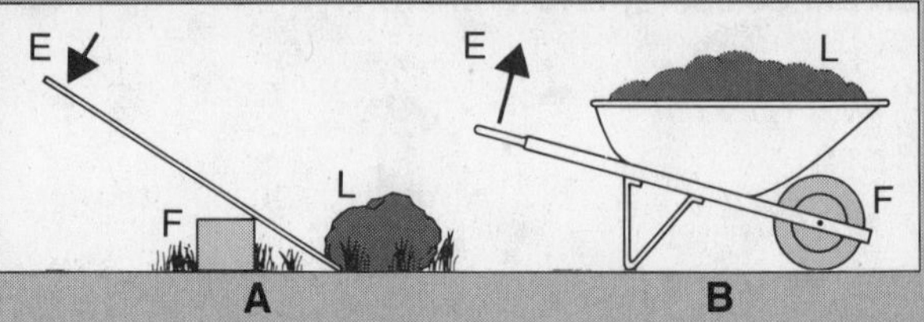

1. In which case will the effort move in the opposite direction of the load?

   (1) A only
   (2) B only
   (3) A and B

   ① ② ③

2. In which case will the effort move the greater distance compared with the distance the load will move?

   (1) A only
   (2) B only
   (3) A and B

   ① ② ③

Item 3 refers to the paragraph below. It asks you to apply a physics concept.

Sally is five feet, two inches tall. Her brother stands nearly six feet. They are going to exercise at a health club. In one activity, they will both lift one of Sally's five-pound dumbbells from the floor to a position above their heads ten times.

3. If the amount of work done is figured by multiplying the force by the distance through which the force acts, who will do more work by lifting the weights?

   (1) Sally
   (2) Sally's brother
   (3) Sally and her brother will do the same amount of work.

   ① ② ③

Check your Springboard answers on page 224.

If you answered all three Springboard items correctly, go on to "The Real Thing." If you missed any, take time to review this lesson before going on.

66 The Real Thing 99

Item 1 refers to the following information.

In a training class, skydivers were shown this table telling how fast a body would fall from a plane before opening a parachute.

Time in seconds:	0	1	2	3	4	5
Velocity in foot-seconds:	0	32	64	96	128	?

1. What would be the velocity of the diver in foot-seconds at the end of the fifth second?

   (1) 152
   (2) 160
   (3) 224
   (4) 256
   (5) 12,800

   ① ② ③ ④ ⑤

Item 2 refers to the following information.

Gas inside a closed container will increase its pressure against the walls of its container if the amount of gas or its temperature is increased.

On a warm summer day, a truck driver checks the air pressure in his tires before starting on a long trip. He travels for 250 miles before making a rest stop.

2. Which of the following is an accurate prediction about the air pressure in the truck's tires at the moment the driver stops?

   (1) All four tires have the same pressure as when he started.
   (2) The pressure in all four tires is lower than when he started.
   (3) The air pressure is higher in some tires and lower in others.
   (4) All four tires have higher air pressure than when he started.
   (5) The spare tire has a higher pressure than it did before he stopped.

Check your answers and record your score on page 225.

LESSON 25

Waves

You've learned that energy is the ability to do work. You've seen, too, that work results when a force is applied to cause motion in the same direction as the force. In this lesson, you'll read about energy traveling in waves. Before you begin, glance at the Warm-up at the end of this section. It will focus your thoughts on important information.

Properties of Waves

Have you ever tossed a rock into a pond and watched the waves travel to the shore in widening circles? As the rock strikes the water, it forces some water to lower depths. The forced-down water causes water around it to rise. This begins an up-and-down motion of the water molecules. The motion is called vibration. The energy in the vibrating molecules sets molecules next to them in motion, and the waves move outward in all directions.

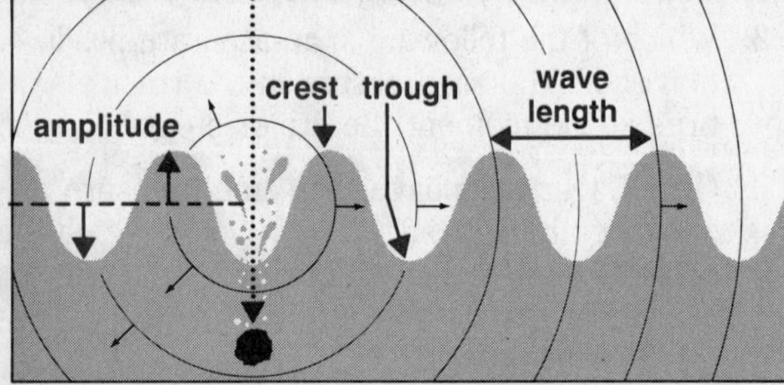

If you floated a stick in the waves, it would bob up and down. It would rise on the crest of a wave and then drop into the trough as each wave passed. Find the wave crests and troughs in the diagram above.

The distance from the crest of one wave to the crest of another is called a wave length. The number of waves that pass a given point in a certain unit of time is the wave frequency. The amplitude of the wave is the height *or* depth of the wave as measured from the normal level of the water (or whatever substance the wave happens to be passing through). Besides liquids such as water, waves also travel through gases such as air and solids such as wood.

Waves also have velocity, which means the distance a wave will travel in a certain period of time. Water waves have a low velocity. They move very slowly. Other kinds of waves travel at incredible speeds, and so they have extremely high velocities.

Warm-up

Study the diagram below. Then answer the questions that follow in complete sentences. Review the information in this section if you need to.

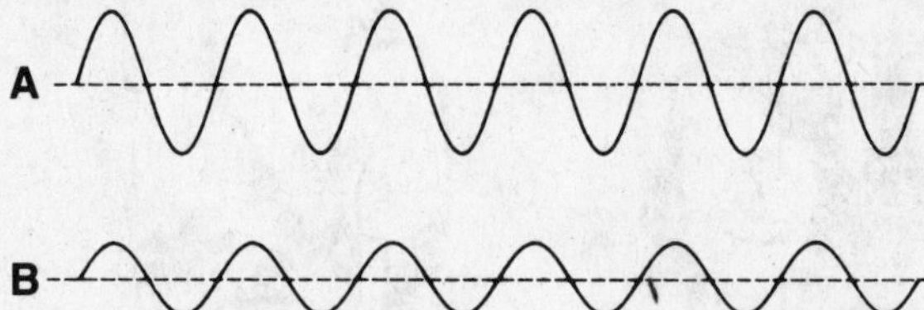

1. Which wave has greater amplitude?

____

____

2. How do the frequencies of the waves compare?

____

____

Warm-up Answers
1. Wave A has greater amplitude. **2.** The two waves have the same frequency.

The sounds that you hear are traveling to your ears in waves. In the next section, you'll read about some important properties of sound waves. Take time to look ahead to the Warm-up at the end. It can guide you to important points in the section.

Sound Waves

The music played on a clarinet, a drum, and a violin sound different. Yet each instrument has vibrating parts that set up waves in the air. These sound waves start at a given source and travel outward in all directions.

Sound waves will not travel in a **vacuum.** A vacuum is a space empty of all solids, liquids, or gases—including air. There must be a medium through which sound can travel. It may seem that the speed of sound traveling through air is terrific. Yet air is a rather poor conductor, or carrier, of sound waves. At room temperature, sound travels through the air about 1,130 feet per second. It travels through wood, however, about 12,620 feet per second and through iron at nearly 17,000 feet per second.

In good conductors, sound travels farther as well as faster. Water and most solids are better sound conductors than air. But there are a few exceptions. Solids such as rubber, cork, and felt tend to absorb rather than conduct sound waves. That property is why people sometimes use these materials to reduce noise levels in rooms.

Sound waves have three main properties—pitch, intensity, and quality. Pitch depends on the frequency of the sound waves. Low-frequency waves produce low-pitched sounds, like the tones of a bass fiddle. High-frequency waves produce high-pitched sounds, like those of a violin or flute.

If you have ever turned down the volume on a radio to lower the sound, you have reduced the intensity of the sound waves coming from it. The amplitude of sound waves determines their intensity. Waves of high amplitude strike hard against your eardrum and other surfaces. Turning down the radio lowers the amplitude and force of the waves and so reduces the intensity of the sound.

To understand the quality of a sound, imagine beautiful tones coming from musical instruments. If a piano, a horn, and a violin were all to play the same musical note, you would be able to tell that the sounds were produced by three different instruments. Although the musical notes played had the same intensity and the same pitch, you would not confuse the sound of the piano with the sound of the horn or violin. The difference in these sounds is called quality.

Coming to Terms

vacuum a totally empty space

Warm-up

Answer each question in a sentence or two of your own.

1. If someone on the shore of a lake blows a whistle, an underwater swimmer hears the sound before a person in a rowboat in the water above him does. Why?

____

____

2. If the intensity of a sound is decreasing, what is happening to the sound waves?

____

____

Sample Warm-up Answers
1. The swimmer hears the sound first because sound travels faster through water than through air. **2.** The amplitude of the sound waves is also decreasing.

Now you'll learn about some of the properties of light, which also travels in waves. Before you begin, look ahead to the Warm-up. It will help you find important points as you read the next section.

The Wave Nature of Light

Can you imagine something traveling so fast that it could circle the earth's equator in about one-seventh of a second? That is about the speed at which light waves travel. It is equal to 186,000 miles per second.

Light travels like waves going in straight lines. You can easily prove that light has this property. Look at the first word in this sentence. Now place your hand between your eye and the word on the page. You won't be able to see the word. The light cannot bend around your hand and carry the image of the word to your eye. Light waves will travel to your eye only in a straight line.

Unlike sound, light can travel through a vacuum. If it couldn't, light from the sun and stars would not reach the earth through the emptiness of outer space. Light waves can also travel through air, glass windows, and clear plastic wrap. All these substances are transparent. Light waves readily pass through any transparent substance.

Light will also pass through a piece of waxed paper. But if you hold a sheet of waxed paper in front of your eyes, you won't be able to see images on the other side of it clearly. That is because the light waves scatter after they pass through the waxed paper. The waxed paper diffuses the light waves. Fog and frosted glass also diffuse light. Substances that diffuse light as it passes through are said to be translucent.

Your hand, a sheet of aluminum foil, and cardboard are all examples of opaque substances. Light waves will not travel through opaque substances.

Luminous objects are the primary source of light waves. The sun is a luminous object that produces light energy used here on earth. Burning light bulbs are common luminous objects in your home.

For hundreds of years, scientists disagreed about just what light is. As you have just read, light often behaves like a wave. However, because other waves do not travel in a vacuum, some scientists thought that light waves traveled through a substance called ether. Other scientists suggested that light was really made up of tiny particles traveling in straight lines. Now scientists know that ether does not exist. They now believe that in many ways light acts like a wave, but in other ways it acts like a series of particles. Physicists are still trying to understand what light is.

Warm-up

Answer each question in a complete sentence.

1. Give three examples of translucent substances.

____

____

2. Give two examples of luminous objects.

____

Cause-and-Effect Relationships

You've read that a cause is what makes something happen, and an effect is what is made to happen. Sometimes it is easy to identify a cause. For example, if you plunge your hand into the still water of a pool, you can see immediately that your action causes ripples to move outward from your hand.

Often, however, a cause is not so easy to spot. Sometimes special equipment or scientific research is needed to locate the cause. In other situations, identifying a cause may be difficult because several factors have combined to produce a single effect. In still other situations, the cause-and-effect relationship may seem confusing because one cause leads to a particular effect, which then becomes a cause itself. A cause-and-effect relationship of this nature is called a chain of events.

Causes and effects are of special interest to physicists because understanding them helps explain so much of what happens in nature.

Sample Warm-up Answers
1. Waxed paper, fog, and frosted glass are all translucent substances. **2.** The sun and a light bulb are luminous objects.

Here's an Example

A cause-and-effect relationship is discussed in the paragraph below.

■ A fisherman sat on a raft poised motionless in a small, calm lake. Soon he heard the roar of an outboard motor, and a motorboat sped across the middle of the lake to the wharf. A few minutes later the raft began to bob up and down in a rhythmic motion.

The effect in the situation described above is the bobbing motion of the raft. The cause is the displacement of the water by the motorboat. It produced ripples that traveled outward from its engine. Those ripples were tiny waves—crests and troughs—and as they moved outward toward the raft, they made it bob up and down.

Try It Yourself

You can use what you have learned about waves to discover many cause-and-effect relationships. For instance, if you think about it, you will see that swimmers can be affected by several types of waves: water waves, light waves, and sound waves.

Read the article below. Then you will be asked to identify a cause-and-effect relationship concerning sound waves.

■ Sound can travel through air. In fact, sound waves causing air molecules to vibrate make it possible for you to hear the ticking of a clock, the whirring of a fan, or any other noises you hear as you read. But sound can move through other materials too, including water, some metals, and even earth. In fact, some Indians could hear the sound of hooves approaching just by putting an ear to the ground. This skill allowed them to know of approaching horses or buffalo long before they could see the animals.

How could Indians know that animals were approaching without seeing them? Could you tell from the information in the passage that the footsteps of large animals, such as horses or buffalo, cause vibrations in the earth? Those vibrations travel quite a distance through the earth as sound waves. The sound waves alerted Indians that large animals were moving in their direction. The footsteps were the cause; the sound vibrations were the result.

On the Springboard

Item 1 is based on the information given. Use your skill at identifying cause-and-effect relationships to answer both it and item 2.

1. During an electrical storm, it is quite common to see a flash of lightning and then hear the thunder shortly afterward. Which of the following is the most likely explanation for the delay of the sound?

   (1) The sound has a greater distance to travel.
   (2) Sound waves are stronger than light waves.
   (3) Light waves travel faster than sound waves.

Item 2 refers to the following paragraph.

The intensity of a sound depends on the force with which it hits. The pitch is determined by the frequency of the sound waves.

Enrico Caruso, the great tenor singer, used to have a parlor trick that he would perform with the sound of his voice. He would take an empty wine glass and sing a note into it, gradually increasing the power of his voice until the glass shattered into pieces. He would then gallantly present his hostess with the stem of the glass as a souvenir.

2. What caused the glass to shatter?

   (1) the intensity of sound waves
   (2) warmth from Caruso's breath
   (3) the pitch of Caruso's voice

(1) (2) (3)

Now turn to page 224 and check your answers to On the Springboard.

If you answered the Springboard items correctly, you did well. Go on to "The Real Thing." If you missed any, make sure that you understand the reasoning behind the correct answers before you go on.

“The Real Thing”

1. During a storm at sea, the wind gives energy to the waves. A wave's amplitude soon increases. Which of the following would be one result of the increased amplitude of the waves?

(1) an increase in wind speed
(2) a decrease in wind speed
(3) a decrease in sound waves
(4) an increase in a ship's forward speed
(5) an increase in a ship's up-and-down motion

<u>Item 2</u> is based on the following article.

Microwaves are waves of extremely high frequency that cannot be perceived by humans. Among many uses, they carry television signals, are used in garage door openers and burglar alarms, and heat food in microwave ovens. More and more, machines that produce microwaves are used in homes, businesses, and industries today. Scientists do not know for certain whether microwaves are a health hazard to humans, but research with small animals shows that microwaves *do* cause damage to their nervous and reproductive systems.

2. Which of the following states a reason that microwave pollution may become an increasing problem in the future?

(1) Microwaves grow stronger with age.
(2) Loud microwaves may damage human hearing.
(3) An increasing use of microwave gadgets will expose people to more microwaves.
(4) Whatever affects small animals will have the same effect on people.
(5) Conventional ovens are gradually replacing microwave ovens in homes.

<u>Item 3</u> is based on the following information.

The Doppler effect is an apparent change in pitch, caused by the motion of certain rapidly moving objects. As the object approaches, the sound waves move an increasingly shorter distance to one's ears, and the pitch sounds higher. As the object passes and moves away, the sound waves must travel a longer distance and so appear to have a lower pitch.

3. Which of the following sounds is caused by the Doppler effect?

(1) The alternating high and low pitch of a siren.
(2) The sonic boom produced by a jet plane.
(3) The changing pitch of a train whistle as it passes at a fairly rapid pace.
(4) The variety of pitches heard when a guitar player's fingers move quickly.
(5) The change in volume of a human voice.

<u>Item 4</u> refers to the article below.

Ultrasound is the name given to sounds so high that the human ear cannot detect them. Ultrasound can be used in medicine to detect certain ailments and can also be used to check the development of an unborn child. Ultrasound waves sent into the mother's womb bounce back and create an outline of the baby's image on a screen.

4. Which of the following would <u>not</u> be revealed by an ultrasound image?

(1) the baby's motions
(2) the presence of twins
(3) the baby's weight
(4) approximate body size
(5) approximate head size

Check your answers and record your score on page 225.

☑ A Test-Taking Tip

Pay attention to key words in questions on the GED Science Test, especially words like *not* and *except.* These words are used when you are supposed to pick the answer that does *not* fit the statement or question. A few questions on the GED Test may include such words.

LESSON 26

The Behavior of Waves

You've already read about what waves are and some of the different kinds of waves. Now you'll read about some of the things that certain waves do. Before you read the first section, preview the Warm-up.

Reflection and Refraction

To get a mental picture of how light waves behave, think of an imaginary line moving in the same direction a light wave is traveling. This imaginary line is called a ray. Several parallel rays form a beam.

You can follow rays of light to learn about their behavior. One of the interesting behaviors of light is **reflection,** which means bouncing. Reflected light rays behave very much like a bouncing ball. If you throw a basketball straight down, it will bounce straight up. If you throw the ball so that it hits the floor at an angle of 45 degrees, the ball will bounce away at the same angle, but in the opposite direction.

You can show that light behaves like the bounced ball by shining a flashlight in a mirror. First, shine the light straight toward the mirror. The ray of light moving toward the mirror is an incident ray. This incident ray will bounce straight back to your hand. Now shine the flashlight toward the mirror at an angle of 45 degrees. This time the incident ray will bounce away from the mirror at the same angle but in the opposite direction. This ray is the reflected ray.

Sound waves can also be reflected. If you've ever heard an echo in a canyon or a quiet hallway, you've heard reflected sound.

Light does not travel through all substances at the same speed. For example, when light moves from air into water, it slows down. This change in speed causes a ray of light to bend. The bending of light as it passes into a different material is called **refraction.** If a ray of light moves directly into a material that slows it down, the light ray will not change its course. But if the light ray enters the material at an angle, causing one side of the ray to slow down before the other, the light ray changes direction. It is bent, or refracted. You can easily see refraction by placing a pencil in a glass of water as shown in this drawing.

Refraction of Light

Coming to Terms

reflection the bouncing of a ray off a surface in an equal but opposite direction

refraction the bending of a ray

Warm-up

What happens when you shine a flashlight toward a mirror at an angle of 60 degrees? Use a complete sentence to answer the question.

____

____

____

Sample Warm-up Answer
When you shine a flashlight toward a mirror at an angle of 60°, the light will be reflected from the mirror at an angle of 60° in the opposite direction.

In the next section you'll be reading about some special properties of waves. Use the Warm-up before you begin to help focus your attention as you read.

Diffraction and Polarization

If someone stands directly in front of you while you're watching your favorite television show, you'll surely want that person to move. The light from the TV set will not bend around the person and enter your eyes, because, as you've already read, light travels in straight lines.

There are certain instances, however, when light rays do bend a little. This bending of light waves is called **diffraction.** Light waves are diffracted when they pass by the edges or through a tiny opening in an opaque substance. As they go past the edge, some "spill over" the side. Sound waves do the same, but the bending of light waves is a million times smaller than that of sound waves. The human eye usually cannot notice it.

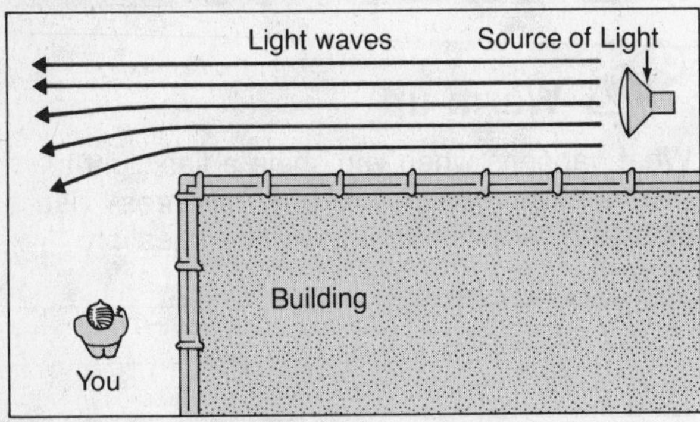

Diffraction of Light

A beam of light contains many light waves. Some waves are vibrating vertically; some are vibrating horizontally; others are vibrating at various slanted angles. **Polarization** occurs when light waves vibrate in the same pattern. You can understand this if you look at the first illustration of polarization. The waves entering the first vertical slot are polarized: they are all vibrating in the same pattern—vertically. They continue to vibrate through the second vertical slot. But see what happens when the vertically vibrating wave goes through the horizontal slot in the second illustration. The vertically vibrating wave will not pass through the horizontal slot.

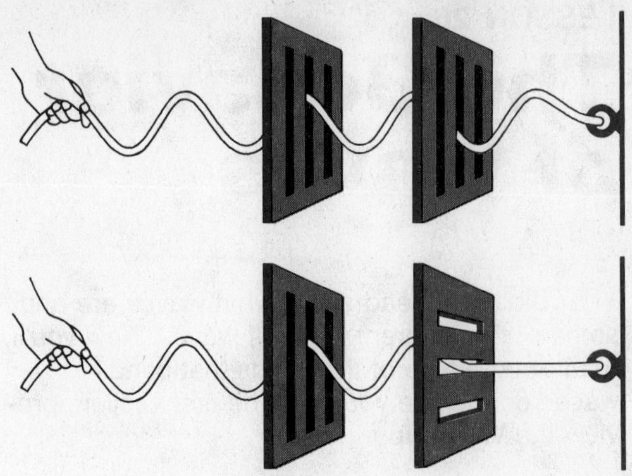

Polarization of Light

Manufacturers can make sheets of a certain material that treats light waves in the same ways shown in the illustrations. If two sheets of this material are placed together so that the fine slots line up in the same direction, light passes through both sheets. But if the sheets are placed so that the slots are perpendicular to each other, polarized light entering the first sheet will not pass through the second sheet. Some sunglasses and camera filters use this material to reduce glare reflecting from objects.

Coming to Terms

diffraction the extremely slight bending of light waves as they move past the edge of something opaque

polarization the vibration of light waves in one particular direction

Warm-up

Give your answer to the question below in a complete sentence or two.

Why would diffraction not occur when light passes through a clear glass window?

____

____

Sample Warm-up Answer
Glass is transparent. Diffraction occurs around the edges of opaque substances.

Distinguishing Facts from Opinions and Hypotheses

You probably remember from earlier sections of this book that a fact is a statement that has been proved true. An opinion, in contrast, is a statement of personal judgment or belief.

You've also learned that a hypothesis is a statement meant as a possible explanation. It can always be tested in some way. An example of a hypothesis is the sentence "Earthquake waves may be strong enough to destroy large buildings." That statement can be tested with equipment that scientists use to measure movements within the earth and through careful observation.

On the Springboard

<u>Items 1–2</u> refer to the statements below. As you work with the following items, keep in mind how facts, opinions, and hypotheses differ from each other.

Below are three statements about a pair of polarized sunglasses.

A. These sunglasses are made of a special material that helps filter out some polarized light.
B. These sunglasses are a necessity for automobile drivers.
C. These sunglasses might even be improved by tinting the material.

1. Which of the statements above is a hypothesis about the sunglasses?

   (1) A only
   (2) B and C only
   (3) C only

   (1) (2) (3)

2. Which of the statements above is a fact about the sunglasses?

   (1) A only
   (2) B and C only
   (3) C only

   (1) (2) (3)

You can check your answers to On the Springboard on page 224.

Did you complete both items correctly? If so, congratulations. You're ready to try "The Real Thing." If you got one or both wrong, review the skills sections of Lessons 8 and 20 first.

☑ A Test-Taking Tip

Some test takers find it difficult to "switch gears" as they move from one type of question to a different type. On the GED Science Test, items from biology, earth science, chemistry, and physics will be mixed together. Items testing different skills will also be mixed together. If you are uncomfortable when you have to move from one type of item to another, try closing your eyes and taking just a moment to relax after completing each item.

"The Real Thing"

Items 1–2 refer to the following article.

Some materials used in building construction absorb sound waves, reducing the sounds that people hear in the room. Other types of building materials actually reflect sounds instead of absorbing them. If there are many different sources of sound in a room—many basketball players involved in a game, for instance, with hundreds of cheering fans—the reflections may bounce off the walls, and the room may become uncomfortable just because of the many reflected sound waves.

An architectural firm designed a new gymnasium for a school. The walls were to be made out of cinder blocks. Then the designers added interior panels of a very porous, sound-absorbing material. When they presented the plan to the school board, the architects made these claims about the gym:

A. This is one of the most pleasant gymnasiums you'll ever be in.
B. The walls will reduce the noise level in the gym.
C. The walls could actually improve players' performance by reducing distractions.
D. Players and spectators alike will love this gymnasium.

1. Which of the statements above are based on opinion?

(1) A and B only
(2) A and C only
(3) A and D only
(4) B and D only
(5) C and D only

(1) (2) (3) (4) (5)

2. Which of the architects' claims could be analyzed using statistical evidence?

(1) A only
(2) A and B only
(3) B and C only
(4) C only
(5) C and D only

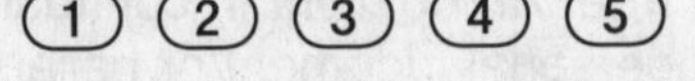

Item 3 refers to the following information.

Resonance is the effect that occurs when a particular tone causes an object to vibrate. Such an incident reveals that the object naturally has the same standard wave frequencies as the tone that sets it to vibrate.

3. Which of the following is an example of resonance?

(1) As a singer produces higher and higher notes, her voice becomes softer.
(2) As a dog barks, some strings on a harp standing nearby begin to vibrate.
(3) A motorcycle engine becomes quieter as it passes by.
(4) Raindrops falling rapidly on the roof gradually blend into one sound.
(5) Guitar strings vibrate more slowly for notes of lower pitches.

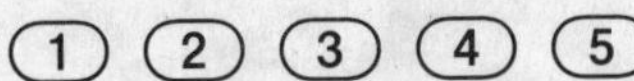

Check your answers and record your score on page 225.

LESSON 27

Electromagnetism

In this lesson you'll read about a useful form of energy—electricity. Preview the Warm-up before you read the first section. It will help you focus on some important details.

Electricity

Can you imagine a world without the modern uses of electricity? There would be no radio, television, or electric lighting. There would be no microwave ovens, automobiles, or modern printing presses.

Actually, everything has an electrical basis because all matter is made of atoms. As you learned earlier in chemistry, atoms have protons and electrons. An atom that has the same number of electrons as protons is a neutral atom. But atoms can gain or lose some of their electrons. When this happens, an atom becomes electrically charged. An atom that loses electrons acquires a positive charge. An atom that gains electrons acquires a negative charge.

You can actually tear electrons away from some kinds of atoms and transfer them to other kinds of atoms. Such transfers produce charges of **static electricity.** If you rub a glass rod with a piece of silk, the silk will gain electrons. It will become negatively charged. The glass rod will give electrons to the silk. Since the rod loses electrons, it becomes positively charged.

When you rub a hard-rubber rod with a piece of wool, electrons leave the wool. They are transferred to the rubber rod. In this case, the wool now has a positive charge, and the rod has a negative charge.

Suppose that you charge a hard-rubber rod by rubbing it with a piece of wool. You suspend the negatively charged rubber rod so that it can rotate freely. Then you charge another rubber rod with wool and hold it near the end of the suspended rod. What happens? As you may have guessed, the negatively charged rods repel each other; the suspended rod swings away.

Now suppose that you use a piece of silk to put a positive charge on a glass rod. You suspend the rod and then charge another glass rod. Hold it near the end of the suspended glass rod and what happens? The positively charged rods also repel.

But what happens when you hold a charged rubber rod near the suspended glass rod? The glass rod swings toward the rubber rod. The charged rods have just demonstrated a basic electrical principle: Like charges repel each other; unlike charges attract each other.

Does all this sound like information you've already studied in *Earth Science* under magnetism? You'll find out soon *why* electricity and magnetism sound so similar.

Coming to Terms

static electricity stationary electricity contained in charged bodies or produced by them

Warm-up

Write your answers in a sentence or two.

1. What is the result when atoms in certain substances gain or lose electrons?

____

____

____

2. What basic principle of electricity can be shown with charged glass and rubber rods?

____

____

Sample Warm-up Answers

1. A substance that gains electrons will have a negative charge. A substance that loses electrons will have a positive charge. **2.** Like electrical charges repel each other. Unlike electrical charges attract each other.

You've just read about static electricity, or charges that stay in the same place. Now you'll read about electricity that moves, or flows. Try looking at the Warm-up before you read the next section. Focus on the terms and principles mentioned in the questions.

Electrical Currents and Circuits

Electrical currents run the appliances that you use in your home. An **electrical current** is a flow of free electrons from one atom to another. Some substances, including metals in particular, have electrons that are free to move easily. This property makes metals good conductors of electricity. But the atoms in some other substances hold on to their electrons so tightly that very few electrons move. Such substances are nonconductors, or insulators. Rubber is a good insulator.

There are two kinds of electrical current: direct current (DC) and alternating current (AC). Direct current flows away from its source in one direction at all times. Alternating current flows and reverses its direction many times a second. The electricity that enters your home is AC.

Electricity flows in paths called **circuits.** A circuit has three main parts—a source of power, an object or objects that use the power, and a connector that connects the power source to the object that uses the electricity.

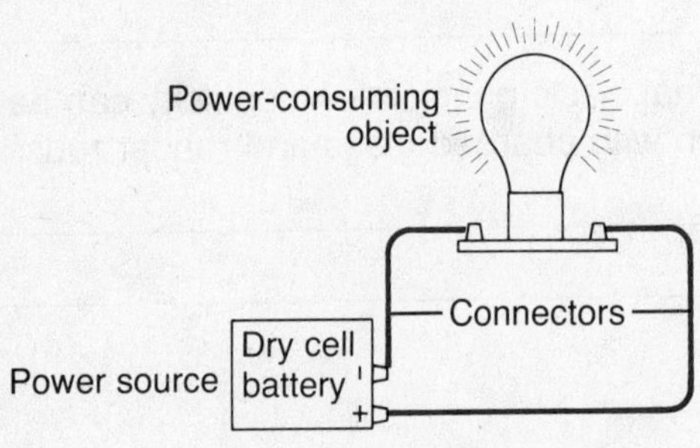

A Simple Circuit

A current must be able to follow a complete path back to its power source. If a circuit is incomplete, or open, current will not flow. Electricity will flow only when the circuit is complete, or closed. Look at the diagram of a series circuit. All of its parts are connected one after another. If you removed one of the light bulbs, the electricity would stop flowing from one part of the circuit to another. The current could not return to its power source. The circuit would be open. What would happen to the other light bulbs? They would go out.

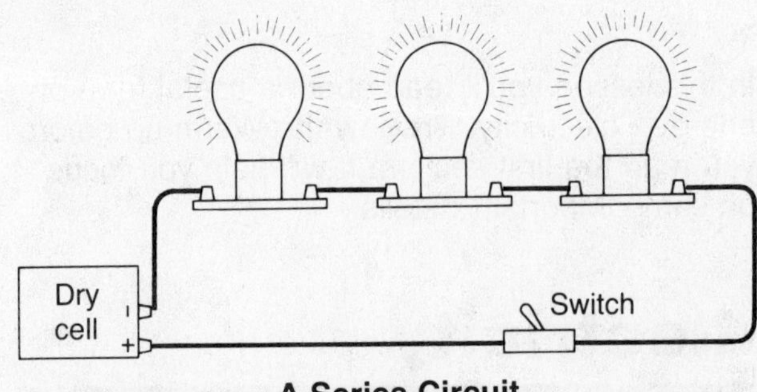

A Series Circuit

Now look at the diagram of a parallel circuit. If you removed one light bulb, the other would continue to glow because the current could still complete the circuit. You have parallel circuits in your home. If a light bulb in a lamp near your television goes out, your television set continues to operate.

A Parallel Circuit

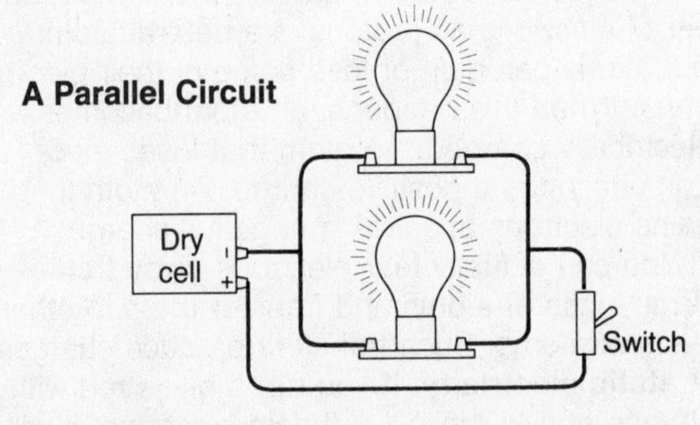

Coming to Terms

electrical current the flow of free electrons in a conductor

circuit a path taken by a current of electricity that goes from the power source to the power-using object(s) and back to the power source

Warm-up

Write your answers in your own complete sentences.

1. How does the behavior of electrons in electrical conductors differ from that of electrons in insulators?

____

____

2. If a gap occurs in an electrical circuit, what will happen to a toaster that gets its power from that circuit?

____

____

In the next section, you'll review some of the things you learned earlier about magnets. Then you'll see how magnetism and electricity are related. Before you read, though, look ahead to the Warm-up and the points that it emphasizes.

Magnetism

Magnet Cove is a special place of interest in the state of Arkansas. People visit there to see an iron ore called magnetite, or lodestone. A piece of magnetite is a natural magnet. It exerts a force on iron, steel, cobalt, and nickel, all of which are magnetic materials. Magnetism, the force that magnetite exerts on the materials, is a form of energy.

You can buy magnets in many different shapes. Some are bar shaped; some are U-shaped; some are shaped like horseshoes. Regardless of its shape or size, every magnet has a north pole and a south pole. As you have already learned, a force acts between the poles. Like poles repel each other, and unlike poles attract each other.

Magnetism and electricity are closely related. Magnetism can produce electricity. If you were to move a bar magnet through a coil of wire, an electric current would flow through the wire. Using magnetism to produce an electric current is a process called **electromagnetic induction.**

On the other hand, electricity can produce magnetism. When an electric current is flowing through a coil of wire, a magnetic field surrounds the wire. This field is the area in which the magnetic force operates. This kind of magnetic force is called **electromagnetism.**

A coil of wire carrying an electrical current is called a solenoid. The solenoid is a major part of an electromagnet. An electromagnet can be made quite easily by wrapping a coil of wire around an iron nail and connecting the ends of the wire to the terminals of a dry cell.

There are two ways in which you can increase the strength of an electromagnet. First you can increase the number of turns in the wire. The second way is to increase the amount of current.

Electromagnets have many uses. They are used in doorbells, telephones, and tape recorders. They are used in electrical motors. They are also used in huge generators that provide electricity for towns and cities.

Coming to Terms

electromagnetic induction the process of using magnetism to produce electricity

electromagnetism a magnetic force surrounding a wire carrying an electrical current

Warm-up

Use complete sentences when you write the answers to the questions below.

1. If you had a coil of wire and a bar magnet, how could you produce electricity?

____

____

2. Name some important uses of electromagnets.

____

____

Sample Warm-up Answers
1. Electrons in good electrical conductors move freely from one atom to another. Electrons in insulators move hardly at all.
2. A gap in the electrical circuit will keep the toaster from getting the current it needs to heat up.

Sample Warm-up Answers
1. If you move the magnet through the coiled wire, electric current will flow through the wire. **2.** Doorbells, telephones, motors, and electric generators all use electromagnets.

Assessing Supporting Data

It's not always easy to make everyday decisions, especially when you don't have all the facts at hand. The same is true in science. To reach any sort of conclusion, it's necessary to have enough information—data that are reliable and that apply to the question being considered.

How can you evaluate data? First, you need to decide whether the information applies to your topic. Next, consider the source of the information. Does it come from the speech or writing of an authority on the subject? Does it come from an encyclopedia or other reference book? Either of those could be excellent sources. You also need to determine whether there are enough data to support a conclusion.

In evaluating evidence, timeliness is also very important. Some information that authorities believed even ten or fifteen years ago may have been disproved or revised because of recent evidence.

When you are assessing the data used to reach conclusions, your own common sense will be your best guide. Read the material and decide whether the reasoning and data used seem logical to you.

On the Springboard

As you complete the Springboard activities, be sure to evaluate all the evidence given.

1. Which of the following does not support the conclusion that electricity and magnetism are closely related?

   (1) If you move an electric current through a wire, a magnetic field surrounds the wire.
   (2) Electricity and magnetism are both very useful in industry.
   (3) Inside an atom, each electron moves, giving the atom a magnetic field.

   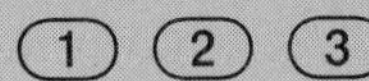

Item 2 refers to the following passage.

A homeowner finished putting a new electrical outlet in his kitchen and then plugged in a fan. The fan lifted out of his hands and then stopped. A smell of burning insulation rose from where it lay. Next the man tried plugging a desk lamp into the new outlet. A bright flash occurred, then nothing.

The warranties on the appliances claimed that they had been tested and would work on 120-voltage current. The voltage meter on the new outlet showed that the outlet delivered a voltage reading of 240. The man concluded that adequate electricity was being supplied.

The homeowner complained that they don't make things like they used to. He decided to take the appliances back to the store and ask for his money back because the fan and lamp were brand new when he bought them.

2. Which of the following supports the conclusion that the man's work was faulty, not the appliances?

   (1) He pointed out that appliances were made better in the past.
   (2) He tried out two appliances, not just one, in the new outlet.
   (3) He put in a 240-voltage outlet but used 120-voltage appliances.

   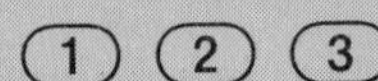

Check your Springboard answers on page 224.

If your answers are correct, go on to "The Real Thing." If you made an error, be sure to read the explanation that goes with the answer.

❝ The Real Thing ❞

<u>Items 1–3</u> refer to the following passage.

If too much electric current flows through a circuit, the circuit wires may overheat and begin to burn. If a gap in a circuit occurs, the circuit is open, and the current cannot flow. Fuses or circuit breakers are therefore used to open a circuit when too much current is flowing through it. Extra current will heat and melt a piece of metal in a fuse, thereby opening the circuit. A circuit breaker will trip and switch off the current automatically if there is too much current. The cause of the extra current must be located. Then the fuse can be replaced or the circuit breaker returned to its normal position. The circuit will then be closed.

1. A woman turns on a light in her living room, and the lights, the television set, and the dishwasher all go off.

   Based on this evidence, the woman should conclude that

   (1) she must stop using one or more appliances
   (2) she needs a new light bulb
   (3) she should replace all her circuit breakers
   (4) an electrical storm is approaching and overloading her circuits
   (5) the wires in her appliances are beginning to burn

   (1) (2) (3) (4) (5)

2. Which of the following could be used as evidence that a circuit is open?

   (1) A timer has just turned on a few lights because the family is away for the evening.
   (2) A dimmer switch is used to vary the amount of brightness of an overhead light.
   (3) A three-way light bulb is turned on to its brightest level to create adequate light for reading.
   (4) A night light in a child's room stays lit all night.
   (5) One light in a string of bulbs burns out, so none of the bulbs will light.

3. An electrical fire may result if

   (1) too much current flows through wires
   (2) a circuit is kept closed too long
   (3) a fuse burns out
   (4) a circuit breaker switches off
   (5) electric wires are not kept plugged into an outlet

Check your answers and record your score on page 225.

LESSON 28

Nuclear Physics

In chemistry you read quite a lot about the atoms that make up elements and compounds. Physicists, too, work with atoms. In this lesson you'll see how. Before you read the first section, look at the Warm-up activity at the end. Keep it in mind as you read.

Subatomic Particles and Accelerators

You can see the sun, the stars, and other planets. Yet they are so large that it is difficult to imagine their true size. Molecules and atoms, on the other hand, are so tiny that it is just as hard to imagine their size. Electrons, protons, and neutrons are even tinier. They are the smaller particles that make up individual atoms, so they are called **subatomic particles.**

Even with the help of powerful microscopes, scientists cannot see atoms and subatomic particles or how they interact. But they can use **accelerators** to observe the results of the behavior of subatomic particles. Some people call accelerators "atom smashers." You have probably heard both terms in news reports.

There are several different kinds of accelerators, but each operates on the same principle. First, the accelerator gives particles in an electric field a great amount of energy. The speeding particles may be protons, neutrons, or electrons. The energy accelerates the particles, or causes them to move at incredible speeds. The accelerator aims the particles at a target, such as carbon. When the accelerated particles strike their target, they smash the nuclei and subatomic particles of the nuclei in the target. These smashed particles leave their tracks on photographic plates. Scientists then study the photos to learn how subatomic particles behave. They can also see how particles react with other particles. From these collisions, they have discovered that even tinier particles make up protons, neutrons, and electrons. They've named these incredibly small pieces of matter quarks.

One kind of particle accelerator—a cyclotron—moves subatomic particles in a circular path. A cylindrical magnet bends their path into a circular pattern. Cyclotrons accelerate particles to extremely high energy levels.

One very powerful accelerator occupies 480 acres on the campus of Stanford University in California. This is a linear accelerator. It is a long object, about two miles from end to end.

The synchrotron is another kind of accelerator. Electrons speed through its doughnut-shaped tunnel at terrific velocities. They move close to the speed of light, in fact. Giant magnets keep the electrons in their path. When the electrons strike their target, tantalum, the tantalum releases X rays. The X rays then hit a target of liquid hydrogen. The protons that are the nuclei of the hydrogen break apart. Different subatomic particles move away from the smashed protons. Synchrotrons have given scientists yet another view of the atom and its nucleus.

Coming to Terms

subatomic particle a tiny particle that is part of an atom, such as a proton, a neutron, or an electron

accelerator a machine used to study the atom and subatomic particles

Why is an accelerator sometimes called an atom smasher? Write your answer in a complete sentence below.

____

____

____

Sample Warm-up Answer
An accelerator can be called an atom smasher because it uses speeding particles to strike a target and smash apart nuclei and subatomic particles of the nuclei in the target.

Now you'll learn about the energy locked in the atom and how machines called nuclear reactors unlock this energy. Perhaps you've seen a nuclear reactor plant near where you live. The energy it produces may provide the electrical power you use in your home. Take time to read the Warm-up question first. Let it focus your thoughts as you read the next section.

Fission and Fusion

Nuclear reactors produce incredible amounts of heat. The heat energy runs the generators that produce electricity. The function of a nuclear reactor is to split the nuclei of atoms. When this splitting, or **fission,** occurs, tremendous amounts of heat energy are released. This energy is called nuclear energy.

Scientists knew for many years that great amounts of energy would result if they split one atom after another—in a chain reaction. But they did not know how to control the chain reaction. It was not until 1942 that Enrico Fermi, an Italian-American physicist, and a group of scientists achieved a controlled reaction at the University of Chicago. This information was used to create the first atomic bomb, which used the idea of splitting the atom.

A radioactive element such as uranium-235 is commonly used during fission. A stream of neutrons is shot at the nuclei of the uranium atoms, splitting them. Great amounts of heat and energy are released. In addition, subatomic particles become free to group into atoms of certain other elements. Some neutrons remain free. These neutrons go on to strike more uranium atoms and split their nuclei. The result is more energy, more different atoms, and more neutrons that are free to strike still more uranium atoms. On and on it goes. The process is a chain reaction.

The diagram on this page shows how a chain reaction starts with the fission, or splitting, of the first atom of uranium-235. Notice that a number of neutrons are freed from the splitting of just one atom's nucleus.

Nuclear **fusion** is another kind of nuclear reaction. So far, scientists have not been able to design practical fusion reactors, but they know how fusion works. It is the opposite of nuclear fission. Instead of breaking atoms apart, fusion joins the nucleus of an atom to the nucleus of another atom of the same element. Fusion is sometimes called a thermonuclear reaction because so much heat is released. *Therm* is a Greek term that refers to heat.

Fusion occurs on the sun, accounting for its great heat and light energy. When four nuclei of the sun's hydrogen atoms fuse, they form a nucleus of helium. In the process, the hydrogen nuclei give off incredible amounts of heat energy.

Fusion is also used in hydrogen bombs on earth. Because much more energy is released by fusion than by fission, hydrogen bombs are more powerful than atomic bombs.

Coming to Terms

fission the splitting of the nucleus of an atom

fusion the combining, or fusing, of the nucleus of one atom with the nucleus of another atom of the same element

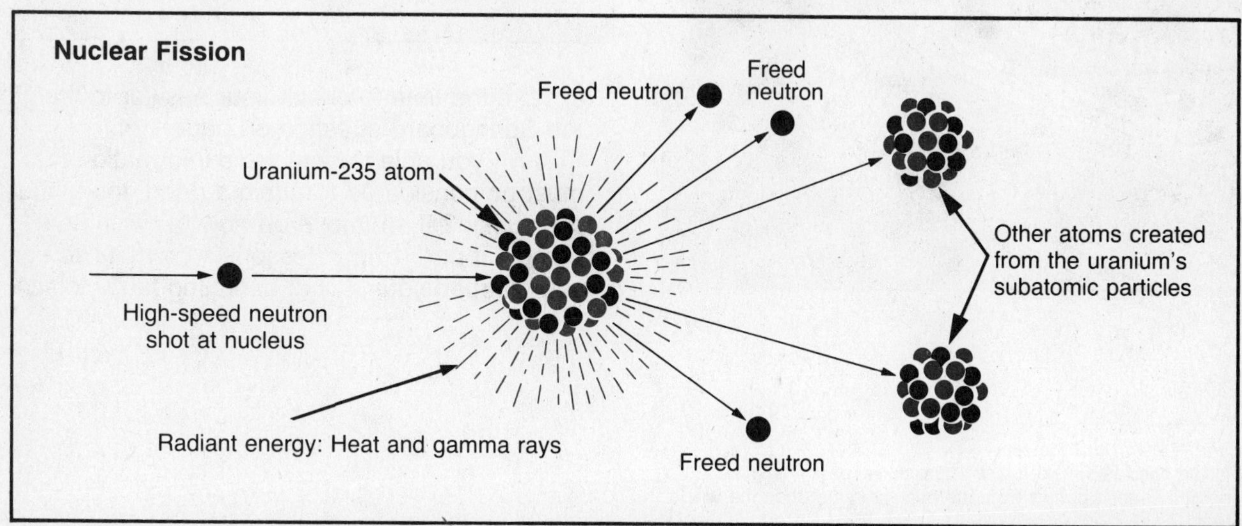

Warm-up

In a sentence or two, explain why *nuclear energy* is a better term than *atomic energy* to refer to the heat released during fission and fusion.

____

____

____

Faulty Logic

You expect that when a computer receives correct information, it will process the data and produce a logical result. Of course, if incorrect information is fed into the computer, or if the program is faulty, you will obtain unreliable results.

The same can be said of human reasoning. If you start with accurate information and use logic, you can expect to come up with reliable results. If there is an error in your information or in your thinking, however, the result will be faulty logic.

Remember from Lessons 11 and 17 the different mistakes people can make in their reasoning. Be alert for them as you do the activities in this lesson.

On the Springboard

Item 1 refers to the following letter to an editor.

Every year our country requires massive amounts of electrical energy for businesses, industries, and homes. Most electricity comes from coal-burning plants; about 10 percent is produced by nuclear power plants.

Nuclear power plants have eliminated a number of the problems that coal-burning plants have. Nuclear plants help conserve dwindling deposits of coal. They are also cleaner, since they don't release the particle matter and other air pollutants that coal-burning power plants do. Clearly, nuclear power is what we need for a safe, healthy environment.

Below are three facts about nuclear energy.

A. Nuclear fission produces radioactive wastes.
B. The use of nuclear power is fairly new.
C. Nuclear fission involves a different process from nuclear fusion.

1. The statement that nuclear power is "what we need for a safe, healthy environment" may be failing to take into account which of the facts above?

(1) A only
(2) B only
(3) C only

Take the time to check your answer to the On the Springboard question on page 224.

Were you able to detect the information that must be considered to attain a good, thoughtful conclusion? If so, move on now to "The Real Thing." If not, review Lessons 11 and 17 to help you sharpen your skill at detecting faulty logic.

Sample Warm-up Answer
Fission and fusion take place in the nuclei of atoms. The energy released comes from the nucleus rather than the whole atom.

“The Real Thing”

Item 1 refers to the following passage.

Water is an important part of the operation of nuclear power plants. Water heated by the tremendous heat of the nuclear reaction turns to steam. This steam spins the turbines that drive generators, and it is the generators that actually produce electricity. Large amounts of water are also used to cool down the enormous heat of the reaction.

1. Based on the information above, which of the following would be a poor location for a nuclear power plant?

(1) near a large river
(2) in a desert far from population centers
(3) within 100 miles of a large city
(4) near the ocean shore
(5) on a lake in a farming region

Items 2–3 are based on the passage below.

Radioactive materials decay when the nuclei of their atoms break down and give off harmful radiation. After Antoine-Henri Becquerel discovered that some elements were naturally radioactive, other physicists began to study radioactivity and its sources. Some of these scientists worked directly with radioactive materials, observing them directly for long hours and even touching the materials with their bare hands. Later, many of these researchers developed various symptoms of radiation disease.

2. The scientists' lack of concern in working with radioactivity was most likely due to

(1) disregard for their own safety
(2) failure to realize that they were dealing with dangerous materials
(3) the desire to be the first to understand radioactivity
(4) the lack of equipment to shield them from the radiation
(5) the belief that radiation was actually beneficial

(1) (2) (3) (4) (5)

3. According to the information above, radioactivity cannot be totally avoided because

(1) it occurs in nature
(2) it is needed to produce nuclear power
(3) scientists must study its properties
(4) all elements eventually decay
(5) radiation sometimes escapes from laboratories

Check your answers and record your score on page 226.

Answers: On the Springboard

24 Basic Principles of Physics Predicting Outcomes

(page 204)

1. (1) You would push *down* on one end of the lever, and the load would move *up*.

2. (1) The arm of the crowbar will move almost to the ground, but the rock will move only a little. On the other hand, the handle of the wheelbarrow will move to a vertical position while the sand will dump to the ground.

3. (2) To answer the item correctly, you must apply the definition of work: The amount of work done equals the force multiplied by the distance through which the force acts. Since Sally's brother is taller, the distance through which he lifts the weight is greater than it is for Sally; therefore, her brother does more work.

25 Waves Cause-and-Effect Relationships

(page 209)

1. (3) It is true that light waves travel faster than sound waves. When lightning strikes, the light waves and sound waves begin traveling outward at the same moment, but the light waves travel more quickly and reach your eyes before sound waves reach your ears.

2. (1) Intensity is determined by force. As Caruso's voice became louder, the force of the sound waves increased until they were strong enough to break the delicate glass.

26 The Behavior of Waves Distinguishing Facts from Opinions and Hypotheses

(page 213)

1. (3) This option suggests a way that the glasses could be improved; someone could test to see whether tinting actually would improve them. Therefore, the statement is a hypothesis.

2. (1) Only option (1) is a statement that could be proved true.

27 Electromagnetism Assessing Supporting Data

(page 218)

1. (2) The item asks for the one option that does *not* support the idea that electricity and magnetism are closely related. Being useful has nothing to do with being related. Options (1) and (3) are both clear illustrations that electricity and magnetism are related.

2. (3) The man had installed an outlet that permitted a 240-volt current to flow into the appliances, but they had been built to operate on only 120 volts. The current was too strong for them. It caused them to overwork, and they burned out immediately.

28 Nuclear Physics Faulty Logic

(page 222)

1. (1) Radioactive wastes are harmful and difficult to get rid of adequately, so they must certainly be taken into account before declaring that nuclear energy is safe and healthy.

Answers: "The Real Thing"

As you check your answers, you may notice that some question numbers are in color. Those questions pertain to the skill taught in that lesson. The skill in each lesson is labeled with a head that is in color. You'll probably want to go back and review the skills you had difficulty with before you complete this section.

24 Basic Principles of Physics
Predicting Outcomes
(page 205)

1. (2) With each second, a diver would be falling another 32 feet faster (subtract each velocity from the one after it, and you'll see this pattern). Therefore, after 5 seconds the diver would be falling at 128 + 32, or 160, feet per second.

2. (4) As a truck travels, heat from the day and from contact with the road causes the air molecules inside the tires to move about more quickly. The space in which they can move about is limited by the tire wall, so their movement raises the pressure. All four tires would have higher pressure than at the beginning of the journey.

KEEPING TRACK
Top Score = 2
Your Score = ☐

25 Waves
Cause-and-Effect Relationships
(page 210)

1. (5) Picture what happens on a stormy sea. The amplitude of a wave is its height. As the amplitude increases, any object riding on the surface would be moved farther up, as a result of a higher crest, and farther down, as a result of a lower trough.

2. (3) As more microwave appliances are used, more microwaves enter the atmosphere. That means a much greater chance of exposure to microwaves and also a greater chance of exposure to a greater concentration of microwaves in any given place at any given time.

3. (3) Because of the Doppler effect, you hear the sound from a moving object change from a higher pitch to a lower one. Option (3) is the only answer that describes such a situation.

4. (3) The image created by ultrasound waves shows the outline of the baby, so motions, size, and the presence of twins would be visible. The ultrasound image cannot, however, determine the weight of the baby.

KEEPING TRACK
Top Score = 4
Your Score = ☐

26 The Behavior of Waves
Distinguishing Facts from Opinions and Hypotheses
(page 214)

1. (3) Statements A and D are both based on personal value judgments; they are both statements of opinion.

2. (3) Statement B is a fact that could be proved using meters that measure noise. Statement C is a hypothesis that could be tested by comparing the team's statistics before and after.

3. (2) Resonance is an effect that occurs when one thing sets up sympathetic vibrations in another. The tone of a dog's bark would set up vibrations in the harp strings that have the same pitch.

KEEPING TRACK
Top Score = 3
Your Score = ☐

27 Electromagnetism
Assessing Supporting Data
(page 219)

1. (1) The fact that a number of appliances go off at the same time is evidence that a circuit has been overloaded and therefore broken by either a fuse or a circuit breaker.

2. (5) When a circuit is open, current cannot flow. Only option (5) describes a situation in which current is not flowing.

3. (1) This information is given in the very first sentence using different words.

KEEPING TRACK
Top Score = 3
Your Score = ☐

28 Nuclear Physics Faulty Logic

(page 223)

1. (2) Water is needed for a nuclear power plant to operate, according to the information given. So a desert would be a poor site for one.

2. (2) The researchers' lack of concern about handling radioactive materials was most likely due to their ignorance of the hazards. They knew that they were experimenting with something unique—something that had properties unlike other elements they had dealt with. In fact, that is just what made their research so interesting to them.

3. (1) The passage tells you that Becquerel discovered *naturally* radioactive elements.

KEEPING TRACK
Top Score = 3
Your Score = ☐

Keeping Track

Now enter all your scores from the Keeping Track boxes on the lines below. Compare your scores with the top scores.

Lesson	Top Score	Your Score
Lesson 24 Predicting Outcomes	2	_____
Lesson 25 Cause-and-Effect Relationships	4	_____
Lesson 26 Distinguishing Facts from Opinions and Hypotheses	3	_____
Lesson 27 Assessing Supporting Data	3	_____
Lesson 28 Faulty Logic	3	_____
TOTAL	15	_____

Which lessons did you do particularly well in? Which lessons, if any, might you need more work in? Review the answer explanations and skill sections for any skill you still have problems with. Then go on to the Extra Practice in Physics that follows.

Extra Practice in Physics

Directions: Choose the one best answer to each item.

1. Solar calculators have become very popular in recent years. Below are four statements from an advertisement for a solar calculator.

   A. contains a material that is sensitive to light
   B. will fit into a shirt pocket
   C. the most convenient calculator you can buy
   D. does not require any batteries

   Which of the claims above is an opinion rather than a fact?

   (1) A only
   (2) B only
   (3) B and C only
   (4) C only
   (5) C and D only

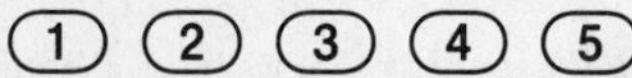

Item 2 refers to the following passage.

When a certain amount of gas is placed in a closed container, it expands to fill the container. If the gas warms up, the pressure of the gas will increase. If the temperature decreases, the pressure will do the same. The reverse relationship is also true: If the pressure changes, a change in temperature will follow.

A tank of oxygen is delivered to a hospital. It sits outside in near freezing temperatures for two days before it is brought inside. The pressure of the gas is measured as soon as the tank is brought inside. The gauge registers 600 pounds per square inch (psi). Twenty-four hours later, the pressure is measured again. The gauge now reads 950 psi.

2. What best explains the change of pressure in the oxygen tank?

   (1) The temperature of the gas increased after the tank was brought inside, and so the pressure increased.
   (2) One of the two readings is incorrect; pressure cannot change in a closed container.
   (3) As the tank warmed up, the gas increased in volume.
   (4) A decrease in pressure would follow a decrease in temperature.
   (5) Some of the gas escaped from the cylinder when the first measurement was taken.

Item 3 refers to the following information.

It is generally known that a compass needle will point north. It does not point to the geographical North Pole, but to the magnetic north pole. The Chinese tell stories of their sea-going ancestors whose compasses pointed south. For a long time, no one believed these stories. Then scientists discovered that periodically the magnetic poles of the earth reverse themselves.

3. What assumption made scientists unwilling to believe the stories about the ancient Chinese sailors?

   (1) Compasses are a very old invention.
   (2) Magnets have two poles: a north pole and a south pole.
   (3) Local iron deposits in the earth can affect the direction in which the compass needle points.
   (4) Magnetic poles of the earth cannot change.
   (5) Compasses always line up with the north and south poles of the earth.

Items 4–6 are based on the diagram and article below.

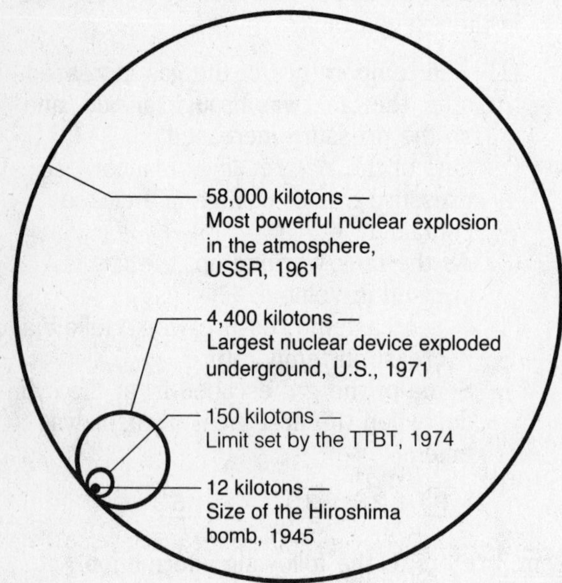

The size of a nuclear explosion is measured in kilotons of energy. The diagram above shows the size of the explosion produced by the Hiroshima bomb compared to the sizes of the most powerful nuclear explosions ever produced in the atmosphere and underground. The diagram also shows the limit on nuclear explosions that was set by the Threshold Test Ban Treaty (TTBT).

The Threshold Test Ban Treaty was signed in 1974 by the United States and what was then the Soviet Union for the purpose of regulating the testing of nuclear devices. This agreement limits the amount of explosive energy that may be released during any test and also specifies where tests can take place and what technical data must be made public after a test.

Scientists can keep track of underground tests because the explosions trigger vibrations deep inside the earth and along its surface. They measure these vibrations to determine how much energy was released. However, scientists are now realizing that geologic conditions deep below the test site may affect how far and how fast the vibrations travel. These conditions differ at each of the test sites approved by the treaty. Accurate calculations of the energy released during a nuclear explosion must take these conditions into account.

The TTBT became a controversial issue because many people believed that the Soviets were testing nuclear devices more powerful than those allowed by the treaty. However, in terms of underground tests, scientists who have reviewed all of the data believe that earlier reports overestimated the sizes of the tests and that the Soviets probably produced nuclear explosions that were close to, but not larger than, the limit set by the treaty.

4. Based on the information in the diagram, which of the following statements about the limit set by the TTBT is correct?

(1) The nuclear bomb released over Hiroshima was larger than the limit allowed by the TTBT.
(2) The limit allows for the largest underground nuclear explosion ever.
(3) TTBT puts a 150-kiloton limit on underground nuclear explosions.
(4) The most powerful underground nuclear explosion that ever took place was twice the limit set by the TTBT.
(5) Neither the United States nor the Soviet Union has ever exceeded the TTBT limit.

(1) (2) (3) (4) (5)

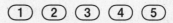

5. According to the author of the passage, which of the following conclusions has been drawn by certain scientists?

(1) The Soviets have observed the TTBT.
(2) The TTBT has saved the world from nuclear war.
(3) Geological characteristics should determine the best test sites.
(4) The limit set by the TTBT should be set higher.
(5) Nuclear testing should be above ground.

(1) (2) (3) (4) (5)

6. The article implies that scientists in the United States could gather fairly accurate information about tests conducted by the Soviets. Which of the following statements best supports that statement?

(1) The TTBT specifies where the tests can be held.
(2) The Soviets always publicized "peaceful" nuclear explosions.
(3) Vibrations from underground tests can be measured far from the test site.
(4) New measurements suggest that the energy released from Soviet tests has been overestimated.
(5) Some of the test explosions are very close to the limit set by the TTBT.

(1) (2) (3) (4) (5)

Items 7–10 are based on the information given below.

Electricity is a form of energy produced by the movement of electrons through a material. This flow of electrons is called current. Below are five terms that relate to electricity.

(1) capacitor = device that holds an electric charge by accumulating electrons
(2) circuit = complete loop through which an electric current can flow
(3) conductor = material through which electrons can move easily
(4) ground = material through which electrons can move easily; acts as a connection between the earth and some object and prevents the build-up of electrical charge in that object
(5) insulator = substance through which electrons do not flow readily

The following items give examples of these terms. For each item, select the one term that best fits the example given. Any term may be used more than once or not at all.

7. In a camera's electronic flash unit, a battery inside the unit produces electrons that are then stored. When these electrons are released, they flow through the lamp in the flash unit and trigger the light to go on.

   The part of the flash unit where the electrons are stored and then released to produce a current is

   (1) a capacitor
   (2) a circuit
   (3) a conductor
   (4) a ground
   (5) an insulator

   1 2 3 4 5

8. A truck carrying gasoline drags a chain along the road.

   The chain acts as

   (1) a capacitor
   (2) a circuit
   (3) a conductor
   (4) a ground
   (5) an insulator

9. When a new dishwasher was turned on, it overloaded a circuit breaker and began to smoke. The repairman found that several wires in the dishwasher had crossed over each other and changed the pathway of the current. He separated the wires and wrapped each in electrical tape. When he tried it out again, the dishwasher worked well.

   The tape wrapping around each wire acted as

   (1) a capacitor
   (2) a circuit
   (3) a conductor
   (4) a ground
   (5) an insulator

10. When the cord from a toaster is plugged into the wall outlet, the current flows freely from the house through the appliance.

    The pathway through which the current flows is

    (1) a capacitor
    (2) a circuit
    (3) a conductor
    (4) a ground
    (5) an insulator

Item 11 refers to the following diagram and information.

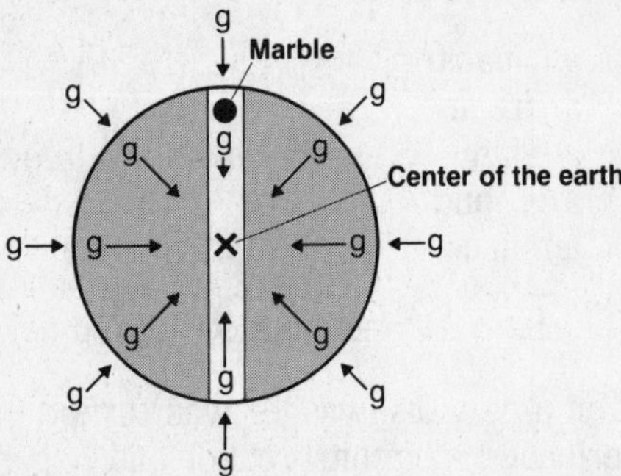

Gravity is a force of attraction that exists among all objects. Every object attracts every other object. Most objects are too small for their gravitational force to be measured or even noticed. Because the earth is large, its gravitational force is very strong. Gravity holds things on the earth's surface as it draws everything toward the center of the planet.

11. Imagine that a very narrow tunnel has been drilled straight through the earth, as shown in the diagram. A small marble is dropped into this tunnel. The marble will most likely
    (1) travel straight through the tunnel at the same speed
    (2) be going much faster than its starting speed when it comes out the other side
    (3) never reach the other side
    (4) be traveling very slowly when it falls out the other side end of the tunnel
    (5) slow down near the earth's center, but will speed up again when it reaches the end of the tunnel

    (1) (2) (3) (4) (5)

Item 12 refers to the following information.

The Reagan administration decided to ask Congress to set aside $4.5 billion for an experimental machine called a Super-conducting Super Collider. Inside the SSC, as this device is called, protons traveling at incredibly high speeds would collide with each other. Physicists believed that the results of these collisions would help them understand the basic particles and forces of nature.

12. Which of the statements below indicates that values were involved in the desire to fund the SSC?
    (1) The SSC would be the largest and most expensive experimental device in the world.
    (2) This proton accelerator would have twenty times more energy than any accelerator to date.
    (3) The machine would contain 10,000 magnets, which would be cooled by helium.
    (4) The protons that collide in the accelerator would be moving almost as fast as light travels.
    (5) The project would guarantee the U.S. the lead in high energy research.

    (1) (2) (3) (4) (5)

Answers to Extra Practice in Physics are on page 233. Record your score on the Progress Chart on the inside back cover.

Answers: Extra Practice

Biology
(pages 109–112)

1. (4) The article states that aerobic exercise requires the use of many muscles continuously over a period of time. Option (4), swimming, is the only activity listed that fits the description. **AP**

2. (3) The article mentions that a buildup of lactic acid causes muscle cramping and that when an affected muscle is allowed to rest, lactic acid is carried away. **CP**

3. (2) This statement is based on an individual opinion, or value judgment. The term *more rewarding* cannot be tested or measured scientifically. Option (5) mentions an opinion, but it could be tested to see if "many people" have that opinion; therefore, option (5) is better classified as fact rather than opinion. **EV**

4. (3) The chain of events described in the article shows that running uses up oxygen. The lack of oxygen causes cells to break down glucose without oxygen, in other words, to function anaerobically. **CP**

5. (5) The article explains that any exercise that uses many muscles for a period of time—and that includes long-distance swimming—will increase the oxygen available to body cells. **EV**

6. (4) A cell that has taken in food seeks to achieve a balance by releasing wastes. None of the other options would help the cell achieve the necessary balance, or homeostasis. **AN**

7. (4) According to the chart, plants produce their own food, but fungi do not. Instead, fungi absorb nutrients from living or dead materials. **CP**

8. (2) As one-celled organisms, foraminiferans would belong to either the moneran or protist kingdom. Since they are complex rather than simple cells, they would have to be protists rather than monerans, which are simple cells. **AP**

9. (1) Fungi and animals require other sources to get their food (ultimately, plants). Plants and some types of monerans and protists can make their own food; they can survive on their own. **EV**

10. (3) The flu virus enters through the mouth or nose. There is no evidence that it can enter through the skin. **CP**

11. (3) A virus is spread from an infected person to a healthy one. If no one has the smallpox virus to pass on to another person, there is no longer a need for the vaccine to prevent the spread of the virus. **EV**

12. (2) An antibiotic is a substance that kills living bacterial cells. However, a virus is not a cell; it does not carry out any of the normal life functions, such as reproduction, response, use of energy, or growth. Since it is not technically alive until it takes over a host cell, a virus itself could not be killed. **AP**

13. (5) Failing to cover the bottom sides of the test leaves would cause error in the experiment because carbon dioxide could still enter the leaves through openings on the bottom sides. **AN**

14. (3) The rocks and sand are a nonliving part of an ecosystem. By collecting wastes that contaminate the water, they can affect the livng organisms in the aquarium. **AP**

15. (1) This item describes the cycle of a population—all the lemmings that live together in a certain area. **AP**

16. (5) The biosphere includes all communities on earth. A gradual warming trend of the entire earth could certainly affect all the species on or near its surface. **AP**

17. (4) A biome is a large group of ecosystems with similar types of climate and communities. All the earth's deserts make up one biome—the desert biome. **AP**

18. (2) The animals and plants that live near the shore of a pond are a group of populations that live in the same area and depend on each other for food; in other words, the animals and plants form a community. **AP**

Earth Science
(pages 158–161)

1. (4) Only this statement takes into account the several different factors involved in predicting the weather. Option (2) states only one of these problems. Options (1), (3), and (5) are false. **CP**

2. (1) The passage states in the second paragraph that satellites have made more weather information available, but they don't cover the entire globe. Using more satellites should make forecasts more accurate because they will give more data. **CP**

3. (4) To different people, the beauty of a diamond may lie in its size, its shape, its arrangement with other stones, or its reflective surfaces. These are *all* opinions. The other options are facts and can be proved by physical or chemical tests. **AV**

4. (5) The information indicates that as the temperature of a metal increases, blue is the last color—the hottest color—that the metal will reach. This suggests that the hottest stars will radiate mostly blue light and therefore appear blue. **CP**

CP = Comprehension **AP** = Application **AN** = Analysis **EV** = Evaluation

5. (4) Taken together, electricity and industry account for 31 percent, or about one-third. **CP**

6. (3) The title of the graph lets you know that the graph shows the percentages of the ways oil is used in the United States. The percentages do not show how oil *can* be used; theoretically, all crude oil could be made into heating oil if there were a need for it. **EV**

7. (1) Only if people demand the same amount of transportation fuels or more will they experience a shortage. If people begin to demand less, less fuel will be produced, and they won't feel that there is a shortage. The meaning of *shortage* depends on the demand, not on the actual amount produced. **AN**

8. (3) Ultraviolet light is absorbed by ozone in the upper atmosphere. If less ozone is present, les UVL will be absorbed by the atmosphere, so more of it will reach the ground. **AN**

9. (4) The passage says that scientists believe that pollution is stopping oxygen from changing into ozone and that the main pollutant is a chemical used in certain products. The word *believe* is a clue that a suggested explanation—a hypothesis—is being offered. The other options are facts from the passage. **EV**

10. (3) The coral reefs must have formed under the surface of shallow salt water. Either the sea moved back, or the reef was lifted up to form part of the land in Texas. All the other options contradict the information given in the paragraph. **EV**

11. (3) The minerals that were once dissolved in water in the soil have accumulated on the bottom of the pot. This fits the definition of deposition. **AP**

12. (4) The small stones flaked from the surface of the stones in the patio. Only exfoliation explains how the small rocks formed from the larger stones. **AP**

13. (1) The rocky debris was formed by the scraping action of the glacial ice against solid rock. Abrasion is the only process that involves grinding action. **AP**

14. (2) Over time the soil on the hillside has crept downhill slowly, and the fence posts have moved with it. Creep is the only process that involves slow downhill movement due gravity. **AP**

Chemistry
pages 195–197)

1. (2) The living yeast cells produce carbon dioxide gas, which causes the bread to rise. When the high temperatures of baking kill the yeast, no more gas is produced, and the bread rises no further. **CP**

2. (4) The addition of sugar to bread dough encourages the growth of yeast and, therefore, the production of CO_2 gas. More sugar will help guarantee that a beginner's loaf of bread will rise. **AP**

3. (4) Surface tension makes it possible for light objects to remain on the surface of the water. A lightweight insect is able to walk across a body of still water on the "skin" formed by surface tension. **AN**

4. (3) Soap reduces the attraction of water molecules for each other. As a consequence, surface tension is weakened, and the needle is no longer supported by the "skin" of molecules on the surface. **AP**

5. (4) Either a base or an acid can be a good cleaning agent. However, when the two are mixed, they neutralize each other, or take away each other's power. Mixing an acid and base together would yield a solution that could not clean as well as either would do by itself **CP**

6. (4) Statements A and C could be tested scientifically. A simple laboratory test can indicate whether an acid is present in a substance. Laboratory tests and observation with a microscope could indicate whether bacteria are removed from skin by the action of the soap. Statements B and D, however, are statements of personal opinion and cannot be proved. **AN**

7. (2) The rings around the nucleus in the diagram show that electrons orbit, or move in a circle, around the nucleus. **CP**

8. (3) Because of the swift motions of electrons, it is impossible to know exactly where any given electron is at a precise moment in time. Instead, the cloud rings show the areas that cover the electrons' path. Electrons can be anywhere within a cloud at any particular moment. **EV**

9. (3) Malleability is the ability to be shaped, including being made into the thin layers of aluminum foil. **AP**

10. (1) When silver is polished, it has a hgih luster—so high, in fact, that a person can see his or her reflection in the surface. **AP**

11. (4) Iron is a good conductor of heat, so it is often used in cookware. **AP**

12. (2) A substance that can be drawn into thin wires without snapping or breaking is described as ductile. Platinum is ductile enough to be made into extremely fine wire for jewelry. **AP**

CP = Comprehension **AP** = Application **AN** = Analysis **EV** = Evaluation

Physics

(pages 227–230)

1. (4) Whether or not the solar calculator is more convenient than other types of calculators is an opinion. All other options are facts that can be proved by testing them. **AN**

2. (1) An increase in temperature caused an increase in the pressure of the gas. All other options are incorrect or irrelevant. The volume of the gas did not change (3) because the container was closed, but temperature and pressure *can* change in a closed container. **CP**

3. (4) Until the 1960s, no one knew that the magnetic poles of the earth reverse themselves infrequently. So scientists who heard the Chinese stories were very doubtful that compasses that had once pointed south would now point north. **AN**

4. (3) This answer can be read directly from the diagram. All the other options misinterpret the diagram. **CP**

5. (1) The last sentence explains that some scientists believe that early reports on the size of nuclear explosions were mistaken. They have therefore concluded that the Russians have probably not broken the agreement. **CP**

6. (3) Scientists do not have to depend on the information given out by the Soviets because the vibrations caused by the explosions indicate their size. The passage states that these vibrations can be measured a long way from the test site. **EV**

7. (1) The electrons are stored, or allowed to accumulate, in the camera. This fits the definition of a capacitor. **AP**

8. (4) The tires of a truck, rubbing along the surface of a road, build up an excess of charge. This excess of charge could cause a spark. A spark could set gasoline on fire. A ground chain prevents this accumulation of charge on the tires by allowing electrons to move between the earth and the truck. The definition of a ground specifically states that the ground connects an object with the earth. **AP**

9. (5) The tape insulated the wires from each other and allowed the current to flow correctly. **AP**

10. (2) A circuit is defined as the complete loop through which electric current can flow. Plugging an appliance into a wall outlet forms a complete circuit. **AP**

11. (3) The marble will never reach the other side of the tunnel because it will be trapped in the center of the earth by the force of gravity. Notice on the diagram how all gravity is focused on the earth's center. For the marble to move past the center and on to the other side, it would have to resist gravity. **AP**

12. (5) This option alone explains why the SSC would be desirable or important for the United States. The value involved is keeping the United States ahead of other countries in scientific research. **EV**

CP = Comprehension **AP** = Application **AN** = Analysis **EV** = Evaluation

The Posttests

You are now ready to take the final step in your study for passing the GED Science Test. Both Posttests in this book resemble the actual GED Science Test in the number and kinds of questions asked. When taking each Posttest, take no more than the allotted time for one entire test. Remember to guess whenever you don't know an answer. To get the best possible score, don't leave a question unanswered.

Take the first Posttest. Figure your score using the Answer Key on page 257, and then find your score on the Progress Chart. You may want or need to take the second Posttest based on your score. If you want to review parts of this book, use the Skill Chart on page 257 to determine which lessons cover skills that were particularly difficult for you.

If possible, try to make arrangements to take the actual GED Science Test as soon as you can after achieving passing scores on the Posttests in this book. Your test-taking skills will be sharp, and you will feel more confident.

SCIENCE POSTTEST A

The Science Posttest consists of 66 multiple-choice questions intended to measure general concepts in science. The questions are based on short readings that often include a graph, chart, or figure. Study the information given and then answer the question(s) following it. Refer to the information as often as necessary to answer the questions.

You should take no more than 95 minutes to complete the test. Work carefully, but do not spend too much time on any one question. If a question is too difficult for you, omit it and come back to it later. There is no penalty for guessing.

To record each answer, fill in the space that matches the number of the answer you have chosen.

EXAMPLE

A physical change is one in which the chemical composition of a substance is not altered. A chemical change, in contrast, results in one or more new substances with different chemical makeups. Which of the following is an example of a physical change?

(1) butter melting
(2) tarnish on silverware
(3) gasoline being used in a car engine
(4) photographic film being developed
(5) photosynthesis in plants

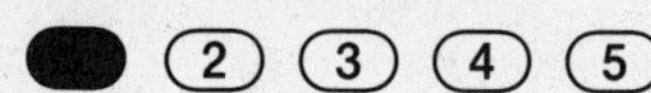

The answer is "butter melting"; therefore, answer space (1) has been marked.

Explanations for the answers are on pages 254–256. Answers to the questions are in the Answer Key on page 257.

Items 1–6 are based on the information given below.

Immunity is the ability of the body to resist disease. Below are five terms that are related to immunity and disease.

(1) acquired immunity = resistance to a disease that results from having had the disease
(2) immunization = introduction of a weak or dead disease-causing organism into the body for the purpose of developing resistance
(3) immunodeficiency = inability of the body to resist disease
(4) infection = invasion of the body by disease-causing microorganisms
(5) inflammation = redness, swelling, heat, and pain that occur when the body responds to injury, irritation, or microorganisms

Each of the following items is an example of one of the terms defined above. For each item, choose the term that best fits the example. Any term may be used more than once or not at all.

1. A woman had chicken pox as a child. She never gets the disease again.

   The woman does not get chicken pox a second time because of

   (1) acquired immunity
   (2) immunization
   (3) immunodeficiency
   (4) infection
   (5) inflammation

   ① ② ③ ④ ⑤

2. Some children have had to live inside large plastic bubbles that are germ-free. If they come out of these special chambers, death will occur in a short time.

   These children probably suffer from

   (1) acquired immunity
   (2) immunization
   (3) immunodeficiency
   (4) infection
   (5) inflammation

   ① ② ③ ④ ⑤

3. The number of cases of tetanus in this country decreased to almost zero once the injection of killed tetanus bacteria became a routine public health practice.

   The injection of these bacteria is called

   (1) acquired immunity
   (2) immunization
   (3) immunodeficiency
   (4) infection
   (5) inflammation

   ① ② ③ ④ ⑤

4. People who receive transplants of hearts or kidneys must continually take drugs to keep them from rejecting the new organs. Because of these drugs, however, people with transplants may die from common diseases such as colds.

   These drugs cause a condition of

   (1) acquired immunity
   (2) immunization
   (3) immunodeficiency
   (4) infection
   (5) inflammation

   ① ② ③ ④ ⑤

5. During World War I, wounded soldiers commonly lost arms or legs due to gangrene when microorganisms grew in the bullet wounds.

   The gangrene was probably due to

   (1) acquired immunity
   (2) immunization
   (3) immunodeficiency
   (4) infection
   (5) inflammation

   ① ② ③ ④ ⑤

6. A sitter forgets to change a baby's diaper. Later, the baby screams when his parents clean the diaper area.

   The baby probably cried because of

   (1) acquired immunity
   (2) immunization
   (3) immunodeficiency
   (4) infection
   (5) inflammation

   ① ② ③ ④ ⑤

GO ON TO THE NEXT PAGE.

7. Scientists believe that long ago all the land of the earth was united in a single mass. Because of movements in the earth's crust, this giant mass broke into the fragments that we know today as the seven continents.

   Which of the following findings would support the theory that the earth's land once existed as a single enormous continent?

   (1) A buried forest has been found on an island near the North Pole.
   (2) Some plants are now found in only one region of the world.
   (3) Many similar kinds of rocks are found throughout eastern Europe and the Middle East.
   (4) Identical types of fossils have been found in Africa and South America.
   (5) Long ago an ice age occurred, and glaciers covered most of the earth's land.

   (1) (2) (3) (4) (5)

8. An art masterpiece is suspected of being a fraud. Several people are invited to analyze the painting to determine whether the picture is genuine or fake. Which of the following could not be scientifically verified?

   (1) fiber content of the canvas
   (2) artistic importance of the picture
   (3) pigments present in the paints
   (4) type of paint used
   (5) approximate age of the painting

   (1) (2) (3) (4) (5)

Items 9–12 are based on the following passage.

Teflon is a synthetic substance called a polymer. This polymer is a chain of thousands of small molecules of carbon and fluorine atoms. Teflon is used in the manufacturing of many items, including medical devices and cooking ware. It is useful because nothing will stick to it. This property of being "non-sticky" is the result of bonding the fluorine atoms to the carbon atoms. Once fluorine is combined with all the carbon, the molecule becomes so inert and stable that nothing else will react with it. Teflon will not burn, no bacteria or fungi can grow on it, no acid will dissolve it, and it does not melt until the temperature reaches 620°F. It is so slippery that large sheets of Teflon have been used to make artificial ice skating rinks.

During the process of making Teflon, chemists can alter the polymer by adding other chemicals along with the fluorine. This gives the polymer new properties. For example, some Teflon is made that has one inert end and one sticky end. When it is applied to fabrics, it forms a protective coating because the sticky end binds to the cloth and the inert end prevents water, dirt, or oil from reacting with the material.

9. The word *inert* is used to describe Teflon because Teflon

   (1) is brittle
   (2) contains carbon atoms
   (3) sticks to many things
   (4) is slippery
   (5) does not react with other chemicals

   (1) (2) (3) (4) (5)

10. In which of the following ways might a Teflon molecule with one sticky end be used?

    (1) hand soap
    (2) paint for exterior use
    (3) all-purpose glue
    (4) non-skid floor covering
    (5) fabric softener for absorbent towels

    (1) (2) (3) (4) (5)

11. Five statements about Teflon are given below. Which one represents an opinion rather than a fact?

(1) Teflon is not a naturally occurring substance.
(2) The properties of Teflon can be changed.
(3) Hydrochloric acid will not damage a Teflon surface.
(4) Because foods do not stick to the surface, Teflon-coated cookware is better than other types of pans.
(5) Teflon-coated containers do not react with the material stored inside.

(1) (2) (3) (4) (5)

12. What is the main reason for the inert nature of Teflon?

(1) the absence of bacteria
(2) its high melting point
(3) its usefulness in cooking
(4) the ease with which it can be made
(5) the chemical bonding of fluorine and carbon

(1) (2) (3) (4) (5)

13. An environment exerts both biological and physical influences on an organism. The biological influences are the living surroundings of the organism. The physical influences are the nonliving surroundings.

Which of the following is a biological factor in the environment of a maple tree?

(1) microorganisms in the soil
(2) temperature
(3) sunlight exposure
(4) moisture
(5) acidity of rainfall

(1) (2) (3) (4) (5)

Items 14–16 refer to the following graph.

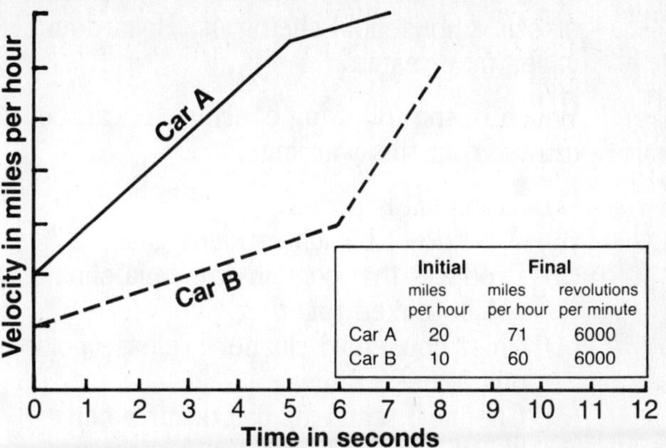

	Initial miles per hour	Final miles per hour	Final revolutions per minute
Car A	20	71	6000
Car B	10	60	6000

Two cars, A and B, were tested to determine how they accelerate in second gear. The results are shown above.

14. What is the starting velocity of car B?

(1) 0 (2) 2 (3) 10 (4) 20 (5) 1,000

(1) (2) (3) (4) (5)

15. Car A pulls away from a stop faster than car B, but B has more passing power on the freeway.

Which of the following statements best explains this observation?

(1) Car A accelerates more quickly at low velocity than it does at high velocity.
(2) The acceleration of car A is always greater than that of car B.
(3) Car B accelerates better at high velocity than it does at low velocity.
(4) Car A reaches top speed sooner than car B does.
(5) Car A accelerates faster than car B at low speed, but at high speed B accelerates faster than A.

(1) (2) (3) (4) (5)

16. Which of the following cannot be determined from the information in the graph?

(1) engine RPM when the test ended
(2) engine RPM at zero seconds
(3) how long it took each engine to reach 6,000 RPM after the test started
(4) final speed of each car
(5) speed of each car at four seconds

(1) (2) (3) (4) (5)

GO ON TO THE NEXT PAGE.

17. The warning on a bottle of bleach reads as follows: Do not mix with ammonia, cleaners, or other household chemicals. Hazardous gases may result.

    Which of the following conclusions can be drawn from this warning?

    (1) Ammonia is poisonous.
    (2) A bottle of bleach contains gas.
    (3) Products that contain ammonia should not be mixed together.
    (4) Most household cleaners release poisonous fumes.
    (5) Chemical reactions can occur when bleach is mixed with other chemicals.

Items 18–20 refer to the information below.

A food chain is a group or organisms related to each other in their feeding habits. One organism is eaten by a second one, which in turn is fed upon by a third one.

The food chain starts with energy from the sun. As each organism grows and is eaten, only about 10 percent of the sun's energy is transferred at each step.

18. A mouse ate corn containing 100 calories. How much energy did a cat gain from the corn when it ate the mouse?

    (1) 1 calorie
    (2) 10 calories
    (3) 50 calories
    (4) 75 calories
    (5) 100 calories

19. Which of the following statements best explains why so little energy is transferred up the food chain?

    (1) At each level, the organism uses most of the energy to maintain its own life activities.
    (2) Energy can be stored in sugar molecules and used at a later time.
    (3) Large animals require more food than small ones.
    (4) Plants contain very little energy.
    (5) People can't use energy from the sun directly.

(1) (2) (3) (4) (5)

20. People who live in areas of the world where food is scarce eat very little meat and depend on grains and other plants.

    Based on the ideas presented, which of the following statements best supports such eating habits?

    (1) It is easier to grow plants than raise animals.
    (2) Plants taste better than meat from animals.
    (3) Plants take up less space than grazing animals.
    (4) More than 90 percent of the energy in plants never reaches people who eat the animals raised on the plants.
    (5) Plants store energy in sugar molecules.

(1) (2) (3) (4) (5)

---

21. Below are five statements about a new coffee maker. Which one of these is an opinion rather than a fact?

    (1) The coffee will taste best if the coffee maker is cleaned once a month.
    (2) The coffeemaker brews 3 to 10 cups of coffee.
    (3) The coffee is maintained at 140°F.
    (4) One thousand watts are required to heat the water.
    (5) The strength of the coffee can be adjusted to suit different tastes.

22. Many scientists are concerned that destruction of tropical rain forests by loggers, farmers, and miners will lead to the extinction of many kinds of plants and animals.

    Which of the following statements indicates that values are involved in efforts to preserve the rain forests?

    (1) Tropical rain forests support nearly 50 percent of plant and animal species.
    (2) Many medicines are made from chemicals found in tropical plants.
    (3) Tropical plants provide seeds for developing new types of plants.
    (4) Plants and animals are worth saving even if people have no use for them.
    (5) A century ago, rain forests covered twice as much area as they do today.

(1) (2) (3) (4) (5)

Items 23–26 are based on the following graph.

Earthquakes in Kaoiki, Hawaii

The time line shows the occurrence of earthquakes in Kaoiki, a small area located between two very active volcanoes in Hawaii. The black dots mark the dates on which earthquakes that originated in Kaoiki occurred. The white circle indicates an earthquake that occurred somewhere in the area, but not enough evidence was available to conclude that the quake originated in Kaoiki.

23. Which of the following statements best summarizes the data shown on the time line?

(1) Each of the earthquakes recorded in the Kaoiki area was stronger than the previous one.
(2) During the years 1941–1984, an earthquake occurred approximately every ten years in a small area of Hawaii.
(3) Since 1920, seven earthquakes have occurred in the same area.
(4) Many earthquakes occur in the Kaoiki area of Hawaii.
(5) The occurrence of earthquakes in Hawaii is unpredictable.

(1) (2) (3) (4) (5)

24. According to the time line, earthquakes occur at very regular intervals. Approximately when would the next earthquake be expected to occur?

(1) 1989
(2) 1994
(3) 1999
(4) 2001
(5) 2005

(1) (2) (3) (4) (5)

25. Which of the following statements represents a hypothesis that may be arrived at using the data rather than a fact?

(1) An earthquake occurred in Kaoiki in 1941.
(2) Five earthquakes occurred during a 43-year period.
(3) The location of the 1930 earthquake in Hawaii is not definitely known.
(4) An earthquake should have occurred at Kaoiki about 1920.
(5) Six earthquakes have been recorded in or near Kaoiki.

(1) (2) (3) (4) (5)

26. Which of the following natural events is most similar to the occurrence of earthquakes in Kaoiki?

(1) Mount St. Helens erupted in Oregon in 1980.
(2) Tornadoes are common in the Midwest but not the Northeast.
(3) The number of sunspots peaks about every eleven years.
(4) Heavy snowfall is more characteristic of northern latitudes.
(5) Mudslides can be a problem in California.

(1) (2) (3) (4) (5)

GO ON TO THE NEXT PAGE.

27. Bacteria in milk from a sick cow can cause severe diseases in people. Pasteurization is a process that involves heating the milk to about 150 degrees to kill these bacteria.

A woman who knows what pasteurization is hears an advertisement on the radio for natural unpasteurized milk. At the store she carefully avoids the brand of milk that came from the dairy that did not pasteurize its product. Which of the following assumptions is she most likely making?

(1) Pasteurization ruins the flavor of the milk.
(2) Some of the nutritional value of the milk is lost during pasteurization.
(3) The dairy would not be aware that a cow is sick.
(4) Dairy herds are routinely tested for disease-causing bacteria.
(5) Pasteurization is a modern process.

(1) (2) (3) (4) (5)

Items 28–31 refer to the information below.

Five physical properties of waves are defined below.

(1) amplitude = the energy of a wave as revealed by its height
(2) frequency = the number of waves that pass a point in a certain length of time
(3) pitch = how high or low a sound is
(4) vibration = repeated movement back and forth or up and down
(5) wavelength = the distance from one wave to the next

Each of the following items gives an example that illustrates one of these terms. For each item, choose the term that is best described by the example. Any term may be used more than once or not all.

28. As the volume control is turned up, the sound from a stereo becomes louder.

The sound waves are increasing in

(1) amplitude
(2) frequency
(3) pitch
(4) vibration
(5) wavelength

(1) (2) (3) (4) (5)

29. A person can feel a train approaching when he puts his hand down on the railroad track.

The person feels the train coming because it produces a(n)

(1) amplitude
(2) frequency
(3) pitch
(4) vibration
(5) wavelength

(1) (2) (3) (4) (5)

30. A high note on a violin produces 2,500 waves per second.

The speed at which the sound waves from the violin are being produced is called

(1) amplitude
(2) frequency
(3) pitch
(4) vibration
(5) wavelength

(1) (2) (3) (4) (5)

31. A guitar player thinks her instrument is out of tune.

The player thinks there is a problem with her guitar's

(1) amplitude
(2) frequency
(3) pitch
(4) vibration
(5) wavelength

(1) (2) (3) (4) (5)

Items 32–34 are based on the following graph.

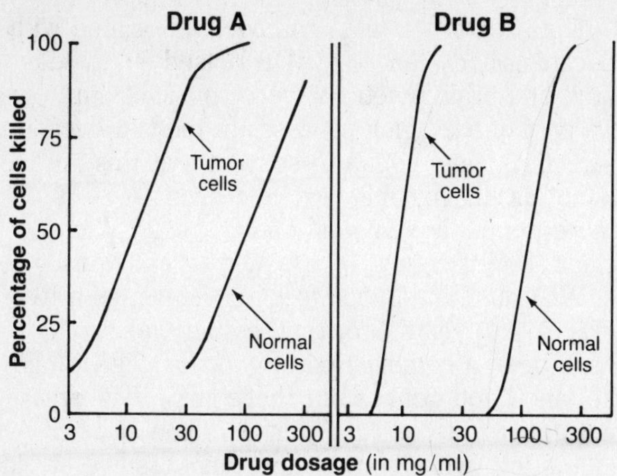

The graph shows how two anticancer drugs compare in their ability to kill tumor cells. The killing effect of the drugs on both tumor cells and normal cells is measured at several doses of each drug.

32. Which one of the following statements cannot be verified from the graph?

(1) the percentage of tumor cells killed by drug A at a dose of 30 mg/ml
(2) whether normal cells are killed by a certain dose of either drug
(3) whether any dose of drug B will kill both normal and tumor cells
(4) which drug kills more tumor cells at a certain dosage
(5) how many kinds of tumor cells each drug will kill

(1) (2) (3) (4) (5)

33. Which of the following is a statement of values concerning drug therapy, not of fact?

(1) Some types of cancer can be controlled with drug treatment.
(2) Drug therapy is often used along with other forms of treatment.
(3) Cancer drugs may have side effects.
(4) Side effects can include pain and loss of hair.
(5) The chance to live is more important than the pain due to drug therapy.

(1) (2) (3) (4) (5)

34. A physician discovers that he has cancer. His family urges him to begin drug therapy. The physician knows that cancer drugs act by killing cells that are dividing. He is reluctant to undergo treatment. His family does not understand why.

Which one of the following statements indicates that his family may not fully understand how cancer drugs work?

(1) Drug therapy works against some types of cancers.
(2) Many drugs used in cancer therapy cause cells to die when they divide.
(3) Cancer cells are killed by the drugs because they rarely stop dividing.
(4) All dividing cells, including normal ones, are killed by cancer drugs.
(5) A cell that divides often is more likely to be killed by the cancer drug.

GO ON TO THE NEXT PAGE.

35. Seawater contains an average of 2.7 percent salt. However, the concentration of salt can change depending on the area of the ocean. Deep ocean water has a constant salt content, but the amount of salt is below average where fresh water from a river enters the ocean and above average where water from the ocean evaporates or freezes, leaving the salt behind.

Given that information, where would the ocean be expected to have a lower than average salt content?

(1) by an island
(2) in the middle of the ocean
(3) at the ocean floor
(4) near a melting iceberg
(5) near the North Pole

36. When the temperature of a gas increases, its pressure also increases, assuming that the volume stays the same. This happens because the gas molecules gain energy. This extra energy causes them to move faster and collide more frequently with each other and with the sides of a container.

A can of spray paint contains paint and gas under pressure. When the nozzle on the top of the can is pressed, several things happen. Some of the gas escapes, blowing the paint out, and the can becomes cold. Which of the following statements would best explain why the can becomes cold?

(1) As the gas pressure decreases, its temperature drops.
(2) The liquid in the spray cools the can.
(3) The gas exists at a higher temperature than the liquid.
(4) Liquids exist at more constant temperatures than gases do.
(5) As the liquid is compressed, its temperature drops.

① ② ③ ④ ⑤

Items 37–40 refer to the following passage.

Until recently, aging has been associated with declining body functions. Decreased heart, kidney, and brain functions were considered a natural part of the aging process. In the last decade, scientists have begun to suspect that this decline is not an unavoidable part of growing old. As more people live longer, one fact has become clear: Different people age at different rates.

Why do some people not age as fast as others? A few years ago, the best answer would have been a combination of good luck, good habits, and good genes. But these answers were not entirely accurate. After all, some athletes die young, while some heavy smokers live to old age.

The real answer is probably much more complicated. Biological, psychological, and environmental factors all influence what happens to a person as he or she grows older. New studies are concentrating on chemical pathways by which emotions and attitudes affect the body. Feelings such as loneliness and a loss of control over one's own life may play a very real part in the decline associated with age.

This new emphasis in no way denies that physical change occurs as one ages. By fifty years of age, some lung capacity is lost, and blood vessels are narrower. However, significant declines do not occur in the absence of disease or damage.

37. Which of the following statements best summarizes the passage?

(1) Scientists are learning that little can be done to halt the inevitable process of aging.
(2) Aging is probably due to emotional, biological, and environmental factors that influence people differently.
(3) Much of the biological decline of aging is probably due to a lifetime of unhealthful habits.
(4) Physical decline is probably not very important in aging.
(5) Mental decline occurs faster than physical decline in the aging process.

38. Which of the following statements represents an opinion rather than a fact about aging?

(1) Lungs do not function quite as well after the age of fifty.
(2) More people are living longer these days.
(3) Decline in body functions is usually the result of disease or damage, not aging.
(4) Genetics, physical fitness, and emotional factors all contribute to aging.
(5) A 75-year-old person is too old to hold a position of responsibility.

(1) (2) (3) (4) (5)

39. Until the last decade, what assumption was made about aging?

(1) Changes such as declining organ functions are inevitable in aging people.
(2) Severe biological decline does not have to happen as a person ages.
(3) Athletes generally live longer than other people.
(4) Smoking can actually lead to a longer life.
(5) People cannot expect to live much beyond their sixties.

(1) (2) (3) (4) (5)

40. Many researchers believe that stress can trigger changes in the body. Below are five statements about how people respond to stress.

A. Stress can trigger the release of hormones that affect blood pressure and heart rate.
B. People who have friends and family to support them recover more quickly from stressful situations.
C. In times of stress, the brain may release mood-altering chemicals.
D. When people experience stress, the number of disease-fighting white blood cells in their blood decreases.
E. People who are allowed to make their own decisions appear more youthful.

Which of these statements support the conclusion that stress and emotions can affect bodily functions in specific ways?

(1) A only
(2) E only
(3) A and B only
(4) B and C only
(5) A, C, and D only

(1) (2) (3) (4) (5)

---

41. A man discovers seashells embedded in rocks on the top of a mountain and concludes that at one time the mountain was covered by an inland sea. Which of the following statements suggests that another explanation might be possible?

(1) Over a long period of time, mud that covered the seashells hardened into rock.
(2) The mountains were formed by the uplifting of the earth's crust that was once part of the ocean floor.
(3) A huge undersea mountain range runs the entire length of the Atlantic Ocean.
(4) Over time mountains are worn down by weather and water and new surfaces are exposed.
(5) Many islands are actually the tops of undersea volcanoes that stick up above the surface of the water.

(1) (2) (3) (4) (5)

GO ON TO THE NEXT PAGE.

Items 42–44 refer to the information below.

Boats float and rocks sink in a lake. These characteristics are due to the density of boats, rocks, and water. Density is the weight of a substance divided by the volume it occupies. Different substances may have different densities. If equal volumes of two liquids have different weights, the heavier liquid has a greater density. A liquid that is less dense than water will float on water, and a liquid that is more dense than water will sink.

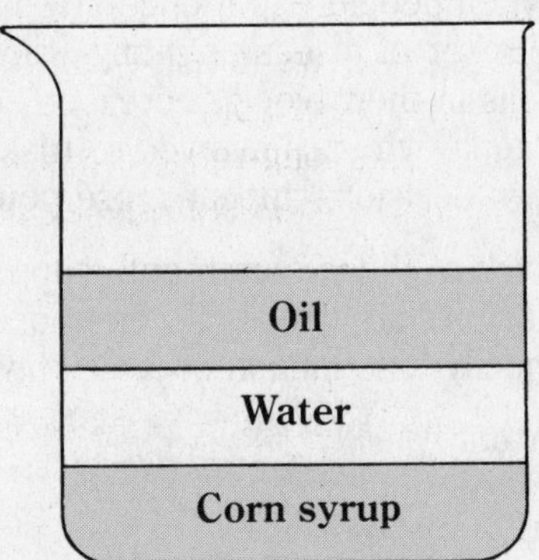

42. If water, cooking oil, and corn syrup are very carefully poured into a glass, one at a time, three distinct layers will form, as shown in the diagram. What will happen if a drop of corn syrup is added to the glass containing the three liquid layers of water, oil, and corn syrup?

(1) The drop of corn syrup will float on the top layer.
(2) The drop will pass through the oil and water and mix with the corn-syrup layer.
(3) The drop will be trapped between the water and oil layers.
(4) The drop will mix with the oil layer.
(5) The drop will sink to the very bottom of the glass.

(1) (2) (3) (4) (5)

43. Blood is made primarily of red blood cells, white blood cells, and a liquid called plasma. Medical laboratories often need to separate blood into its three main parts. This separation can be easily done because each part has a different density. Blood is carefully added to a test tube containing a medium called Ficoll-Hypaque, as shown in A.

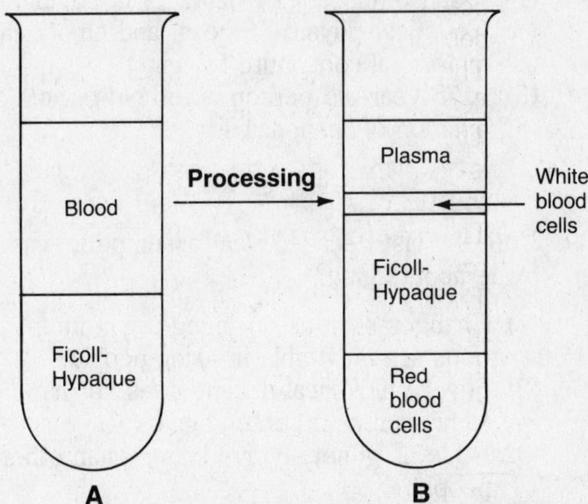

After A is processed, the blood separates into the three parts shown in B. Which of the following statements about the densities of the three parts is correct?

(1) Plasma is the densest component.
(2) White blood cells are more dense than red blood cells.
(3) Red blood cells are denser than either white blood cells or plasma.
(4) All blood cells are equally dense.
(5) Red cells are less dense than whole blood.

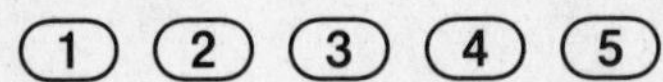

44. Many scientists believe that the ocean floors float on top of the earth's mantle—a thick layer of very dense rock—and that the continents float on top of the ocean floors.

Which of the following statements best justifies the observation that the continents rise above the ocean floors?

(1) The continents are smaller than the ocean floors, so the continents are less dense.
(2) The ocean floors are held down by the density of the water on top of them.
(3) The continents consist of granite, which is less dense than the rock that forms the ocean floors.
(4) The mantle is made of very dense rock.
(5) The material in the earth's mantle is more dense than the rock in the ocean floors.

---

45. Aspirin and acetaminophen are the chemicals that reduce pain in some pain-relief products for children. Although these chemicals appear to be equally effective, many doctors now recommend products that contain acetaminophen and not aspirin. What does this fact suggest?

(1) Acetaminophen works better than aspirin.
(2) Aspirin may cause side effects that do not occur with acetaminophen.
(3) Aspirin is an addictive drug.
(4) Aspirin and acetaminophen actually are the same chemical under different names.
(5) Children should not be given products containing chemicals.

① ② ③ ④ ⑤

46. Preserving food by radiation has been practiced on a small scale for twenty years. As this process is used on more foods, public attention is beginning to focus on it.

Below are five statements about using radiation to preserve food. Which of these statements is an opinion rather than a fact?

(1) Food exposed to radiation does not become radioactive.
(2) Radiation may change the texture of the food.
(3) Radiation will not eliminate the need for insect sprays in the fields.
(4) Radiation slows the ripening of some fruits and vegetables.
(5) Because its long-range effects are unpredictable, radiation should be banned.

GO ON TO THE NEXT PAGE.

Items 47–51 are based on the following information and diagram.

Cockroaches and owls are most active at night. Robins wake with the first light of day. Bean plants lift and lower their leaves at a regular time each day. Such biological cycles occur approximately every 24 hours and are called circadian rhythms. They seem to be linked to the cycle of the sun. The sunlight resets the cycles each day to keep them synchronized with the environment. However, when plants or animals are kept under conditions of constant light, their biological activities continue to cycle, though they may speed up or slow down.

The biological nature of these rhythms is not understood, but some facts are known. For example, there are usually several circadian rhythms going on at the same time. The rhythms stem from specific regions in the body. These regions are called "clocks," and one clock can control several rhythms. A clock is located in the eyes of squids and snails, and in the brains of lizards, birds, and mammals.

As many as four circadian rhythms have been identified in algae. If lighting conditions change, the clock also changes, but all four rhythms maintain their time relationship to each other. The following diagram shows three of the four circadian rhythms of algae.

Biological Cycles of Algae

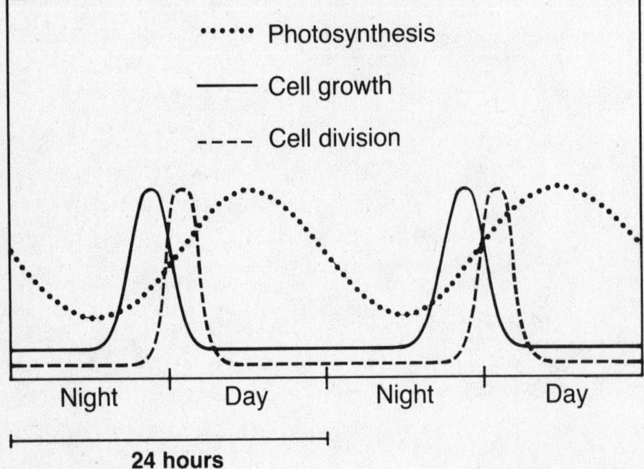

Biological clocks also exist in humans. Sleeping, waking, and eating are mainly circadian rhythms. Less apparent rhythms include changes in body temperature and in the release of certain hormones at particular times each day.

47. Which of the following statements best summarizes the information given in the graph about the algae?

(1) Several distinct processes in the algae are controlled by circadian rhythms.
(2) Many biological processes occur in the algae.
(3) Photosynthesis in algae controls many of the organism's other processes.
(4) Photosynthesis occurs once a day in algae.
(5) The circadian rhythms in algae will reset if the biological clock is disturbed.

(1) (2) (3) (4) (5)

48. Which of the following human activities shows a rhythm most similar to that of cell division in algae?

(1) eating
(2) sleeping
(3) bathing
(4) waking
(5) working

49. "Jet lag" is a condition of tension, tiredness, and irritability first described by people who traveled across many time zones. However, scientists now believe that jet lag can occur any time the body is readjusting its biological clock to a new time setting.

A group of people who often might experience jet lag are those who

(1) get up early
(2) change work shifts
(3) go to bed late
(4) feel most awake in the afternoon
(5) keep a strict daily routine

1 2 3 4 5

50. Which of the following is a conclusion that can be drawn from the passage?

(1) Sunlight influences but does not directly cause biological rhythms.
(2) The biological clock appears to be reset each day by the cycle of the sun.
(3) In some animals, the location of the clock in the body is known.
(4) Biological rhythms can be speeded up or slowed down.
(5) The biological clock can be reset if lighting conditions change.

1 2 3 4 5

51. In an experiment, a group of people lived in rooms with no windows for many days, and the lights were never turned off. During the first two weeks, the sleep and body temperature cycles averaged 25 hours. After two weeks, however, the temperature cycle remained 25 hours long, but the sleep cycle lengthened to 33 hours.

Which of the following statements best explains this observation?

(1) There are at least two clocks in people.
(2) People do not have circadian rhythms.
(3) Circadian rhythms function only when the sun resets the clock.
(4) People sleep more than they actually need to.
(5) The exact location of the clock in people has not been determined.

1 2 3 4 5

---

52. Shoulder harnesses are safety devices on most cars. The purpose of the harness is to hold the passenger in the seat and prevent him or her from smashing into the dashboard or windshield during a collision.

Which of the following principles best explains why a shoulder harness is necessary?

(1) The faster an object is moving, the harder it is to stop.
(2) A car has a different speed after a collision.
(3) In a crash a person cannot react fast enough to brace himself or herself.
(4) When a vehicle stops suddenly, a passenger will continue moving forward.
(5) A broken windshield will always curve into the car.

GO ON TO THE NEXT PAGE.

Items 53–56 refer to the following passage.

The world appears to have enough low-cost light oil at the present time. However, these supplies will eventually be depleted. When this occurs, countries will have to recover their vast resources of heavy oil and bitumen from the earth and refine them into a usable light oil. Bitumen is a very heavy, sticky oil that contains much sulfur. In North America, the Canadian province of Alberta contains the largest concentration of heavy oil and bitumen, which is found mainly in oil sands. How heavy oil and bitumen are recovered depends on how deeply they are buried.

Ten percent of the bitumen is close enough to the surface to be mined from open-pit mines. After the oil is removed, the sand is returned to the pit. Currently, 15 percent of Canada's oil is produced from bitumen by open-pit mining.

Deeply buried deposits of bitumen make up about 90 percent of Canada's heavy oil resources. However, it is very difficult to get this bitumen because it is so thick and sticky that it is almost a solid. The technology to recover it involves heating the bitumen deep in the ground and pumping it to the surface through wells before it cools. The process is somewhat like recovering light oil, except that light oil is easy to reach because it occurs naturally as a liquid in porous rocks beneath the ground.

The production of refined oil from bitumen and heavy oil is an expensive process and one that does not pay for itself at the current low price of conventional light oil. Alberta is working on the problem so that when the world's reserves of light oil run out in the future, Alberta will be ready to produce synthetic light crude oil from its vast bitumen resources.

53. How is it possible to mine deeply buried bitumen?

(1) Its thickness makes it easy to cut and dig up.
(2) Heat changes bitumen into a liquid-like substance.
(3) It rises to the surface with naturally occurring light oil.
(4) It sticks to pipes drilled into the ground and then brought up.
(5) It can be mined in open sand pits.

54. What assumption does the government of Alberta make when it finances the development of new oil-producing technology?

(1) Alberta has the largest supply of alternative oil resources in North America.
(2) Unrefined bitumen can be directly used as a fuel source.
(3) As light oil supplies are used up, the price of oil will rise, and oil production from bitumen will pay for itself.
(4) Only some of the oil reserves can be reached by open-pit mining techniques.
(5) Techniques that are currently used for oil production can produce oil from bitumen and heavy oil reserves.

55. Which of the following statements is a hypothesis that Alberta is testing?

(1) The production of light oil from bitumen and heavy oil can be made less expensive.
(2) In open-pit mining, the bitumen must be extracted from the sand.
(3) Bitumen is a very heavy, tarry oil with a high sulfur content.
(4) The deeply buried bitumen must be heated because it is thick and sticky.
(5) Between 10 and 20 percent of Canadian oil is produced from bitumen.

1 2 3 4 5

56. Which of the following statements indicates that values play an important role in the development of technology for using oil reserves?

(1) The major expense in developing the deep oil reserves involves moving the bitumen to the surface for processing to light oil.
(2) The natural resources of bitumen and heavy oil are the largest in North America.
(3) Fifteen percent of Canada's total oil production comes from open-pit mining of bitumen.
(4) Production of bitumen from deep deposits was seven times greater in 1985 than in 1980.
(5) It is important for Alberta to produce light oil from bitumen so that Canada will be less dependent on other countries.

1 2 3 4 5

57. Below are four statements about spider webs from a biology textbook.

A. A spider's web is a beautiful, complex work of engineering.
B. Spiders use silk threads to make protective cocoons for their eggs.
C. A web can be a lethal trap for insects.
D. Spiders inherit the instinct to spin webs.

Which of the statements shows that the textbook is blending opinion with fact?

(1) A only
(2) B only
(3) C only
(4) D only
(5) C and D only

58. A news article reporting the discovery of a galaxy gives the following information: the galaxy is about 12 billion light-years—the distance a light ray travels in a year—from the earth. Analysis of the light from this galaxy reveals that it is composed mainly of hydrogen gas and a few young stars.

A person who knows very little about astronomy reads this article and thinks that the galaxy is actually forming today. Which of the following statements helps explain that he does not fully understand the report?

(1) Analysis of light from a long distance is not a reliable technique.
(2) The new galaxy can be seen using only very powerful optical telescopes.
(3) The galaxy formed 12 billion years ago, and its light is only now reaching the earth.
(4) Stars are formed primarily from hydrogen gas.
(5) Most galaxies formed billions of years ago.

GO ON TO THE NEXT PAGE.

Items 59–61 are based on the following information and diagram.

A person visiting Mexico was frightened when a snake crossed his path and then turned toward him. The man grabbed a stick and clubbed the snake. When he was sure the reptile was dead, he sat down and examined it. He made the following observations. The rings around the body formed the following pattern: black, red, black, yellow; black, red, black, yellow. The scales were smooth, all about the same size, and cycloid in shape. No other markings were seen.

Later, he found a book about snakes and used the following key to identify the snake he had killed.

Key to Families

1. Red, yellow, and black rings about body, red bordered by yellow. .... **elapids**, p. 196
   If red, yellow, and black rings, red bordered by black .... *see* **2**
2. Scales smooth, cycloid, of uniform size .... **blind snakes**, p. 136
   Not as above .... *see* **3**
3. Deep pit between nostrils and eye. .... **pit vipers**, p. 198
   Not as above .... *see* **4**
4. Large scales on top of head .... **colubrids**, p. 140
   Small scales on top of head .... **true boas**, p. 138

59. What family did the snake belong to?

(1) elapids
(2) blind snakes
(3) pit vipers
(4) colubrids
(5) true boas

① ② ③ ④ ⑤

60. Which of the following statements best summarizes the information on the key?

(1) Smooth scales of similar size and shape are characteristic of blind snakes.
(2) The size of the scales on a snake's head distinguishes colubrids from true boas.
(3) Colored rings and their arrangement separate elapids from blind snakes.
(4) Snakes are best distinguished by their coloration, their scales, and the presence of a pit.
(5) Pit vipers have a deep pit between their nostrils and eyes, but colubrids and true boas do not.

① ② ③ ④ ⑤

61. What assumption did the man most likely make when he killed the snake?

(1) Most snakes feed on rats and mice.
(2) Snakes are dangerous.
(3) Snakes feed very infrequently.
(4) Some types of nonpoisonous snakes very closely resemble poisonous ones.
(5) Some snakes that appear ferocious are actually quite harmless.

① ② ③ ④ ⑤

---

62. Almost all rose bushes sold today were developed by humans. Some roses might have very desirable characteristics, such as color, disease resistance, or flower size, but they do not grow well because they have very weak root systems. Other rose plants have very strong roots but bloom poorly. So buds from the attractive roses are grafted onto the healthy roots of the other bushes. The rose bush that results has all the good qualities of both plants.

Which of the following is true of most rose bushes that are commercially available today?

(1) They have shallow roots.
(2) They are resistant to disease.
(3) Some desirable characteristics are given up to insure a strong root system.
(4) They are a combination of two different plants.
(5) They do not grow well.

① ② ③ ④ ⑤

Items 63–65 refer to the following diagram and information.

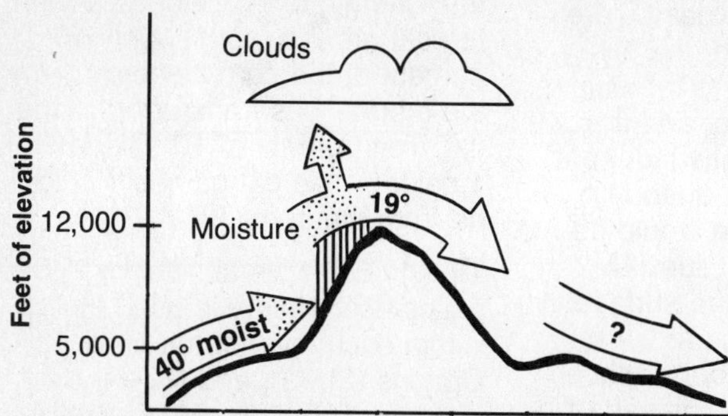

When damp air blows against a mountain, it rises. As it moves higher, it gets colder. For every 1,000 feet the air rises, its temperature drops 3 degrees. Clouds also form because moisture condenses as air becomes colder. When the air has reached the top of the mountain, it is quite dry. As the dry, cold air moves down the other side of the mountain, it heats up about 5½ degrees for every 1,000 feet of descent. It heats up more because the moisture is gone.

63. Which of the following best summarizes what the diagram shows?

(1) what happens to moist air as it crosses a mountain
(2) how air loses moisture
(3) why rain falls
(4) why the temperature of air changes
(5) why air becomes colder as it crosses a mountain

(1) (2) (3) (4) (5)

64. The diagram shows that moist air arriving at a mountain has a temperature of 40°F at an altitude of 5,000 feet. The air rises to 12,000 feet to cross the mountain. Which of the following best describes the condition of this air when it arrives back down at 5,000 feet on the other side of the mountain?

(1) 40°F; dry
(2) colder than 19°F; moist
(3) warmer than 40°F; dry
(4) warmer than 40°F; moist
(5) between 19° and 40°F; dry

(1) (2) (3) (4) (5)

65. What kind of land would most likely occur on the right side of the mountain?

(1) marshland
(2) an ocean
(3) a forest
(4) a desert
(5) bare rock

(1) (2) (3) (4) (5)

---

66. Camels, like all animals, need water to live. Yet they are known for being able to go up to ten days without eating or drinking. Many people believe that camels store water in their humps, but others disagree.

Which of the following statements would help prove that water is not stored in a camel's hump?

(1) The hump becomes smaller when there is nothing to eat or drink.
(2) The hump gets smaller when there is no food but water is available.
(3) A camel can live for months on green grass and no water.
(4) A camel's hump may contain up to fifty pounds of fat.
(5) The hump becomes larger when the camel eats and drinks.

(1) (2) (3) (4) (5)

END OF EXAMINATION

Answers: Posttest A

1. (1) The woman developed a resistance to chicken pox when she had the disease as a child. This acquired resistance, or immunity, lasted her entire life. **AP**

2. (3) These immunodeficient children must live in germ-free bubbles because they have no ability to develop resistance to disease-causing organisms. They can die from just a cold. **AP**

3. (2) The injection of killed bacteria fits only the definition of immunization. Resistance did develop because the number of cases of disease decreased greatly. **AP**

4. (3) The drugs decrease the transplant recipient's ability to develop resistance to disease. Only immunodeficiency could cause this lowered resistance. **AP**

5. (4) The gangrene-causing organisms invaded the wounds, causing infection and disease. **AP**

6. (5) Inflammation alone explains the pain that makes the baby cry. Inflammation follows irritation, but it does not necessarily indicate that microorganisms have invaded the body. **AP**

7. (4) South America and Africa are now widely separated by water with no land bridge between them, but identical fossils suggest that at one time the two continents were united. The other options do not support or disprove the theory. **EV**

8. (2) The importance of the picture could not be determined by any scientific analysis. Importance is determined by artistic evaluation. All other options could be verified by chemical analysis. **AN**

9. (5) The first paragraph states that a Teflon molecule is "so inert and stable that nothing else will react with it." Although options (2) and (4) are true of Teflon, none of the options except (5) explains what *inert* means. **CP**

10. (2) If an exterior paint were made of sticky Teflon, the sticky end would stick well to the surface it was applied to, and the inert end would resist wind, heat, weather, and acid. A soap (1) made of sticky Teflon would be difficult to rinse out. Glue (3) would stick only to one surface; it would not hold two surfaces together. The Teflon floor surface (4) would be slippery instead of non-skid. Towels treated with sticky Teflon would not absorb water (5). **AP**

11. (4) Whether the food cooked in Teflon cookware is better is an opinion. All other options restate facts given in the passage. **AN**

12. (5) The passage tells you that chemists combine fluorine with carbon to make Teflon. The molecule that is produced is stable and very inert. **CP**

13. (1) Microorganisms in the soil are part of the living things in the environment of the tree. Options (2)–(5) are all physical factors in its environment. **AP**

14. (3) This number can be read directly from the inset table on the graph. **CP**

15. (5) Only this statement correctly compares the acceleration pattern of the two cars at both low speeds and high speeds. **EV**

16. (2) The inset panel tells final engine RPM (1) and final speed (4). The test ended when engine RPM reached 6,000; the time at which the test ended (3) for each car can be read directly from the graph. Option (5) can be determined indirectly: The initial speeds are stated, so it is clear that each division on the graph equals 10 mph. From this information, the speed at four seconds could be determined. **CP**

17. (5) When bleach is mixed with other cleaning chemicals, chemical reactions often occur. Hazardous gases are formed during these reactions. **AN**

18. (1) The corn contained 100 calories. When the mouse ate the corn, he gained 10 percent of that energy, or 10 calories. When the cat ate the mouse, only 10 percent of the corn's energy from the mouse was transferred to the cat. Ten percent of 10 calories is 1 calorie. The cat gained 1 calorie from the corn. **AP**

19. (1) Only this answer explains how energy is used up within each level of the chain. Options (2), (3), and (5) are true statements but do not answer the question. **AN**

20. (4) Only (4) indicates that at each level of the food chain energy is lost. Much of the energy in the plants is lost to people when the plants are first eaten by animals. **EV**

21. (1) "Best-tasting" coffee is a personal judgment. How often the coffee maker should be cleaned depends on how often it is used, the local water conditions, and many other factors. This statement is an opinion. All the other options are facts that can be verified scientifically. **AN**

22. (4) This statement urges saving the rain forests because they have value other than economic worth. All the other options are facts. **EV**

23. (2) The line emphasizes the regular interval between the five earthquakes known to originate in Kaoiki. Options (3), (4), and (5) do not mention this pattern. The time line does not indicate how strong any of the earthquakes were (1). **CP**

24. (2) The graph shows that earthquakes occurred every ten to eleven years since 1941. Because the last known quake occurred in 1984, the next one would be predicted for 1994 or 1995. **CP**

25. (4) The graph begins with known quakes in 1931. If the theory that a quake occurs every ten to eleven years is correct, the year 1931 minus 11 years equals the year 1920. Scientists hope that by studying historical documents they will find reports of a quake that occurred in the Kaoiki area in 1920. **AN**

26. (3) The earthquakes in Kaoiki occur at regular intervals. The sunspots also peak at regular intervals. **AP**

27. (3) If the dairy is unaware that a cow is sick, the milk may contain disease-causing organisms. Options (1) and (2) are reasons the woman *would* buy unpasteurized milk. If she assumed the herds are tested routinely (4), she might not avoid unpasteurized milk. Option (5) is irrelevant. **AN**

28. (1) A louder sound means that the waves are larger and contain more energy. Amplitude is a measure of the size of the wave. **AP**

29. (4) The train is producing movement of the particles that make up the track. Such movement is a vibration. **AP**

30. (2) The speed at which the waves are produced determines how many waves will pass a certain point within a certain time. This fits the definition of frequency. **AP**

31. (3) Pitch is the property of waves that determines the high and low sounds the listener hears and whether they are "in tune." **AP**

32. (5) The graph gives no information about how many different kinds of tumor cells each drug was tested on. The graph does indicate at what doses each drug was tested and what percentages of normal and tumor cells were killed by each dosage. All options except (5) can be determined from the graph. **CP**

33. (5) This is a statement involving values because the importance will vary depending on each individual's values. **EV**

34. (4) This option indicates that cancer drugs do not distinguish between normal and tumor cells and often cause death in normal cells. This death of normal cells causes side effects. **AN**

35. (4) Near a melting iceberg, which is frozen fresh water, there would be a greater than average amount of fresh water, so the amount of salt in the water would be lower than average. Options (1), (2), and (3) are areas where the salt content would be average. In polar regions (5), the salt content would be greater than normal because when water freezes, it freezes as pure water and leaves the salt in the water that remains unfrozen. **AP**

36. (1) Pressing the nozzle releases some of the pressure in the can. Temperature and pressure of a gas are directly proportional; a decrease in pressure causes a decrease in temperature. **(AN)**

37. (2) The passage emphasizes that researchers now believe that how a person ages depends on many different factors. Physical (4) and mental (5) decline are only two of these factors. According to the passage, (1) and (3) are false statements. **CP**

38. (5) This statement is an opinion since there is no scientific evidence to support the idea. The passage emphasizes that people age at different rates. **AN**

39. (1) Until the last decade, aging was considered a gradual loss of body function. Mental and emotional decline followed these physical changes. Now researchers believe that the opposite is true: emotional and psychological factors influence the biological processes associated with aging. **AN**

40. (5) Hormone levels (statement A), mood-altering chemicals from the brain (statement C), and fewer white blood cells (statement D) are all measurable changes that are due to stress. Statements B and E are generally believed to be true statements about aging, but they do not indicate specific bodily changes. **EV**

41. (2) The man believes that water carried the seashells to the mountains and then receded. Option (2) suggests that the mountains were formed by being lifted up from the ocean floor and that the seashells were present in this soil material. **EV**

42. (2) The corn-syrup drop will pass through the less dense layers of oil and water, but it will stop when it reaches the corn-syrup layer. Options (1), (3), and (4) are incorrect based on the information supplied. Option (5) is also incorrect. The drop will stop once it reaches the corn-syrup layer because it has the same density. Only a drop of liquid of *greater* density than corn syrup would fall to the bottom of the glass. **AP**

43. (3) Red blood cells collect in the bottom of the tube because they are the most dense part of blood. **AP**

44. (3) Only this option says that the continents are less dense than the ocean floors that they rise above. That follows the principle of the density of a material determining its level. **EV**

45. (2) Doctors would recommend acetaminophen either because it works better or because aspirin is in some way harmful. The information is given that the two drugs are equally effective. **AN**

46. (5) Banning the process is an opinion. Many people are in favor of the process and think it should be used on even more foods. All the other options are facts that can be confirmed using scientific techniques. **AN**

47. (1) The graph shows three different processes in the algae that cycle with a circadian rhythm. Option (2) is incomplete because it ignores the cyclic rhythm of these three independent processes. **CP**

48. (4) Cell division in algae tends to occur as night turns to day. That pattern is also followed by humans when they wake up. **AP**

49. (2) People who change their work shifts often have their biological clocks reset each time they change their eating and sleeping schedules to fit the new shift. This fits the definition of jet lag, a feeling that results from resetting the clock. No other option indicates that the biological clock is disrupted in any way. **AP**

50. (1) This statement is a conclusion supported by facts given in the passage. In fact, options (2)–(5) help support it. See also the last two sentences of the first paragraph. **AN**

51. (1) The temperature cycles on one rhythm, while the sleep pattern cycles on another. Therefore, there must be one clock to control each rhythm. **AN**

52. (4) The passenger will continue moving at the speed at which the car was moving before the collision. The seat belt should hold him or her in the seat. No other option explains this. Options (1) and (2) are true statements, but (1) does not explain why the passenger will not stop with the car. Option (2) is irrelevant. Even at slow speeds, a person is not strong enough to hold himself or herself in the seat if the car stops suddenly (3). Option (5) is not true. **AN**

53. (2) The paragraph says that the bitumen is difficult to obtain because it is thick and sticky. Heat makes it more liquid-like, so it can then be pumped to the surface through wells. **CP**

54. (3) The final paragraph of the passage says that the oil-producing process does not pay for itself at the current price of oil. When oil is scarce, the price will increase, and the production of light oil from bitumen will become profitable. **AN**

55. (1) This is a hypothesis suggested in the final paragraph. Alberta is working to produce less-costly oil. **AN**

56. (5) Only this option indicates why Alberta is developing this expensive research program. The country values its self-sufficiency and wants to remain independent of other nations. All other options are facts that are not influenced by values. **EV**

57. (1) This description of a spider's web is partly opinion. All the other statements are facts that can be verified by scientific methods. **AN**

58. (3) The galaxy is 12 billion light-years from the earth. This means it has taken the light from the galaxy 12 billion years to reach our planet. Therefore, we are seeing this galaxy as it looked 12 billion years ago. There is no ways of knowing what is occurring in the galaxy right now. Perhaps it does not even exist any longer. **EV**

59. (2) Section 1 of the key distinguishes snakes on the basis of their ring color and arrangement. The red rings on the snake were bordered by black. The key instructs the user to "see 2." Section 2 is concerned with the size and arrangement of the scales on the body. The scales of the dead snake fit the description of "smooth, cycloid, of uniform size." By using the key, you can identify the snake as a blind snake. **CP**

60. (4) The key is arranged as follows: Section 1 describes the rings around the body. Section 2 describes the scales on the body. Section 3 describes the presence of a pit. Section 4 describes the scales on the head. Option (4) summarizes these identifying markings. All other options are true statements about how the markings of different kinds of snakes are dissimilar. They all support the summary stated in (4). **CP**

61. (2) At a glance the man could not tell whether the snake was poisonous. He killed the snake because he assumed it might harm him. **AN**

62. (4) The roses are a combination of buds from one plant and strong roots from another. Options (1), (3), and (5) are false statements about the roses that are commercially available today. Option (2) may or may not be true; this is only one of the desirable qualities mentioned. **CP**

63. (1) The information describes that when moist air arrives at a mountain, it rises, becomes colder, gives up its moisture, and warms up as it flows down the other side of the mountain. Options (2), (3), (4), and (5) indicate only parts of the process. **CP**

64. (3) The air has lost its moisture, so it will be dry. As the air rose 7,000 feet, it cooled 21° (3° × 7 = 21°). Coming 7,000 feet down the other side, it gained 38.5° (5½° × 7 = 38.5°). It will be warmer. **AN**

65. (4) Since the air on the right side of the mountain would tend to be warm and dry, desert land would most likely occur. **AP**

66. (2) This option indicates that lack of food causes the hump to shrink. If water is available but food is not and the hump gets smaller, the hump must contain an energy source. Actually, this has been proved to be true. The camel's hump does not contain water but fat, which is used as an energy source by the animal when necessary. **EV**

CP = Comprehension **AP** = Application **AN** = Analysis **EV** = Evaluation

Answer Key

Circle the numbers of all the questions you answered incorrectly or did not answer at all on the Answer Key below. Then count how many questions you answered correctly and find that score on the Progress Chart on the inside back cover.

1. (1)	**17.** (5)	**34.** (4)	**51.** (1)
2. (3)	**18.** (1)	**35.** (4)	**52.** (4)
3. (2)	**19.** (1)	**36.** (1)	**53.** (2)
4. (3)	**20.** (4)	**37.** (2)	**54.** (3)
5. (4)	**21.** (1)	**38.** (5)	**55.** (1)
6. (5)	**22.** (4)	**39.** (1)	**56.** (5)
7. (4)	**23.** (2)	**40.** (5)	**57.** (1)
8. (2)	**24.** (2)	**41.** (2)	**58.** (3)
9. (5)	**25.** (4)	**42.** (2)	**59.** (2)
10. (2)	**26.** (3)	**43.** (3)	**60.** (4)
11. (4)	**27.** (3)	**44.** (3)	**61.** (2)
12. (5)	**28.** (1)	**45.** (2)	**62.** (4)
13. (1)	**29.** (4)	**46.** (5)	**63.** (1)
14. (3)	**30.** (2)	**47.** (1)	**64.** (3)
15. (5)	**31.** (3)	**48.** (4)	**65.** (4)
16. (2)	**32.** (5)	**49.** (2)	**66.** (2)
	33. (5)	**50.** (1)	

How did you do on Posttest A? If you didn't pass or just barely passed, there are several things you can study to improve your test score. For instance, read the answer explanations carefully for the questions you missed. The answers may point out errors in your thinking or may indicate that you misread information. You can also use the Skill Chart below to determine which skills are most difficult for you, and then review the lessons that give you practice in those areas. You also may review the section on diagrams, graphs, and tables at the front of the book for tips on understanding illustrated information. After looking again at those pages, take Posttest B and compare your scores on the Progress Chart.

If you did well on Posttest A, you're probably ready to take the GED Science Test. However, you'll no doubt feel more comfortable with the test and more confident on your ability if you do Posttest B as further practice. If you can't take the GED Science Test soon after you study this book, you can use Posttest B as a refresher just before exam time.

Question Number	Skill	Lesson
12, 15, 19, 20, 34, 36, 41, 51, 52, 65	Seeing cause-and-effect relationships	5, 15, 25
1, 2, 3, 4, 5, 6, 10, 18, 24, 26, 28, 29, 30, 31, 35, 48, 49, 59, 64	Applying ideas	6, 19, 24
9, 13, 14, 42, 53, 62	Restating information	2, 12
22, 33, 56	Understanding the role of values in beliefs and decision making	18, 23
8, 11, 21, 25, 38, 46, 55, 57	Distinguishing between facts, opinions, and hypotheses	8, 20, 26
17, 43, 45, 50	Working with conclusions	7, 14, 21
7, 16, 32, 40, 44, 66	Evaluating data	10, 22, 27
23, 37, 47, 60, 63	Summarizing	4, 13
27, 39, 54, 61	Recognizing assumptions	9, 16
58	Seeing faulty logic	11, 17, 28

SCIENCE POSTTEST B

The Science Posttest consists of 66 multiple-choice questions intended to measure general concepts in science. The questions are based on short readings that often include a graph, chart, or figure. Study the information given and then answer the question(s) following it. Refer to the information as often as necessary to answer the questions.

You should take no more than 95 minutes to complete the test. Work carefully, but do not spend too much time on any one question. If a question is too difficult for you, omit it and come back to it later. There is no penalty for guessing.

To record each answer, fill in the space that matches the number of the answer you have chosen.

EXAMPLE

A physical change is one in which the chemical composition of a substance is not altered. A chemical change, in contrast, results in one or more new substances with different chemical makeups. Which of the following is an example of a physical change?

(1) butter melting
(2) tarnish on silverware
(3) gasoline being used in a car engine
(4) photographic film being developed
(5) photosynthesis in plants

The answer is "butter melting"; therefore, answer space (1) has been marked.

Explanations for the answers are on pages 278–280. Answers to the questions are in the Answer Key on page 281.

Items 1–4 are based on the following passage.

Returning a spacecraft to earth intact is a difficult operation. How can the craft be slowed down for landing? The ideal method would be to use braking rockets similar to those used to launch the craft. Unfortunately, this type of braking system would require putting a gigantic rocket into orbit simply to land the spaceship.

All spacecraft so far have used an aerodynamic system—one that uses the earth's atmosphere as a brake. This method relies on the physical law that an object will come to rest only when its kinetic energy—energy of motion—is converted to some other form of energy, such as light, sound, or heat.

A spacecraft moving 18,000 miles per hour contains an enormous amount of kinetic energy. This energy is converted mainly into heat as the craft plows back into the earth's atmosphere and friction with the air begins to slow it down. Space engineers developed several ways to remove this heat so that the spacecraft would not burn up: (1) A heat shield in front of the craft heats up to several hundred degrees Celsius and radiates heat back into the air. (2) Part of the outside shell of the craft is burned off as the shell absorbs the heat. (3) The surface of the craft heats up the air in contact with it, leaving behind a stream of hot air.

Although the aerodynamic landing system is not ideal, it will be used for a long time because it is less costly and more fuel efficient than other braking systems.

1. According to the passage, what must be true if a space vehicle is to stop?

   (1) The craft's kinetic energy must be reduced to zero.
   (2) The spaceship must absorb atmospheric heat.
   (3) Heat, light, and sound energy must be absorbed by the vehicle.
   (4) A landing rocket must be launched to release heat energy.
   (5) Heat energy of the air must change into other forms of energy.

   1 2 3 4 5

2. According to the passage, braking rockets could slow down and stop a landing spaceship. Such a braking rocket would be necessary for a spaceship landing on

   (1) a faraway planet
   (2) a planet with a strong pull of gravity
   (3) a planet with a cold surface
   (4) a planet with no atmosphere
   (5) earth under adverse weather conditions

   1 2 3 4 5

3. Which of the following actions is most similar to a returning spaceship moving through the earth's atmosphere?

   (1) a fish swimming through water
   (2) a basketball shot toward a hoop
   (3) a man walking down a hill
   (4) a cup dropped from a table
   (5) a car's tires approaching a stop sign

4. Which of the following statements from the passage indicates that values influence people's behavior and decisions?

   (1) Aerodynamic braking will be used for a long time because of its fuel economy and low cost.
   (2) Returning a spacecraft to earth is difficult.
   (3) Kinetic energy must be converted to other energy forms.
   (4) The successful reentry of a spacecraft into the earth's atmosphere depends on physical principles.
   (5) Power braking would require carrying a large rocket to land the spaceship.

   1 2 3 4 5

GO ON TO THE NEXT PAGE.

5. Three kinds of warblers live in the same kind of tree in Maine during the same time of year. However, they coexist because they nest in different sections of the tree. The Myrtle warbler lives in the bottom branches, the Cape May warbler lives in the middle branches, and the black-throated green warbler lives near the tops of the trees.

A particular large bird of prey soars over the forest in Maine and feeds on small birds such as warblers. If the population of this bird suddenly increased, which of the following results would be expected about the warbler population?

(1) All three kinds of warblers would also increase in number.
(2) The Cape May and black-throated green warblers would increase in number, but the Myrtle warbler would decrease.
(3) The black-throated green warbler would decrease in number more than the Cape May and Myrtle warblers.
(4) The Cape May warbler would decrease in number, while the Myrtle and black-throated green warblers would increase.
(5) All three kinds of warblers would decrease equally in number.

① ② ③ ④ ⑤

6. An article in a magazine describes volcanoes in all of the ways listed below.

A. monumental acts of creation
B. nature's most spectacular bulldozers
C. builders of the land
D. makers of the sea
E. producers of the atmosphere

Which of these descriptions shows that the article is blending opinion with fact?

(1) A only
(2) A and B only
(3) A, C, and E only
(4) B and D only
(5) C, D, and E only

① ② ③ ④ ⑤

Items 7–9 are based on the following diagram and information.

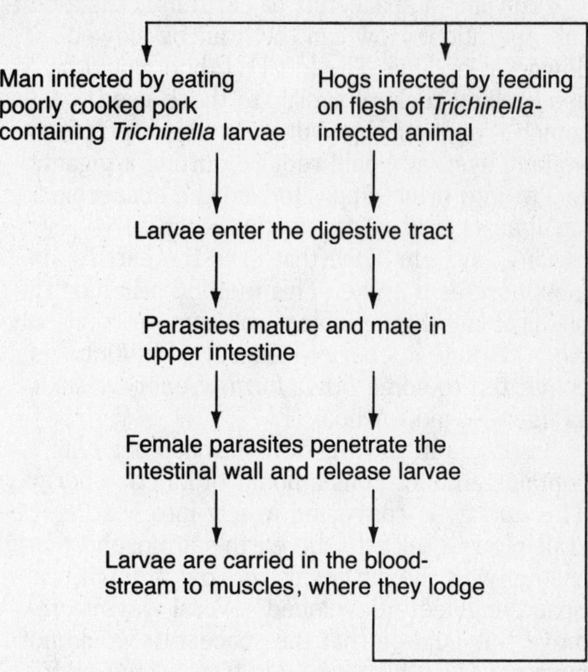

Trichinosis is a disease caused by the parasite *Trichinella spiralis*. The diagram above shows the life cycle of the parasite and the pathway it follows in nature to cause infection.

7. According to the diagram, in which one of the following ways could a human become infected with *Trichinella?*

(1) handling pork products
(2) eating poorly cooked pork that contains *Trichinella* larvae
(3) being bitten by a hog
(4) eating meat that contains mature parasites
(5) spreading infection from person to person

8. Below are five suggestions for eliminating trichinosis. Which of the five would not be an effective means of preventing infection?

(1) Cook pork thoroughly.
(2) Adopt a meat inspection program for pork products.
(3) Stop sales of meat from any herds in which *Trichinella* is found.
(4) Wash hands thoroughly before eating pork.
(5) Use only thoroughly cooked scraps of pork as feed for pigs.

(1) (2) (3) (4) (5)

9. One of the symptoms of trichinosis is muscle pain and loss of muscle function. Which of the following statements would support this medical finding?

(1) Large numbers of larvae lodge in muscle.
(2) The disease is transmitted by eating poorly cooked muscle tissue from infected hogs.
(3) Many diseases affect muscles.
(4) Muscles are penetrated by the adult parasites.
(5) Muscle is the only tissue of the body that is exposed to the parasite.

(1) (2) (3) (4) (5)

---

10. City trucks commonly clear icy streets by spreading salt. Which of the following chemical principles best explains why this procedure is effective?

(1) When salts are dissolved in water, the water freezes at a lower temperature.
(2) Cold molecules move more slowly than warm molecules.
(3) When salt dissolves in water, it fills in some of the spaces between water molecules.
(4) Salt molecules dissolved in water will disperse until they are evenly distributed throughout the water.
(5) In the process of freezing, water molecules form crystals.

(1) (2) (3) (4) (5)

11. A student of ecology is doing a survey of the migratory habits of a rare species of geese. From her observation point she counts ninety birds flying south for the winter. From this same point she counts seventy flying north the following spring. She concludes that the population of this species is decreasing.

Which of the following states the assumption she made?

(1) Some of the geese could no longer reproduce.
(2) No new geese were born in the winter.
(3) All the geese flew north by exactly the same route they flew south.
(4) Some of the geese remained in the south.
(5) All the geese that flew south were healthy.

(1) (2) (3) (4) (5)

12. When moist air arrives at a mountain, it rises and cools. Because cold air cannot hold as much moisture, rain falls. What sort of climate conditions would probably be found on the other side of the mountain?

(1) wet
(2) dry
(3) hot
(4) cold
(5) mild

(1) (2) (3) (4) (5)

GO ON TO THE NEXT PAGE.

<u>Items 13–16</u> are based on the following information.

Nearly all substances can exist as solids, liquids, or gases. The process of going from one form to another is called a phase transition. Five phase transitions are defined below.

(1) condensation = the change of a substance from a gas to a liquid
(2) evaporation = the change of a substance from a liquid to a gas
(3) melting = the change of a substance from a solid to a liquid
(4) solidification = the change of a substance from a liquid to a solid
(5) sublimation = the change of a substance from a solid to a gas

Each item below contains an example of a phase transition. For each item, select the one process that the example demonstrates. Each process may be demonstrated more than once.

13. Molten steel hardens in a casting.

The steel goes through the process of

(1) condensation
(2) evaporation
(3) melting
(4) solidification
(5) sublimation

14. Grease drips from hamburgers barbecuing on a grill.

The process that causes the dripping grease to form is

(1) condensation
(2) evaporation
(3) melting
(4) solidification
(5) sublimation

1 2 3 4 5

15. A tray of ice cubes is left in a freezer. After two months, the ice cubes are one-half their original size.

The ice cubes became smaller because of

(1) condensation
(2) evaporation
(3) melting
(4) solidification
(5) sublimation

1 2 3 4 5

16. Dew makes the grass wet on summer mornings.

The process by which dew forms is called

(1) condensation
(2) evaporation
(3) melting
(4) solidification
(5) sublimation

---

17. Different strains of a flu virus can exist. A person's immunity to one flu virus does not protect that person against an altered form of the same virus.

A special news report states that "the current Taiwan flu virus is a special threat to people under thirty-five years of age." Which of the following does the news announcement imply?

(1) This flu virus is unlike any viruses that have caused epidemics before.
(2) Young people are less likely to develop immunity to flu viruses.
(3) There was an outbreak of the same Taiwan flu virus thirty-five years ago.
(4) The Taiwan virus is a very common flu virus.
(5) People under thirty-five get ill more easily than older people.

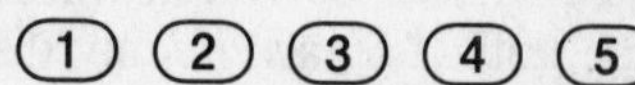

Items 18–20 refer to the following table.

Sound Level Chart

Decibel	Bel	Type of Sound	Times as Loud as 0 Decibels
0	0	The least sound heard by a normal human ear	
10	1	The rustle of leaves in a light breeze	10
20	2	An average whisper 4 feet away from hearer	100
30	3	Broadcasting studio when no program is in progress	1,000
40	4	Night noises in a city	10,000
50	5	Average residence	100,000
60	6	Normal conversation at 3 feet	1,000,000
70	7	An accounting office	10,000,000
80	8	A noisy city street	100,000,000
90	9	A moderate discotheque	1,000,000,000
100	10	A food blender	10,000,000,000
110	11	A pneumatic drill	100,000,000,000
120	12	A jet engine	1,000,000,000,000

18. A person wants to make a tape recording of the sounds of daily surroundings. The tape will include leaves rustling in a summer breeze, whispered conversation, typewriters and adding machines in a business office, and sounds of a busy downtown area during lunch hour. Through what minimum decibel range must the recording equipment be sensitive?

(1) 0–50
(2) 0–120
(3) 10–80
(4) 10–100
(5) 20–90

(1) (2) (3) (4) (5)

19. One could use the chart to obtain all the following information <u>except</u>

(1) the relationship of a decibel to a bel
(2) how much louder 40 decibels is than 20 decibels
(3) the sound level associated with different settings
(4) the intensity level at which sounds become uncomfortable
(5) how many times greater a sound at 9 bels is than a sound at 0 decibels

(1) (2) (3) (4) (5)

20. A buyer looking at new cars reads that at 60 mph the internal noise level of one model is 69 decibels. The internal noise level of a competitive model is rated at 80 decibels. The man decides that the difference between 69 and 80 cannot be very important, since 80 is only about 15 percent greater than 69. What is wrong with the man's consideration of the facts?

(1) Eighty decibels is really a 30 percent increase in noise level over 69 decibels.
(2) The values listed on the cars are calculated under laboratory conditions and do not apply to routine driving.
(3) Both 69 and 80 decibels are well within the noise comfort range.
(4) Eighty decibels is the same sound intensity as normal conversation.
(5) One car is actually more than 10 times noisier inside than the other.

(1) (2) (3) (4) (5)

GO ON TO THE NEXT PAGE.

<u>Items 21–22</u> refer to the following information.

Mining companies often scrape away layers of soil to obtain minerals lying below the earth's surface. Some companies store the removed soil in a pile. This means that surface soil ends up at the bottom of the pile. When the mineral excavation is completed, the miners return the soil to its original spot.

Such mining practices have created problems. Biologists know that certain organisms live at very specific depths in the soil. Many of these organisms recycle nutrients and produce fertilizers for plants. Turning the soil upside down during excavation destroys the environments of these soil organisms, so they soon die. Although companies carefully replace the stored soil in the hole, the organisms have already been killed. Nutrients are no longer recycled, and the land becomes barren.

21. When mining companies replace the excavated soil, they are assuming that

(1) replacement of the soil will restore the land to its original fertile condition
(2) microorganisms are extremely sensitive to their environmental conditions
(3) microorganisms are an essential part of land productivity
(4) soil fertility is dependent on the nutrients and fertilizers present
(5) turning the soil upside down may interfere with the ability of organisms to survive

(1) (2) (3) (4) (5)

22. Persons who object to mining methods that excavate soil probably place a high value on

(1) the latest technology in mining
(2) conservation of soil resources
(3) underground metals and minerals
(4) the use of artificial fertilizers
(5) keeping fuel costs low

(1) (2) (3) (4) (5)

23. The Bermuda Triangle is in the Caribbean Sea. The popular press has carried articles claiming that mysterious events occur within the Bermuda Triangle and cause the loss of ships and airplanes.

A reader concludes that the triangle is a very dangerous area. Which of the following statements best indicates that the reader's conclusion may be <u>incorrect</u>?

(1) Articles cite the loss of more than 2,000 craft in the Bermuda Triangle, dating from the mid-nineteenth century.
(2) The large number of articles written on the subject has strengthened public opinion that dangerous, secret forces exist in the Bermuda Triangle.
(3) Close study of the original data indicates that writers have changed the details of events to fit the story of unnatural hazards in the Bermuda Triangle.
(4) Written articles often cite radio messages to document unexplained events in the Bermuda Triangle.
(5) No mysterious force acting in the area known as the Bermuda Triangle has as yet been identified.

(1) (2) (3) (4) (5)

24. An electron beam that sweeps rapidly back and forth across the screen produces the picture that we see on a television set. In the United States, a total of 525 lines make up each image on a television screen.

A consumer comparing color TV sets in an appliance store observes that the picture on a 9-inch screen is much sharper than the picture on a 26-inch screen. Which of the following statements best explains this difference?

(1) The electron beam is more focused on a large screen.
(2) The 525 lines that make up the picture are farther apart on a larger screen than on a smaller screen.
(3) More than 525 lines are used with a smaller screen.
(4) The electrons occupy less space on a large screen.
(5) The pictures are actually equally sharp, but the color is dimmer on the larger screen.

(1) (2) (3) (4) (5)

Items 25–27 are based on the following weather map.

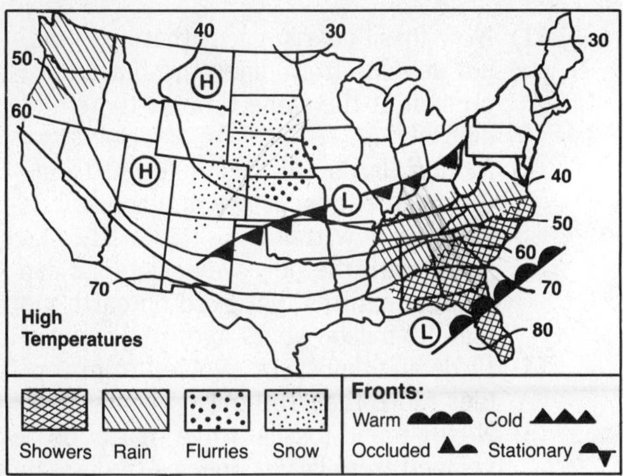

25. For which area of the country is snow predicted?

(1) Northwest
(2) Rocky Mountains
(3) Central Plains
(4) Northeast
(5) Midatlantic Coast

① ② ③ ④ ⑤

26. When cold air and warm air fronts meet, thunderstorms often result. The area of the country where thunderstorms might be expected within the next few days would be the

(1) Northwest
(2) Southwest
(3) Great Lakes
(4) Northeast
(5) Southeast

① ② ③ ④ ⑤

27. A woman who lives in the mountains of Idaho looks at the map and then tells her husband, "We'll be having snow within the next couple of days." What assumption is she making?

(1) Idaho often has snowstorms at this time of year.
(2) A high-pressure area usually means a storm is coming.
(3) The cold front in the middle of the country will reach Idaho soon.
(4) An ideal temperature range for snow to form is 20°–30°F.
(5) The rain in Washington will turn to snow when it reaches the mountains in Idaho.

① ② ③ ④ ⑤

Items 28–29 refer to the information below.

Water evaporating from a surface tends to cool that surface. Pine needles contain structures like little mouths, called stomata. Stomata open and close to help regulate how much water the plant releases into the air.

28. What would stomata best allow a plant to do?

(1) stay cool on a hot day
(2) grow toward a water source
(3) become warmer on a cool day
(4) shed water on a rainy day
(5) produce energy

① ② ③ ④ ⑤

29. What process in the human body is most similar to the release of water through a plant's stomata?

(1) digesting
(2) perspiring
(3) drinking
(4) urinating
(5) salivating

① ② ③ ④ ⑤

GO ON TO THE NEXT PAGE.

Items 30–33 refer to the following passage.

In 1861, someone found a 150-million-year-old fossil of a pigeon-sized bird that resembled a dinosaur with feathers. The ancient creature had a brain and a scaly head like a dinosaur but the wishbone, wings, and feathers of a bird. Scientists named the animal *Archaeopteryx* and assumed it was the ancestor from which all modern birds evolved.

For many years, scientists agreed that dinosaurs existed before birds. Although many dinosaurs were large and heavy, some were very small. The small creatures ran quickly on two long back legs and grasped food with short forelegs. Scientists hypothesized that over a span of 60 million years, these dinosaurs evolved into birds. Their short forelegs became wings. Their scales became feathers.

In August 1986, two newly discovered incomplete fossil skeletons caused scientists to change their hypothesis. The newly found fossils have characteristics of modern birds that *Archaeopteryx* lacked, but they are 75 million years older than *Archaeopteryx*. A large brain case, wide eye sockets, and a breastbone anchoring the muscles used in flight are hallmarks of a modern bird. The fossils found in 1986 show these characteristics; *Archaeopteryx* does not. If the identification of the new fossils is correct, it appears now that birds evolved much earlier than scientists had believed.

30. Which of the following statements best summarizes the information contained in the passage?

(1) New fossil data suggest that birds did not develop from dinosaurs but were present at the same time as the earliest dinosaurs.
(2) Modern birds are very different from their earliest ancestors and are still developing new traits.
(3) Fossils are the only way scientists can study creatures that lived on earth more than 60 million years ago.
(4) Birds and dinosaurs evolved from reptiles more than 150 million years ago.
(5) Newly found fossils prove that birds developed from larger species of dinosaurs than scientists had originally thought.

(1) (2) (3) (4) (5)

31. In order to hypothesize that birds descended from dinosaurs, scientists first had to make which of the following assumptions?

(1) Modern birds must have developed from earlier animals.
(2) Older fossils would show more advanced traits than younger ones.
(3) Dinosaurs had the ability to fly.
(4) Dinosaurs were light, active creatures.
(5) Birds are the oldest life form on earth today.

(1) (2) (3) (4) (5)

32. Which of the following is one of the hypotheses stated in the passage?

(1) *Archaeopteryx* had several features in common with dinosaurs.
(2) Birds existed much earlier than scientists previously thought.
(3) Based on the *Archaeopteryx* fossil, scientists developed a theory for the evolution of birds from dinosaurs.
(4) Newly discovered fossils are much more birdlike than *Archaeopteryx* and yet are much older.
(5) Fossils indicate that ancient birds had enlarged brain cases, breastbones, and wide eye sockets.

(1) (2) (3) (4) (5)

33. Below are five items that would interest a researcher studying fossils of the earliest birds.

A. how old the fossils are
B. how large the birds grew
C. how far the birds could fly
D. how the birds resembled dinosaurs
E. what the birds ate

Which points of information could the researcher establish through scientific analysis?

(1) A only
(2) A and B only
(3) A and E only
(4) D and E only
(5) A, B, and D only

(1) (2) (3) (4) (5)

34. There are two types of foods that have many calories—foods high in sugars and foods high in fats. It has been assumed for a long time that high sugar consumption leads to obesity. There is now evidence to indicate that this assumption of cause and effect is incorrect.

Which of the following observations helps support the belief that the assumption is probably wrong?

(1) Sugar is very fattening.
(2) Pies and cakes contain fattening substances other than sugar.
(3) The body can store sugar for later use.
(4) Overweight people tend to eat more high-calorie foods than people of normal weight.
(5) Some people of normal weight consume more sugar than overweight people do.

(1) (2) (3) (4) (5)

GO ON TO THE NEXT PAGE.

Items 35–37 refer to the graph and passage below.

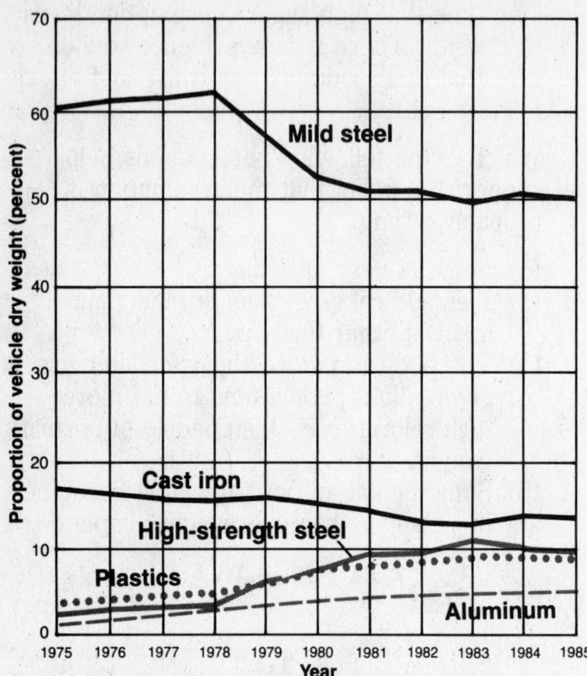

The lightweight-materials content of the average car manufactured in the United States has increased sharply since the mid-1970s. The data shown in the graph are for an average passenger car produced by one major manufacturer and are typical of all U.S. automakers. Lightweight materials are shown in gray. Heavy materials are indicated in black.

35. Which of the statements below best summarizes the materials content of the average passenger car manufactured in 1981?

(1) Lightweight materials accounted for about 22 percent of the car's weight, while heavy materials made up about 65 percent.
(2) Heavy materials made up 52 percent of the car, while lightweight materials made up the remaining 48 percent.
(3) Sixty-two percent of the weight was due to steel and 30 percent due to lightweight materials.
(4) The percentage of different materials remained the same from 1981 to 1985.
(5) The overall use of high-strength steel, mild steel, and cast iron decreased as these heavy substances were replaced by lightweight materials in autos.

(1) (2) (3) (4) (5)

36. Which of the following statements is a conclusion about cars made during the 1980s that can be drawn from the graph?

(1) Cars in the 1980s became increasingly expensive.
(2) Cars made in the 1980s were more difficult to handle than those in the 1970s.
(3) Cars made during the 1980s required more fuel per mile than those in the 1970s.
(4) Cars made during the 1980s weighed less than cars made during the 1970s.
(5) Cars in the 1980s could carry fewer and fewer passengers.

(1) (2) (3) (4) (5)

37. An insurance company is studying the graph. Which of the following factors would it be most interested in?

(1) the melting point of all the materials
(2) the difference between high-strength steel and mild steel
(3) the kinds of molecules used to create the plastics
(4) the amount of impact that the lightweight materials can withstand
(5) how well the lightweight materials resist rust

(1) (2) (3) (4) (5)

Items 38–43 are based on the following information.

Genetics is the study of DNA, the hereditary material of the genes in a cell. Five terms that deal with the genetics of a cell or organism are defined below.

(1) genotype = the collection of all the genetic material present in the cell
(2) mutation = any change in the chemical units that make up DNA
(3) phenotype = the physical appearance of a cell or organism
(4) replication = the process in which genetic material is duplicated so that further growth of the organism can occur
(5) reproduction = the process by which one cell becomes two

Each of the items below contains an example of one of the terms defined above. Select the term that is best represented by the example. Each term may apply to more than one example.

38. A small spot of mold appears on a piece of bread. By the next day it is much larger.

The mold spot increases in size because of

(1) genotype
(2) mutation
(3) phenotype
(4) replication
(5) reproduction

① ② ③ ④ ⑤

39. A cocker spaniel and a poodle are bred. Each pup receives half of its genetic material from each of its parents.

The term that best describes why each pup has all its particular traits is

(1) genotype
(2) mutation
(3) phenotype
(4) replication
(5) reproduction

① ② ③ ④ ⑤

40. A particular strain of wheat grows to be six feet tall and is golden brown in color.

The color and size of the wheat are part of its

(1) genotype
(2) mutation
(3) phenotype
(4) replication
(5) reproduction

① ② ③ ④ ⑤

41. More DNA is detected in cells growing under ideal conditions than in cells placed on a starvation diet.

The different amounts of DNA in the cells is due to differences in

(1) genotype
(2) mutation
(3) phenotype
(4) replication
(5) reproduction

① ② ③ ④ ⑤

42. A researcher divides some seeds into two groups. One group receives a very high dose of X-irradiation. Both groups are then planted. None of the irradiated seeds grow.

The irradiated seeds do not grow because of

(1) genotype
(2) mutation
(3) phenotype
(4) replication
(5) reproduction

① ② ③ ④ ⑤

43. All the maple trees in a grove have similarly shaped leaves.

The similar appearance of all the trees is described as

(1) genotype
(2) mutation
(3) phenotype
(4) replication
(5) reproduction

① ② ③ ④ ⑤

GO ON TO THE NEXT PAGE.

Items 44–46 refer to the following diagram and information.

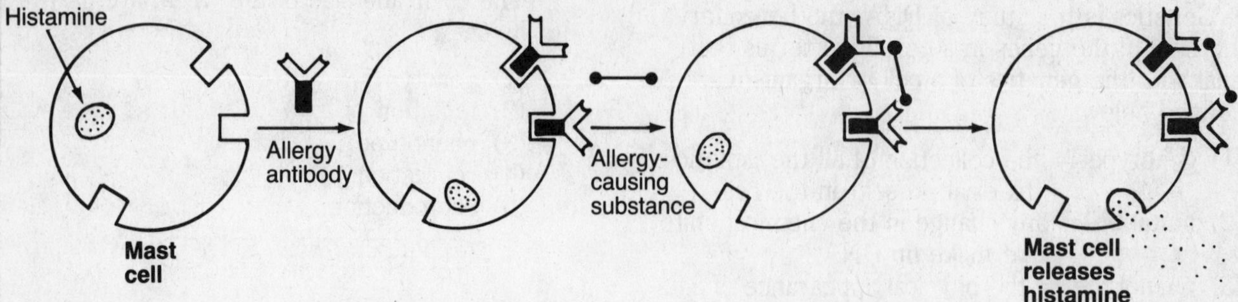

Normally, immune responses help protect an organism's body. However, some immune responses, such as allergies, do not seem to be protective. Allergies can occur in some people when they eat certain foods, receive certain drugs, or come into contact with dust or pollens.

Allergies stem from several processes in the body. In some individuals, the body produces allergy antibodies that stick to white blood cells called mast cells. When a person comes into contact with a substance to which he or she is allergic, that substance reacts with the allergy antibodies. The mast cells release histamine as a result of this reaction. Histamine is responsible for the runny nose, itchy eyes, and difficult breathing associated with allergy.

44. Based on the information above, what must happen for an allergic reaction to occur?

(1) The allergy antibody must attach itself to the mast cell.
(2) Pollen in the air must trigger the production of disease-carrying antibodies.
(3) Histamine must be attacked by the allergy antibody.
(4) Histamine must be attacked by the allergy-causing substance.
(5) The body must be unable to produce antibodies to fight off diseases.

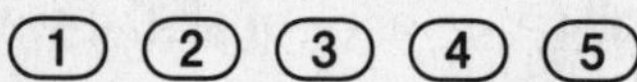

45. Which of the following statements best summarizes the information contained in the passage and diagram?

(1) Histamine in the bloodstream can produce a variety of allergic reactions.
(2) The difficult breathing, itchy eyes, and runny nose of allergic reactions occur when mast cells release antibodies.
(3) Common drugs and plant substances can cause allergic reactions in some people.
(4) Allergies result from a series of special reactions involving mast cells, antibodies, and histamine.
(5) Allergic reactions are immune reactions that protect the body from irritating substances.

46. Antihistamines are drugs that reduce the severity of allergic reactions. An antihistamine can make an allergic response less severe because the antihistamine

(1) blocks the release of histamine from mast cells
(2) stimulates antibody production
(3) stimulates mast cells to attract more antibodies
(4) prevents mast cells from releasing antibodies
(5) causes allergy-causing substances to bond with antibodies

47. A photographer decides to develop film at home. He has never done it before, so he tries an experiment with three rolls of film. He develops the first roll at 15°C for 12 minutes, the second roll at 25°C for 6 minutes, and the third roll at 35°C for 3 minutes. The films all appear identical after development.

What does his experiment imply about film development?

(1) Doubling the temperature reduces the developing time by half.
(2) Increased temperature requires increased developing time.
(3) When the temperature is decreased, the film develops in less time.
(4) Increasing the temperature decreases the time needed to develop the film.
(5) Decreased temperature means the film will take twice as long to develop.

(1) (2) (3) (4) (5)

48. Scientists sometimes try to produce rain in dry regions through cloud seeding. They use airplanes to spray chemicals into clouds or release chemicals on the ground so that wind drafts carry them upward to the clouds. The chemicals cause moisture in the clouds to condense and fall to the ground as precipitation.

For cloud seeding to work, which of the following factors must be assumed?

(1) The land area is excessively dry and parched.
(2) There is already enough moisture in the clouds to condense and fall.
(3) The air is warmer than the land region over which it lies.
(4) The chemicals released into the clouds will speed up molecular action.
(5) The force of gravity in that region is too weak to allow rain to fall without help.

(1) (2) (3) (4) (5)

Items 49–50 refer to the diagram below.

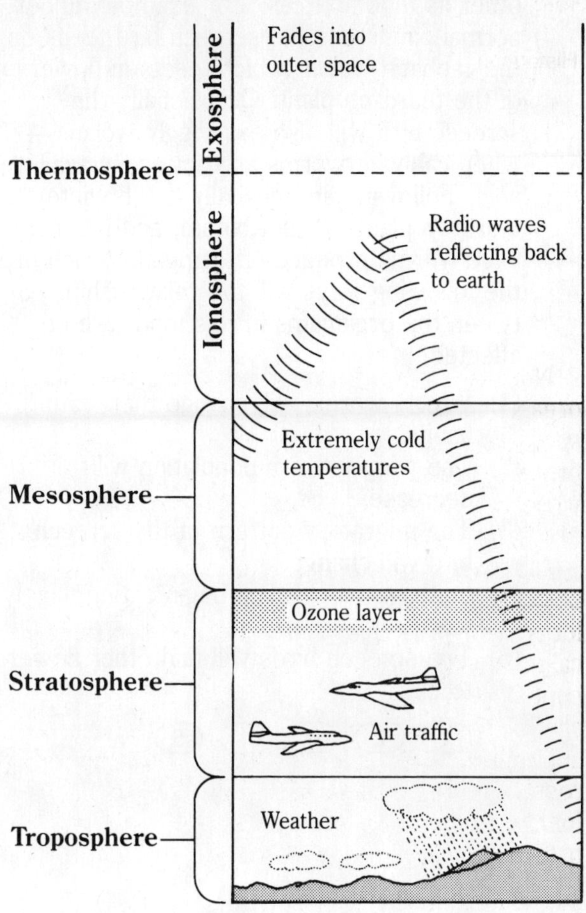

49. If a television communications satellite is working correctly, it may be assumed that it is in which layer of the atmosphere?

(1) ozone layer only
(2) ozone layer and mesosphere only
(3) mesosphere and ionosphere only
(4) stratosphere and troposphere only
(5) ionosphere only

(1) (2) (3) (4) (5)

50. Based on the diagram, in which layer of the earth's atmosphere do most clouds appear?

(1) troposphere
(2) ozone layer
(3) stratosphere
(4) mesosphere
(5) ionosphere

GO ON TO THE NEXT PAGE.

51. Animals are highly dependent on one another as food sources. For example, under normal conditions the screech bird feeds on the cabbage worm, which feeds on flowers of the teardrop plant. Occasionally the screech bird will also eat wiggly worms—when cabbage worms are not easily available. Following an unusually harsh winter, teardrop plants do not bloom, and few cabbage worms produce offspring. In which of the following ways will the relationships between the organisms in this food web be affected?

(1) Wiggly worms will change their eating habits.
(2) The wiggly worm population will decrease.
(3) The migratory pattern of the screech bird will change.
(4) Cabbage worms will begin eating wiggly worms.
(5) The screech birds will find other flowers to eat.

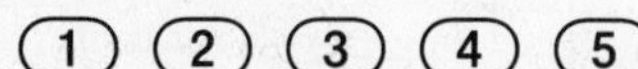

Items 52–53 are based on the following passage.

High tide occurs on earth when the gravitational pull of the moon causes a tidal bulge. The moon's gravitational pull raises millions of tons of water, which wash far inland across ocean shores. Large ships have taken advantage of tides for years to move in and out of harbors. But so far people have used tidal energy only occasionally to provide energy on land. Now scientists are taking a closer look at the power of tides.

Falling water has energy. As high tide recedes, large amounts of water fall. Scientists think this action could generate power in several ways. For example, dams might trap high tides as they rise. Then, when the tide falls, the water could be channeled through turbines to generate electricity. Another proposed method would resemble the mill wheels people of earlier centuries used on many rivers. The tides could turn reversible paddle wheels when they came in, and then again when they went out.

Scientists predict that tidal energy will be clean and leave behind no waste products. They are still studying to determine the effects tidal dams might have on ecology.

52. Tides have tremendous power because

(1) they make water move uphill
(2) they are actually currents that act like rivers
(3) oil and coal supplies cannot be replaced
(4) so many shoreline dams harness moving water
(5) the moon's gravitational pull gives raised water potential energy

(1) (2) (3) (4) (5)

53. Tidal power might prove to be superior to nuclear power because

(1) it creates no toxic wastes
(2) people everywhere can use tides
(3) hydroelectric power plants are so inexpensive
(4) traditional paddle wheels make it simple to capture
(5) the moon's gravity is more powerful than nuclear energy

(1) (2) (3) (4) (5)

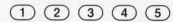

54. A vector is an insect or other organism that transmits a disease-causing organism. Rickettsias are small microorganisms that cause the disease Rocky Mountain spotted fever. They have been found in cattle ticks. The ticks, which are relatives of spiders, carry the rickettsias in their digestive system. The rickettsias have no effect on cattle, but a person infected with rickettsias becomes extremely ill.

The vectors of Rocky Mountain spotted fever are

(1) rickettsias
(2) microorganisms
(3) ticks
(4) spiders
(5) cattle

(1) (2) (3) (4) (5)

55. Parvo is a new disease that appeared early in the 1980s. It spread rapidly across the country, causing epidemics among the dog population. Many puppies and young dogs die from the disease if untreated. Parvo infections in adult dogs cause mild to severe illness but are usually not lethal.

Below are four statements relating to the parvo virus or the illness it causes.

A. The virus is similar to another virus that causes a severe disease in cats.
B. New vaccines used to protect against parvo virus are 99 percent effective.
C. The disease usually affects the dog's digestive system.
D. Insufficient funding has been allotted to the study of the disease.

Which of these statements can be verified using scientific analysis?

(1) A and B only
(2) B only
(3) B and C only
(4) A, B, and C only
(5) A, B, C, and D

(1) (2) (3) (4) (5)

Item 56 is based on the information and diagram below.

Gravity is the force of attraction existing between two objects. The gravitational force increases as the mass of the objects increases or as the distance between them decreases. The diagram below shows a simple experiment that demonstrates the force of gravity. Two spheres of equal mass are suspended on a free-swinging rod. If a third sphere of equal mass is held near one of the suspended spheres, the force of gravity causes that suspended sphere to move.

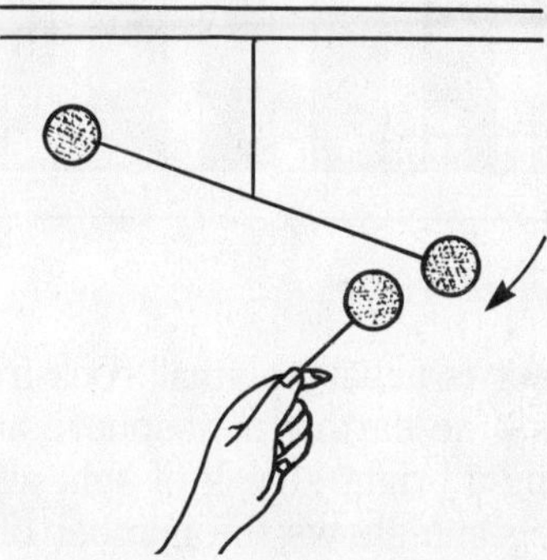

56. The interpretation of this experiment is based on which of the following assumptions?

(1) The gravity of suspended objects is greater than the earth's.
(2) The objects are not attracting because of magnetism.
(3) All objects are attracted toward the earth.
(4) All three objects used in the experiment must be of the same size.
(5) A large object exerts more gravitational pull than a small one.

GO ON TO THE NEXT PAGE.

Items 57–58 refer to the graph and information.

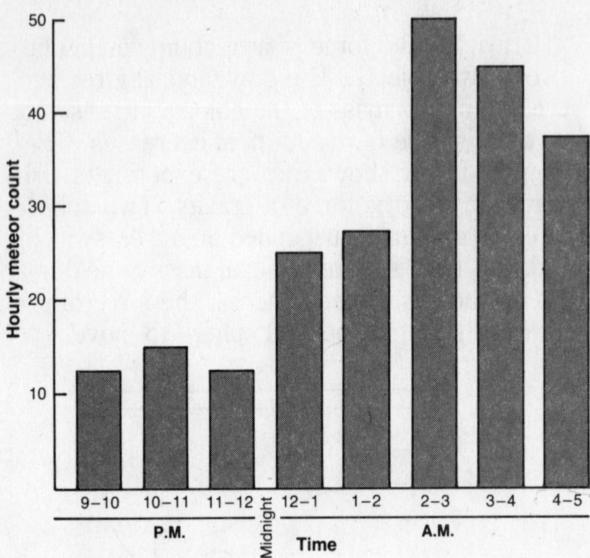

A meteor is usually a small rock from space that enters the earth's atmosphere and burns up, causing a bright streak of light across the sky. The graph shows the number of meteors a group of amateur astronomers observed during one night.

57. Which of the following statements best summarizes the information in the graph?

(1) Many more meteors were sighted during the hours after midnight.
(2) Midnight to one o'clock A.M. is the peak hour for sighting meteors.
(3) Fewer than fifty meteors were sighted each hour.
(4) The number of meteors varies greatly from hour to hour.
(5) No pattern is apparent in the number of meteors that can be sighted in a single evening.

① ② ③ ④ ⑤

58. An amateur astronomer counts meteors each night during mid-August when the Perseid Meteor Shower is known to occur each year. She then sends all her data to the American Meteor Society. Several of her reasons for doing this are listed below. Which of the statements indicates that values are involved in her hobby?

(1) The origin of a meteor shower can be determined most accurately if it is observed from several different locations on earth.
(2) When data gathered by amateurs at many different places are put together, facts not apparent to an individual observer can be determined.
(3) An experienced amateur can determine the peak time of shower activity.
(4) An amateur's reward is knowing that he or she has made a useful contribution to science.
(5) The hourly counts of meteors observed by amateurs indicates the density of the meteor cloud.

Items 59–60 refer to the information below.

Many Americans are now eating less beef and more chicken because chicken meat contains less fat and cholesterol. The beef industry is responding to this by developing new breeds of cattle. Industry planners hope that the meat from these animals will offer the dietary advantages of chicken and retain the taste and texture of beef.

59. Below are five statements about these newly available meats. Which represents an opinion rather than a fact?

(1) Chianina averages 36 percent fewer calories than regular beef.
(2) Zebu has a more pleasant flavor than pure beef.
(3) Beefalo is produced by crossing bison with cattle.
(4) Chianina and regular beef have about the same amount of cholesterol.
(5) Brae contains less fat than regular beef.

(1) (2) (3) (4) (5)

60. According to the information given, what factor is most responsible for Americans' switch to chicken?

(1) the desire for a change
(2) the inexpensiveness of chicken
(3) the delicious taste of chicken
(4) difficulty in cooking beef
(5) concern for their health

(1) (2) (3) (4) (5)

GO ON TO THE NEXT PAGE.

Items 61–66 are based on the graph and information given.

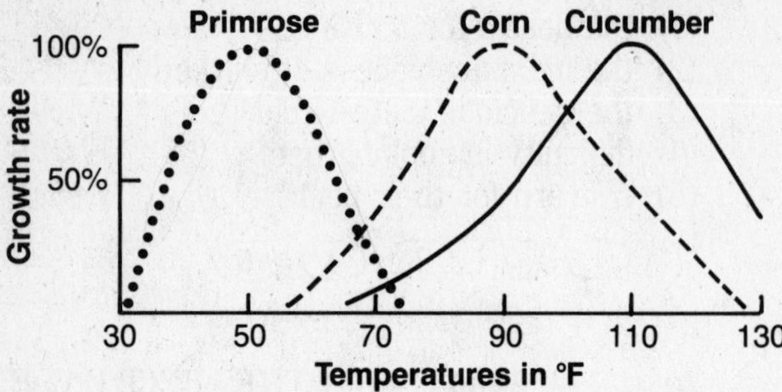

A group of agricultural researchers conducted an experiment to study the growth rates of plants at various temperatures. In their laboratory, they divided primrose, cucumber, and corn plants into a number of different groups. During the experiment, they kept the different groups of primrose plants at different but constant temperatures for twenty-four hours every day. They did the same for the corn and cucumber plants. The graph shows the growth rates that they recorded for the different groups of all three kinds of plants.

61. According to the graph, at what temperature did primroses grow best?

(1) 40°F
(2) 50°F
(3) 60°F
(4) 70°F
(5) 80°F

① ② ③ ④ ⑤

62. Judging from the data in the graph, what sort of climate would favor the growth of cucumbers?

(1) cold nights, cold days
(2) cold nights, warm days
(3) very warm nights, very warm days
(4) warm, rainy days
(5) warm nights, cool days

① ② ③ ④ ⑤

The questions that follow consist of statements about the study and graph. Classify each of the statements into one of the categories defined below. More than one statement may have the same classification.

(1) the problem = the main issue being studied
(2) a method = a procedure used to study the problem
(3) a finding = a result obtained as part of the study
(4) an assumption = a supporting idea for which no proof is given in the study
(5) irrelevant information = material that does not relate to the problem under study

63. Corn grows best at a constant temperature of 90 degrees.

This statement should be classified as

(1) the problem
(2) a method
(3) a finding
(4) an assumption
(5) irrelevant information

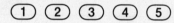

① ② ③ ④ ⑤

64. Corn is in more demand than either primroses or cucumbers.

This statement should be classified as

(1) the problem
(2) a method
(3) a finding
(4) an assumption
(5) irrelevant information

① ② ③ ④ ⑤

65. Plants were divided into a number of different groups.

This statement should be classified as

(1) the problem
(2) a method
(3) a finding
(4) an assumption
(5) irrelevant information

(1) (2) (3) (4) (5)

66. Temperature may affect the growth rates of plants.

This statement should be classified as

(1) the problem
(2) a method
(3) a finding
(4) an assumption
(5) irrelevant information

(1) (2) (3) (4) (5)

END OF EXAMINATION

Answers: Posttest B

1. (1) The second paragraph states that the vehicle will come to rest only when the kinetic energy of the ship has bean converted to some other form of energy, so the energy of motion would then equal zero. **CP**

2. (4) The passage described an aerodynamic braking system that relies on earth's atmosphere to act as a brake for the spaceship. The atmosphere absorbs the heat energy released by the ship. If a spaceship is to land on a planet that has no atmosphere, it would need its own braking system of landing rockets. **AP**

3. (5) The fires of a car slow down and consequently heat up as the car approaches a stop sign. The entire passage deals with how a spaceship must slow down and transfer its heat to the atmosphere before it can land. **AP**

4. (1) Fuel economy and low cost are values that influence the method used to land the spaceship. As noted in the passage, aerodynamic braking is not the ideal way of landing a ship. **EV**

5. (3) The black-throated green warblers would probably be caught more often because they live near the tops of the trees, where the birds of prey can spot them more easily. Their number would therefore decrease more than the other warblers. **AN**

6. (2) Volcanoes actually reshape the land (statement C), produce the sea floor (statement D), and release gases that account for about 25 percent of the gases in the atmosphere (statement E). All of these statements could be tested and verified. Words like *monumental* and *spectacular* are clues that statements A and B are partly opinions. **AN**

7. (2) People become infected with *Trichinella* only by eating meat that is not cooked thoroughly enough to kill the parasitic larvae. Meat, which is muscle tissue from animals, does not contain mature parasites (4). **CP**

8. (4) Washing hands before eating pork will not get rid of the parasites. Thorough cooking will kill the infectious larvae (1). A meat inspection program (2) would detect *Trichinella* in meat before it is bought. If meat from infected herds could not be sold (3), the infection could not be spread to humans. Using only cooked pork scraps as feed for the pigs (5) would prevent reinfection of the pigs with the parasites. **AN**

9. (1) Huge numbers of the larvae accumulate in muscle tissues, where they penetrate the spaces between the muscle fibers. The fibers can no longer move freely, and pain occurs. **EV**

10. (1) Water that contains a large amount of salt freezes at a lower temperature than pure water, so salt keeps the water on the streets from freezing so quickly. Options (2)–(5) are all true statements, but they have nothing to do with this particular example. **(AN)**

11. (3) The student assumed that she had counted every bird that flew south and every one that flew back north. She assumed that they had all flown directly over her observation point both times. **AN**

12. (2) The air will lose its moisture when it hits the mountain and rises. When it flows over to the other side of the mountain, it will have very little water in it. The climate will be dry. **AN**

13. (4) The molten, or liquid, steel hardens and becomes a solid. **AP**

14. (3) Grease forms because the solid fat in the meat becomes a liquid (melts) over the heat of the barbecue. **AP**

15. (5) The ice cubes become smaller because over a period of time the crystals of ice in the cubes turn to water vapor. The cubes do not melt and then evaporate. They pass directly from solid phase to gas. This fits only the definition of sublimation. **AP**

16. (1) Dew is water vapor in the air that turns to liquid because of the cool night temperature. It forms on grass in the morning. Vapor changing to liquid fits the definition of condensation. **AP**

17. (3) People over thirty-five years old would have some immunity to this virus only if they were exposed to the *same* virus before. **CP**

18. (3) The sound of rustling leaves is rated at 10 decibels. The sound of a noisy city street is rated at 80 decibels. These are the quietest and the noisiest of the sounds to be recorded. The recording equipment must be sensitive over the range of 10–80 decibels. **CP**

19. (4) The table does not show whether a particular type of sound or sound level is comfortable or uncomfortable to the human ear. **CP**

20. (5) According to the table, 70 decibels is 10 million times louder than zero decibels. Eighty decibels is 100 million times louder than zero decibels. Therefore, 80 decibels is 10 times louder than 70 decibels. So 80 must be more than 10 times louder than 69. **EV**

CP = Comprehension **AP** = Application **AN** = Analysis **EV** = Evaluation

21. (1) The excavators assume the land will be the same after excavation as it was before it. If any of the other options were assumed, the excavators might not carry out their operations at all. **AN**

22. (2) Persons who object to the effects of mining excavations are probably well informed about the environmental hazards to the soil. **EV**

23. (3) The person reading the articles assumes that they report the events correctly. This often is not true. **AN**

24. (2) The size of the screen determines how far apart the lines are. The closer together the lines are, the clearer the screen image will be. **AN**

25. (3) This question can be answered directly from the weather map. **CP**

26. (5) Cold and warm fronts are found only in the southeast part of the country on this weather map. **AP**

27. (5) The map indicates there is rain in Washington State. The woman assumes this storm will move eastward into Idaho and turn to snow. None of the other options logically follows from information given on the weather map. **AN**

28. (1) Stomata could increase evaporation and its cooling effect. **AN**

29. (2) Releasing water from surface openings called stomata is very similar to releasing water from pores in the skin, which is what perspiration is. Both help regulate temperature. **AP**

30. (1) The passage is about new fossils that have changed old ideas about the development of birds. **CP**

31. (1) This states one aspect of the theory of evolution. The scientists were trying to fit the development of birds into the pattern of evolution. **AN**

32. (2) Only this statement is a hypothesis, a testable conclusion. The others are restatements of facts from the passage. **AN**

33. (5) The age of the fossils can be determined by scientific tests. The size of the birds and their resemblance to dinosaurs can be established by examining the fossils. There would be no way to determine, however, what the birds ate or how far they could fly. **AN**

34. (5) If eating a lot of sugar were actually a cause of obesity, then obese people would eat more sugar than normal-weight people Option (1) supports sugar as a cause of obesity. Options (2), (3), and (4) do not support or disprove the assumption. **EV**

35. (1) This answer can be read from the graph. Options (2), (3), and (5) are untrue. Option (4) happens to be true, but it does not summarize the content of the cars in 1981. **CP**

36. (4) This statement is the only conclusion among the options listed supported by the data in the graph. Cars with a greater percentage of lightweight materials would weigh less. **AN**

37. (4) The insurance company would most likely be concerned with how a car is affected in an accident. The effect of impacts on cars made of a greater percentage of lightweight materials would interest the company. **AP**

38. (5) Only reproduction would account for an increase in size. **AP**

39. (1) Their genotypes determine what traits the pups inherited. If you confused this with phenotype, remember this: the phenotype is the appearance of the pup; the genotype is the genes that determine that appearance. **AP**

40. (3) The color and size are physical characteristics, a part of the wheat's appearance. A physical characteristic is part of the wheat's phenotype. **AP**

41. (4) The cells on a starvation diet must not replicate their DNA as much as cells growing under ideal conditions replicate theirs. **AP**

42. (2) The seeds did not grow because of changes in their DNA caused by the irradiation. **AP**

43. (3) The phenotype of the trees is their appearance. **AP**

44. (1) The diagram shows that the allergy antibody must be attached to the mast cell before histamine is released. **CP**

45. (4) Many different processes must occur before a person actually experiences an allergic reaction. Options (1) and (3) are true statements but give details rather than summaries. Options (2) and (5) are false statements. **CP**

46. (1) If less histamine is released from mast cells, an allergic reaction will be less severe. None of the other options would have this effect. **AN**

47. (4) The following pattern can be seen in the example: Each time the temperature of development is increased 10°, the development time is cut in half. **CP**

48. (2) If there is little moisture in the clouds, no rain can fall from them. The chemicals do not produce moisture; they can only cause what moisture is already there to condense. **AN**

49. (5) The drawing shows that the ionosphere reflects radio waves back to the earth; therefore, the satellite would have to be in the ionosphere if it is to function. **CP**

50. (1) The diagram shows clouds present at different levels of the troposphere. **CP**

51. (2) Because there are no teardrop plants, there will be very few cabbage worms. The screech bird will eat wiggly worms instead. The wiggly worm population will decrease. **AN**

52. (5) The first two sentences of the second paragraph describe directly how tides get potential energy. The first paragraph describes how the gravity of the moon causes tides on earth. **CP**

53. (1) The third paragraph of the passage says that scientists believe tidal energy would be clean and create no wastes, unlike the dangerous wastes left by nuclear power plants. **CP**

54. (3) Ticks carry the disease-causing rickettsias, so they are the vectors. **CP**

55. (4) Statements A, B, and C can be verified by tests and statistics. Statement D cannot be verified because it is a matter of opinion whether the funding has been sufficient. **AN**

56. (2) The interpretation assumes that the only attraction between the two objects is due to gravity. Options (3), (4), and (5) are true but irrelevant. Option (1) is a false statement. **AN**

57. (1) Only this statement both accurately summarizes the graph and determines that there is a pattern. **CP**

58. (4) The amateur enjoys her hobby because she values making a scientific contribution. All other options are facts and do not involve values. **EV**

59. (2) Flavor is a matter of opinion. All other options are statements that could be verified by scientific methods. **AN**

60. (5) The first sentence tells you that Americans are eating more chicken because it "contains less fat and cholesterol." That reason reflects concern for their health. **CP**

61. (2) This information comes directly from the graph. **CP**

62. (3) The plants in the experiment were maintained at a constant temperature day and night. Cucumbers grow best at temperatures around 110°. This wouldbe very warm, both day and night. Option (4) is irrelevant because the experiment did not describe water needs. **CP**

63. (3) This statement is a finding because it is a piece of information that resulted from the study. **AP**

64. (5) This statement is irrelevant information. It has no relation to the problem being addressed. **AP**

65. (2) This statement describes part of the method used in the study. The different groups were then exposed to different temperatures. This is how the researchers studied the problem. **AP**

66. (1) This statement is the problem, or issue, that the researchers were studying—precisely *how* temperature affects the growth rates of particular plants. **AP**

Answer Key

Use this Answer Key as you did the one for the first Posttest. Circle the numbers of the answers you got wrong, count the answers you got right, and record your score on the Progress Chart on the inside back cover. Use the Skill Chart on this page if you would like a final review of the lessons that discuss the types of questions you missed.

1. (1)	**17.** (3)	**34.** (5)	**51.** (2)
2. (4)	**18.** (3)	**35.** (1)	**52.** (5)
3. (5)	**19.** (4)	**36.** (4)	**53.** (1)
4. (1)	**20.** (5)	**37.** (4)	**54.** (3)
5. (3)	**21.** (1)	**38.** (5)	**55.** (4)
6. (2)	**22.** (2)	**39.** (1)	**56.** (2)
7. (2)	**23.** (3)	**40.** (3)	**57.** (1)
8. (4)	**24.** (2)	**41.** (4)	**58.** (4)
9. (1)	**25.** (3)	**42.** (2)	**59.** (2)
10. (1)	**26.** (5)	**43.** (3)	**60.** (5)
11. (3)	**27.** (5)	**44.** (1)	**61.** (2)
12. (2)	**28.** (1)	**45.** (4)	**62.** (3)
13. (4)	**29.** (2)	**46.** (1)	**63.** (3)
14. (3)	**30.** (1)	**47.** (4)	**64.** (5)
15. (5)	**31.** (1)	**48.** (2)	**65.** (2)
16. (1)	**32.** (2)	**49.** (5)	**66.** (1)
	33. (5)	**50.** (1)	

Question Number	Skill	Lesson
5, 12, 44, 46, 47, 51	Seeing cause-and-effect relationships	5, 15, 25
2, 3, 13, 14, 15, 16, 24, 26, 28, 29, 37, 38, 39, 40, 41, 42, 43, 49, 53, 62, 63, 64, 65, 66	Applying ideas	6, 19, 24
1, 7, 18, 25, 50, 52, 54, 60, 61	Restating information	2, 12
4, 22, 58	Understanding the role of values in beliefs and decision making	18, 23
6, 32, 33, 55, 59	Distinguishing between facts, opinions, and hypotheses	8, 20, 26
8, 36	Working with conclusions	7, 14, 21
9, 10, 19, 23, 34	Evaluating data	10, 22, 27
30, 35, 45, 57	Summarizing	4, 13
11, 17, 21, 27, 31, 48, 56	Recognizing assumptions	9, 16
20	Seeing faulty logic	11, 17, 28

Index

When a word and page number are in **bold** type, the word is defined in a Coming to Terms on that page.